THE WORLD'S MOST

INFAMOUS KILLERS

THE WORLD'S MOST

INFAMOUS KILLERS

CHANCELLOR PRESS

This hardback edition first published 2003 by Chancellor Press
an imprint of Bounty Books, a division of
Octopus Publishing Group Ltd,
2-4 Heron Quays, London E14 4JP

The material in this book has previously appeared in:
True Crimes: Lady Killers
(Chancellor Press, Octopus Publishing Group Ltd, 1993)

True Crimes: Serial Killers
(Chancellor Press, Octopus Publishing Group Ltd, 1993)

ISBN 0 7537 0806 X

Printed in Great Britain by Mackays of Chatham

Contents

REASONS TO KILL

POISONOUS WOMEN

METHODS OF MURDER

GUILTY OR INNOCENT?

PARTNERS IN CRIME

Introduction

THIS book is not a treatise on the psychology of the serial killer, nor an attempt to describe the latest work being done by such bodies as the FBI's Behavioral Sciences Unit or the National Center for the Analysis of Violent Crime. It does not discuss how to build up a profile of a killer to fit a particular crime.

It is, instead, a recognition that murder is a fascinating subject for the armchair student; how else to explain the world's continuing fascination with the story of Dracula, or the large sales of the Sunday newspaper scandal sheets, or the prominence given to sensational cases of murder on the television? Collected here are the stories of some of the most prolific and shocking murderers to have made the world's headlines over the years.

We hope you enjoy reading them.

Cesare Borgia

RODERIGO LANZOL BORGIA was an Italian cardinal who was to become Pope Alexander VI. Meanwhile he kept a mistress, the courtesan Vannozza Cattanei, who shared a luxurious palace with him and gave him five illegitimate children. Among these were Cesare Borgia, born in 1476, and the youngest of all, Lucrezia Borgia, born in 1480.

Cesare became a cardinal, a military leader and politician. Pampered as a child, he never came to terms with the fact that sometimes in life it is not possible to have everything one wants. Cesare was handsome, his mother and sister adored him, and his father indulged him. This wasn't enough for Cesare, who wanted the whole world to love and obey him, particularly the latter. He wanted to have every woman to whom he took a fancy: his sister was probably one of the first of his sexual conquests, while his brother's wife would later become another. When he was a soldier the virgins of captured towns would be rounded up for his pleasure.

If by chance Cesare could not get his way he would throw a tantrum and, if so moved, would resort to murder to remove obstacles from his path. If he could not dispose of his enemies openly – for example, torturing soldiers who had looted his mother's house – he would kill quietly. For this purpose, he became an expert on poisons. Cesare knew how to kill quickly with a poison which caused death like a heart attack, and also how to kill slowly, so that he could enjoy watching his victim's gradual disintegration. His easy-going father preferred his brother Juan, so Cesare had Juan murdered. When Lucrezia was married off by her father to Alfonso of Aragon, Cesare was so jealous at losing the singular devotion of his young sister that he engineered the death of Alfonso, too. He later resumed his close

Cesare Borgia

relationship with Lucrezia and her first child was almost certainly his son.

Cesare was not only handsome, he was energetic and intelligent. He was a great patron of the arts and promoted the work of Leonardo and the young Raphael. His ultimate ambition was to rule Italy, dispensing favours to those he liked and removing those he didn't. His ruthlessness was such that after his return from a period at the French court where he fancied he had not been treated in the manner appropriate to his view of himself, he executed many of the servants who had accompanied him so they could not relate to others at home the stories of the various slights he had endured. Thus were removed not only political opponents but even those who were just embarrassments.

Cesare Borgia, whose dozens of victims included many who were poisoned, was himself poisoned and, although he was not to die, the event marked the beginning of his downfall. He and his father were taken ill after they had dined with Cardinal Adriano de Corneto, who himself fell sick – although it is not known if the cardinal's illness was a cover-up. While Cesare recovered, his father, the Pope, did die. Cesare was imprisoned by the new Pope, and his supporters, his army and his influence were lost. On his release he went to Spain but was imprisoned again, for the murder of his brother. He escaped and, with Lucrezia's help, joined forces with his brother-in-law, but he was badly injured in a battle and left to die. He was only 32.

Lucrezia lived for another ten years, married again and was renowned for her kindness. However, because of the lifelong support she gave Cesare throughout his career, she has acquired the reputation of being an accomplice in his murders and is regarded as a poisoner herself, although there is no evidence she ever killed anybody. There is no doubt, though, that Cesare Borgia was a classic case of a serial killer.

Vlad the Impaler
and Elizabeth Bathory

BRAM STOKER could not have known how widespread were the deep fears and fantasies that his classic horror story *Dracula* would stir. The idea that a human could be literally thirsty for blood caused such a frisson as to provoke endless variations on the vampire theme in books and films. Yet a real man and woman from the 15th and 16th centuries were Dracula figures whose atrocities can hardly be imagined.

The original Dracula was Vlad Tepes, ruler of Wallachia, which is separated by the Carpathian Mountains from Transylvania in what is now part of Romania. His father had been given the name Dracul, which means 'Devil' or 'Terrible One'. When Tepes came to the throne in 1456 he inherited a country where the nobles were at war with each other, his own father and brother having been slain in these conflicts. He began his reign by exterminating his enemies and his enemies' families in the most barbaric way – torturing and burning. He solved the problem of the local poor and sick by inviting them to dine, and then locking up the palace and setting it on fire. However, his favourite form of execution was impaling his victims on long upright spikes. As they struggled, or even moved at all, so their weight would fix them more securely on the spike, and they would gradually work their way down the spikes until they died. This perversion earned him the nickname of Vlad the Impaler. There is no doubt he achieved sexual satisfaction from this torture, and he liked to take his meals in the presence of these poor victims and listen to their cries of agony. He would vary the positions in which the doomed were placed on the

11

spikes, and – the Dracula hallmark – he would drink his victims' blood.

Vlad the Impaler was himself murdered in 1476, but his grave in the monastery at Snagov was never found.

About 100 years after Vlad's reign of terror, Elizabeth Bathory was born in Hungary to rich aristocrats and was brought up in the Carpathians, just to the west of Vlad's empire. When she was 15, in 1575, she married General Count Nadasdy, the 'Black Hero' of Hungary. They lived in a castle at Csejthe but the General was often at the wars, leaving the Countess to her own devices, which included satisfying a well-developed sexual appetite and establishing a large colony of cats, which she believed were endowed with supernatural powers.

The Countess acquired a taste for blood accidentally when she wounded a maid who had upset her. Some of the blood splashed upon the Countess's skin and, when it was washed away, she fancied that her skin glowed. When her husband died young in 1600, the Countess developed her new taste for blood. Except for a 'witch-nurse', some carefully chosen servants and a collection of 'enchanted' cats, she lived in seclusion. Local peasant girls began to vanish and soon rumours circulated of girls kept to provide blood for the Countess's baths, which she took to keep her skin young.

On New Year's Eve 1610, Count Thurso, the Countess's cousin and Hungary's prime minister, visited Castle Csejthe with soldiers and police to investigate the rumours. The discovery he made was horrifying.

Girls were chained up everywhere. Many were dead and the corpses stank; many were on the point of death, with the blood drained from them. Many more were well-fed, clearly being prepared for their task of providing blood in the future. Some of these were already 'in production', punctured with small holes at the neck, chest or stomach, from where the blood was drawn off. There were also many instruments of torture, such as scissors, chains, handcuffs and a gruesome 'iron maiden' – a device like a mummy case with many spikes pointing inwards, so that when a victim was placed inside and the case was closed, she would be punctured in several places at once. And around all the girls, alive, bleeding, or dead, the cats picked their way.

It was estimated that some 300 women had been put to death by the Countess. While alive they had been fed on their own flesh, grilled. 'We have the right to do what we wish to those beneath us,' she said. 'We are of royal blood.'

The Countess was 50, but her skin was that of a much younger woman. She was walled up in her room for the rest of her life and fed through slits in the wall. Without her blood baths she lived only three more years.

Burke and Hare

TO 'BURKE', according to the dictionary, is to murder by suffocation so as to leave no mark. The word comes from William Burke, famous with his partner William Hare for selling bodies to the medical profession for dissection. Yet Burke and Hare were not the bodysnatchers or grave-robbers of legend; they acquired their bodies by murder. Only Burke was punished, as Hare, the main instigator of the trade, turned King's evidence.

Burke and Hare were Irishmen who, like many others, came to Scotland to work on the Union Canal between Glasgow and Edinburgh. They met in 1826 when both were living in squalor in neighbouring lodging houses in Edinburgh's West Port. The activities which earned them notoriety began by chance on 29 November 1827 when a fellow lodger of Burke, an army pensioner named Donald, died while owing Hare £4, a large sum in those days. Desperate to regain the money in some way, Hare decided to sell Donald's body to Dr Knox of the Anatomy School. The grave-robbing trade was already well established, but it was a skilled and arduous practice, carried out by men who were called 'Resurrectionists'. Hare's idea was to cut out the 'middleman' of the parish undertaker so, while the body was in its coffin in the house, awaiting collection, he removed it with the help of friend Burke and substituted tree bark. The two men trundled the body round to Dr Knox at 10 Surgeons' Square and were delighted to get £7.10s for it, with the hint that more of the same would be gratefully accepted; Dr Knox had a great number of students, and bodies for dissection were not easy to obtain.

Burke and Hare discovered that the latter held true for them, too. They could hardly sit around waiting for fellow lodgers to die, so when one of them, a miller, was taken ill with a fever they smothered him. Dr Knox paid £10, which became the standard fee. Hare's common-law wife Maggie and Burke's mistress, Helen McDougal, joined the 'business', but after another lodger had been released from the suffering of jaundice, the quartet ran out of sick acquaintances.

The problem was solved by luring poor people off the streets for a party, rendering them insensible with whisky (usually while Burke, who had a fine voice, sang) and despatching them to the next world before trundling them along to 10 Surgeon's Square, the premises of Dr Knox. This was done by Hare placing his hands over the victim's nose and mouth from behind and pulling the victim to the floor, when Burke would sit on the victim's chest as he or she suffocated. The £10 revenue per transaction more than paid for the expenses of whisky, and soon the four of them were living in relative style.

There were upsets and misunderstandings. Helen McDougal, discovering Burke apparently enjoying himself with two buxom 18-year-old prostitutes, needed a lot of persuading that Burke was merely about his business and was only subdued by a clip round the ear with a wine glass. As Burke and Hare wheeled a tea chest carrying the body of one of the girls to Dr Knox they were followed by some scruffy street-boys, who shouted out that they had a body in the box. Dr Knox was so impressed by the young and voluptuous body that he preserved it in whisky for a special occasion, and a student invited an artist to sketch it.

On another occasion, after Hare had acquired a diseased and decrepit old horse to help take the bodies of a woman and her 12-year-old son to Dr Knox, the horse collapsed, and Burke and Hare had to hire a porter to help them complete the journey. At £16 the pair of corpses, they could afford it. The visit of Ann McDougal, a distant relative of Burke's, provided more income, as did Burke's washer-woman. Another 'double' was scored when the daughter of an old prostitute, already in the tea chest, came searching for her, and was reunited with her mother for ever.

The criminals took dreadful risks. An 18-year-old called Daft Jamie, well-known in the area as what used to be called the 'village idiot', was a victim. His body was, of course, immediately recognized by Dr Knox and his students. Daft Jamie put up a great struggle because he did not drink whisky, so Burke and Hare devised a wax mask to hold over their victims' faces to make suffocation easier.

The game was up when two new lodgers in Burke's house, Mr and Mrs Gray, discovered the body of a woman who had been brought to the house the previous day. Helen McDougal was asked about it, and tried to bribe them to keep quiet with a few shillings and a hint of £10 a week for them if they wanted. But the Grays went to the police.

The trial of Burke and Helen McDougal was held on Christmas Eve and continued until 9.25 am on Christmas morning, when the jury brought in their verdicts. The conviction of Burke was a formality after both the Hares had turned King's evidence. Helen McDougal escaped the gallows through the peculiar Scottish verdict of 'Not Proven'.

A crowd of 25,000 spectators cheered when Burke was hanged in a downpour on 28 January 1829. His body was dissected for the education of the students of Dr Monro, Dr Knox's rival, then publicly displayed. His skeleton is still at the University of Edinburgh. His three collaborators narrowly escaped lynching. The two women were smuggled out of the country – McDougal to Australia and Mrs Hare to Ireland. Hare fled to London, where workmates discovered who he was and threw him into a lime pit. He was last seen as a blind matchseller.

A year after Burke's execution the law that required every corpse to have a Christian burial was repealed. Two years later an act was passed enabling bodies, under certain circumstances, to be sent to medical schools for dissection – so the trade that Burke and Hare made famous ceased.

Hélène Jegado

HÉLÈNE JEGADO was an illiterate French peasant girl who murdered anyone who displeased her and a few more besides by mixing arsenic in their food. She was eventually tried for three murders and three attempted murders but she was implicated in no less than 23 deaths, one of them that of her own sister.

As a young girl she was sent into service, a dismal life of hard work and few pleasures which she tried to brighten by stealing from her employers. She was dismissed from several jobs but always managed to find new employment because she appeared so submissive and pious. At one time she joined a convent as a novice but before long small items began to go missing and were traced to the newcomer, so she was sent away.

Her murderous impulses began to emerge when she was in her 30s. She worked as a maid for one clergyman after another and in each household, illness and death spread like a virus. 'Wherever I go, people die!' she lamented, putting on a convincing show of grief as yet another body was carried out. There was no reason why she should be suspected; after all, she had nothing to gain from the deaths. She was just as likely to poison her fellow servants as the families of her employers, so the deaths assumed a random pattern and were always written off as due to one of the many diseases prevalent in the mid-19th century.

In 1849 she was working for the Rabot family in Rennes, but was given notice when she was caught pilfering. Next day the three members of the household suffered violent stomach cramps and vomiting. For once, Hélène's skill as a poisoner had deserted her and her victims lived to give evidence against her later.

She moved to take another job in the same city, this time with Professor Théodore Bidard. Shortly after her arrival a younger maid fell ill and, with Hélène as her nurse, she was soon dead. Hélène told M. Bidard that sooner than have a stranger filling her friend's place, she would do the work of both girls and he was touched by her devotion. The following year another servant, Rosalie Sarrazin, was taken on and the two girls became close friends but things changed when Rosalie took on the household accounts, sitting studiously over her books at the table while the illiterate Hélène watched enviously. In the summer of 1851 Rosalie was taken ill with the familiar gastric symptoms and she died in July.

This time the doctor had his doubts about the cause of death but Hélène might still have escaped detection save for an unguarded exclamation when the magistrates, accompanied by police, arrived to investigate. Her first words were, 'I am innocent!' The magistrates pointed out that no one had accused her of anything yet, but soon afterwards she was arrested.

There was surprisingly little hard evidence against Hélène Jegado. It was never proved that she had ever obtained arsenic and no convincing motive was established, but the circumstantial evidence was overwhelming and she was sent to the guillotine in December 1851.

Dr William Palmer

THE CLASSIC British case of systematic poisoning is that of Dr William Palmer who, when he was born in 1824, was the only legitimate child of the several in the family. When his father died, each child inherited £7,000 of ill-gotten gains, although they could not claim their money until they were 21. William was a happy if self-willed lad who at 17, when apprenticed to a chemist, stole from his employers to pay for his girlfriend's abortion. His mother made good the sum, saving his honour if not his job, but when, soon afterwards, a man whose wife William fancied died after drinking some brandy in his company, he decided to leave his village of Rugeley in Staffordshire and go to London. He qualified as a surgeon at Bart's Hospital, and returned to Rugeley to practise medicine from his rooms opposite the Talbot Arms.

Palmer had developed an expensive taste for horse-racing and gambling and soon found his inheritance disappearing, so he married Annie Brooks, who had an inheritance of her own. Her father, Colonel Brooks, was one of five brothers who all committed suicide separately, in the Colonel's case leaving his wife and daughter well off. Mrs Brooks was a drunkard with whom Annie had broken relations but after a while there was a reconciliation and she was persuaded to come and live with her daughter and Palmer. Within two weeks she had died, and Palmer gained access to her wealth: seven houses and more capital for his horse-racing. By now, he owned his own stables.

Palmer seemed to become surrounded by sudden death. An uncle died the day after Palmer visited him (as far as it is known, Palmer didn't benefit): two of Palmer's illegitimate children died: and an acquaintance who came to stay with Palmer for the races (and to collect a debt) passed away also. Even his wife Annie, extremely happy at first, began to remark upon the coincidence. Four of her own children died young. When a friend called Bly, who was owed £800 by Palmer, died, so allowing Palmer to deny the debt, Annie asked 'What will people say?' Soon Annie herself died, and Palmer collected £13,000 from an insurance policy he had lately taken out.

Gossip about Palmer was widespread in Rugeley, of course, where people had not failed to notice these happenings, and it was not abated when the housemaid gave birth nine months after Annie's death, nor when the baby shortly died.

Palmer's gambling meant he always needed money, and now he struck a deal with his brother Walter, who had also married into money but was spending it rapidly on gin, which threatened to end his life early. Palmer suggested to his brother that he insure his life for a small sum on the understanding that he, Palmer, would keep him well stocked with gin, to be repaid in full when Walter died and the policy could be cashed. Walter agreed and even went on the wagon temporarily to convince the insurers he was a good risk. He soon died, whether from the copious gin he was given or from something else nobody knew. The policy, however, far from being a small one, proved to be another for £13,000, the company having declined Palmer's wish to make it £82,000. The insurance company disputed the claim, together with another on a friend of Palmer's for £25,000, and Palmer's cash flow became even more of a problem.

One day Palmer went to Shrewsbury races with his friend John Cook, whose mare, Polestar, won. Cook returned to Rugeley with Palmer to celebrate, but became ill after drinking a brandy. Palmer installed him in the Talbot Arms under his own care, then went to London to collect from a bookmakers the money owed to Cook. On the morning after his return, Cook took pills Palmer had prescribed, went into a convulsion and died. Palmer soon produced a money order for £4,000 in his favour signed by Cook. However, Cook's stepfather was suspicious, claimed it was a forgery, and demanded an autopsy.

Although only a little antimony rather than the suspected strychnine which Palmer was alleged by witnesses to have bought was found in the body, the circumstantial evidence at the inquest led to a verdict of 'wilful murder' and Palmer was arrested. The bodies of his wife and brother were exhumed and plenty of antimony was found in the former's body, although there was none in that of Walter.

Palmer was tried for the murder of Cook at the Old Bailey, and although the medical evidence was poor – seven medical men declared there was strychnine in the body, 11 that they could find nothing – Palmer was found guilty. There was a crowd of 50,000 at Stafford Gaol on 14 June 1856 to see him hanged. The citizens of Rugeley petitioned for the name of their now infamous village to be changed, but it is still there.

Frederick Deeming

FREDERICK DEEMING was born in the 1840s, the youngest of seven children. His father gradually went mad, and Deeming himself was odd enough to be known as 'Mad Fred' as a boy. The balance of his mind, like his father's before him, deteriorated until, in his last years, he committed some callous crimes.

Deeming became a ship's steward at 18, and never lost his inclination to travel round the world. Unfortunately, in most places he visited he lived as a confidence-trickster, assuming numerous aliases and posing as rich men, usually with a title. He cheated jewellers by masquerading as a diamond mine owner, an idea he probably got when working in South African goldfields. The death of his mother in 1875 affected him deeply, and he began to see visions of her. He went back to sea, and suffered some mental illness in Calcutta.

Back in his native Liverpool, he married and then, with his wife, went to live in Australia. However, after fathering four children he abandoned the family in Sydney, leaving his wife to beg on the streets, and began to make his way back to England. In 1890 he was posing as Lord Dunn in Antwerp, trying to raise cash by cheating diamond merchants. He returned to Liverpool but did not stay long, going off to Rainhill, just outside the city. Here he found himself accommodation by posing as Albert O. Williams, an Inspector of Regiments searching for a house to rent for his employer Colonel Brooks. He rented a property called Dinham Villa from a Mrs Mather and stayed in the local hotel while pretending to await Colonel Brooks. In this short period he courted Mrs Mather's daughter Emily.

Deeming's surprise when his wife and four children turned up one day was considerable. Having bravely made her way to Liverpool,

Mrs Deeming had been directed to Rainhill by Deeming's brothers. However, Deeming persuaded Mrs Mather to allow his 'married sister' and her family to stay in Dinham Villa for a day or two before going abroad. He also gained permission to move into Dinham Villa himself to re-cement the floor in one room, as it was not level enough for Colonel Brooks' rich carpets. Soon the family disappeared and the room had an excellent new cement floor.

Deeming now speeded up his courtship of Emily, married her, announced his intention to take her to Australia, threw a farewell party and left, leaving Colonel Brooks, who, of course, was never to arrive, to pay the bills.

The scene now shifts to a house in Windsor, a suburb of Melbourne, later in the year. A Mr Druin, an Englishman with a Liverpool accent, had been renting it, but had left suddenly. The house was being shown to a prospective new tenant, who turned it down because of a nasty smell in one bedroom. The owner and agent later returned to investigate the smell, and found it came from beneath the hearthstone. As they began to raise it, the smell became so overpowering they called the police. Buried in the concrete were found the remains of a woman.

In the grate, police found a torn luggage ticket issued by a shipping line at Melbourne, covering the luggage of two people. It was issued to Albert Williams, and the police issued a warrant for Williams' arrest. In rubbish at the back of the house they also found a screwed-up invitation for a party at the Commercial Hotel in Rainhill – the very farewell party Deeming had thrown before leaving for Australia. The Australian police quickly compared notes with those at Rainhill. Dinham Villa was entered, and the new floor was discovered to be giving off a dreadful smell. Under the concrete were the bodies of a woman and four children. Deeming's brothers identified them as being Deeming's family, whom they had directed to Rainhill only a few months earlier.

Meanwhile, back in Australia, Deeming had gone to Adelaide and taken a ship to Sydney. On board he met 19-year-old Kate Rounsefell,

EXECUTION Of DEEMING.

Alleged Confession.

Last Moment

Contemporary poster of the execution of Frederick Deeming

who was on her way to see her sister in Bathurst. Deeming, now 'Baron Swanston', swept her off her feet, stayed with her for 24 hours in Sydney, proposed, was taken to see the sister and was accepted. When Baron Swanston left, Miss Rounsefell agreed to meet him after her visit at his hotel in Melbourne.

When she arrived there, the fortunate Miss Rounsefell found a telegram from her sister urging her to go no further. The reason soon became clear: Baron Swanston's picture was in the newspapers. He was described as Albert Williams, wanted for questioning about the murder of his wife.

Deeming did not turn up, anyway. He had fled to a mining town called Southern Cross, over 1500 miles away in Western Australia. He was nevertheless recognized and arrested and brought back to Melbourne, a long journey by train and ship during which he was in constant danger from an incensed public.

Thousands jammed the docks at Melbourne, and Deeming had to be smuggled ashore after a decoy had been sent in the opposite direction. He was brilliantly defended by Alfred Deakin, who later became prime minister of Australia. The main defence was insanity, but judge and jury would not let him escape. He was hanged on 23 May 1892, to the cheers of thousands. It was alleged later that three houses in which he had lived in South Africa also harboured female bodies under the floor.

H.H. Holmes

AMERICA'S classic serial killer is Hermann Mudgett, otherwise H.M. Howard or, most famously, H.H. Holmes. He was a man who would indulge in any sort of crime, but who graduated mainly through confidence trickery and fraud to well-planned murder in a purpose-built 'castle'.

Holmes began life in 1860 in New Hampshire, studied medicine in Michigan and began to practise in New York. He was married at 18, and perpetrated what was probably his first big swindle at medical school by faking the death of a partner in crime with the use of a body stolen from the school, the pair to share the insurance money.

In 1886 he moved to Chicago and assumed the name of Holmes in order to escape his wife and child. He bigamously married the pretty and well-off Myrta Belknap, but was soon discovered forging her uncle's signature, which led to a separation. Holmes found another route to quick riches by teaming up with the owner of a drugstore, a Mrs Holden. Soon he became a partner, and then became the owner when she disappeared.

Holmes profited vastly from the sale of patent medicines and with the proceeds began to build his spectacular 'murder castle' opposite the drugstore. It was ostensibly a massive hotel, built in anticipation of housing visitors to the Columbian Exposition of 1893. The ground floor was stores, while the second and third floors contained 100 rooms or so, some for Holmes' use as living accommodation and offices, others for guests. In fact, by picking arguments with successive builders and replacing them during construction, Holmes was able to erect a warren of secret rooms and passages.

Some of the rooms in Holmes' hotel were gas chambers, without windows and with strong doors. There were peepholes and Holmes could control the gas from outside. Some rooms had chambers built below false floors, while others had chutes to convey bodies to the basement. The basement was fitted with quicklime pits and vats of acid. The execution chambers were even fitted with alarms which warned Holmes in his own quarters of escape attempts.

The victims for Holmes' hotel were nearly all young women who met him socially and accepted his swift proposals of marriage or applied for jobs which he advertised in the press. Those who were found suitable (that is to say risk-free) were installed in one of his rooms while he set about realizing their assets. He would resort to torture on women not immediately forthcoming with their valuables. When Holmes had acquired a victim's goods, and had satisfied his sexual desires, she would be despatched to the basement.

A jeweller who took a corner of the drugstore to repair watches moved out when he discovered his wife, Julia, and her 18-year-old sister had both become Holmes' mistress. The sister disappeared soon after becoming pregnant. Soon Julia herself became jealous of Holmes' stunning new secretary, blonde Emily Cigrand. She was despatched with her eight-year-old daughter, and Miss Cigrand followed only three months later; her demise may have been hastened by the appearance of pretty Minnie Williams, an heiress worth $20,000. Minnie moved in with Holmes, and she too brought a sister to stay who later disappeared.

Holmes had been unable to get out of the debt incurred by his building works and after the Exposition was over he tried to recoup $60,000 from an insurance company for damage to the upper storeys. However, he was thwarted after an investigation and when details of his past began to come to light he fled from Chicago with Minnie, who had made her fortune over to him, and Benjamin F. Pitzel, a partner in many of Holmes's swindles. In Denver, Holmes married again, the bride being lovely Georgiana Yoke, and at about this time Minnie disappeared.

Holmes bought a drugstore in St Louis after raising loans on Minnie's property. He insured the stock, which Pitzel promptly removed by arrangement, but the insurance fraud was discovered and Holmes was gaoled (for the only time in his career of swindling). In gaol, Holmes met Marion Hedgepeth, a notorious gunfighter and train robber. Holmes asked Hedgepeth if he could recommend a crooked lawyer, and outlined his next insurance fraud to him. The latter recommended Jephta D. Howe, for which service he was promised $500.

On his release, Holmes (now calling himself Howard) moved with Pitzel to Philadelphia, and rented a house near the morgue. The plan was a repeat of Holmes' first fraud. Pitzel would set up in business as R.F. Perry, there would be an accident and the body of Perry would be found. Holmes would collect the insurance, and the two would split the money. No doubt Pitzel believed the body would be stolen from the morgue, but in the event it was his own that was found. Holmes identified the body, and the lawyer collected the cheque on behalf of the family. Holmes paid him off and kept for himself, of course, a double share.

Holmes now had to remove Pitzel's family to escape detection, for the latter's wife was in on the scheme, and there were five children. On the pretext of taking them to their father, Holmes took the three middle children to Indianapolis, where he disposed of the boy. He then took the two girls to Toronto, where they too were killed. Meanwhile, Hedgepeth had decided he was never going to get his $500, so he told the authorities of Holmes' plan in a bid to get his sentence reduced. The insurance company realized they had been swindled, and some smart detective work led them to find Holmes in Burlington, Vermont, where he was living with Georgiana. Mrs Pitzel and her two remaining children were living nearby, awaiting their chance, they thought, to join the rest of the family.

Holmes was taken to Philadelphia, while more detective work found the bodies of the three Pitzel children. A thorough search was now undertaken of Holmes' 'castle' in Chicago. Nobody knows how many bodies the bones and remnants found there belonged to. One newspaper estimated 200, a figure quoted by many accounts since. Holmes sold a 'confession' to a Chicago newspaper for $5000, but later disowned it. He claimed 27 victims but, as he named some people who were still alive, and ignored others who were known to be dead, this list is worthless.

Holmes was hanged on 7 May 1896 for the murder of Pitzel, Philadelphia declining to allow Chicago the pleasure of executing him for the more horrific crimes carried out in his 'castle'. Altogether, Holmes probably killed upwards of 40 people. Had he not foolishly boasted to Marion Hedgepeth, he could possibly have added many more to his list over the next few years.

Johann Hoch

NOBODY knows exactly how many women Johann Hoch poisoned, but 15 to 20 is the most reasonable estimate. His reasons and methods were always the same. Changing his name from one wife to the next, he would make the acquaintance of his victim, marry her, if necessary poison her, and abscond with her wealth. He did not always kill: the number of his marriages is also unknown, but 55 in 15 years is not far off.

Hoch was born John Schmidt in 1862 in Horweiler, Germany, but was taken to the USA when young. Having deserted his first wife and three children, he embarked on his systematic way of life and death around 1890. His favourite means of attracting likely candidates for his plans was an advertisement in German-language newspapers – a good way to meet homesick countrywomen. The advertisement which attracted the last victim read:

> Widower, quiet and home-loving, with comfortable income and well-furnished house, wishes acquaintance of congenial widow without children. Object: matrimony.

Hoch was an intelligent man who used arsenic to kill. He was careful and patient, so that the victims gradually got worse, and the doctors diagnosed the kidney disease nephritis, for which there was then no cure. Hoch made sure the corpses were heavily embalmed, because at that time all embalming fluids contained arsenic, and if by chance a suspicious authority exhumed a body for study the presence of arsenic would be explained.

In the middle of his rampage, Hoch was almost exposed. He was arrested in Chicago under the name of Martin Dotz for suspected bigamy and the swindling of a furniture dealer. His picture appeared in a newspaper and was recognized by a Reverend Haas of Wheeling, West Virginia. Haas knew the balding man with the moustache as Jacob Huff who, three years earlier, had arrived in Wheeling and quickly married Mrs Caroline Hoch, a well-off widow. The Revd. Haas had officiated at the ceremony. It wasn't long before the new Mrs Huff became ill, and in three months she was dead. The Revd. Haas had seen Huff give his wife a white powder, and was suspicious. After the death, Huff collected the insurance, withdrew his wife's money from the bank, sold the house and disappeared. According to the Revd. Haas, he faked a suicide by leaving a note and his clothes on the bank of the Ohio River.

All this was related to Inspector Shippy in Chicago, who put it to 'Dotz' that he was Huff. Hoch immediately agreed, but then thought better of it and said no more. Mrs Huff's body was exhumed but nothing could be proved. While 'Dotz' was serving a year's imprisonment for his swindle, the Chicago police tried to trace his life and activities between Wheeling and Chicago. Discovering a trail of marriages and early deaths, and convinced of the truth of the story of the Revd. Haas, they now felt sure they had a mass murderer in custody. However, no solid proof of murder could be unearthed and Hoch had to be released.

It was a narrow escape, and Hoch realized another mistake would be his last. For this reason, perhaps, he speeded up his operations, not wishing to remain too long in any one place. Ironically, it was in Chicago that he made his final mistake, and he was using the name Johann Hoch – Hoch being, of course, the name of the previous wife he had killed in Wheeling. It was a peculiarity of Hoch that he often used as his alias the name of one of his wives, a macabre and dangerous trait. It was not this that finished him, however.

A Mrs Marie Walcker answered a seemingly innocuous advertisement for a wife. In a few days she was married, and within a month was dying. Her sister Amelia came to visit her on what turned out to be her last day. Hoch embraced her, and told her his wife was dying and that he couldn't face being alone. He proposed marriage. Amelia was stunned, but, as Hoch said: 'The dead are for the dead.' They were married four days later. Hoch took her money and disappeared. That was his mistake. The trusting and sorrowful Amelia reported him missing to the police. Hoch's picture was published in various newspapers. Suddenly from everywhere there were claims from women that the missing man was their husband under another name, or from other sources that he was the short-term husband of a friend or relative who had died soon afterwards. Bodies were exhumed and arsenic found. A big police hunt was launched.

Hoch was found in New York. He was the new boarder, 'Henry Bartels', of a widowed landlady to whom he had proposed 20 minutes after their meeting. Incriminating articles were found in his room and many ex-wives came forward to testify against him. He was charged with the murder of Marie Walcker, whose embalmer, as it happened, had switched two weeks before to one of the new embalming fluids which did not contain arsenic. It was the clincher. 'It's all over with Johann,' said Hoch, as he was sentenced to be hanged. His last day was 23 February 1906, and 100 people witnessed his death.

In 1955 some bones were found in the wall of a cottage in which he had lived – a place searched without success by the police seeking evidence at the time.

Joseph Vacher

VACHER was the classical killer of the horror movies, an unspeakably ugly tramp who was almost certainly mad and who performed outrageous atrocities on his victims, always working in a frenzy but in a deadly silence. In France he was called 'Jack l'eventreur du sud-est' – Jack the Ripper of the south-east.

He was born on 16 November 1869 at Beaufort, Isère, the fifteenth child of his family. He claimed after his capture that at eight years of age he was bitten by a mad dog, and that this, plus the fact that he took in one swig a bottle of medicine from the local quack, permanently upset his brain. It is likely there was an incident with a mad dog, but exactly what it was is unknown. He began work as a farmhand, but found himself in trouble for attempting to rape a youth. After he developed an inflammation of the scrotum, he underwent an operation which necessitated the removal of part of a testicle; his mutilation later of male victims echoed this experience. He joined the army and a liking for knives and an aggressive readiness to use them at first won him promotion to sergeant, but then landed him in hospital for observation.

On his release, Vacher courted a girl who finally preferred a rival. He shot her three times, and then turned the gun on himself. She recovered quickly and Vacher, who shot himself in the head, merely gave himself a hideous face. The bullet lodged behind his right eye, which thereafter was permanently bloodshot and raw, without a lower lid, and continuously weeping. A scar ran from below his lower lip to the right side of his upper lip, which was raised and twisted. Since his face was pale with yellow patches and part of it was paralysed, it presented a repulsive contorted appearance. This shooting, added to his previous history, meant that in July 1893 he was committed to Saint-Ylie asylum, where his behaviour was ferociously aggressive and his cunning enabled him to escape from time to time. However, after being transferred to an asylum at Saint-Robert, he was discharged as cured on 1 April 1894.

Vacher's first murder occurred about six weeks later and, for the next three years, he roamed the countryside as a tramp, carrying an accordion to which he sang, and a sackful of other odd objects including a cudgel, a pair of scissors, several knives and a cleaver.

On 20 May 1894, 21-year-old Eugénie Delhomme awaited her boyfriend in a quiet country road near Beaurepaire, south of Lyon. Instead, along came Vacher and Eugénie was later found behind a hedge, strangled, raped and disembowelled. Six months later, in August, the body of a 13-year-old girl, Louise Marcel, was found in a stable. Her throat had been cut and her body mutilated. In May 1895, Adèle Mortureux, aged 17, was treated in the same way. There were strong suspects for all these murders and, in the case of the last two, there were arrests – but nobody was sent for trial. In August 1895, 60-year-old Jean-Marie Morand was raped and killed in her lonely cottage while her son was in the fields. Like all the other victims, she had been disembowelled. The crimes had come at six-month intervals, but now Vacher struck again after only a week – a young shepherd, Victor Portalier, was repeatedly stabbed. This time a description of Vacher was circulated on the strength of people at the local farms reporting that this wretch had called on them begging for food.

It is difficult to understand how Vacher escaped capture, especially as next month he was disturbed by an approaching cart as he killed 16-year-old Aline Alise. The driver saw his bloodstained face and offered assistance, but Vacher claimed to have had a fit and fallen, and that he had recovered. The driver went on, and Vacher returned to mutilating the corpse. A week later he sexually assaulted and then killed another shepherd boy, aged 14.

Vacher was all but caught in March 1896 when he attacked 11-

year-old Alphonsine-Marie Derouet on her way to early morning mass. Her screams were heard by a gamekeeper who tackled Vacher, but could not capture him. However, the police now had a very accurate description of Vacher, although later that day a policeman on a bicycle stopped Vacher as he tramped along a road and, incredibly, did not recognize or detain him.

It is just as remarkable that, eight days later, Vacher was arrested for vagrancy, and still not recognized. After a few weeks in prison, he was free again. The killings were resumed: in September 1896, Marie Moussier, the 19-year-old wife of a shepherd, in October a 14-year-old shepherdess, Rosine Rodier. In May 1897 Vacher killed a 14-year-old fellow tramp, Claudius Beaupied, in an empty house although the body was not found until Vacher confessed to the murder six months later. In June it was the turn of 14-year-old Pierre Laurent, who was castrated.

On 4 August 1897 Vacher's atrocities finally came to an end. Mme Marie-Eugénie Plantier was out collecting pine cones with her husband and children when Vacher attacked her from behind. She got his hand from her mouth long enough to shout, at which her husband ran up, picked up a stone and smashed it into Vacher's twisted mouth. Vacher produced his scissors and wounded Plantier but, with the assistance of the latter's wife, children and a peasant working nearby Vacher was finally subdued. Two other peasants helped take him to the local inn, where he played his accordion to the locals while awaiting the police.

Vacher was charged with the killing of Portalier, and admitted all his previous crimes, pleading insanity and citing the incident with the dog. He was studied by a team of doctors headed by the famous Alexandre Lacassagne, who found him sane; with hindsight, it seems they were wrong. Vacher was sentenced to death on 28 October 1898 and on 31 December was dragged to the guillotine.

Peter Kürten

A MILD-MANNERED, soberly dressed, intelligent man, Peter Kürten nevertheless caused terror in Düsseldorf in the late 1920s, and his deeds fascinated and horrified the whole world. A psychiatrist to whom he frankly related his crimes and his feelings after his arrest described Kürten as the 'king of sexual perverts'.

Kürten saw plenty of raw sex as a child because his father was a drunkard who violently forced himself on his wife in the presence of the children, of whom there were eventually 13. Kürten's sexual activity appears to have started at the age of eight, when a local dog-catcher showed him how to masturbate his dogs. He claimed to have committed his first murder at the equally tender age of nine, pushing a schoolfriend off a raft and holding down the head of a would-be rescuer, so that both boys drowned.

The family moved to Düsseldorf in 1894 when Kürten was 11. By the time he was 13 Kürten was practising bestiality with farm animals, and discovered his greatest satisfaction when stabbing a sheep while having intercourse. From then on, blood and sex were combined in his dreams and many animals of local farmers suffered. Kürten's father was imprisoned for the attempted rape of his own daughter and Kürten himself tried to have an incestuous relationship with the same unfortunate girl.

Kürten ran away from home at 14 after stealing from his employer and went to live with a prostitute, who taught him how to abuse her for her pleasure. He was subsequently imprisoned for two years for his theft, during which time his fantasies of blood and lust increased. On his release at the age of 16, he sexually assaulted a woman in the Grafenberger woods in Düsseldorf and then strangled her. However, although he left her for dead, she must have recovered because no crime was reported.

As Kürten's prison terms mounted up, so his fantasies took a revengeful twist, and he dreamt of poisoning whole schools of children. In his periods of freedom he enjoyed indulging in arson, and watching its victims' despair. His first proven murder occurred in 1913, when he was 29. He was burgling a tavern when he came across a 10-year-old girl, Christine Klein, asleep in bed. He strangled her and then cut her throat, leaving behind a bloodstained handkerchief bearing the initials 'PK'. Sadly, the girl's father was called Peter, and it was assumed the handkerchief was his. Suspicion fell on the father and then on his brother, Otto, with whom he had quarrelled bitterly the previous evening. The brother was tried for murder but acquitted on insufficient evidence. Not surprisingly the family never recovered from this trauma.

After spending most of World War I in prison Kürten went to Attenburg in 1921 and married there, his wife being an ex-prostitute who had reformed after shooting a man who jilted her. Kürten also managed to reform to some extent; he got a job in a factory, gave up petty crime and became an active trade unionist. However, he constantly relapsed into his old ways with sexual attacks on women and perversions with animals, only managing to avoid prison sentences for the former crimes because his wife testified to his good character. He later described the thrill of cutting off a swan's head and putting its neck in his mouth to catch the blood.

In 1925 Kürten returned to Düsseldorf, arriving while the city was enjoying a blood-red sunset, which he later said he took as an omen. His wife joined him a few weeks later, but if she had had a hand in his improved behaviour her influence was waning; between 1925 and 1928 he committed several attacks on women and a number of crimes of arson, and was imprisoned again. Between 1900 and 1928 his various spells in prison had totalled nearly 20 years. He was deliberately undisciplined when in captivity, seeking solitary confinement

Police photo of Peter Kürten, the 'Düsseldorf Vampire'

where he could enjoy his fantasies. Then in 1929, when he was 45, he embarked on the series of attacks which soon panicked Düsseldorf.

They began on 3 February, when he attacked a Frau Kuhn and stabbed her 24 times. Her screams saved her life – but only just. On 8 February he killed eight-year-old Rosa Ohliger, stabbing her repeatedly with a pair of scissors. In the evening he returned to the body and tried to burn it, using petrol. The body was found next morning under a hedge and it was evident that the scissors had been used in a sexual attack.

Five days later Kürten met a drunken man, Rudolf Scheer, going home from a beer cellar. He stabbed him repeatedly with the scissors and drank his blood. Soon afterwards he tried to strangle two women with a noose and their descriptions led to the arrest of a mentally handicapped man who confessed to the murders and was placed in a mental home. As if appreciating an escape, Kürten kept his worst impulses in for six months until August, when he began again, launching three separate attacks within half an hour on two women and a man as they walked home in the evening. They all survived his attack, but a domestic servant, Maria Hahn, was not so lucky; she allowed herself to be taken to some fields and was stabbed to death, after which Kürten drank her blood. Her naked body was not found for three months and Kürten later admitted that he had buried it twice, having dug it up six days after the murder with a view to crucifying it on a tree for all to see. He had the spikes with him, but found the task too difficult so reburied the body in a new place.

On 23 August Kürten met two stepsisters, Luise Lentzen, 14, and Gertrud Hamacher, five, returning across some allotments from the local fête. He gave the older girl some money and asked her to fetch him some cigarettes. While she was gone he strangled the younger girl and cut her throat, and when her stepsister returned she met the same end. Their bodies were found next day – the same day that another domestic servant, 26-year-old Gertrud Schulte, accepted Kürten's invitation to take her to a fair. On entering some woods, Kürten attempted to rape her. As she fought she cried, 'I'd sooner die', at which Kürten replied, 'Well, die then', and stabbed her repeatedly with a knife which eventually broke, leaving half of it in her back. She survived, and was able to describe Kürten as fortyish and pleasant-looking in a quiet way; in fact, Kürten was thought of as a dandy by those who knew him.

By now police knew they were searching for a man of unexceptional appearance who nursed a blood lust so strong that nobody in Düsseldorf was safe from a sudden savage and prolonged attack with a sharp implement. The world's newspapers compared the 'Düsseldorf Monster' with the unsolved case of Jack the Ripper. Although the police had descriptions of the Monster, and even one victim who accused Kürten himself, the sheer volume of the information and clues handicapped them. Thousands of suspects were suggested to them by the public, and they interviewed around 10,000 people.

In September another servant, a class of young woman which seemed to fascinate Kürten, was bludgeoned to death with a hammer. Her name was Ida Reuter, and in November another servant, Elisabeth Dorrier, met the same fate. Two more women were attacked with a hammer but survived.

On 7 November Kürten reverted to the knife in killing a five-year-old girl, Gertrud Albermann. She had also been strangled but, for good measure, had been slashed 36 times. Her body was undiscovered for a couple of days and, perhaps in imitation of Jack the Ripper – whose case Kürten had studied – a newspaper was sent a map and a description of where her body would be found. Kürten also gave the location of the body of Maria Hahn, murdered three months before. These disclosures fanned the publicity and the fear surrounding the Monster.

Kürten was quiet now for another six months, until another domestic servant entered his life on 14 May 1930. Twenty-year-old Maria Budlick had lost her job in Cologne and took the train to Düsseldorf to find employment. She met a Frau Bruckner who gave her her address and offered to help her find accommodation, but that evening she failed to meet Frau Bruckner and accepted instead the assistance of a man who volunteered to take her to a hostel where she could get a bed. When the route led into Volksgarten Park, Maria, who knew of the Monster, became alarmed and resisted going further, despite the man's entreaties. A quietly spoken man came to her assistance and she was happy to allow him to find her a room instead. In the meantime she accompanied him to his flat and had a glass of milk and a ham sandwich with him before they took the tram to the hostel. Ironically, the last part of the journey was also through some woods – the same Grafenbergen woods in which Kürten claimed to have strangled a girl some 33 years earlier. This time Maria was not too worried about accompanying her new acquaintance – but her error nearly proved fatal. Kürten insisted on sex and, during intercourse, he began to squeeze the terrified Maria's neck.

Maria was lucky in that she was still conscious when Kürten reached a climax. He immediately became polite and concerned, as (he later confessed) was his normal behaviour after reaching satisfaction. He asked Maria if she could remember where he lived should she need his help again, and she said, 'No', a half-truth which saved her life. Kürten directed her to the hostel and left her.

Maria Budlick did not report her experience to the police, but she did write to Frau Bruckner to tell her of the traumatic encounter she had had. However, she misspelled Frau Bruckner's name, and it was a Frau Brugmann who received the letter and read it. She appreciated the implications and took the letter to the police, who went to see Maria Budlick in the hostel. By such strange coincidences was the first step taken in the apprehension of the Düsseldorf Monster.

Maria Budlick could remember the distinctive name of the street where she had been taken for a snack: Mettmannerstrasse. After some searching with the police she decided No. 71 was familiar, and the landlady showed them a room at the top of the block which she recognized. As they were returning downstairs Kürten entered the hallway and, on seeing Maria, turned pale and hurried out again. The landlady gave the police her tenant's name but, of course, there was still no proof that he was the Monster.

Frau Kürten was fetched from the restaurant where she was used to working until late at night (thus unwittingly giving Kürten the evenings unencumbered for his activities) but she could throw no light on the affair. She was, of course, resigned to Kürten's frequent gaol sentences – for sexual offences as well as burglary – so was only routinely worried about this latest development. Soon afterwards Kürten met her at the restaurant, and confessed to her that he was the Düsseldorf Monster. Frau Kürten took some convincing as, later, did the neighbours, who saw him as a gentle person who got on well with children.

Kürten arranged to meet his wife next day outside a church. She went to the police and led them to him, thus claiming the large reward offered for the capture of the Monster. Kürten was surrounded by armed police, whom he greeted with a smile, saying, 'Don't worry. There's no need to be afraid.' It is possible that this form of capture was planned by Kürten so that the reward would provide for his wife's old age.

Kürten was charged with nine murders and seven attempted murders. He admitted them all, and was fully cooperative in helping police and the chief psychiatrist to piece together the record of his crimes. He stood trial in April 1931, giving evidence from a cage; he was well-dressed and spoke in a matter-of-fact voice, helping the judge to present the facts. It was only when he began to cast aspersions on the morals of some of his female victims that the judge treated him without sympathy. Kürten confessed to 68 vile crimes, some not previously known to the police, all the details of which he could recall clearly. The recollection no doubt gave him renewed pleasure.

He was 48, and was considered sane and indeed clever. One witness said he was also a nice man. The contrast between his manner in

the court and the events he was describing was genuinely shocking.
He was found guilty, of course, and cooperated fully with the police
psychiatrist before his execution by guillotine on 2 July 1931. He
looked forward to a final 'pleasure to end all pleasures', he said –
being able to hear for a split second the blood spurting from his neck,
as it had from the swan he had beheaded in the park.

Neville Heath

NEVILLE GEORGE CLEVELY HEATH was born in Ilford, Essex, in 1917, the son of a hairdresser who plied his trade at Waterloo Station and provided his family with a comfortable middle-class home. Neville was only a mediocre pupil at school, but came into his own at 18 when he was commissioned in the Royal Air Force. He was a good-looking young man with blond hair and a film-star cleft in his chin, was proficient at sports, became a pilot, and generally had the air of an aristocratic, insouciant man-about-town.

Alas, he lacked the income to indulge the role, and began embezzling mess funds and bouncing cheques to pay for the extravagances which he clearly regarded to be his rights. He deserted, was arrested and taken back to his station, escaped in a stolen car and was finally dismissed from the service. As a civilian he continued to offend, was sent to borstal when 19, and on his release enlisted in the Royal Army Service Corps. He was again commissioned but, while a captain in the Middle East soon after the outbreak of World War II, was cashiered for more financial frauds and put on board a ship bound for England.

However, Heath jumped ship at Durban and under the name Armstrong joined the South African Air Force. He married Elizabeth Pitt-Rivers, daughter of a prominent South African family, and soon had a son. In 1944 he was seconded to Bomber Command in England. In trouble again for issuing dud cheques, he returned to South Africa, where he was arrested for fraud. He agreed to a divorce from his wife, giving her custody of their son in return for £2000 and, soon afterwards, was deported to England. He arrived on 5 February 1946, and within five months was charged with murder.

Heath had shown minor signs of a liking for sadism from

44

schooldays – such as stamping on the fingers of a schoolgirl, and spanking another with a ruler. Sadistic practices among consenting adults are not often displayed to others, of course, but Heath had been in England for only 18 days when the manager of London's Strand Palace Hotel entered a bedroom because an electrician had heard screams from within. There was Captain James Cadogan Armstrong of the South African Air Force, otherwise Heath, beating a woman with a cane. She preferred no charges, although the police interviewed her, and the couple seemed on good terms later.

Armstrong's companion may have been Margery Gardner, a married woman who had left her husband and baby in Sheffield to seek fame in London. She wanted to be an actress but, at 31, was leading a precarious life, relying on casual men friends for meals and beds. She was a masochist, and her meeting with Heath provided both of them with some satisfaction. As for Heath, he was using the aliases of Blyth, Denvers and Graham as well as Armstrong, and passing himself off as an officer from the RAF or SAAF. He had the uniforms complete with wings to back up his deception, and was living by financial fraud again.

Margery Gardner certainly shared a night with 'Lieutenant-Colonel' Heath in May at the Pembridge Court Hotel in Notting Hill, where she was tied up and flogged, to the satisfaction of both parties. On 15 June, a 19-year-old girl, Yvonne Symonds, met 'Lieutenant-Colonel' Heath at a WRNS dance and was attracted to him. They booked into the Pembridge Court Hotel as Mr and Mrs N.G.C. Heath, although on this occasion Heath was well-behaved.

Yvonne Symonds went off to join her parents on holiday in Worthing and on the following Thursday, 20 June, Heath was back at Room 4 of the Pembridge Court with Margery Gardner. Both were drunk – they had been drinking together all evening, and Heath had also been consuming vast amounts of liquor ever since lunchtime. He left the hotel in the early hours of the morning.

At 2 pm next day the chambermaid entered the room, having

received no answer to her knock. It seemed to her that one bed had not been used and the other was still occupied. Feeling uneasy, she called the assistant manager, who pulled back the sheet a little to discover an unmistakably dead woman.

What the police uncovered when they arrived was a badly mutilated naked body. There were 17 deep lash marks caused by a diamond-patterned riding whip, her breasts had been bitten away and there was a seven-inch tear in her vagina, probably caused by a short poker in the fireplace. She had been bound hand and foot.

Heath, meanwhile, had followed Yvonne Symonds to Worthing, where he rang her hotel. He had been named in the newspapers as the man wanted for questioning and had to invent a story to cover himself; consequently, he told Yvonne that on the night of the murder he had met a friend, Jack, who was looking for somewhere to take a girl. Remembering he still had the key to Room 4 in the Pembridge Court Hotel (where he and Yvonne had stayed) he had lent the key to Jack. Some time later, Heath told Yvonne, he had received a call from a Chief Inspector Barratt informing him of the murder; he had gone to the hotel to help the police and had even seen the body. On being asked how the girl had died, Heath said: 'A poker was stuck up her. It must have been a maniac.'

Yvonne was convinced by Heath's manner of the truth of what he said. However, the Sunday papers carried the story that police urgently wanted to interview him, and she rang him back at the Ocean Hotel, where he was staying, to tell him her parents were worried. Heath said that he had hired a car and was returning to London immediately to help with police enquiries. Yvonne was never to see him again.

Heath did not go to London, however, but wrote to Scotland Yard, giving a story similar to that he had told Yvonne. He claimed he had lent his key to Mrs Gardner so that she could use his room until 2 am to go to bed with a man. She was to leave the hotel door open for Heath to join her later. At 3 am, he said, he had found her in the state in which the police had discovered her, and had packed his bags and left. He did not want to see the police because there would be a fraud charge against him, but he had the whip and was forwarding it separately, as there would be fingerprints on it other than his. He never did return the whip.

Heath's letter was postmarked Worthing, but by the time the police arrived there, interviewed Yvonne Symonds and visited the Ocean Hotel, Heath had gone, leaving a uniform and some medals. He was now Group Captain Rupert Brooke (an odd name for a handsome young man trying to blend into the background to choose), and was staying at the Tollard Royal Hotel in Bournemouth. On the sea front he met 19-year-old Doreen Marshall, a former Wren who was recovering from a spell of flu by having a holiday at the nearby Norfolk Hotel. Heath took her walking and invited her back to his hotel for tea.

That evening they had dinner, and a lot to drink. During the meal other guests noticed a change of mood in Doreen Marshall, who seemed upset. She and Heath retired to the writing room, where they remained under the observation of other guests, including a Mr and Mrs Phillips. At midnight, when the latter couple decided to retire, Doreen Marshall asked Mr Phillips if he would call her a taxi, which he did at the desk on the way up. However, soon after Heath cancelled it, telling the porter he would walk his guest back to the Norfolk Hotel. 'I'll be back in half-an-hour,' he said, which a still-unhappy Doreen Marshall changed to 15 minutes.

The porter waited for Heath till 4 am, then checked his room, to discover him sound asleep. Heath had used a ladder against the wall at the back of the hotel to climb in, he explained to the manager in the morning, claiming he had been playing a joke on the porter.

Doreen Marshall never returned to the Norfolk. A suspicious and observant Mrs Phillips, seeing Heath next day wearing a silk scarf, asked if she could see it closely, and noticed scratch marks on Heath's neck. Two days after Doreen Marshall's dinner with Heath, the manager of the Norfolk rang his counterpart at the Tollard Royal,

Mr Ivor Relf, to inform him of his guest's disappearance, and Mr Relf asked Heath if the missing Miss Marshall from Pinner might be his guest of earlier in the week. Heath laughed it off, saying his old friend did not come from Pinner. Nevertheless, the manager suggested Heath should go the the police, and with great bravado Heath rang the police to say he would come down to look at a photo of the missing girl to see if she were the one he had entertained to dinner.

'Group Captain Rupert Brooke' admitted at the police station that the girl was indeed the same, and related how he had seen her part of the way home and indeed had seen her again entering a shop the following morning. Completely at ease, and being as helpful as possible, he invented the name of an American army officer who, he said, was also her friend.

Heath was about to leave (and presumably rapidly disappear again) when there occurred one of those coincidences which often mark murder cases. Doreen Marshall's father and married sister arrived to aid enquiries. The two sisters were very alike and, on seeing this striking likeness, Heath was so moved that he began to shiver. The detective-sergeant interviewing him noticed this and suggested to him that Brooke and Heath were one and the same person. The murderer at first denied this but when it was pointed out that he looked very like the photographs of Heath he confessed to his identity.

Heath was detained for further enquiries. He asked if he could go with a policeman to his hotel for his jacket. An inspector went for it instead and found in the pocket a cloakroom ticket from Bournemouth West station dated 23 June. The suitcase was collected from the station and in it were found items of clothing, including a blood-stained scarf, and the diamond-patterned whip which had been used to such vicious effect on Margery Gardner.

A couple of days later Doreen Marshall's body was found. A young woman, Kathleen Evans, noticed her dog investigating something in the undergrowth at Branksome Dene chine, and disturbing a cloud of flies. When the same thing happened next day she brought her father

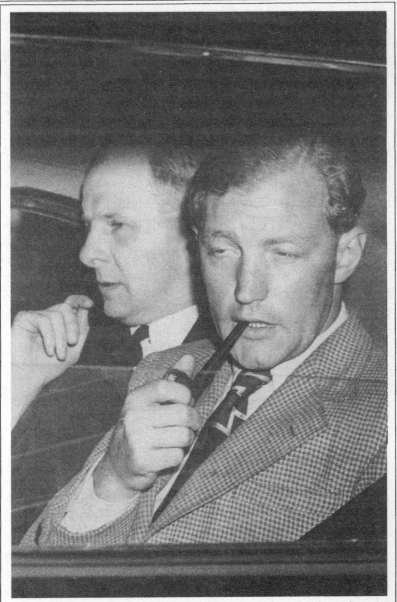

Neville Heath being driven away from court under police escort

to investigate. They found the naked body of Doreen Marshall with the hands tied and throat cut, covered by some of her clothes. Among her injuries were a bitten-off nipple and lines of deep, jagged cuts.

Heath was tried for the murder of Margery Gardner (at the time a person could be charged with numerous murders, but tried for only one at a time). He pleaded not guilty on the grounds of moral insanity. This defence relied on the fact that at the time of the crime the perpetrator was so mentally unbalanced as not to know that he was doing wrong. Heath was so clearly in control of himself that the jury took less than an hour to find him guilty.

He saw no one while awaiting hanging, but wrote to his mother to say that he would sit up during his last night to greet the dawn, which to him had happy associations of early aircraft patrols or late returns from nightclubs. His last dawn was 16 October 1946. When offered a traditional last whisky he replied, 'You might as well make it a double, old boy', continuing his impersonation of an officer and a gentleman until the end.

Charles Schmid

TUCSON is a diverse city; a centre of commerce and of the food-processing industry, it is popular too with tourists and retired people. It is also the university town of Arizona, and supports a large floating population of students. In the early 1960s it was a place where drugs, alcohol and easy sex were available, and there developed an underground teenage society whose activities were based around these. One of the leaders of this society was Charles Schmid who, in 1964, was 22 years old.

Schmid was a bizarre character. He was only 160 cm (5 ft 3 in) tall, and wore high-heeled cowboy boots into which he tucked pads to give him an extra centimetre or two. He was red-headed, but dyed his hair black to present a meaner appearance. He also used make-up, and even affected an artificial mole on his cheek. His behaviour was wild and his stories were wilder. Teenage girls hovered around him, attracted by his easy arrogance, and he was called the 'Pied Piper of Tucson'. His parents were well off, he even had his own 'pad' – a shack-like building at the foot of his parents' garden – and owned a souped-up battered car. One of his tales was that he ran a ring of prostitutes, to whom he had taught 100 different ways of having sexual intercourse. He found a job in the nursing home his parents owned for one young admirer, Mary French, and persuaded her to pay her wages into his bank account.

It was in this atmosphere of 'anything goes' that on the night of 31 May 1964 Schmid told his companions Mary French and John Saunders that he had the urge to kill a girl – any girl – and that they should all do it that very night. Mary French went in search of 15-year-old Alleen Rowe, and asked her to join them for a drive in

Schmid's car. Alleen had told her mother previously that she had been invited to join a 'sex club' and was clearly anxious to become part of the in-crowd, so she was not slow to accept the invitation.

The four drove into the desert, where French stayed in the car while Schmid and Saunders took Alleen to a quiet spot. Schmid raped the girl and calmly told Saunders to hit her over the head with a rock. Before Saunders could obey the terrified girl ran for it, so it was Schmid himself who chased and caught her and smashed in her skull. They buried her in a shallow grave and returned to their drinking, Schmid telling Mary French that he loved her. A strange aside to the story is that Alleen's father, in another part of the country, dreamt about his daughter being murdered, and phoned his wife to tell her of the dream.

Schmid had bragged to his companions beforehand that he could literally get away with murder, and now his boast was that indeed he had. The news, of course, spread in teenage society and many claimed later that Alleen Rowe's fate was common knowledge, but none of this reached the ears of any responsible persons, or if it did it was dismissed as just rumours. So far as the police were concerned, Alleen was just another missing person.

In 1965 Schmid became friendly with a handsome blonde girl, 17-year-old Gretchen Fritz. Schmid, who boasted of the freedom with which he distributed his own sexual favours, was beside himself with misery when the flighty Gretchen rang to tell him she had just made love with somebody else. However, Gretchen later became infatuated with Schmid, who soon found her something of a millstone round his neck.

In mid-August 1965 Gretchen took her 13-year-old sister with her to a drive-in movie, and then went to visit Schmid in his shack. Schmid strangled both sisters and dumped the bodies in the desert. Again, be could not keep quiet about his daring; he boasted to Richard Bruns, a 19-year-old friend. Bruns demanded to see the bodies as proof, so Schmid drove him into the desert, where they buried the bodies more securely.

Once more the sex-and-drugs teenage crowd of Tucson heard the stories but they kept them to themselves, even when undercover police tried to join their circles. Schmid himself, when questioned by outsiders, maintained that the two sisters had run away to California.

It was inevitable that sooner or later there would develop a weak strand in this web of deceit and insider knowledge. It was Richard Bruns who cracked; he acquired the notion that his own girlfriend, whom he knew Schmid had approached unsuccessfully, would be the next on the death list and he began to have terrifying nightmares about it. On 9 November, three months after the double murder, he could stand it no more; he was in Columbus, Ohio, while his girlfriend was still back in Tucson, in reach of Schmid. Bruns went to the police in Columbus and said he could tell them of several murders that had taken place in Tucson.

On 11 November, Schmid, Saunders and French were all arrested and, when the last two turned state's evidence, Schmid's fate was sealed. In any case, Bruns was able to show the police where the two skeletons were. Alleen Rowe's body was never found. Schmid was sentenced to death for the murder of the Fritz girls, and to 55 years in prison for the rape and murder of Alleen Rowe. Saunders received life imprisonment and French five years for their parts in the murder of Alleen Rowe. The picture of Tucson teenage society which emerged at the trial flabbergasted the older citizens of the town.

Capital punishment was subsequently abolished in Arizona for some years so Schmid avoided the death penalty, receiving two terms of life imprisonment instead. He escaped from the Arizona State Prison in November 1972 with another triple murderer and they stayed on a ranch, holding the owners hostage, for a day or two. However, when they split up they were soon recaptured.

Jacques Mesrine

JACQUES MESRINE developed a simple ambition: to be the most famous criminal in the world. Possibly he succeeded. His crimes certainly contained more flair and daring than anybody else's. The public half-admired him, but to the French authorities he was simply 'Public Enemy Number One'.

Mesrine was born near Paris in 1937, and was noted at his schools (he was expelled twice) more for his energy and aggression than for his intelligence. At 18 he married a beautiful black girl from Martinique named Lydia, who was expecting another man's baby, but he would not accept being tied down and was divorced after being conscripted into the army at the age of 19. In Algeria he proved a brave fighter, and won the Military Cross. Life afterwards seemed dull, so he joined the OAS, a right-wing organization opposed to Algerian independence, and took to crime, being sentenced to three years in prison for burglary in 1962. He was still only 25 but had already made a second marriage to a Spanish girl called Soledad, with whom he had a daughter, Sabrina (who was to remain devoted to him through everything) and two sons. On his release after a year, he took a job in an architect's office but, on being made redundant, went back to crime, despite his wife's pleas that he should keep on the right side of the law. In 1966, he left his family (whereupon Soledad returned to Spain) and lived with a prostitute, Jeanne Schneider, who adored his bravado and became a perfect partner in crime. In November 1967, while staying at a hotel in Chamonix, they brought off the audacious armed robbery of a wealthy Arab, a fellow guest. However, Mesrine's flamboyance was becoming a trademark and a manhunt was mounted in France, so in February 1968 he and Jeanne moved their operations to Canada.

There they worked for a 69-year-old crippled millionaire, Georges Deslauriers, as chauffeur and housekeeper. When they were dismissed they kidnapped him for a $200,000 ransom, but a drugged drink Mesrine gave him failed to work, and Deslauriers found his crutches and escaped. They then made the acquaintance of a wealthy widow, Evelyne le Bouthillier, who was subsequently murdered. The pair fled to the USA but were caught and brought back. Mesrine escaped from prison while awaiting trial for murder and released Jeanne, but they were recaptured. Acquitted of the murder, Mesrine received ten years and Jeanne five for the kidnapping.

The expensive new prison – with more warders than prisoners – was said to be escape-proof but, after a year, Mesrine led three others out in a spectacular escape which was front-page news in Canada. With his fellow-escapee Jean-Paul Mercier, Mesrine determined to win more glory by returning to the prison and freeing the others but they were intercepted by a police car and after a gunfight were repulsed.

Next they successfully robbed a Montreal bank, then, on being surprised by forest rangers while having target practice in some woods, they killed the rangers and took their guns.

Mercier was accompanied by his girlfriend Suzanne and Mesrine offered to free Jeanne to join them too, but in view of the murders and the subsequent manhunt she decided to serve her sentence. Mesrine found himself a new girlfriend, the beautiful 19-year-old Jocelyne Deraiche, and the foursome moved to Venezuela via the USA. With papers obtained through the OAS network they set up headquarters near Caracas, intending to raid US banks from there. However, Interpol was on their trail and, while Mercier and Suzanne (who needed an operation) returned to Canada, Mesrine and Jocelyne flew to Spain and, from there, drove back into France.

Mesrine continued his marauding from several bases in Paris, on one occasion wounding a police officer after a gunfight in a bar. He was captured in March 1973 using a flat rented from a judge – a typical piece of bravado. He boasted – no doubt falsely – of 39 murders and was once again top news in France, especially when he promised to be free in three months. What the police did not know was that he had studied the courthouse at Compiègne to which he was brought on 6 June and a pistol had been smuggled into the lawyers' lavatory. Mesrine acquired it and forced his way out with the lawyer as hostage. A friend was waiting in the courtyard with an Alfa Romeo, and Mesrine escaped in a hail of bullets which wounded him in the arm.

With Jocelyne, Mesrine now moved to a flat near the police head-quarters in the seaside resort of Trouville, where he befriended a policeman. Among his accomplishments was, of course, a mastery of disguise. Eventually the homesick Jocelyne, who was too conspicuous with her Canadian accent, returned to Canada where she was sub-sequently imprisoned for helping Mercier (serving a term for the murder of the forest rangers) escape. Mesrine continued his audacious robberies in Paris, usually committing two on the same expedition, to maximize profit without undue risk. He even visited his sick father in hospital, disguised as a doctor. He cultivated an image of gallantry and was charming to a female cashier who was scared when she pressed an alarm button accidentally; he assured her that he liked music while he worked. Finally, in September 1973, his driver was captured and the police discovered Mesrine's hide-out, where he was recaptured in a blaze of publicity.

Mesrine was not tried for $3\frac{1}{2}$ years, during which time he wrote a book and smuggled it out for publication, causing the French govern-ment to bring in a new law prohibiting criminals from profiting by their offences. At the trial, in May 1977, he was again the star, at one stage removing from the knot of his tie a plaster impression of the keys of his handcuffs. The court was electrified but the judge, whom he had ridiculed, was not so amused. He was sentenced to 20 years.

La Santé, in Paris, was another 'escape-proof' prison. On 8 May 1978 Mesrine was in the interview room awaiting his lawyer, when, from a ventilation duct, he produced pistols, a knife, tear gas and a rope. Meanwhile a fellow prisoner, François Besse, put a guard out of action by squirting soapy water into his eyes. A third prisoner, Carman Rives, was released, and warders in the staff office were overpowered. The three convicts donned the warders' clothes and told workmen fitting new grilles to the windows to move the ladders to the outside wall. With these and the rope they scaled the wall, but Rives was shot dead by police. Mesrine and Besse hijacked a passing car and escaped.

A huge manhunt for Public Enemy Number One was launched after this sensational escape. Mesrine continued his daring and quixotic raids with Besse as an ally. In Deauville they were both injured in a shoot-out with police, Besse badly so, but by taking hostages, commandeering cars and even stealing a rowing boat they got to Paris while police helicopters scanned the route.

Mesrine then robbed a company which had won libel damages over his book, and a plan to kidnap the judge who had sentenced him failed only because of the inexperience of his helpers. Foiled of this personal revenge, Mesrine kidnapped a rich industrialist, Henri Lelièvre, an operation which realized 6 million francs and gave him the means to relax in London for a while.

In August 1979 an anti-Mesrine squad was formed in Paris as the authorities realized that Mesrine was becoming a national anti-hero, undermining the law. In September Mesrine met a journalist named Jacques Tillier and wounded him as a warning, believing him to be an informer. Tillier could provide sufficient details of Mesrine's accomplice, Charly Bauer, for police to identify and find him, and soon police knew Mesrine's hide-out. The whole block and much of the surrounding area was staked out by plain-clothes police.

On 2 November 1979 Mesrine emerged with his girlfriend, Sylvie Jeanjacquot, and her white poodle. They drove off in a BMW. Soon they found a blue lorry, with tarpaulin covering the back, cutting across them to turn right. Another lorry was behind. Suddenly the tarpaulin was thrown back and four police marksmen fired 21 shots point-blank at Mesrine. A car pulled up alongside and another police-man fired a shot into Mesrine's head, although he was already dead; Sylvie Jeanjacquot and her dog were severely wounded. Minutes after the attack was launched the police were literally dancing with joy in the street.

Charles Manson

SHARON TATE, wife of the film director Roman Polanski, was spending a quiet evening with friends in her Hollywood home. She was eight months pregnant and while her husband was away in Europe, Voytek Frykowski, a writer, and his girlfriend, coffee heiress Abigail Folger, were staying with her. On the evening of 9 August 1969 Sharon's ex-lover Jay Sebring and a friend of Frykowski, 18-year-old Steven Parent, had joined them for a quiet drink. All five were brutally butchered that night by members of Charles Manson's 'family', obeying their leader's commands.

Two girls – Susan Atkins and Patricia Krenwinkel – and an ex-football star, Tex Watson, broke into the house though the nursery prepared for the baby while a fourth member of the family, Linda Kasabian, stayed on watch outside. 'I am the Devil and I'm here on the Devil's business,' Watson announced to the shocked group of friends. Sebring tried to tackle him, but Watson shot him through the lung, then pursued Frykowski, who tried to run for it. He knifed him in the back, shot him twice, then battered him over the head with his gun butt. Sharon Tate and Abigail Folger were both screaming in panic; Abigail ran out into the garden pursued by one of the women, who stabbed her over and over again. Sharon Tate was the last to die and as she pleaded desperately for the life of her unborn baby Susan Atkins laughed, 'Bitch, I don't care!' All three joined in the savage attack that followed, when Sharon Tate was stabbed 16 times, in the neck, chest, back and the womb. Afterwards a towel dipped in her blood was used to write the word 'Pig' on the living room wall.

The group then went back to report their success to Manson, though it was only when they heard the report on television that they knew who they had killed. Susan Atkins was thrilled to find that one of their victims was as famous as Sharon Tate. The senseless brutality of the murders sent shock waves through America, reinforced two nights later when supermarket owner Leno LaBianca and his wife were killed in a similar manner. Rosemary LaBianca was stabbed 41 times, her husband 12 times and the word 'War' was cut into his abdomen. The words 'Death to Pigs' and 'Helter Skelter' were written on the walls in blood.

The killers were only identified when Susan Atkins, while in custody on a charge of car theft, told her cell-mate about her involvement with the Tate–LaBianca killings. This was a valuable piece of information for a remand prisoner trying to bargain for release and it was soon passed back to the investigating officers. What they heard led them to the hippie group led by the magnetic Charles Manson, who demanded unquestioning obedience from his followers.

Manson was born in Ohio in 1934, the illegitimate son of a prostitute who was gaoled for beating up and robbing her clients. By the age of 11 he was already a juvenile delinquent and was sent to reform school. Sentences for armed robbery, pimping and car theft ensured that he spent much of the next 21 years behind bars. By the age of 32, when he was at last free, he was confused and bitter, unable to adapt to normal life: 'I didn't want to leave gaol but they insisted,' he said.

He spent his first few days and nights of freedom riding on buses

Charles Manson during the Tate–LaBianca trial

but eventually gravitated to the Haight-Ashbury district of San Francisco, then the centre for the 'flower power' hippie movement. He found himself in his element, taking hallucinogenic drugs and practising free love; he grew long hair and a beard, developed an interest in hypnotism and the occult and began to see himself as a Messiah. He gathered a group of young people around him and made the headquarters of the 'family' in abandoned shacks behind a ranch in the Californian desert. Sex orgies and drug-taking were commonplace; alcohol and contraceptives were banned. Women were subservient and had to submit sexually to any man who wanted them. All the members of the group were completely dominated by him. 'He is the king and I am his queen,' Susan Atkins was to say later. 'The queen does what the king says . . . Look at his name, "Man's Son" – now I have visible proof of God, proof the church never gave me.'

He had such command over his followers that he was able to direct them to commit crimes, beginning with theft and car stealing, progressing to terrorizing rich people in their homes and eventually to murder. He drew up a 'hit list' of wealthy and privileged people as well as those he imagined had slighted him, and his code-name for the day of reckoning, when all scores would be settled, was 'helter skelter', taken from a Beatles record.

In July 1969 he sent three of his followers to rob and kill musician Gary Hinman who was thought to keep a large amount of cash in his house. Though Hinman was tortured the money was never found, but he was forced to sign over his two cars to the group before he was stabbed and left to bleed to death. Soon afterwards a member of the group was stopped while driving one of Hinman's cars and arrested. Manson announced, 'Now is the time – helter skelter.' Within a week, the seven brutal murders had taken place.

Manson went on trial with Susan Atkins, Patricia Krenwinkel and another female follower, Leslie Van Houten, who had taken part in the LaBianca killings. It was the first of many trials involving members of the Manson family: there were 84 witnesses and it lasted over nine months.

Linda Kasabian, who had turned state's evidence, was a crucial witness. She had lived in 11 drug-oriented communes before she joined the Manson family and felt that she belonged at last, believing that Manson was 'the Messiah come again'. She told how, when she was left on watch outside Sharon Tate's home, she heard loud screaming, then saw the wounded Frykowski crawling towards her: 'He had blood all over his face . . . and we looked into each other's eyes for a minute . . . and I said, "Oh god, I am so sorry. Please make it stop." And then he just fell to the ground in the bushes.'

Manson showed his power over the women of the family by coercing the three girls into confessing to the murders, declaring that he was innocent. When the lawyers for the girls would not cooperate and refused to question them, the girls insisted on telling their stories verbatim. The judge ruled that the jury must leave, so that this testimony could later be edited and the inadmissible parts removed before they heard it. The girls countered by refusing to testify unless the jury was present.

Manson then decided to take the stand and, in the absence of the jury, spent 90 minutes expounding his philosophy. His 'family' he said, 'were just people that you didn't want, people that were alongside the road; I took them up on my garbage dump and I told them this: that in love there is no wrong'. He was bitter about a society that has discarded him long ago and now regarded him as a fiend. 'I don't care what you do with me,' he declared. 'I have always been in your cell.' Once Manson had had his say, he told the girls not to testify and, of course, they obeyed.

The prosecutor, in his summing up, called Manson 'one of the most evil, satanic men who ever walked the face of the earth'. All four defendants were found guilty and sentenced to death but, as the California Supreme Court voted to abolish the death penalty for murder in 1972, their sentences were commuted to life imprisonment.

The Zebra Murders

THE TERRIFYING activities of the Black Muslim group calling themselves 'Death Angels' were highlighted in San Francisco, USA, in 1973–4, when 15 white victims died at the hands of black killers: hence the nickname of 'Zebra murders'. The murderers were aspiring members of the group and were simply fulfilling their initiation rites, which meant killing a specified number of 'white devils', men, women and children alike. The victims were chosen at random on the street, in telephone booths or stores, or standing at a bus stop. They had never seen their killers before and had no chance to protect themselves.

The first attack was on Richard and Quita Hague, who were walking down a San Francisco street in October 1973 when several black men jumped out of a van and bundled them into the back. Quita was raped and hacked to death with a machete. Richard, too, was attacked with a machete but in spite of serious wounds, he lived. In the same month Frances Rose, aged 28, was driving along a city street when a black assailant opened the passenger door of her car and shot her. A few weeks later a grocery store owner was tied up and shot in the head.

In December there were six killings, including that of an 81-year-old man. The same guns were used in several of the murders and the police were by now fairly certain that they were looking for a group of killers working together as would-be members of the 'Death Angels'. There was already a horrifyingly long list of unsolved murders in the same pattern in California: over 130 men, 75 women and some 60 children were already likely victims of the murderous group.

Four people were killed within a couple of hours on 28 January: two men and two women aged between 32 and 69. A fifth, 23-year-old

Roseanne McMillan, who survived her wounds, said that a smiling black man had approached her, said 'Hi', then taken out a gun and fired. The last two murders, and three more attempted ones, came in April. A young couple were gunned down on their way to a grocery store: 19-year-old Thomas Rainwater died instantly while 21-year-old Lindy Story was partially paralysed for life. Two more young men were wounded on Easter Sunday and the last death came on 16 April 1974, when Nelson Shields received three bullets in the back.

The full-scale investigation mounted by the police, stopping and questioning thousands of blacks and searching them for weapons, inflamed racial feelings and produced no tangible results. The break-through came only when Anthony Harris, one of the group of killers, volunteered a confession and named eight other Zebra murderers. All were arrested, but four were later released because the evidence against them would not stand up in court. The remainder – Jesse Cooke, Larry Greene, Anthony Harris, J. C. Simon and Manuel Moore – were charged with murder. Two of them, Harris and Moore, had met while in prison and had decided before their release to earn membership of the 'Death Angels'.

The trial began on 5 March 1975 and established a record as the longest in California's legal history, running until 9 March, 1976. Over 180 witnesses gave evidence, chief among them Anthony Harris, who spent 12 days on the stand. All four were found guilty and sentenced to life imprisonment. The fully-fledged members of the Death Angels, those who had already reached their killing total, were never caught.

Peter Sutcliffe

OVER a period of five years a sadistic killer committed so many violent crimes on women in the area from Leeds to Manchester that women turned out on the streets to demonstrate against the impotence of the police to catch the killer. When the police received taped messages purporting to come from the killer taunting them on their inability to catch him, the ingredients of a sensational case were in place. The savagery with which the killer mutilated his victims' bodies led to him being called the 'Yorkshire Ripper'.

The realization that there was a maniac at large developed as the attacks increased in number. The first occurred on 5 July 1975, when Anna Rogulskyj was attacked in Keighley. On 15 August 1975 Olive Smelt was assaulted in Halifax. Both women were hit on the head with a hammer and slashed with a knife, but both survived after brain surgery.

Wilma McCann, a 28-year-old prostitute, was not so lucky; she was killed with a hammer 90 m (100 yd) from her home in Leeds on 30 October 1975 and then stabbed several times. Some three months later the body of another prostitute, Emily Jackson, aged 42, was found in the same condition, except that the wounds inflicted after death were even more horrific – 50 lacerations caused by a knife and a Phillips screwdriver. A wellington boot had stamped on her, so the police knew the killer's shoe size. This second murder was also in Leeds, and the police acknowledged the two were linked.

In May 1976 a woman survived an attack in Leeds, and the next murder was not until 5 February 1977 when the body of Irene Richardson, a 28-year-old part-time prostitute, was discovered in a playing field by a jogger. The details were as before, with the careful arrangement of her boots on her thighs contrasting with the way her body had been slashed with a knife.

It was now that the name 'Yorkshire Ripper' was applied to the killer, and Leeds prostitutes began to live in fear. The next killing was in nearby Bradford; Patricia Atkinson, a 32-year-old divorcee, was murdered in her home in the vice district. As well as the identifying atrocities being present, her sheets showed the imprint of a wellington boot of the same size as before.

George Oldfield, Yorkshire's most experienced detective with 31 years in the force, was put in charge of a massive murder hunt. The public really became involved towards the end of June 1977 because the next victim, back in Leeds, was a 16-year-old girl on her way home from seeing friends. Sadly for her, the route took her near the red-light district. The outcry against the killings was now deafening.

With a huge police operation involving over 300 officers in progress, another woman was attacked in Bradford in July 1977. She survived but, unfortunately, the description she gave of her assailant proved to be unlike that of the Ripper. From now on the Ripper was not to strike consecutively in the same town and the next murder was across the Pennines in Manchester. Jean Jordan, a 21-year-old prostitute, was struck 11 times and killed near some allotments but, as the Ripper dragged the body to some bushes, he was disturbed by the arrival of another car and fled. The body was not discovered, and he returned to it eight days later to search for the new £5 note he had given her, which he realized might be a giveaway. He could not find her handbag and, in frustration, attacked the body savagely with a piece of broken glass, trying to remove his hammer trademark by cutting off the head. He failed. The body was found next day, and the £5 note soon afterwards.

The bank that had issued the note was traced, and all the employees of companies which had been supplied notes from the batch to pay wages were interviewed. Among them was Peter Sutcliffe, who was seen twice but aroused no suspicions.

A woman was attacked in Leeds in December, and on 21 January a prostitute, Yvonne Pearson, aged 22, was murdered on waste ground at Bradford. Her body, which had been jumped upon as well as suffering the usual mutilations, was not discovered for two months. Ten days after this murder, Helen Rytka, an 18-year-old prostitute who practised in tandem with her twin sister, was killed viciously in a Huddersfield woodyard. A short time later, the Ripper returned to the still undiscovered body of Yvonne Pearson and placed a newspaper, dated four weeks after her murder, beneath her arm. He possibly made the body more visible, too. In May, a 41-year-old prostitute Vera Millward was murdered in Manchester.

In August Peter Sutcliffe was interviewed by the police twice more, once because his car registration number was on a list compiled of vehicles in Leeds and Bradford, and once when police were checking tyre marks. His rare blood group, B, and small shoe size (seven) were not checked against what the police thought they knew of the Ripper. By now the police had interviewed thousands of men, and the reward for information stood at £15,000.

The Ripper was now quiet for 11 months, but the murders resumed in April 1979 in Huddersfied with an attack on a 19-year-old building society clerk, Josephine Whitaker. The murder of such a young girl after the long break provoked another outcry. In June the police broadcast a tape they had received, apparently from the Ripper, which followed three letters that had arrived since March 1978; it had been the flaps on the envelopes that had given away the Ripper's blood group. The voice on the tape taunted George Oldfield with his failure to catch him and promised another victim in September or October. Experts studied the accent, and from now on it was assumed the Ripper came from Sunderland. The tape was broadcast around pubs and clubs in Leeds and Bradford, while parts of the letters were published in the hope that a member of the public would identify the writing.

Oldfield had a heart attack in July as the pressure told on him, and

Sutcliffe was once again interviewed, as his car had been recorded in the relevant Bradford area on 36 occasions. However, Sutcliffe was not from Sunderland, and escaped detection again. A month later a student from Bradford University, 20-year-old Barbara Leach, was killed while taking a walk at night. It seemed the Ripper was not now waging a campaign against prostitutes, but was attacking girls merely for being out in the evening.

The Ripper did not strike for nearly a year after this, during which time the police concentrated again on the £5 note. The number of companies which might have issued it was reduced to three. Sutcliffe was interviewed four more times during this period.

In August 1980 Marguerite Walls, a 47-year-old civil servant who had been working late in the office, was on her way home in Leeds when she was killed. In October the Ripper attacked Upadhya Bandara, a doctor from Singapore but, having put a rope around her neck, he inexplicably apologized and left her. On Guy Fawkes night he knocked down a 16-year-old girl but her boyfriend heard her scream and the Ripper was chased off.

Less than a fortnight later another student was killed. Jacqueline Hill got off a bus near the Leeds University hall of residence in which she lived when the Ripper struck. By now the five-year lack of success in catching the Ripper had become a scandal, and a 'super squad' was formed.

It was routine police work that finally caught the Ripper. On Friday, 2 January 1981, two policemen saw a possible prostitute climb into a car in Melbourne Avenue, Sheffield. They decided to investigate. The driver, calling himself Peter Williams, asked if he could relieve himself in some bushes and was allowed to, but his purpose was to hide a knife and hammer behind an oil storage tank. While he was away the policemen discovered the car plates were false, and took 'Peter Williams' and the prostitute, Olivia Reivers, to the police station, where 'Williams' went to the lavatory again, and hid a second knife in the cistern.

Peter Sutcliffe on his wedding day

The arrested man admitted his name was Peter Sutcliffe and was held overnight. Next day, the Ripper squad was called. It was established that Sutcliffe's blood group was B, and the police discovered he had been interviewed often during the investigation. All day Saturday he was questioned, and then kept another night. Meanwhile Sergeant Bob Ring, one of the policemen who had brought Sutcliffe in, heard that the Ripper squad were interviewing him in depth, and suddenly realized the significance of the man's wish to relieve himself at Melbourne Road. Hurrying back there, he searched around and found the hammer and knife.

On Sunday afternoon, after several hours of talking, it was suddenly sprung on Sutcliffe that the hammer and knife had been found. Sutcliffe straight away admitted that he was the Yorkshire Ripper and made a long statement, which took 17 hours, explaining his motives.

Sutcliffe had been a small, weak baby when he was born on 2 June 1946, the oldest of the five children his parents would have. His black eyes were his most startling feature. He was intelligent but was small and was bullied as a child. Later he had little success with women, although he was extremely vain. Among his menial jobs was that of a grave-digger at Bingley Cemetery; because of his beard, his colleagues nicknamed him 'Jesus'. He met a dark, pretty, 16-year-old Czech girl, Sonia Szurma, and courted her for seven years before they were married in Bradford in 1974.

Some time around 1969, two events took place which had a great effect on Sutcliffe. His mother, whom Sutcliffe adored, was dramatically exposed by his father in front of the whole family after Sutcliffe senior discovered she was having an affair with a neighbour, a policeman, an event which Sutcliffe's father afterwards said he thought had turned his son's mind. The second significant event was that Sutcliffe went with a prostitute after a row with Sonia. Humiliatingly, he was unable to achieve intercourse, and was furthermore cheated by the girl who failed to give him £5 change from a £10 note. This inspired his first attack on a prostitute; he found her two weeks later and hit her over the head with a sock filled with stones.

There was a similar attack in 1971, in the red-light district of Bradford, when he was out driving with his best friend, Trevor Birdsall. On the way home, he admitted to Birdsall what he had done. Birdsall was also with him on the night in 1975 that Olive Smelt was attacked, and at one stage he told his wife that he suspected Sutcliffe was the Ripper.

Sutcliffe's defence to the charge of 13 murders and seven attempted murders was based on insanity. He claimed that God had spoken to him from a particular headstone while he was working at the cemetery, and had instructed him to go out and kill prostitutes. 'Cleaning the streets' was how he later explained it to his brother.

The Attorney General, Sir Michael Havers, was said to be ready to accept a bargain plea of manslaughter, believing him to be suffering from paranoid schizophrenia, but Mr Justice Boreham threw that out, no doubt on the grounds that only a full-scale trial would satisfy the public after such a traumatic five years. Coincidentally, Sonia had been diagnosed as schizophrenic after a breakdown two years before their marriage; this handicapped Sutcliffe's defence, as the jury were invited to believe that Sutcliffe's 'symptoms' were merely copied from Sonia, who had imagined she was a second Christ.

Many of the investigative mishaps were aired at the trial. At T. and W. H. Clarke, the road haulage company where he worked, colleagues had jokingly referred to Sutcliffe as the Ripper because of the number of times he had been questioned by the police. In his cab was a handwritten note which read: 'In this truck is a man whose latent genius if unleashed would rock the nation, whose dynamic energy would overpower those around him. Better let him sleep?' Sutcliffe even revealed that on one occasion, when he was asked about the size seven wellington boots which had left their imprint at two murders, he was actually wearing them – but the policeman interviewing him had not noticed.

Despite the medical evidence, the jury found Sutcliffe guilty on all counts and on 5 May 1981 he was sentenced to life imprisonment, with the recommendation that he should serve at least 30 years.

An intriguing unanswered mystery concerns the tape message, of which Sutcliffe denied all knowledge, and which sent the police so drastically on the wrong trail (they had 50,000 responses to its broadcast). In 1993 a North Shields widow, Olive Curry, revealed that when Sutcliffe was arrested in 1981 she recognized him as a man she had met often in 1978 when she worked in the canteen at the North Shields Fisherman's Mission (the haulage company I. and W.H. Clark confirm Sutcliffe was often in the area at that time). Sutcliffe, said Mrs Curry, was always with a friend he called Carl or Trev. Mrs Curry had heard the tapes and, on seeing Sutcliffe, realized that the voice was that of Sutcliffe's friend. She said that she had informed the police of this in 1981 but had heard no more. She subsequently wrote to Sutcliffe about this and visited him in prison; Sutcliffe wrote hundreds of letters to her, stopping only when she revealed her story to the press. Sutcliffe then himself wrote to the *Sunderland Echo* to deny he had an accomplice. However, Mrs Curry remains convinced, and perhaps there is a final twist to the story to come.

Jim Jones

UNLIKE most mass murderers, Jim Jones did not kill with his own hands. However, in his efforts to create an earthly paradise for his followers he was ready to order the deaths of anyone who opposed his will and finally, when he saw that his religious empire was doomed, he ordered the 900 cult members to commit mass suicide. Perhaps he had set out as a benign religious leader who would create a better and fairer society but, as he felt the joy of power over his congregation, it had all gone disastrously wrong.

Jim Warren Jones had founded the People's Temple in a run-down area of Indianapolis, USA, in the late 1950s, preaching a gospel of racial integration that would create a classless society. As his congregation grew he launched himself into the profitable faith-healing market, healing the sick and crippled by the dozen and raking in the dollars. Eventually he set up a new Temple in downtown San Francisco, using the support of prominent politicians and often preaching to crowds of 5000 or more.

Then came the defections, with ex-members of the Temple claiming that Jones was forcing his followers to sign over all their money to him. They exposed his faith cures, describing how they had pretended to be blind or wheelchair bound, only to jump up when Jones laid hands on them, crying that they could see or walk for the first time. They also told stories of Jones presiding over bizarre sex rituals and claiming the right to take any woman in the congregation to his bed. He ordered youngsters who did not show sufficient respect to be beaten or tortured with electric cattle prods.

Eventually the tide of criticism threatened to swamp Jones and his Temple so he led his followers to a new home in Guyana, setting up a

Jim Jones

community on a tract of savannah grassland surrounded by jungle, where there would be no one to interfere. However, a year later a California Congressman, Leo Ryan, pressured the US State Department to persuade the reluctant Guyanese government to let him go to Jonestown and interview the cult members. Ryan had received many reports from his constituents that young people were being held in the commune against their will and beaten and abused if they did not obey Jones's orders, so he was determined to discover the truth for himself. He arrived at Jonestown on 17 December 1978 with a group of reporters and cameramen, to find the perimeters of the remote settlement patrolled by armed guards. Jones explained that they were necessary to keep out bandits. The cult members looked gaunt and hungry but most still professed complete devotion to Jones and his ideals. When Ryan gave a personal guarantee of protection to anyone who wanted to leave, only 20 commune members volunteered.

Jones knew that if one of his congregation returned home, the truth about Jonestown would emerge, and he could not allow that to happen. As the party was preparing to leave from Port Kaituma airport, 18 km (8 miles) from Jonestown, they were ambushed. A tractor emerged from the bush on to the tarmac and gunmen opened fire from it, moving in to shoot victims already lying on the ground at point-blank range. Congressman Ryan was killed instantly and NBC reporter Don Harris died as he took the full force of the blast from an automatic rifle. Cameraman Robert Brown, who had continued filming after the massacre began, only stopped when fatally hit by a bullet. A young photographer from the *San Francisco Examiner* also died in the hail of bullets.

According to an eye-witness, once Jones heard that some members of Ryan's party had escaped and realized that the authorities would soon take action, he decided that his followers should take part in one final ritual: mass suicide. He had always told them that this was the only way out if the existence of the commune was threatened and over 900 men, women and children gathered to hear him talk about the beauty and dignity of death.

'We were too good for this world,' he told them. 'Now come with me and I will take you to a better place.'

The elders of the Temple produced large vats of cyanide mixed with Kool-Aid, a popular soft drink, and the mixture was ladled out by the commune's doctor and nurse. Members lined up to collect the lethal mixture, singing gospel songs. Babies died first, as parents spooned the poisoned drink into their mouths, then the children, then finally the adults drank, wrapping their arms round one another to stay close in death.

When Guyanese soldiers arrived next morning they found Jones's body sprawled across the altar, a bullet through his brain. They also found a number of bodies lying near the trees at the edge of the clearing, with bullets in their backs; many of those who tried to flee had been executed before they could reach safety.

Kenneth Bianchi and Angelo Buono

THE FIRST victims of the 'Hillside Strangler' were found bound, raped and strangled on the hills above Los Angeles in October 1977. Both 19-year-old Yolanda Washington and 15-year-old Judith Miller were prostitutes and their deaths caused little public interest. At first the police thought they were looking for a killer of street women but their ideas changed rapidly with a string of murders in November: seven more bodies were found and only one, Jill Barcomb, was a prostitute. The others were a waitress, four students and two schoolgirls, 12-year-old Dollie Cepeda and 14-year-old Sonja Johnson. Three of the bodies were found together on 20 November, thrown naked on to a rubbish dump so that the boy who found them thought they were discarded fashion mannequins. All had been tied up before being strangled and police now knew that they were looking for two murderers, for the girls had been raped by two different men.

In December, the naked body of call-girl Kimberley Martin was found on a vacant lot in the city; she had disappeared after going to meet a client who gave a fictitious telephone number. One of the tenants in the apartment block she had visited, 26-year-old Kenneth Bianchi, told the police that he had heard screams.

The last of the set of murders was that of Cindy Hudspeth, a 20-year-old waitress whose body was found in the boot of her car, which had been pushed over a cliff in February 1978. She was naked and, like the other girls, had been raped by two men. After that everything went quiet, the female population of Los Angeles began to relax and the police hoped that the killings were over. But the killers were to surface again in Bellingham in the state of Washington where two girls, Diane Wilder and Karen Mandic, were offered a job minding a house for a few hours while its alarm was repaired and were later found strangled, their bodies thrown in the back of Karen's car. Karen had told her boyfriend that they had been hired by Kenneth Bianchi and though he denied all knowledge of the girls, a search of his home turned up a number of items linked to the victims and he was arrested.

At first Bianchi denied everything, then he took refuge in claims of multiple personality: he was completely innocent and it was his alter ego, Steve, who had killed the girls. Eventually, at a sanity hearing in October 1979, it was decided that Bianchi was shamming and that he should be indicted for murder. At that point, Bianchi decided to plead guilty and agreed to testify against his partner in crime, his cousin Angelo Buono, in return for a life sentence to be served in California, rather than Washington's harsh Walla Walla prison. He protested that he was full of remorse for his actions: 'In no way can I take away the pain I have given others, and in no way can I expect forgiveness from others.'

Bianchi, who was something of a charmer with a history of lying and stealing, was the subservient half of the partnership, hero-worshipping his cousin Buono who was 17 years his senior, oversexed and brutal and never happier than when he was ill-treating women. In the 1970s the cousins went into business together as pimps. They promised a 16-year-old girl called Sabra Hannan work as a model then forced her, by beatings and threats of death, to act as a prostitute. Later they recruited a 15-year-old, Becky Spears, terrorizing her and forcing her to submit to all manner of sexual acts.

Intent on broadening their operation, they paid an experienced prostitute for a list of clients, only to find that it was false. They set out for revenge but, as they could not find the prostitute who had cheated on them, they settled for her friend Yolanda Washington. They found raping and strangling her such a great experience that they wanted to repeat it over and over again. Bianchi, who had always cherished an ambition to join the police force, had often posed as a policeman to corner his victims. They had picked up Judith Miller on the pretence of arresting her for prostitution, and had told the two schoolgirls that they were investigating a burglary in the neighbourhood and needed to question them.

It seems that by early 1978 Buono was tired of the killing games and even more tired of Bianchi, and when Bianchi's common-law wife decided to move back to her home town of Bellingham, Buono persuaded him to follow her. If that had been the end of the 'Hillside Strangler', the murderers might never have been caught, but Bianchi found life flat and dull without the stimulus of raping and killing and thought that carrying out a couple of murders alone and unaided would earn him respect from his cousin. With typical carelessness, he chose as his victim Karen Mandic, who worked in the store where he was employed as a security guard.

Once in gaol, Bianchi hatched a plot to clear himself. A writer, Veronica Compton, had asked for help with a play about a female serial killer and through letters and visits revealed an obsession with torture and murder. She happily agreed to Bianchi's plan to prove that the Hillside Strangler was still at large: she would drive to Bellingham and strangle a woman, then leave behind some of Bianchi's sperm, which had been smuggled out of prison in a rubber glove. Fortunately, her selected victim proved too strong for her, and she was arrested and sentenced to life imprisonment.

Buono's trial lasted for two years; Bianchi alone spent five months in the witness box, contradicting himself over and over again and even claiming that he was innocent after all. Buono's lawyer argued that Bianchi was solely responsible for the murders and was only implicating his client for the sake of a plea bargain.

The jury remained unconvinced and Buono was found guilty and sentenced to nine terms of life imprisonment. Bianchi was held to have violated the terms of his plea bargain and was sent to Walla Walla prison, where he was to need special protection from the other prisoners.

In pronouncing sentence, the judge told Bianchi and Buono: 'I am sure you will probably only get your thrills from reliving over and over again the torturing and murdering of your victims, being incapable, as I believe you to be, of feeling any remorse.'

Dennis Nilsen

DENNIS NILSEN was an intelligent, shy man who felt that all his life he had suffered rejection in one form or another. Usually extremely lonely, he liked making friendships and helping others less well off than himself, and extended his concern to animals. He liked to expound his caring views – he hated Thatcherism – but at the same time possessed a dominant personality that demanded admiration and acquiescence. Events and circumstances combined with this strange and complex personality to make him the serial killer with possibly the highest number of victims in Britain.

Nilsen's sense of rejection began early. He was born on 23 November 1945 in Fraserburgh, Scotland, fathered by a Norwegian sailor who came to Scotland in 1940 when Norway was overrun by the Germans. His father was a hard drinker and, though his parents married, Dennis did not see much of him. The person who meant most to him in his early life was his grandfather, Andrew Whyte, with whom he and his mother, brother and sister lived. He was left there after his mother divorced and remarried – his first experience of rejection. In 1951 his grandfather died, and the six-year-old Dennis, without preparation, was invited to see the corpse. It was a shattering experience which shaped his life, and united images of love and death in his mind.

Nilsen rejoined his mother but left home as soon as possible and at the age of 15 joined the army catering corps, where he became a good-looking, amusing companion, albeit too retiring to make close friendships. He photographed his closest acquaintance feigning death in action. It was the first sign of fantasies about death, and also perhaps of a mental instability which had shown itself in his mother's forebears. He had a girlfriend for a while and thought about marriage, but was too shy to propose and broke off the relationship. He enjoyed his 11 years in army catering which, incidentally, gave him a skill in dissection which he was to use again.

Nilsen left the army because he didn't like the British treatment of the Irish and joined the police, where he saw plenty of dissected corpses, which fascinated him. He had homosexual tendencies which made it difficult for him to ignore the aggressive and routinely intolerant views of many officers on the subject, and he left after about a year. He subsequently joined the Department of Employment and worked at a Job Centre, where he met many young men living a lonely life. His fantasies about death had now reached the point where he would colour his lips blue, smother his body in talc to give it a white appearance and lie looking at himself in the mirror.

When Nilsen was 30 he met a much younger man, David Gallichan, and for two years they shared a garden flat at 195 Melrose Avenue, Cricklewood. They acquired a dog, Bleep, adopted a stray cat and led a happy and orderly life. It was not a sexual relationship, but Nilsen was devastated when, in 1977, Gallichan took a job in Devon and moved away. Nilsen once more felt rejected and began to spend much of his free time drinking.

On New Year's Eve 1978, Nilsen met an Irish teenager in a pub and took him home. They became insensibly drunk. In the morning Nilsen awoke first, and knew that when the youth awoke, he would become another of those who would leave him. Picking up his tie, he strangled him until he was practically dead, then finished him off by holding his head in a bucket of water. He than carried the body to the bathroom, washed it tenderly and thoroughly, dried it carefully and dressed it in

Dennis Nilsen (left)

fresh underclothes. He lived with the corpse for a week then placed it under the floorboards, where it stayed for an amazing eight months, with, according to Nilsen, very little decomposition. After that he took it down the garden and burned it, together with some rubber to disguise the smell.

Nilsen was amazed at getting away with murder and panic-stricken at the same time; he determined to reform and give up drinking. Yet just three months later he attempted a similar murder with a Chinese man named Andrew Ho, who managed to break free from the strangulation attempt and went to the police. Nilsen was again amazed that the police accepted his explanation that Ho's allegations were merely Ho's attempt to get even after they quarrelled.

A young Canadian, Kenneth Ockenden, was Nilsen's next victim, on 3 December 1979. Because he was expected home for Christmas and had disappeared suddenly from his hotel, Ockenden was the only one of Nilsen's victims for whom there was a well-publicized search. The details of the killing followed what became a pattern. After killing Ockenden Nilsen carefully washed the body, dressed it in fresh underwear and kept it for a couple of weeks, watching television in the evening with the body beside him on the bed. He undressed the body, wrapped it in curtains and placed it under the floorboards when the time came to sleep.

After a fortnight, Nilsen cut up the body and kept parts under the floorboards and parts in a wooden garden shed where he built a pile of bricks into a sort of tomb. He would daily spray inside the shed with disinfectant, and burn the fragments piecemeal.

Nilsen now killed more frequently. He usually met his victim in a pub, took him home where they both got drunk, then Nilsen would strangle him with one of his ties, wash and dress the body and finally chop it up for the shed and the fire. Between May 1980 and May 1981 there were nine more victims. The last at Melrose Avenue was an epileptic, Malcolm Barlow, whom Nilsen found sitting on the pavement near the house in September 1981, his legs having given way.

He took him in for coffee and called an ambulance for him. Next day, Barlow was waiting on the doorstep when Nilsen returned from work. Nilsen asked him in and strangled him, it being easier than calling an ambulance again. At the time, there were parts of six bodies already under the floorboards.

Soon afterwards Nilsen, a sitting tenant in the flat, was offered £1000 to move, and accepted. He had one final bonfire and, in October 1981, moved to an attic flat in 23 Cranley Gardens, Muswell Hill, another of London's more respectable districts. Some of the people who died at Melrose Avenue were never identified and had Nilsen died or changed his way of life, nobody would ever have known about the murders.

Nilsen did intend to reform: many stayed with him and lived, especially in his early days at Muswell Hill. The first murder there was in March 1982, when the victim, John Howlett, put up such a fight that he nearly overpowered his killer. Nilsen chopped up the body and boiled chunks of it in a big black pot. In May Carl Stotter did escape. He was to go to the police after Nilsen's arrest, as were two more men who had escaped Nilsen's murder attempts.

Late in 1982 Nilsen killed a man who fell asleep while eating an omelette. Parts of the body were boiled and stored while others were gradually flushed down the lavatory. The last victim was Stephen Sinclair, on 26 January 1983.

A week later the residents of 23 Cranley Gardens complained that the drains were blocked. On the evening of 8 February a plumber came to inspect. What he found 3.5 m (12 ft) down under the manhole cover outside seemed to him to be about 40 pieces of nauseating human flesh. He came back next morning with his boss, to find only some small pieces of flesh and bone. The police were called.

During the night Nilsen had played his last card, going down the manhole and removing the flesh. He had thought of covering it with chicken flesh, but could not buy enough. He went to work next day wearing the scarf of his last victim, Stephen Sinclair. As he left the office, where he was now supervisor, he told the staff that tomorrow he would be either dead or in prison. They thought it a strange joke. When he got home, the police were waiting to interview him.

The interview wasted little time on niceties. 'What has happened to the rest of the body?' asked the inspector. 'In there,' said Nilsen, pointing to the wardrobe. Inside were two bin liners containing human remains. In the car on the way to the station the inspector asked: 'Are we talking of one body or two?' 'Fifteen or 16 altogether,' replied Nilsen. This matter-of-factness contrasts with his concern for his faithful dog, which was put down a week after the arrest.

Nilsen made a detailed statement: he had an attentive captive audience at last. Later, in prison, he wrote a full and frank description of a murderer's feelings. At his trial the defence argued that the circumstances of his upbringing had left him with a severe personality disorder, but Nilsen himself insisted that he was sane and he was convicted by a majority of 10–2 of six murders. He was sentenced to life imprisonment on 4 November 1983.

George Stephenson

In 1987 George Stephenson was found guilty of murdering the Cleaver family in their home in Hampshire, England, where he had left them bound and helpless, then set fire to the house so that they would be burned alive. It was an act of 'indescribable brutality and cruelty' said the judge, Mr Justice Hobhouse, and he told Stephenson: 'You showed no mercy and deserve none.'

The bodies of 82-year-old Joseph Cleaver, his wife Hilda, who had been confined to a wheelchair for 14 years, and 70-year-old nurse Margaret Murphy had been found in the master bedroom, so badly burned that they had to be identified from dental records. Thomas Cleaver, aged 47, had managed to crawl out of the bedroom in search of air, but had been suffocated by smoke. His wife Wendy, age 46, had been beaten, raped and strangled: her body had been doused with petrol but remained unburned.

The story that unfolded in court was one of revenge and greed. Thirty-five-year-old Stephenson had been employed as a handyman at Burgate House, the Cleavers' imposing mansion in extensive grounds beside the River Avon, but had been sacked three weeks before the murders, so he decided to avenge himself. On 1 September 1986 Stephenson and two companions, George and John Daly, entered the house while the family were at the dining table. They always dined promptly at 8 pm and Stephenson knew that the front door was left open at this time, in case friends cared to drop in.

All three men carried pickaxes and they shepherded four members of the family into the main bedroom and tied them up before they dragged Wendy Cleaver into the next room, where she was raped by all three men and finally throttled. The intruders then searched for the safe but failed to find it and had to make do with cash and jewellery worth less than £100, as well as three shotguns and the family stock of liquor. Before they made off they set fire to the master bedroom, intending to burn down the house. However, the plan misfired; the house was so solidly built that the fire failed to penetrate much beyond the room itself and the murders were discovered when staff arrived next morning.

Stephenson was an immediate suspect and when his picture was shown on television he went to the police. At first his story was that he had told some bikers about the Cleavers and their money on the day of the murders, but forensic evidence was to link him to the scene. At the trial, Stephenson maintained that he had not realized that anyone had died until he saw the television broadcast: 'It was like a mirror; I was looking at myself. Up until that moment I hadn't any idea what had happened. I was expecting the police to contact me because I thought I would get pulled for a burglary.'

The three men pleaded not guilty, with John Daly withdrawing his alleged confession to the murder of Wendy Cleaver. They failed to convince the jury and Stephenson received four life sentences for murder – though he was found not guilty of killing Wendy Cleaver – and the judge recommended that he should serve at least 25 years. John Daly was sentenced to life imprisonment and George Daly to 22 years.

_____

Jeffrey Dahmer

Around midnight on 22 July 1991, in the Marquette University area of Milwaukee, two patrolling police officers spotted a distraught-looking black man staggering in the street with a handcuff dangling from his wrist. Thinking he had escaped from police custody, they apprehended him and asked for an explanation. The man, 32 year-old Tracy Edwards, told them he had just fled from a nearby apartment where someone he described as a 'weird dude' had put handcuffs on him.

They went to the address in order to check Edwards' story, and in doing so stumbled across a grisly scene of horrific proportions. They were greeted at the door of Apartment 213 at 924 North 25th Street by a mild-mannered blonde-haired man in his early thirties, Jeffrey Dahmer. He offered to get the key to the cuffs from the bedroom, implying it had all been part of some homosexual game, but when one of the officers followed him he found the room littered with photographs of dismembered human bodies and what appeared to be skulls stacked in a refrigerator.

The officer called to his colleague to detain Dahmer, who immediately became violent, resisting the officer's attempt to cuff him. When they eventually restrained him, they started to search the premises, beginning with the refrigerator. What they found there – a human head – sent them reeling back in horror, while closer inspection revealed three more heads in the freezer in plastic food bags.

In other parts of the apartment they made more ghoulish discoveries, including two skulls, a cooking pot containing decomposed hands and a human penis, and jars of male genetalia preserved in formaldehyde. In addition there were quantities of chloroform, formaldehyde and ethyl alcohol, plus scores of Polaroid photographs of the male victims in bondage poses before they were murdered and in various stages of dismemberment afterwards.

The shocking find, which was to uncover a long-term history of such slaughter on Dahmer's part, came just a couple of months after another incident which was a 'near miss' for the police, tragically ending with what was to be the murderer's final killing. On that occasion, two women came across a hysterical Asian-looking youth running naked through the early-morning streets; he was clearly terrified of something, and when the police arrived and tried to question him, they were joined by Dahmer, who took the officers back to his apartment to explain that nothing was wrong.

The police believed his story of a homosexual 'domestic' argument, and left him and the dazed (and drugged) youth – Konerak Sinthasomphone – to sort out their differences. Hours later Dahmer had strangled the boy, sexually abusing the corpse before dismembering it, and recording each step in instant photographs for his private pleasure later.

The Sinthasomphone killing turned out to be the last in a thirteen-year series of murders, the details of which Dahmer confessed to after his arrest. He admitted having bizarre fantasies involving murder and necrophilia – always with male victims – thoughout his teenage years, the first actual realisation of those fantasies occurring when he was just eighteen.

It was then, in 1978 (while he was still living at home with his parents in Bath, Ohio) that he picked up a hitchhiker, Steven Hicks, subsequently having a drink with him. When Hicks decided it was time to leave, Dahmer got angry and hit him over the head with a barbell, killing him instantly. He disposed of the body by cutting it up and burying the parts, packed into plastic bags, in woods behind the family home.

After a spell in the Army, Dahmer moved into his grandmother's home in West Allis, Wisconsin in 1981, where some low-key offences involving drinking and (on two occasions) indecent exposure were all that marred a seemingly otherwise normal record of behaviour.

Things were not as they seemed, however. Over the years the fantasies played on his mind, and began to take over rather than go away, until in September 1987 he claimed his second victim Steven Toumi, who he lured to a hotel room for sex before killing him. He stuffed the body in a suitcase and took it to the basement of his grandmother's house, where he indulged in what would become a ritual of necrophilic sex, dismemberment and disposal.

With what was becoming a systematic routine of picking up victims in gay bars, inviting them home, drugging them and killing them, by the summer of 1988 Dahmer had murdered another two men, at which point he was to move from his grandmother's house to his own apartment in Milwaukee.

His killing exploits were interrupted in the September of that year when he was arrested for the sexual exploitation of a child and sexual assault, after a Laotian 13-year-old who he had drugged and molested subsequently reported the incident to his parents and the police. Coincidentally, the boy was the brother of Konerak Sinthasomphone, Dahmer's final victim who he murdered in 1991.

The trial ended early in 1989 with Dahmer pleading guilty, and while he was awaiting sentence he moved back to his grandmother's home where he claimed his fifth victim, Anthony Sears. Unaware of the undiscovered remains of an increasing number of victims, and the horrendous history of perverted violence behind them, in May 1989 the judge in the child assault case handed down a stayed sentence with five years probation and one year in the House of Correction under 'work release,' whereby he was allowed to go to work during the day and return to jail at night.

The leniency on the judge's part was a direct result of an impassioned defence plea on his own behalf by Dahmer, in which he claimed this was his only transgression of this kind, and something that would never happen again if only he was given a chance to make amends. Like many psycopathic killers before and since, he was a convincing liar.

So convincing in fact that the judge granted him an early release from the House of Correction after 10 months, and after moving back to his grandmother's briefly in May 1990 he moved to Apartment 213 at 924 North 25th Street, Milwaukee, an address that was to go down as one of the most notorious in the annals of criminal history.

It was here that the most intense period of Dahmer's homicidal career took place, just over a year, in which he murdered twelve men. The crimes were almost identical in their execution, with Dahmer paying careful attention – indeed more attention – to what he did with the victims after they were dead than the actual murders, which were over and done with in a matter of seconds. It was the necrophilic sex and dismemberment which he recorded carefully in photographic detail, and added to this was another horror – cannibalism. When the police finally searched the apartment, they were at first curious why there was little food there. It soon became obvious, the killer had been living off his victims.

When he came to trial in 1992, the prosecution and defence postions were simple. Nobody could deny Dahmer's guilt, and he eventually pleaded guilty against the advice of his lawyer. While the prosecution was claiming this was a man who was not insane but unspeakably evil, so the defence pleaded that only a madman could have committed such atrocities.

At the end of the proceedings, after five hours of deliberation the jury found Dahmer guilty of all fifteen counts of murder, and deemed to be sane, so he was sentenced to fifteen consecutive life terms in prison, a total of 957 years.

After serving just over two years of his sentence at the Columbia Correctional Institute in Portage, Wisconsin, on 28 November 1994 Dahmer was violently attacked by a fellow inmate – he was found with a mop handle stuck in his eye – and died of his injuries almost immediately.

After Dahmer's death, his father – who had argued for his son to be treated rather than punished back in 1989, even though it would have meant incarceration rather than the leniency of the House of Correction – said his brain should be examined, to learn more about such behaviour and so help prevent it occuring in other potential serial killers in future. It was a move opposed by the killer's mother, however, and the judge eventually ruled against such a course of action.

Javed Iqbal:
The Monster of Lahore

The terrible case of the 100 young boys, many of them literally street urchins, who were seduced, raped and then strangled, their bodies disposed of in a vat of acid, highlighted two crucial critiques of Pakistani society over and above the sheer horror of the case itself.

First of all the dreadful crime called into question the whole problem of street children, and how a modern society could ignore its most vulnerable young to the degree that they were not recorded as missing until the killer himself confessed to their deaths. Secondly, the brutalisation of that same society was seen by many to be epitomised in the sentence handed down to the convicted murderer, a carbon copy of the way he killed and disposed of his victims.

In the centre of the Pakistani city of Lahore, with its population of seven million, lies the market square surrounding one of the great shrines of Islam, the glorious Mina-I-Pakistan. Here pilgrims and tourists jostle with locals, the latter including the inevitable street children who are a sad feature of so many conurbations like Lahore. And the presence of these children – some teenagers, some barely past infant age – is in turn a magnet for predators of various kinds.

There are those adults who will pray on these kids as a source of cheap labour, enlisting them into virtual slavery. There are those who recruit them into vice, in both male and female prostitution; and there are those who will use them for their own sexual gratification, ostensibly as 'house servants', but as often as not doubling as sex slaves. This latter arrangement is not uncommon in Pakistan; although Islam strictly forbids both homosexuality and paedophilia, men take young boys into their service as servants and lovers with a certain degree of impunity.

So it was that Javed Iqbal, a twice-divorced, mild-mannered middle-aged man, would pick boys out of the teeming masses in the market square and take them home to his three-room apartment to work as servants. It was one such 'act of mercy', so he was to claim later to police, that led Iqbal down the terrifying path of mass murder. He had, he maintained, taken in a pair of such street youngsters who returned his generosity by severely beating him up, presumably with the intention of robbing his home.

He claimed he was so viciously attacked that he was left for dead by the boys who fled the scene, and his severe head injuries left him with a serious case of memory loss. Several operations later he was recovered, but in the interim had lost both his home and his car through being unable to work. To make matters worse, his plight so upset his ageing mother that she simply died from the stress. When he looked to the police for help, they instead accused him of sodomy, an accusation he refuted.

It was then that he hatched a plot, as he saw it to avenge his mother's death. He clearly placed the blame squarely at the door of street children generally, and so he set himself a target of killing 100 such unfortunate kids, with the help of four youngsters he recruited to aid him in his horrendous plans.

After he achieved his goal, Iqbal confessed his crimes to the police. In five short months through the latter half of 1999 he had murdered a hundred young boys, ages ranging from nine to the mid-teens, with a systematic precision that was repeated in each case. First of all, usually with the help of one or two of his 'helpers', he would entice a child to his run-down accommodation alongside the Ravi River; where he would ply them with a powerful sedative, lulling them into a false sense of security. At this stage he would ask the victim all manner of questions about his life, his family (if he had one), sounding, to a child who had little care in his life, like someone who for once actually cared. He would even take copious notes of the boys' replies to his questions.

Then, as the sedative took hold and the child was too weak to resist, he would rape him before slowly strangling him with a length of iron chain. Details of each stage, as well as the information given by the children about their backgrounds, were all carefully noted in Iqbal's diary and notebooks which he gave to the authorities. These included the step-by-step description of how he cut the bodies up, and dissolved the pieces in a vat of inexpensive hydrochloric acid.

When the job was done, he would dump the stinking liquid in a nearby sewer; when the smell got too much and neighbours began to complain, he emptied the vat into the river.

With his target complete, Javed Iqbal sent a detailed confession to both a local newspaper and the police. Amazingly, it wasn't until the pressmen were about to descend on his house that the police woke up to the enormity of the crime detailed in the confession, which via their inefficient bureaucracy had ended up in a waste basket!

Only two children's bodies were still in the house, their harder-to-dissolve remains still bobbing around in the acid. It seemed that the villain had deliberately left these for the authorities and press to find, to confirm that his confession wasn't the invention of some crank. The discovery was an indictment of Pakistani society as much as of Iqbal, especially in light of the fact that of the 100 children who had vanished via the mass murders, only 25 had ever been reported missing.

Likewise, when the court handed down a punishment to the killer that was truly 'an eye for an eye', there was much outcry that society was stooping to his level in its desire for revenge. The judge had declared that Iqbal should be publicly strangled to death with the actual chain used on his victims, and his body cut into 100 pieces and dissolved in the same mix of hydrocholic and sulphuric acid that he had used on his victims.

The case was then referred to a higher court after an intervention by the Council of Islamic Ideology ruled that the sentence violated Islamic law that states a body should not be desecrated.

On 8 October 2001 Iqbal and one of his accomplices were both found dead in their adjacent cells, strangled with their own bed sheets. The authorities claimed they had committed suicide, but both seemed to have been beaten beforehand.

The case is still subject to investigation, but the whole gruesome saga of the Lahore mass murders, if nothing else, served to spotlight the problem of the dispossessed young among its population, in the most horrific way imaginable.

George Joseph Smith

GEORGE JOSEPH SMITH seemed to have hit upon a foolproof way of making money – killing his wives and collecting the insurance. Unfortunately he was quite unable to show a little restraint: by bumping off one wife the day after the wedding he was clearly going to draw attention to himself.

Smith was born in Bethnal Green, London, in 1872 and spent his years between nine and 16 in a reform school, which signally failed to reform him because he became a small-time crook, always in and out of prison. His one asset was a capacity for charming women, which was partially derived from his hypnotic eyes. In 1898, as Oliver Love, he married 16-year-old Caroline Thornhill and put her to work as a servant in well-to-do houses so that she could steal. She was soon caught and imprisoned, whereupon he disappeared. However, she later met him by coincidence and denounced him; he served a prison sentence in his turn while she emigrated to Canada.

In 1908, under his real name, he bigamously married Edith Pegler, and remained true to her. He set her up in a home in Bristol, and always returned from his trips 'dealing in antiques' with money for her. Some of this money came from his marriage, as George Rose, to a Miss Faulkner in October 1909 in Southampton. He took his bride to the National Gallery, where he left her for a minute to go to the lavatory. She didn't see him again nor the £300 he took with him together with other possessions.

On 26 August 1910, Smith met and married 33-year-old Miss Bessie Mundy at Weymouth. He was Harry Williams at the time; she was an heiress worth £2500. Smith found that this money was too tied up for him to get it, so he took the £138 that was available and departed, leaving a note for the former Miss Mundy claiming that he had caught a social disease from her, and had to go away to recover. She herself went to live in Weston-super-Mare and, by coincidence, bumped into Smith one day on the front. Such was Smith's persuasive charm that she immediately agreed to live with him again.

In 1912, therefore, they went off to begin a new life at Herne Bay, although in Bessie's case it was not to be a long one. As soon as they arrived Smith bought a second-hand bath, knocking half-a-crown off the price by haggling. Then he and his wife made out wills in each other's favour. They then visited a Dr French about Bessie's 'fits' – although so far as she was concerned she had only a mild headache. The doctor was called twice more two days later, but Bessie seemed all right. Next day, however, the doctor was called to certify her death, as she had drowned in her bath. A policeman and a neighbour were there to aid the stricken husband and, 'drowning during an epileptic fit' was the verdict. The whole operation had taken a week. Smith collected over £2500 and he and Miss Pegler invested in a shop and other property. Smith, by the way, did not pay for the bath; he returned it as unwanted after all.

In November 1913 Smith used his real name again to marry Alice Burnham, a plump 25-year-old nurse, at Portsmouth. Her father (as did most men) took an instant dislike to Smith, which was enhanced when Smith demanded from him £104 that he was looking after for his daughter. Smith had to resort to a solicitor to get it, but he had insured Miss Burnham's life for £500. His treat for her was a trip to Blackpool.

One day the landlady, Mrs Crossley, ran a bath for the couple as they took a walk. The next thing she knew water was coming through the ceiling and Smith was knocking at the front door with some eggs he had just 'bought for breakfast'. Pointing to the water, Mrs Crossley urged him to hurry upstairs. He found Mrs Smith had died in her bath.

The landlady was not impressed by Mr Smith, who had happily played the piano while the inquest arrangements took place, and then treated his late wife to the very cheapest of funerals. When he left, she

George Joseph Smith – the murder of Alice Burnham

wrote in her card-index: 'Wife died in bath. We shall see him again.' The inquest verdict was accidental drowning.

A few months later Alice Reavil married Oliver James at Woolwich. She proved to be lucky. Smith left her in Brockwell Park six days later, taking £78 plus her furniture, including a piano, and those clothes she wasn't actually wearing.

Less than three months after this a clergyman's daughter, Margaret Lofty, married John Lloyd in Bath. Her life had already been insured for £700, and when the couple searched for lodgings in Highgate they had been particular in finding rooms with a bath. With those formalities out of the way Smith was able to take his new bride to the local doctor on her actual wedding day to seek advice about her 'fits'. Next morning they saw a solicitor about her will in his favour. That evening the new bride took a bath.

The landlady heard the splashing while, in the front room, the groom played the harmonium – the tune was the hymn 'Nearer My God to Thee'. Ten minutes later the husband was at the front door. He had 'slipped out for some tomatoes for tea' and forgotten his keys. The bride did not live to enjoy the tomatoes; alas, she was found drowned.

It was a week before Christmas. The inquest was begun but adjourned until 1 January 1915, and the conclusion was that the bride had fainted; giving rise to a verdict of accidental drowning. Unfortunately for Smith, the *News of the World* loved the story, and 'Bride's Tragic Fate on Day after Wedding' made the front page.

Alice Burnham's father and Mrs Crossley, the Blackpool landlady, both noticed that the details were exactly the same as the case of 13 months before. They wrote to the police, and it was not long before bodies were exhumed, other cheated women came forward, and Smith's history was pieced together. Smith was charged with three murders, but under the law could be tried for only one. The prosecution chose Bessie Mundy. Smith claimed accidental death, which allowed the prosecution to cite the other cases as evidence of 'system'. It was proved by experiment (an experiment which came uncomfortably close to the real thing) that it was simple for Smith to drown his brides by lifting their legs with one arm and holding down their heads with the other. The jury took 22 minutes to find him guilty.

Smith had shown a macabre sense of humour by playing 'Nearer My God to Thee' while his last wife took her bath. Another example came at his trial, when his Bristol 'wife' tearfully told how he had advised her not to buy a bath because it is well-known that 'women often lose their lives through weak hearts and fainting in a bath'.

The last laugh was on Smith, though. He was hanged on 13 August 1915 – a Friday. His only legal wife – the one who had emigrated to Canada – had turned up to give evidence at his trial and joyfully remarried the day after he died.

Fritz Haarmann

IT WOULD be difficult to imagine more sickening crimes than those of Fritz Haarmann. Haarmann picked up young boys in the unsettled days after World War I and murdered them, according to him, by biting through their throats. He then cut up the bodies and sold the flesh on the black market as meat for human consumption. Eventually about one body a week was being sold.

Haarmann was born in Hanover on 25 October 1879. He was weakly and was sent to a military school to be toughened up, but was subsequently diagnosed as epileptic and released. He was then put into an asylum after being caught molesting children, but escaped. After that he drifted into crime and served periods in prison, where he spent the duration of the war. On his release he continued his small criminal activities – including selling meat, which was scarce, on the black market – and at the same time got on the right side of the police by becoming a paid informer.

Haarmann was homosexual and as Hanover became a centre of attraction for youths with no jobs or prospects and, because of the losses of the war, in many cases without even a father, Haarmann had an endless supply of boys to satisfy his desires. At the railway station he would always find a lost soul willing to accompany him to his basement room for warmth and a snack. Haarmann, with his police connection, even shrugged off being caught practising his sexual deviances – there were far too many other problems for the police in this shifting, desperate society.

It is not known when Haarman first began to kill the boys. Probably it was at first for the purpose of robbery. The murders accelerated in 1919 when he met a homosexual 20 years his junior who became both a sexual and criminal partner. This man, Hans Grans, was elegant and witty and dominated Haarmann. They shared a flat, where Grans treated Haarmann as if he were a servant. Grans would sometimes select a victim because of some possession, such as a jacket, that he coveted.

Haarmann, for his part, was happy to take the risks of picking up the boys and, once the killing became a habit, realized that his butcher's trade was a good way to get rid of the bodies. He expertly filleted them, chopped them into choice cuts and threw the skulls and other bones into the River Leine. Haarmann developed a taste for his own product, which drove him on to acquire more, while, if his customers noticed the peculiar flavour of the meat – well, practically all the meat available at the time had something wrong with it. One woman was known to have taken meat bought from Haarmann to the authorities, where it was analysed by the police expert. She was told that it was as good a piece of pork as could be obtained in the city!

The end drew near for Haarmann in May 1924, when a human skull was fished out of the Leine. Soon there were three more, and a dredge of the river was organized which turned up some 500 human bones. On 22 June Haarmann was arrested for attempting to molest a boy named Fromm and, while he was in custody, police searched his flat. Items belonging to missing boys were found, plus human blood on the walls.

By now Haarmann had grown tired of his oppression by Grans and confessed, taking pleasure in implicating his partner. Haarmann's trial began on 4 December 1924. He was accused of 27 murders of boys and men whose ages ranged from 10 to 23, but most were between 16 and 18. The dates of the murders ranged from 12 February 1923 to 14 June 1924 – a week before Haarmann was arrested. Haarmann denied some of the murders, but admitted there must have been many more before February 1923 – he was prepared to admit to 40, and clearly couldn't remember them all.

Nearly 200 witnesses were called, most of them relatives identifying the belongings of victims. Haarmann was unrepentant, chatting to the judge, telling Grans to confess, and turning the 14 days into a vulgar show. He shouted at and argued with the witnesses, telling one boy's father that he would never have looked twice at such an ugly boy.

Haarmann could not face a return to an asylum – he demanded the death penalty and, on 20 December, was beheaded. Grans, who was certainly a partner in murder, if not in selling the flesh, received a life sentence and served 12 years.

Henri Girard

HENRI GIRARD was a clever poisoner who, instead of employing the usual well-known deadly poisons, decided to dispose of his victims by giving them natural illnesses, such as typhoid fever. It was a hit-and-miss method as some recovered, and it turned out not to be as detection-proof as he had hoped.

Girard's father was a prosperous chemist in Alsace who, in the 1880s, moved his family to Paris in order to accept an appointment there. The teenaged Henri was enrolled at boarding school but, after being expelled from two establishments for theft, was sent to a reform school. At 18 he joined the army, where he again disappointed, losing his rank as an NCO. On his return to civilian life he indulged in an easy-come easy-go lifestyle of many mistresses and days spent at the races, which entailed first stealing from his father and then dabbling in wine-selling, bookmaking and selling insurance. He was what used to be called a rake, and was extremely popular.

After a fraudulent share-dealing scheme earned him a year in prison, he decided his business partner, one Pernotte, could be more useful to him dead than alive. So, in 1909, he insured Pernotte's life (without the knowledge of Pernotte's family) with two companies for several thousand francs. Pernotte, his wife and two sons soon developed typhoid fever. On feeling better they went away to convalesce, but M. Pernotte did not quite recover despite, or because of, an injection which Girard, who had convinced him of his medical knowledge, gave him.

Pernotte died, at which eyebrows were raised, but Girard nevertheless collected his money and continued his rake's progress. He was living at Montreuil-sous-Bois, just outside Paris, and one of his neighbours was a Monsieur Godet. At Girard's suggestion the two men took out a joint insurance policy, so that if one died the other would benefit. One day, after lunching with Girard, Godet was taken badly ill with typhoid fever. He eventually recovered, but decided not to see Girard again.

Girard was called up into the army when war broke out in 1914, and his raffish lifestyle made him as popular as ever. He continued to try to repeat his successful coup, and insured the life of a fellow soldier named Delmas, who also developed typhoid fever after lunching with Girard. Luckily for him, he had the resources of a military hospital to help him recover.

Girard now turned to another friend, a post-office employee named Duroux. Duroux was flattered by the attentions of his dashing, well-off new friend, and enjoyed a meal at his flat with no ill-effects, to the surprise of Girard, whose technique was clearly not yet perfect. However, two bouts of illness after eating in restaurants with Girard persuaded Duroux to give his friend a wide berth from then on.

Girard married, moved into Paris and for his next victim turned to Mme Monin, an ex-milliner who made hats for his wife, taking out four policies on her life. When she called one evening Mme Monin was given a glass of the wine Girard and his wife were enjoying before they went out. Mme Monin reached home only with the help of policemen and a taxi, for she collapsed in the Metro soon after leaving Girard's house. She died that evening. Girard collected on one policy immediately and on two more after some difficulty, but one company declined to pay. No poison was found in the body of Mme Monin, but Girard was detained while enquiries were made.

Girard's flat was found to contain extensive equipment for bacteriological research. There were also extensive notebooks, from which it was clear he was experimenting on ways of extracting poison from mushrooms and other fungi, and diaries with notes of the condition of his victims.

Police also obtained admissions from his wife that she had stood in for Mme Monin when the medical tests were made for the insurance policies on Mme Monin's life, and a statement from a former mistress of Girard's that the meal given Duroux was thought to be so lethal that she and Girard sent away the servant and washed up the dishes themselves, using large quantities of disinfectant.

Examinations of Girard pronounced him sane and he was committed to stand trial in October 1921, but he died in prison beforehand. He had been clever enough to make himself his last victim.

Dr Morris Bolber

DR MORRIS BOLBER was not a *bona fide* medical practitioner but among the Italian community of Philadephia, USA, in the 1930s he made a comfortable living selling his useless potions. Especially popular with the local housewives was a draught made from ginger beer and saltpetre which was supposed to lessen their husband's sexual drive.

In 1932 he had an idea for increasing his income substantially when Mrs Giacobbe, the grocer's wife, confided in him that her marriage was miserable because her husband was always chasing other women. On the pretence of giving her his special urge-damping potion he supplied her with an aphrodisiac, with instructions to add it to her husband's food every day, with the object of making sure that she became even more disenchanted with her husband. He then arranged for an Italian tailor, Paul Petrillo, who had as few moral scruples as the 'doctor' himself, to seduce the unhappy Mrs Giacobbe.

Petrillo then began to work on his new mistress, convincing her that if only her husband was eliminated they could marry and live happily – especially if she had insured her husband's life for $10,000.

Mrs Giacobbe showed little reluctance. One winter night when her husband came home drunk and passed out on the bed she and Petrillo stripped him and left him lying under the open window so that he caught pneumonia. Even then he might have survived, had not Dr Bolber added a little poison to his medicine. After that, the widow Giacobbe was in no position to refuse when he demanded half of the insurance money.

Everything had gone according to plan and Bolber saw a rich future ahead. He recruited Petrillo's cousin Herman to the team, so that they could spread the net wider. It was Herman who became the lover of Mrs Lorenzo, whose husband was a building worker. Lorenzo was not insured, so Herman impersonated him, arranging a substantial policy. Herman then arranged a temporary job on the same building site as Lorenzo and waited for the right opportunity to push him off a roof.

The third victim was a fisherman named Fierenza and once again one of the Petrillos impersonated him for the benefit of the insurance agent, so that Fierenza himself had no idea that when he died he would be leaving his widow a good-sized nest-egg – to be shared with her evil partners in crime.

In 1933, with a number of murders already to his credit, Bolber joined forces with Carino Favato, known as the 'Philadephia witch', who was reputed to have poisoned three husbands and to be willing to dispose of any unwanted man for a small fee. She had plenty of useful contacts, thus enlarging Bolber's potential market, while he was able to introduce her to the benefits of insuring the victim first.

By then Bolber had decided that contriving so many 'accidents' was becoming too risky and he worked out a new way of killing off unwanted husbands so that their deaths appeared to be from natural causes. He used a canvas bag filled with sand, which would first knock the man out. More blows with the heavy bag would then induce a cerebral haemorrhage without leaving any sign of violence.

Over five years, Bolber and his associates killed some 30 people and enhanced their bank accounts considerably. They might have gone on in the same way indefinitely if Herman Petrillo had not bragged to an ex-convict friend that he had found a sure-fire way to make money: murdering for insurance. The ex-convict, Harrison, evinced great interest and tempted Petrillo into expanding on his methods. Harrison then went straight to the police and told all he knew.

The murderous gang was arrested and each member, anxious not to take the blame alone, was eager to talk about the part the others had played so the police soon built up a fat dossier of crimes. The wives who had been so willing to see their husbands killed were brought in for questioning; some were eventually tried and imprisoned but many were granted immunity in return for turning state's evidence. Doctors who had performed medical examinations for insurance policies identified Herman Petrillo as the man who had posed under various pseudonyms.

After a lengthy trial, Bolber and Favato received sentences of life imprisonment while both Petrillos were sentenced to death and executed in the electric chair.

John Haigh

WAS John George Haigh a common con man with an exaggerated idea of his own learning and cleverness, or was he a badly disturbed man who enjoyed drinking blood? Stories of vampirism kept Britain fascinated in 1949 when Haigh was arrested and charged with murder.

The story centred round the Onslow Court Hotel in London's fashionable South Kensington. Haigh, a dapper man with a neat moustache, charming smile and immaculate hair, who wore smart clothes and highly polished shoes, had been staying in Room 404 for two years. A wealthy widow, 69-year-old Mrs Olive Durand-Deacon, whose husband had been a colonel in the Gloucestershire Regiment, had lived in Room 115 for seven years. They dined at neighbouring tables.

On 14 February 1949 the courtly John Haigh, then 39, invited Mrs Durand-Deacon to visit his factory in Crawley, Sussex. She had expressed interest in manufacturing artificial fingernails, and Haigh said he could help her. In fact Haigh merely rented occasional use of a glorified storeroom, which Mrs Durand-Deacon was to discover when Haigh drove her there in his racy Alvis on the following Friday, picking her up not from the hotel but at the Army and Navy Stores in Victoria.

On arrival Haigh produced a revolver and shot his guest expertly through the neck. He then poked her 89 kg (14 stone) body into a 205 litre (45 gallon) drum, stood the drum up with difficulty, then strolled round to Ye Olde Ancient Priors' Restaurant for poached egg on toast and tea. After his repast he returned to the storeroom and, wearing a rubber apron, gloves and a gas mask and using a stirrup pump, filled the drum with sulphuric acid before driving back to London, leaving the acid to do its work over the weekend.

On Saturday he discovered, to his temporary discomfort, that Mrs Durand-Deacon had mentioned her proposed trip with him to a friend at the hotel, Mrs Constance Lane, so his avoidance of being seen driving off with the wealthy widow had been in vain. He had to tell Mrs Lane that Mrs Durand-Deacon had not kept the appointment and quickly sold his victim's watch and jewellery. By Sunday, Mrs Lane was talking about reporting her friend's disappearance to the police. Haigh drove her round to the station, pointing out that his story would be of use to them. The affable and helpful Haigh impressed the police with his concern.

However, as enquiries gently meandered on, Sergeant Alexandra Lambourne had an uneasy feeling about the too-smart, too-charming Haigh and voiced it to her superiors. Instead of rebuffing her, they investigated his background and found convictions and imprisonments for fraud and theft. They decided to inspect the premises at Crawley. Haigh had already emptied the drum on the Sunday after the murder, but in a hatbox they found various ration books, passports, diaries, a revolver and some bullets. There was also a dry-cleaning ticket which proved to be for Mrs Durand-Deacon's fur coat. Soon Mrs Durand-Deacon's jewellery turned up at a dealers and later that day Haigh was invited to return to the police station.

Haigh was inventing a story to explain the finds when the senior detectives were called from the room. Alone with an Inspector Webb, Haigh suddenly asked: 'What are the chances of anyone being released from Broadmoor?' He had decided that he would plead insanity and get sent to the institution for the criminally insane.

Haigh, who knew but misunderstood the phrase 'corpus delicti', thinking it meant there had to be a body before murder could be proved, told the officer that Mrs Durand-Deacon no longer existed. He said she was sludge at the Crawley works. Haigh then gave the astonished officers a long matter-of-fact statement, in which he told what

John Haigh arriving at court

had happened to Mrs Durand-Deacon, with the additional detail that, after killing her, he had made a careful incision in her neck, drawn off a glassful of blood, and drunk it. He then went on to explain his possession of ration books and documents in the names of McSwan and Henderson.

Donald McSwan was the son of a man who had employed Haigh as an amusement arcade manager in the 1930s. In September 1944, after they had renewed acquaintance, Haigh took him to his basement flat in Gloucester Road, near the Onslow Court Hotel, killed him and disposed of him in acid, as with Mrs Durand-Deacon. A year later he did the same, separately, with McSwan's parents, Donald and Amy. He forged signatures to gain power of attorney over the family's affairs, and sold their property for his own profit. Exactly three years later, in September 1947, he answered an estate agent's advertisement and made an offer for the house of a Dr Archibald and Rosalie Henderson. The deal did not come off, but he started a friendship with the couple and, in February 1948, he killed them and dissolved their bodies in acid at the Crawley workshop. By clever forgery he again allayed suspicion and realized their property assets. In the case of all five murders, said Haigh, he had drunk his glassful of warm blood immediately after the killings.

The police went back to the Crawley workshop. Sunk into about 2 sq m (20 sq ft) of garden was a greasy sludge, about 7.5 cm (3 inches) deep. Professor Simpson, the police pathologist, discovered among it three gallstones and plastic items which the acid had not dissolved. Among these were the strap of Mrs Durand-Deacon's red plastic handbag, and, vitally, her false teeth, which could be positively identified by her dentist.

The game was up for Haigh, but his stories of vampirism had reached the newspapers and caused a sensation. By linking pictures of his arrest with a story of the murders of the McSwans and the drinking of blood, the *Daily Mirror* was fined for contempt of court and its editor went to prison. Haigh was sure that he would be declared insane, and the life story he told was to reinforce the idea of his madness. His parents were Plymouth Brethren, and he was brought up in a house enclosed by high walls, where newspapers, radio and friends of his own age were not allowed. His father had a blue scar on his forehead as a result of being hit by a chip of coal in the colliery where he was foreman, and told Haigh that this was the mark of Satan; his mother, to whom Haigh was devoted, was said to be an angel, with real wings.

In spite of his odd childhood he won a choral scholarship to Wakefield Grammar School and sang in the choir at Wakefield Cathedral. After school, he found work tiresome. At 25 he married a waitress who was also a photographer's model, but when four months later he was imprisoned for fraud, he was never to see her again. When he came out of prison, he lived by fraud and theft. In 1944, the year he set up his own engineering company, he had a car accident in which he had swallowed some of his own blood. This had revived schoolboy dreams of crucifixes which dripped blood and awakened his lust for blood to drink.

While in prison Haigh was observed drinking his own urine, but only one of the medical experts who examined him believed him to be insane – the others concluded it was all an act. He was tried at Lewes in July 1949 and the jury found him guilty after only 15 minutes' retirement. He was hanged on 10 August 1949, 17 days after his fortieth birthday. Four years later his trial judge, Sir Travers Humphreys, retired – and went to live at the ill-fated Onslow Court Hotel.

Perry Smith and Richard Hickock

RICHARD HICKOCK heard about the wealthy Clutter family when he was serving time in Kansas State Penitentiary, USA. His cell-mate Floyd Welles had worked on Herb Clutter's farm and reckoned that his employer normally kept $10,000 in his safe. Hickock questioned Welles closely about the household and discovered that 48-year-old Clutter was a prosperous wheat farmer, a well-known and respected member of the community, who lived with his nervous, highly-strung wife Bonnie and two of his children, 16-year-old Nancy and 15-year-old Kenyon. As he served his sentence, Hickock had plenty of time to plot how to turn the information to his advantage.

On the night of 15 November 1959 Hickock and his accomplice Perry Smith followed Welles' directions to the Clutter farm at Holcomb, Kansas, where four members of the family lay sleeping. Herb Clutter heard the intruders and came downstairs to be faced with two armed men demanding the money from his safe. Mildly and politely, he pointed out that he had no safe but Smith and Hickock dragged him from room to room as they searched.

Then they went upstairs, ignoring Clutter's plea not to disturb his invalid wife, and herded the four members of the family into the bathroom. Except for Kenyon, all were in their nightclothes; he had hurriedly dressed in jeans and T-shirt, though his feet were bare. The robbers decided that it would be safest to leave each of the Clutters in a separate room while they searched further. First they trussed up Herb Clutter and left him lying face down on a cardboard box in the boiler room, then Kenyon was bound and left in the downstairs recreation room. The two women were tied up and left lying on their beds.

The robbers' search was fruitless and by the time they realized

The Clutter family. The picture shows (clockwise) Mr Herb Clutter, teenagers Kenyon and Nancy, and Mrs Bonnie Clutter

there was no $10,000, both men were angry and frustrated. They went into a huddle and decided that leaving the Clutters alive to identify them was just too risky. The killing began with Herb Clutter: Smith stabbed him in the throat then, when he did not die quickly enough, shot him in the head. His wife, son and daughter were all shot as they lay helpless. Only Nancy, whose mouth had not been taped, was able to plead for her life, but in vain. The robbers made off with $50 and Kenyon's radio.

Once news of the murders broke, Floyd Welles told police what he knew and the police hunt for the fugitives was on. Some six weeks later, Smith and Hickock were apprehended driving a stolen car in Las Vegas. 'Perry Smith killed the Clutters and I couldn't stop him,' said Hickock. 'He killed them all.' Though Smith at first maintained that Hickock had killed the two women, he later confessed that he had acted as executioner. He said of Clutter: 'He was a nice gentleman . . . I thought so right up to the moment I cut his throat.'

The prosecutor at their trial exhorted the jury not to be 'chicken-livered' about bringing in a guilty verdict. After they had found both men guilty on each of the four counts of murder and sentence of death had been passed, Smith said to Hickock, 'No chicken-livered jurors they', and both men laughed heartily.

It took almost five years for the two killers to exhaust the legal appeals procedure but both were finally hanged on 14 April 1965.

Captain Julian Harvey

MURDER for gain is an unforgivable crime, the more so when, for example, a bomb is placed on a plane or a train is derailed in an attempt to kill one person, with no concern for the deaths of all the other victims unknown to the murderer.

The person who commits this crime is more properly a mass murderer than a serial killer. Captain Julian Harvey was one such, but it was suspected after his death that it was not his first exercise in sacrificing others for his main purpose, so he could be called a possible serial killer too. It was the emphatic and unexpected way in which he was exposed that makes his case interesting.

Julian Harvey was born in 1916, and, after a career as an officer in the US Air Force, during which he reached the rank of lieutenant-colonel, he began operating a ketch, the *Bluebelle*. On 8 November 1961 he set sail from Fort Lauderdale, Florida, with his wife Mary and the Dupperault family, consisting of Mr Arthur Dupperault, his wife, and three children: 14-year-old Brian, 11-year-old daughter Terry Jo and seven-year-old Renee.

Five days later Captain Harvey was found adrift in a dinghy, which also contained the drowned body of little Renee. He said that the *Bluebelle* had caught fire and blown up the day before, when they were some 80 km (50 miles) from Nassau. The flames had been so fierce that he had been unable to reach his wife or any of the other passengers before he had had to leave the boat. He had fished Renee's body from the sea, but everybody else had disappeared. There was no hope for them.

Although Captain Harvey had shortly before taken out a double-indemnity policy on his 34-year-old wife, nobody considered that the

Terry Jo rescued from her raft after her three-day ordeal at sea

case could be other than a tragic accident at sea. Harvey was attending a coastguard hearing four days later when amazing news reached the inquiry – one of the passengers, 11-year-old Terry Jo, had been rescued from a cork raft.

Terry Jo's story was quite different from Captain Harvey's. She had seen Harvey slaughter her parents, her brother and his own wife. She had seen the bodies of her mother and brother, she said, covered all over with blood. She had been on deck when Harvey opened the vessel's sea-cocks to allow the ketch to sink, but had managed to get away on the raft before the ship had gone down.

On learning of the girl's rescue, Harvey did not wait to hear the story she told. He left the hearing shaking his head, went back to his Miami motel room and wrote a suicide note before slashing his wrists with a razor blade. He was buried at sea.

It was discovered afterwards that Harvey's first wife had also died violently and not alone. In 1945 Harvey had been driving a car containing his wife Joan and also her mother, Mrs Myrtle Boylen, over a river bridge in Florida when it crashed through a railing into the water. He told the investigators that he had been thrown clear, but that the two women had been drowned in the car. Could Captain Julian Harvey have twice killed other people in order to cover up the murder of his wives?

Al Capone

AL CAPONE is the personification of the Chicago gangster popularized in Hollywood films of the 1930s and beyond. He was the head of a mob which more or less owned Chicago, including the police and the law, and he was personally responsible for more than 500 killings.

Capone was born in 1898 in the slums of Brooklyn, the son of a barber from Naples. He left school after beating up his teacher and became a gangster, impressing the older Johnny Torrio, who hired the podgy teenager as a bouncer in a saloon-cum-brothel. In a fight over a woman with Frank Gallucio, another hood, Capone received the long scar on his left cheek which earned him the nickname 'Scarface', the title of one of the films about him.

In 1920 Torrio went to Chicago to help his uncle Big Jim Colosimo to run the brothel business there, and he took Capone with him. When the Volstead Act was passed and the prohibition of liquor opened up great bootlegging prospects for gangsters Colosimo was slow to act, so Torrio decided to eliminate his uncle and Capone took care of the murder.

Torrio's empire grew until there was only one rival for the 'owner-ship' of Chicago. This was the North Side gang, mainly Irishmen led by Dion O'Banion, a florist. In 1923 O'Banion sold Torrio a brewery and then had it raided by the police, causing Torrio's arrest. Later in the year, Mike Merlo, who ran the illicit liquor manufacturing busi-ness under Torrio's protection, died, and the mob ordered $100,000 worth of flowers for the funeral – mostly from O'Banion. Three of Capone's men, under the pretence of buying flowers, shot O'Banion in his shop.

After O'Banion's funeral all-out war existed between the two groups, during which as many as 1000 gangsters lost their lives. Torrio himself was shot, his life being saved only by the jamming of a gun held to his head. After nearly dying in hospital he retired, and the 26-year-old Capone was in charge. His organization employed over 1000 men, paying out $300,000 per week. He was nevertheless not above killing personally, especially to make a point, as when 'Ragtime Joe' Howard, a bootlegger, mistreated his book-keeper. Capone approached Howard in a crowded bar and shot him six times in the head. There were 'no witnesses'.

Liquor, gambling and prostitution were Capone's main concerns, and he was popular; he kept his workforce happy by loyalty, which was returned. He survived numerous murder attempts, including being shot at by the men who nearly killed Torrio, an attempt at poisoning and, most spectacularly, when his headquarters in the Hawthorn Hotel in Cicero, Illinois, was sprayed with machine guns by eight carloads of men from the O'Banion gang. Over 1000 rounds were poured in, but Capone escaped by lying on the floor surrounded by bodyguards.

Capone got away with machine-gunning Chicago's assistant attorney from a speeding car – the gangster trademark – and was never held for long on any charge. Two actions probably prompted the beginning of the end for Capone just when it seemed he was untouchable. The St Valentine's Day massacre in 1929 was meant to eliminate Bugs Moran, the leading light in the O'Banion gang. Capone's men, dressed as policemen, went to a meeting called by the opposition in a garage and, lining the seven gangsters present against a wall, machine-gunned them down. Moran himself was late, saw the fake police car, and escaped. Three months later, at a lavish banquet, Capone denounced three of his men, including two of his top gunmen, as traitors. Taking a club from under his chair, Capone walked round the table and battered the three to death, with nobody lifting a finger.

The public were sickened by these events and the federal government found a way of getting Capone by charging him with income tax

Al Capone winks at reporters as he arrives at the Chicago court for sentencing

evasion. 'I didn't know you paid tax on illegal earnings', was his confident attitude, but the jury he had carefully fixed were replaced at the last minute and he was sentenced to 11 years' imprisonment, first at Atlanta and then in Alcatraz. His health rapidly deteriorated through paresis, a paralysis of the motor functions derived from syphilis. After his release he had eight years of luxurious freedom in his mansion at Palm Beach, but his mind had completely gone. He died peacefully in 1947, aged 48.

Murder Inc.

MURDER INC. was the name given by newspapers to an outfit designed to keep order for the syndicate that divided up crime in the United States in the 1930s. Lucky Luciano and Meyer Lansky were the leading gangsters who formed the syndicate, which was a collection of the younger Mafiosi and the Irish and Jewish gangs that proliferated in the Prohibition Era.

The aim was to control and eliminate the gang warfare that had caused so many deaths in the Capone/O'Banion era, a control that became especially necessary after the repeal of the Volstead Act and the end of bootlegging. The gambling, prostitution, drugs, loans and other racketeering businesses were to be divided up, shared and practised for everybody's mutual benefit. Of course, the old gangs were not always agreeable when it came to allocating spoils, and even when demarcations existed the lines could be crossed, so it was necessary for the heads of the syndicate to have a 'law enforcement' arm. This was a troop of killers who would kill only for business and only on the orders of the syndicate. This was Murder Inc. – a private assassination army.

Lucky Luciano was the most influential figure in the development of organized crime in the USA – in fact, he was the man who did most to add the description 'organized' to crime, and to make the syndicate 'bigger than US Steel'.

He was born Salvatore Luciana near Palermo in Sicily in 1897 and entered the USA in 1906. He offered smaller kids at school 'protection' from bullies – they either paid or he beat them. One who wouldn't pay was Meyer Lansky, a Jewish kid born in 1902 in Grodno, Poland. They fought, then became lifelong allies. While both became

Lucky Luciano at his Naples home, 1958

gangsters, Lansky joined up first with Bugsy Siegel to form the Bug and Meyer gang, which both hijacked liquor and sold protection to bootleggers. They would kill for a price and were, therefore, the forerunners of Murder Inc.

Luciano and Lansky worked to form the syndicate during the 1920s. By eliminating 'Joe the Boss' Masseria and Salvatore Maranzano, the old-style Mafia chiefs, they were in a position to put their plans into operation. Lansky, well-read, studious, devious, clever with money, and Luciano, ruthless, fearless and with a flair for organization, made a perfect complementary pair. Among other 'directors' of the newly formed syndicate were Joe Adonis, an Italian who controlled bootleg liquor in Manhattan and who was unofficially second-in-command to Luciano, New Yorker Dutch Schultz, the king of the numbers racket (an illegal gambling pastime which made huge profits), Louis Lepke, a union racketeer who took control of the garment industry, and Frank Costello, an Italian who looked after the bribery for the syndicate, paying out thousands of dollars to politicians, judges and police. He was known as the Prime Minister of the Underworld.

Lepke, a man who loved violence, was the operating head of Murder Inc., with Albert Anastasia as his second-in-command. Anastasia, known as the Lord High Executioner, could be said to live solely for killing and was also called the Mad Hatter. Below these two were lieutenants like Abe 'Kid Twist' Reles, Louis Capone and Mendy Weiss. Orders for a killing came down through these men to killers like Pittsburgh Phil (alias Harry Strauss), Frank Abbandando, Happy Maione, Buggsy Goldstein and Vito 'Chicken Head' Gurino, who practised by shooting heads off chickens.

No killing was carried out without the approval, explicit or by implication, of the board of directors. A killing was called a 'hit' and the killer the 'hit-man'. An order for a killing was a 'contract' and the victim was a 'bum'.

It was a superb organization in that if a killing were necessary the contract could be given to a hit-man far removed from the directors or the bum. The killer and victim might be from different parts of the country and unknown to each other. The hit-man would arrive, do his job and disappear – how could the law trace the murder back to Luciano or another director?

The professionalism and singleness of purpose of Murder Inc. could allow Bugsy Siegel to promise 'we only kill each other'. The highest-ranked criminal to be killed by Murder Inc. was Dutch Schultz, himself a director of the syndicate. Schultz wanted to eliminate Thomas E. Dewey, the prosecutor who was later just beaten in the election for President of the USA, and when this idea was rejected by the board he set up a plan to do it himself. It was about to be put into operation when Albert Anastasia, in whom he had confided, reported it to Luciano. The board put out a contract on Schultz, and he was shot, with his three companions, at a chop house in Newark, New Jersey.

The number of hits carried out by Murder Inc. in the 1930s is thought to be about 500. Of the founder members mentioned here, Albert Anastasia was shot dead in 1957, with the approval of Meyer Lansky, as he sat in a barber's chair at the Park Sheraton Hotel, New York. Lepke, Weiss and Capone were executed in 1944 for a contract killing. Pittsburgh Phil, the most prolific killer, whose own score possibly surpassed 100, was sent to the electric chair in 1941 for just one of his hits. Abbandando went to the chair in 1942.

The reason many of these original members of Murder Inc. were executed by the state was that in 1940, Abe Reles was picked up on a murder charge with other members of Murder Inc. and word got around that one of them was about to talk. Frightened of being informed upon, Reles, whose own score of killings was about 30, decided to get in first and gave the authorities their first knowledge of Murder Inc.

Reles' testimony allowed 49 murders to be solved, and he was a star witness in numerous trials. In November 1941 he was due to give evidence on Anastasia and Bugsy Siegel but, although he was always guarded by six policemen, he 'fell' out of a hotel window. Twenty years later Luciano revealed that it had cost Costello a bill of $50,000 to the police department to check whether the singing canary could also fly.

Earle Nelson

THE NUMBER of women raped and murdered by Earle Leonard Nelson is unknown, but in the 16 months alone from February 1926 to June 1927 his victims numbered at least 20. Among the names given him during this spell was the 'Gorilla Murderer'.

Nelson was born in 1897 in Philadelphia. His 20-year-old mother suffered from a venereal disease contracted from his father, and died before he was a year old. He was brought up by his aunt Lillian Fabian, who was devoutly religious and said her nephew would be a minister one day; he certainly did become obsessed with the Bible.

At ten he was hit by a trolley car, suffering terrible injuries which left him with a hole in his head that caused intermittent pain throughout his life. As a teenager he alternated Bible-mania with acts of violence, and in 1918 he was committed to a mental asylum after raping a young girl in Philadelphia. He repeatedly escaped from the asylum and remained free from 1919 when, using the alias of Roger Wilson, he married a schoolteacher. Constant lecturing from the Bible and accusations of infidelity finally gave Mrs Wilson a nervous breakdown which sent her to hospital, where Nelson visited her and attempted to rape her. He was ejected from the hospital and disappeared.

What Nelson did for the next six years is unknown. The series of murders which brought him to the public's attention began on 20 February 1926. On that day Miss Clara Newman, a 60-year-old lodging-house owner in San Francisco, was visited by her nephew. He thought she was out until he pushed open a lavatory door and found her naked body propped on the seat. She had been badly assaulted and strangled with her own pearl necklace. The removal of a 'To Let'

127

notice from the window suggested that she had been killed by some-body looking for a room. Two weeks later a very similar murder was committed at a lodging house in San José, and there were three more in June and August in the same San Francisco-Oakland area.

The killer then moved to Portland, Oregon, where three landladies were murdered on consecutive days in October. In November his victims were in Oregon City, San Francisco and Seattle, in December he killed in Council Bluffs, Iowa, and around Christmas time two women died in Kansas City. The second, 28-year-old Mrs Germania Harpin, had an eight-month-old daughter, whom the killer throttled with a piece of rag.

The killer's method was clear: he would enquire at houses showing a 'To Let' sign and if the landlady who invited him in was alone he would strangle and rape her, often hiding the body under a bed. Sometimes he took jewellery, and it was through this that the first description of him was produced. The Portland police published details of some of the stolen jewellery and were brought items three landladies had bought from a young man who had stayed with them. They proved to belong to Mrs Florence Monks, who had been killed in Seattle. The description the ladies gave of the pleasant, quiet, religious young man was that he was short, blue-eyed and dark-complexioned. He had a slightly simian jaw. This last detail, and the ferocity of the killings, led to the 'Gorilla' tag, although other papers called him the 'Dark Strangler' or the 'Phantom'.

In 1927 the trail of bodies led through Philadelphia, Buffalo, Detroit and Chicago. In June the killer crossed into Canada, taking a third-floor room in Smith Street, Winnipeg, where the landlady was a Mrs Catherine Hill. The next day Mr and Mrs Cowan, a couple staying in the same house, reported their 14-year-old daughter Lola had disappeared. Then, in another part of town, William Patterson came home to find his wife Emily missing and informed the police. That night, as he knelt to pray, he saw her hand under the bed and discovered her dead body.

Recognizing the Gorilla Murderer's trademark, the Winnipeg police checked all lodging houses. Mrs Hill mentioned the lodger who had just left, Roger Wilson, a Bible-loving man. The police asked to see his room, and under the bed, giving off a terrible stench, was the mutilated body of Lola Cowan, where it had lain for three days.

The net was tightening on Nelson, because he had changed his clothes at the Pattersons' house, and changed them again at a second-hand shop, so it was known he was wearing corduroys and a plaid shirt. An attempted strangulation in a boarding house at Regina, some 480 km (300 miles) to the west, gave police a clue as to the direction Nelson was taking, and a full-scale hunt was launched between there and the border with the States. He was picked up by two officers, Constables Gray and Sewell, 19 km (12 miles) from the border. He gave his name as Virgil Wilson, and looked so innocent that he was left alone in the gaol, handcuffed to the bars, while the officers phoned Winnipeg to check details. In 20 minutes he had picked two locks to escape. But the police were now on to him, and when they spotted him again next day they made no mistake.

Nelson killed at least 20 women, and there were other killings, particularly three in Newark, New Jersey, which bore his mark. He was tried in Winnipeg for the Canadian murders only and although he was supported by his aunt and former wife in a plea of insanity, after four days was found guilty. 'I am innocent before God and man,' he said from the stand. 'I forgive those who have wronged me. God have mercy!' He was hanged on 13 January 1928.

Gordon Cummins

IN 1942, London was suffering night after night from the raids of German bombers. From sunset to sunrise it was illegal to show any light which would indicate the target to a bomber, and each evening householders put up their special blackout curtains. In February there occurred a series of murders which earned a young aircraftman the title of the 'Blackout Ripper'.

The murders were first discovered in the early hours of 9 February 1942, when a woman's body was found in a brick-built air-raid shelter in Marylebone. She was identified as Miss Evelyn Hamilton, a 42-year-old chemist. Her silk scarf had been bound round her nose and mouth as a gag, and she had been strangled. Her handbag was found nearby. The only clue to her killer was a bruise on her throat which led police to believe her attacker was left-handed.

The following day the body of Mrs Evelyn Oatley was found in her apartment in Wardour Street, Soho. She was an ex-Windmill girl who used the name Nita Ward, and had taken to a little prostitution. Hers was a sex murder. Her naked body had been thrown across her bed. Her throat was cut, and her belly and sexual organs had been savagely attacked with a tin-opener; this lay nearby and showed left-handed fingerprints, as did part of a mirror found in the flat. Mrs Oatley had been last seen in Piccadilly Circus, hailing a taxi with a man.

The two murders caused a frisson of anxiety among London women, particularly those who needed to go out into the dark evening streets. Three days later the neighbours of Mrs Margaret Lowe told police they were worried that they had not seen her. Mrs Lowe was a prostitute who, under the name of Pearl, operated from a flat just off Tottenham Court Road. Police forced the door, and under a quilt on the bed found her naked body. She had been strangled with a silk stocking. Her lower body had been severely mutilated by a variety of instruments which lay scattered around, including a bread knife, other knives and a poker. There were more fingerprints, and confirmation again that the killer was left-handed.

Detectives were still examining the body when they were informed of another, in Sussex Gardens, Paddington. Mrs Doris Jouannet, the wife of a hotel manager, was found dead. Her husband, as was his habit, had slept at the hotel and found her on his return home in the morning. It was a similar case: the naked body sprawled across the bed, the tightly knotted scarf round the neck, the sadistic slashing of the genital area.

The police then turned to two other events that had happened on the same evening as Mrs Jouannet's death. A young married woman, Greta Heywood, had been bought a drink by a good-looking, charming airman in Piccadilly. As they left the pub and went into the dark street, he pulled her into the doorway of an air-raid shelter and began to throttle her. She dropped the torch which most people then carried, and its noise attracted a passer-by. The airman fled but left behind his gas mask, on which was stencilled his RAF number – 525987. Two hours after this attack, Mrs Margaret Mulcahy also met a young airman in Piccadilly, and took him to her apartment in Southwick Street, Paddington. Then, she told police, he tried to strangle her, but she was too strong and screamed and kicked to such effect he ran off. He left behind an RAF belt. Mrs Mulcahy lived just round the corner from Mrs Jouannet.

It was a matter of a few minutes routine to discover the owner of RAF number 525987 – he was 28-year-old Aircraftman Gordon Cummins, stationed at St John's Wood. He was immediately arrested. The fingerprints tallied, and a cigarette case and fountain pen belonging to two of his victims were found in his billet.

As was the practice of the day, Cummins was charged with one murder only – that of Mrs Oatley. There was a major hiccup at the trial when the jury was asked to inspect fingerprints; the superintendent who investigated the case pointed out to the judge that they were from one of the murders not being tried. The judge was forced to halt the case, appeal to the discretion of the press, and restart the trial with a new jury days later. The jury pronounced a verdict of guilty, and the Blackout Ripper was hanged on 25 June 1942.

John Christie

JOHN REGINALD HALLIDAY CHRISTIE was an inadequate youth who suffered a trauma as a teenager when unable to perform the sexual act with a more experienced girl. As a result of this episode he became known among his circle as 'Reggie No-Dick'. In later life he always found it easier to have sex with passive, unconscious or possibly even dead women, and this led to him becoming one of Britain's most notorious murderers.

He was born on 8 April 1898 in Halifax, and was a clever, studious boy. However, at 17 he was caught pilfering and sacked from his job as a clerk with the police, whereupon his father, a disciplinarian who was remote from his children, turned him from the house. After this he drifted around, sometimes sleeping on his father's allotment, until he was called up in World War I, during which he suffered a dose of gas poisoning which left him with a quiet voice.

Christie married in 1920 but, as his record of petty crimes built up, his wife Ethel left him. He was convicted in 1929 of an attack on the prostitute with whom he was living. Eventually he pleaded with his wife to return and, in 1933, she did. They moved to London, took a flat at 10 Rillington Place, Notting Hill, and, in 1939, he became a war reserve policeman. He was at last in his element, as the uniform gave him the air of authority he craved.

In August 1943 Constable Christie met a 17-year-old part-time prostitute, Ruth Fuerst. She had a cold, and he told her he had an ideal cure for a blocked nose. Ethel was away and Christie took Fuerst to 10 Rillington Place. There the cure involved her putting her head under a cloth and inhaling the steam from a bowl of boiling water and friar's balsam. Unknown to Fuerst, it also contained a tube which was connected to the gas; it was by this means that Christie rendered his victim unconscious. Christie committed rape on the insensible Fuerst and then strangled her. When his wife returned unexpectedly he had to relinquish the body and surreptitiously bury it at night in the garden.

In October 1944, when Mrs Christie was again away, Muriel Eady became Christie's second victim. By now he had refined his technique, using an inhaler in the form of a jar of perfumed water, with again, a tube leading to the gas. Eady's body joined that of Ruth Fuerst in the back garden.

In 1948, Timothy and Beryl Evans had moved in upstairs as Christie's subtenants, and Beryl had given birth to a baby, Geraldine. Beryl and Geraldine were murdered in November 1949. Evans was hanged for Geraldine's murder, although many years later he was given a posthumous free pardon. Not all experts are in agreement about these two murders, but the most generally accepted version of events is that Mrs Evans required an abortion, which was then illegal. Christie persuaded the mentally subnormal Evans that he could perform it, and would do so during the day while Evans was at work. Christie's first-aid manuals would have helped him persuade Evans of his credentials. Mrs Evans was perhaps 'helped to relax' with Christie's inhaler. He then raped and strangled her.

When Evans returned from work he was told by Christie that his wife had died during the operation. They carried her body to an empty flat, and Christie impressed on Evans that they were both implicated in breaking the law. Evans was persuaded that the best course would be for Christie to hide the body in a drain outside the house and place the child with a couple he knew, while Evans went back to Wales for a while. Evans duly sold his furniture and left to stay with relatives, but three weeks after the murders went to the police in Merthyr Tydfil and related a version of events. This was that he had returned home from work and found his wife dead after she had tried to give herself an abortion. He said he had disposed of the body down the drain. Police investigated and found the drain cover impossible for one man to lift and the drain empty. On being confronted with this news, Evans implicated Christie and told the latter's version of events.

The police went back to Rillington Place and found a stolen brief-case – sufficient grounds for them to arrest Evans for the time being. They also met Christie, who told them that Evans had had rows with his wife. Another closer search was made of the premises when, it is said, Christie's dog unearthed a bone in the garden and Christie was forced to kick earth back over it and take the dog indoors. In the outside washhouse the bodies of mother and baby were found, the baby with one of Evans' ties around her neck. Evans, who had been in custody for 3 days, then made a further confession, admitting both killings, and was charged.

At Evans' trial, where he was accused of murdering his baby, Christie gave impressive evidence for the prosecution. Evans retracted his contradictory confessions and maintained Christie had killed both his wife and child, persisting in this story even after being found guilty. He was hanged on 9 March 1950.

How much Ethel Christie knew of all this was never established. On 14 December 1952 Christie murdered her – by his own account as a mercy killing, for he said she was suffering convulsions. He kept the body in bed for two days, then hid it under the floorboards.

In the next three months three more women were killed. The bodies of Kathleen Maloney, 26, and Rita Nelson, 25, were wrapped in blankets and propped up in a cupboard in the kitchen. Hectorina MacLennan, 26, also ended up there, sitting on a pile of rubbish, her bra strap hooked to one of the other bodies to keep her upright. Christie wallpapered over the door of the cupboard to disguise its existence. A fortnight after the last murder he left, illegally renting his flat to subtenants who paid three months in advance (£7.13s) but were evicted by the landlord next day.

The top-floor tenant, Beresford Brown, was told by the landlord he

10 Rillington Place, home of John Christie

could clean up the kitchen and use it himself. On the third day after Christie's departure Brown decided to put up a bracket to hold a shelf for his radio and discovered the door beneath the wallpaper. Behind this, he saw a near-naked body.

. After removing the contents of the cupboard, which included a large can of air freshener, police soon found a fourth body – that of Ethel Christie – beneath the living-room floorboards, and then the two in the garden which they had missed four years earlier. By now a human bone was propping up the fence. A warrant was issued for Christie's arrest and a policeman found him staring into the Thames near Putney Bridge. He had been living rough for ten days.

Christie was charged with murdering his wife and admitted murdering all the six women whose bodies had been found, plus Beryl Evans, though not baby Geraldine. He pleaded insanity but was found guilty and hanged on 15 July 1953.

After the trial there was an immediate outcry about the conviction of Timothy Evans. Mr Scott Henderson QC was appointed to carry out an enquiry into a possible miscarriage of justice before Christie's execution took place. He found that the evidence was overwhelming that none had occurred. However, investigative journalism – particularly on the part of Ludovic Kennedy, who disclosed in a book published in 1961 that Evans' defence had been deprived of crucial evidence in the form of the worksheets of men employed in the house at the time of Beryl Evans' death, provoked a further review in 1966 by Mr Justice Brabin. The worksheets had since disappeared but Brabin's review concluded that Evans, on probabilities, had not killed his child but had killed his wife. In October 1966 Evans was granted a free pardon and his body was reburied in consecrated ground.

Heinrich Pommerencke

IN 1959 a wave of fear spread through the young women of southern Germany, for the 'Beast of the Black Forest' was on the loose and he might pounce on any lone female at any time.

The body of 18-year-old Hilda Knothe was found hidden in the bushes in a park in Karlsruhe. She had been brutally raped, the clothes literally ripped off her body, and her throat had been slashed with a razor. A month later an 18-year-old beautician, Karen Walde, was raped and battered to death with a rock.

In June, 21-year-old student teacher Dagmar Klimek was taking a nap in an empty railway carriage when a man slipped in quietly from the corridor and threw himself on her. Waking with a start, she fought back, whereupon he opened the carriage door and threw her out onto the line. He then pulled the communication cord to stop the train and ran back down the track to where Dagmar lay unconscious. He dragged her into the undergrowth and tore off her clothes, raped her, then stabbed her to death.

Only five days later a woman was looking out of the window of a train pulling out of Rastatt station when she saw a girl running down the road, chased by a tall young man in a grey suit. When he caught up with her he pulled her off the road into the woods. The woman assumed that this was natural horseplay between a girl and her boyfriend until, a couple of days later, she heard a radio report that Rita Walterspacher, an 18-year-old secretary, was missing. Her report led to a police search and Rita's body was found hidden under a pile of brushwood. She had been raped and strangled and, just like the other victims, her clothes had been torn off with brute force.

The day after Rita's disappearance a young man called in at a tailor's shop in Hornberg, near Rastatt, to collect a suit that he had ordered earlier. When he had tried it on, he asked the tailor if he could leave his old clothes and the parcel he was carrying in the shop while he did some other errands. He left them in a corner but once he had gone the tailor decided to move them into the back room. When he picked up the parcel he realized that it felt suspiciously like a gun, so he reported it to the police. Sure enough, they found that the parcel contained a sawn-off shotgun. This was a particularly interesting find, as a sawn-off shotgun and been used in a robbery in a local railway station the day before, as well as in several other similar robberies in the area. When the young man, Heinrich Pommerencke, came back to collect to his property he was arrested.

As the police questioned him, they realized that there was a correspondence between the areas in which the burglaries had taken place and those where rape and murder had occurred. Moreover, Pommerencke fitted the description given by women who had been attacked but had managed to escape and that of the train passenger who had seen Rita Walterspacher with her assailant. Quite soon, Pommerencke was confessing to both the burglaries and the rape-murders.

He was born in East Germany in 1937 and spent a solitary childhood; he never made a single friend, he said. When he reached his teens he was too shy and awkward to find himself a girlfriend, though he was tormented by violent sexual urges. By the age of 15 he was hanging around dance halls and making attempts at assaulting girls who left alone, though he usually ran away at the first scream. Later he graduated to rape and at one time he was forced to flee to Switzerland to avoid imprisonment for sex crimes.

He explained that sexy films made him so tense that he needed to relieve his frustration by 'doing something to a woman.' It was after seeing *The Ten Commandments,* where he watched half-naked women dancing around the golden calf, that he followed Hilda Knothe into the park and committed his first murder.

Pommerencke seemed genuinely revolted by his actions, saying,

'Everything I did was cruel and bestial. From the bottom of my heart I would like to undo all this.' This led some psychologists to believe that his apparent stupidity in leaving his gun behind in the tailor's shop may have fulfilled a subconscious need to be caught and punished.

At the time of his trial for 4 murders and 12 attempted murders, as well as 21 rapes and 35 other counts, Pommerencke was only 23 years old. He was sentenced to 6 life sentences, adding up to at least 140 years in prison.

Peter Manuel

PETER MANUEL was a known troublemaker from the age of 11, but when he went on a murder spree in 1956 it took two years to catch him, and an innocent man was charged with some of his crimes.

He was born in Manhattan, New York, on 15 March 1927, of a Scottish Roman Catholic family who had gone to the United States to seek a better life. They all returned to Scotland in 1932 but, five years later, moved to Coventry. When he was 11 Manuel was convicted of crimes that included shopbreaking, and spent much of his time thereafter in approved schools and in borstal. His parents moved close to Glasgow in 1941 when their house in Coventry was bombed, and Manuel, having assaulted a woman with a hammer in 1942, when he was 15, joined them on his release from borstal in 1946.

Manuel was shorter than average, but strong. He had dark hair and dark, piercing eyes. He liked to draw and to write stories, fantasized about his life and was an impressive talker and convincing liar – although an attempt to establish American citizenship in 1954 at the US Consul in Glasgow with stories of being a member of the British security services was soon shown to be untrue.

No sooner was Manuel back in Scotland than he was caught housebreaking and, while awaiting trial, he raped an expectant mother and indecently assaulted two other women. At his trial for these offences he ably conducted his own defence but was sentenced to eight years' imprisonment. He was released, with remission, in 1953.

Manuel returned to crime and began courting a girl in 1953. However, after fixing the date for the wedding as 30 July 1955, his fiancée broke the engagement, having discovered his life of crime. On what would have been his wedding night Manuel attacked a woman in a field. Her screams were heard, and police unsuccessfully searched the area, while Manuel kept the girl quiet at knife-point. By acting sympathetically, the girl kept Manuel talking much of the night, until he threw away the knife and let her go. Manuel was arrested and charged with sexual assault but acquitted.

Manuel's first murder was committed on 2 January 1956. The body of 17-year-old Anne Knielands was not discovered until two days later, when a man found her on a golf course at East Kilbride, just outside Glasgow. She had not been sexually assaulted, but semen stains showed that her killer had achieved sexual satisfaction through violence. Her head had been savagely beaten. While running to report his find, the man who was unfortunate enough to come across the body met some gas board engineers and told them his story. One of them was Peter Manuel, who was thus interviewed by the police. They were immediately suspicious of him, as he had scratches on his face and clothing he was known to possess two months earlier was missing, but Manuel's father confirmed his son was indoors on the evening in question and no real evidence was forthcoming.

In March, Manuel was arrested attempting a burglary after police had received a tip-off. While he was awaiting trial, there were local burglaries on successive nights in September 1956, both bearing Manuel's hallmark: footprints on bedding and tins of food and ashtrays emptied on to carpets. The morning after the second burglary, a daily help found three bodies at a bungalow a few doors away; her employer, Mrs Marion Watt, and Mrs Watt's daughter Vivienne and sister Margaret Brown had all been shot at close range, the older ladies dying in their beds.

Manuel was interviewed and his home searched, but without any evidence being found. Police interest switched to the other occupant of the house, Marion's husband William Watt, who had gone away on a fishing holiday to Argyll, staying at the Cairnbaan Hotel. He had been seen there at 1.00 am and 8 am but police formed the theory that he could have driven home between these hours, killed the three women

Peter Manuel

and driven back. He was charged and held in Barlinnie Prison outside Glasgow, where Manuel was sent on 2 October after being sentenced to 18 months' imprisonment for the attempted robbery in March.

From his cell, Manuel wrote to Watt's solicitor asking him to represent him in an appeal against his sentence for burglary and hinting that he would tell him something that would help him in his defence of Watt. He also related details which convinced the solicitor that Manuel had been present at the murder. An informer then told police that Manuel had bought a gun a week before the murders. After 67 days police released Watt, now sure they had arrested the wrong man. Four days after Manuel's release on 30 November 1957, Watt agreed to meet Manuel, hoping to discover more about his family's murder, but Manuel merely pointed the finger at a criminal he knew and admitted nothing.

On 29 December, less than a month after Manuel's release, 17-year-old Isabelle Cooke was reported missing. A shoe and handbag were found in a water-filled colliery shaft. While police were still searching for her, news came on 6 January of the discoveries of three bodies in a bungalow in Uddingston, only 10 minutes' walk from Manuel's house. Peter Smart, a 45-year-old manager of an engineering firm in Glasgow, his wife Doris and 11-year-old son Michael had been shot through the head at close range while in their bedrooms. They had been killed on 1 January, and neighbours reported that between then and the date of their discovery lights had been switched on and off, so the killer had either stayed there or returned to the scene of the crime. On 4 January, another local couple, Mr and Mrs McMunn, had woke at 5.45 am to see a man at the door of the bedroom. He had fled when quick-thinking McMunn had pretended he had a gun.

Police arrested Manuel on 14 January 1958 and charged him with the murder of the Smarts and the break-in at the McMunns. They also arrested his father for receiving stolen goods. A camera and gloves had been taken from a house near Isabelle Cooke's home, and

Manuel's father, in an attempt to protect his son, had claimed to have bought them in a market.

As the police hoped he would, Manuel now showed feelings for his father. He offered a deal – a confession in exchange for his father's release. He duly wrote a full confession of all the murders and led police to the ploughed field where he had buried the body of Isabelle Cooke, identifying the exact spot. He also showed them where he had thrown the two guns into the river.

Manuel's trial on eight murder charges began on 12 May 1958. Ten days later he sacked his counsel and conducted a brilliant defence himself. He had renounced his confession and part of his defence was that William Watt had murdered his own family, so Watt had to face cross-examination by the killer of his loved ones.

Manuel was found guilty of seven murders, being acquitted of that of Anne Knielands on lack of evidence. He was hanged on 11 July 1958. Seventeen days later, a coroner's jury in Newcastle decided that taxi-driver Sydney Dunn, who had been shot on 8 December 1957, was another of his victims, for Manuel had gone to the city for a job interview.

Jerry Brudos

THOSE who ponder the question of how much of a person's character is inherited and how much is shaped by his or her experiences would find Jerry Brudos an interesting study.

Even at the age of five Brudos had a fixation for women's shoes, which he would play with. As an adolescent, he was excited by women wearing black stiletto heels. At 17 he forced a woman at knife-point to pose nude while he took photographs of her. He was confined to a mental hospital for nine months with a personality disorder, then, when he was released, began to steal women's underwear and shoes. First the underwear came off clotheslines, then he stole from apartments while the owners slept, and if the women woke he would rape them. By the time he committed his first murder, he had a large collection of women's clothes.

Brudos, tall, very strong and freckle-faced, was 28 by this time, married and the father of a child. He had the strange foible of insisting that his wife should walk about the house in the nude.

In January 1968 a 19-year-old encyclopaedia saleswoman called Linda Slawson had the bad luck to walk down Brudos's street in Portland, Oregon, while he was outside his house. She asked Brudos if his was the house where she was expected, and he asked her in. Brudos's mother and child were upstairs, so he took Miss Slawson into the basement, where he knocked her unconscious with a piece of wood then strangled her. He sent his mother out on an errand and then enjoyed himself with the corpse, dressing it in his collection of underwear and photographing it. Then he chopped off her left foot, fitted her shoe on, and stored it in the refrigerator. Finally, he tied a piece of car engine to the body, took it to a bridge over the Willamette River and dropped it in.

On 26 November 1968, Jan Whitney was driving home when her car broke down. Jerry Brudos stopped to help. She wasn't seen again, but a photograph of her hanging by the neck in Brudos's garage was found later. Brudos repeated his sexual games with the corpse and this time kept the right breast. He was later to say that he made paper-weights from the breasts of some of his victims.

A highly intelligent, beautiful 19-year-old student was the next girl to disappear. Karen Sprinker failed to show up for lunch with her mother at a department store and was reported missing. After waiting 24 hours the police found her car on the top floor of the store's car park. Brudos had abducted her, subjected her to various sexual acts before and after killing her, photographed her, cut off and kept her breasts, and dropped the rest of her body in the river.

That was in March 1969, and in April Linda Salee disappeared on the way to a date with her boyfriend. Her car was found on the top floor of a supermarket car park, where Brudos had picked her up by posing as a store detective. He had strangled her and then wired her up to the electricity so that he could photograph her while passing electric shocks through her corpse.

Soon Linda Salee's body was found by a fisherman in the Big Tom River with part of an engine tied to it. Then the corpse of Karen Sprinker was similarly discovered. The police realized that a sick killer was at large and would strike again. A huge operation was mounted, which included asking all Karen Sprinker's fellow students at the Oregon State University if they had seen or heard anything unusual.

At last police found a possible lead. Three girls had received calls from a man claiming to be a Vietnam veteran and asking if they were interested in 'Coke and conversation'. One had actually met him, a tall red-haired man with freckles. The girl was told to stall and get in touch with the police if there were further telephone calls. A fortnight later the man rang again, and the girl arranged to meet him in an hour then warned the police. The police met him instead, learned his name and later, when checking, discovered his conviction and mental history. They decided to watch his house.

One day in May Brudos began to load up his car as if going away. The police quickly got a search warrant and arrested him. Slowly Brudos began to talk, and soon the police had all the gory details of his murders. At his trial Brudos pleaded insanity but psychiatrists pronounced him sane; he was sentenced to life imprisonment in the maximum security Oregon State Penitentiary, where he is a model prisoner.

Albert DeSalvo

ON A WARM June night in Boston, Juris Slesers arrived at his mother's third-floor apartment to take her to a service at the nearby Latvian church. He received no answer to his knock and when, after half an hour, there was still no answer, he was worried enough to force open the door. He found his mother, a 55-year-old divorcee, lying on the floor, naked except for her housecoat, which was flung open. Her legs were spread wide apart and the blue cord of the housecoat was knotted tightly round her neck and finished with a bow under the chin.

At first Slesers thought that his mother had hanged herself on the bathroom door and fallen, but the police decided otherwise, for Anna Slesers had been sexually assaulted, probably with a bottle. The bath was half-full of water, so it looked as though she had been preparing to take a bath when she had answered the door to her murderer. Various drawers had been opened and the contents scattered around, but nothing valuable was missing. It seemed that Mrs Sleser's assailant had merely rifled through her possessions out of interest.

It seemed at the time like a random sex killing, but in fact it was the first of a series of Boston murders bearing the same trademark: the bow tied under the chin of a woman who had been sexually assaulted and strangled in her own home. The 'Boston Strangler' was to remain at large for the next two years, from 1962 to 1964, sending a wave of fear through the city as lone women bolted and barred their doors and slept with knives or guns beside their beds.

Two weeks after Anna Sleser's murder, 63-year-old Mrs Nina Nichols was in the middle of a telephone conversation with her sister when the doorbell rang. She broke off, saying she would ring back when the caller had gone. She never did and when her sister failed to

149

get an answer later in the evening, she asked the janitor to check the apartment. He found Mrs Nichols lying on her back, her legs spread wide and her housecoat and slip pulled up above her waist to expose her body. She had been assaulted with a foreign object – later shown to be a wine bottle – and strangled with her own stockings, which were knotted into a bow. The apartment had been ransacked but apparently there had been no theft.

Panic truly took hold in the city with the discovery of the body of Helen Blake, a 65-year-old retired nurse. Though she was not found until 2 July, when neighbours became concerned that she had not been seen for some time, she had been killed on the same day as Nina Nichols. The next two murders also came as a pair: 75-year-old Mrs Ida Irga and 67-year-old Jane Sullivan, who lived on the other side of the city, were both strangled on 20 August. Mrs Irga's body was arranged on the bed with a pillow under her buttocks, the legs spread and propped up on the rungs of two chairs as though she had been prepared for a gynaecological operation. It had been positioned so that it was the first thing seen by anyone entering the room. Jane Sullivan, a strong, heavy ex-nurse, had put up quite a fight, She was found in the bath in a half-kneeling position, her face in 15 cm (6 inches) of water. Her clothes had been pulled up to expose her buttocks and she had been sexually assaulted with a broom handle.

A special 'Strangler Squad' was formed at police headquarters, patrols were increased to unprecedented levels and hundreds of suspects were rounded up but without result. The search became even more difficult when the killer suddenly departed from his normal *modus operandi*: the next three victims – Sophie Clark, Patricia Bissette and Beverly Samans – were young women and, unlike the earlier victims, they had been raped. Beverly Samans had been stabbed to death, though stockings were tied around her neck in the familiar pattern. Police began to wonder if they were looking for more than one murderer.

Two more strangled victims were found in 1963: 58-year-old Evelyn

Corbin and 23-year-old Joann Graff, who was killed on 23 November, a day of national mourning after the assassination of President Kennedy. In January 1964 the final strangling took place: the victim was the youngest so far, 19-year-old Mary Sullivan, a secretary who was found strangled in the shared apartment she had moved into three days before. Along with the stockings, two brightly coloured scarves were round her neck and between the toes of her right foot was slotted a card reading 'Happy New Year'. Semen was running from her mouth and a broom handle had been rammed into her vagina.

The killing stopped but the investigation went on at full strength. A committee of psychiatrists was set up to build up a profile of the Boston Strangler and many of them inclined to the view that there were two stranglers, one favouring elderly victims, the other out to rape young women. Dr James Brussel was convinced that it was one man, whose personality had changed over the time period of the murders: at first he had been obsessed with his mother and had assaulted the elderly women in childish ways but later, when he felt he had revenged himself on her and grown up emotionally, he had turned his attention to younger women. The murders had stopped because he had finally worked through the need to kill. Dr Brussel suggested that the killer would be physically strong, possibly Italian or Spanish, around 30 years old and a neat dresser with a good head of hair; he thought that he would be caught because, rejoicing in his new-found 'maturity', he would need to talk about his crimes.

He was proved right on most counts when, in February 1965, the police received information from a young lawyer about the confession of an inmate of Bridgewater State Hospital. Albert DeSalvo had been arrested for a series of sex crimes and while under observation at the hospital had boasted of being the Boston Strangler to his cellmate, murderer George Nassar. Of course the police were used to dealing with false confessions but this sounded authentic: DeSalvo was able to supply unpublished details about the crimes and the apartments where they had taken place.

DeSalvo came from an unsavoury background: his father had battered his wife and children regularly and taught them to steal from an early age. He brought prostitutes home and had sex with them in front of the children. Albert's mother was too centred on her own problems to spare any love or attention for the children. He joined the army immediately after leaving school and married a girl he met in Germany, though she divorced him later, complaining of his unreasonable sexual demands; from an early age he had been obsessed with sex and needed intercourse four or five times a day.

In 1960 he had been arrested as the 'Measuring Man'. He had been gaining entry to the apartments of young women on the pretext of being the representative of a model agency. Often he would simply take the girl's measurements, thank her politely and leave: other times he would manage to seduce her, but there were no complaints of assault.

When detectives investigating a series of rapes covering a wide area of New England saw a sketch of the rapist, made with the help of one of the victims, they immediately saw the likeness to the 'Measuring Man' and DeSalvo was arrested again. During 1964 he had carried out some 300 assaults and had also become known as the 'Green Man' because he always wore green work trousers. He would break into the homes of young women, force them to strip at knife-point then kiss and caress them all over, often raping them, but usually apologizing before he left. Several of the victims were able to identify DeSalvo.

Once DeSalvo had begun confessing to the 'Strangler' murders, there was no stopping him. He included two other murders where he had failed to leave his trademark, so they had never been linked by the authorities. One was 69-year-old Mary Brown, stabbed and beaten in her apartment in March 1963, and the other was 85-year-old Mary Mullen, who had collapsed and died of a heart attack when he grabbed her round the neck so he had left her body undisturbed on the couch. As the strangler, his method had been to knock on apartment doors and, when a woman opened the door, he would pretend that he

Albert DeSalvo

had been sent to do some maintenance work. No one who met him doubted his ability to convince the women that he was genuine; he gave the impression of being a very pleasant young man. He had chosen his victims at random whenever he felt the urge and the bow he always tied around the neck was the type he used when tying removable casts on his daughter Judy's crippled hip.

DeSalvo maintained that he had no idea why he killed and that he often felt deep shame. Before the murder of Anna Slesers he had been tempted to rape and kill another woman but had pulled back at the last moment in the face of her fear. He had gone down on his knees, sobbing, 'Oh God, what was I doing? I am a good Catholic man with a wife and children. I don't know what to do.' Instead of calling the police she had told him to go home, but now he wished desperately that she had turned him over to the law immediately. The last and youngest victim, Mary Sullivan, had tried to persuade him not to rape her. 'I recall thinking at the time, yes, she's right. I don't have to do these things any more now.' Afterwards he thought: 'Why? I say to myself, it could have been my daughter, too.'

Most of those who heard the 50 hours of tapes produced by DeSalvo were convinced that he was the Boston Strangler but there was no hard evidence. Witnesses who had seen the killer leaving his victims' apartments failed to identity him and there were no fingerprints to tie him to the scene. In a remarkable piece of plea-bargaining DeSalvo's lawyer Lee Bailey managed to agree that his client would receive a life sentence for the other sexual offences. He hoped that DeSalvo would be committed to a mental hospital for treatment but instead he was eventually sent to a maximum-security prison. Six years later he was found dead in his cell, stabbed through the heart by an unknown assailant.

Richard Speck

WHEN a pretty young Filipino student nurse, Corazon Amurao, opened the door of a Chicago nurses' home on the night of 13 July 1966 she found herself facing a tall, blond man smelling strongly of alcohol. He had a gun in one hand and a knife in the other but his words were, comparatively speaking, reassuring. 'I'm not going to hurt you,' he said as he shepherded Corazon and two other nurses upstairs. 'I'm only going to tie you up. I need your money to get to New Orleans.'

In the back bedroom were three other nurses and the gunman tied them all with strips torn from the bedsheets. Over the next half hour, while he collected all the money he could find, three more student nurses arrived home and they were trussed up alongside their colleagues. Then the intruder began taking them out, one by one. The remaining girls, panic-stricken, tried to roll themselves under the beds but only Corazon Amurao, who was small and slight, managed to hide herself well enough to fool their attacker. When only Gloria Davy was left in the room, apart from Corazon, the man returned and spent 25 minutes raping her before he led her from the room.

Corazon lay were she was for hours before daring to roll out from under the bed and scream from the window for help. When the police arrived they found a scene of carnage. The first girl to die had been Pamela Wilkening, who had been stabbed and then strangled. This first murder seemed to have roused the killer to a pitch of sexual excitement and after that he killed every 20 minutes or so. The girls had been stabbed or strangled or both; one of them, 20-year-old Suzanne Farris, had been stabbed 18 times and her underclothes had been ripped to shreds.

The sole survivor was able to give the police an accurate description of the killer, down to his southern drawl and the tattoo 'Born to raise hell' on his arm. Another important clue was that the knots in the girls' bonds were of a kind used by seamen, so police made enquiries at the office of the Seaman's Union near the nurses' hostel and, sure enough, staff there remembered a man matching the police description enquiring about a ship to New Orleans. He had filled out an application form in the name of Richard Franklin Speck and the fingerprints on the form corresponded with those found at the murder scene.

Speck was 25 and had a long record of burglary and drunk and disorderly offences. He had married at the age of 20 but his wife's infidelities had enraged him to the point where he once attacked a complete stranger, holding a carving knife to her throat, because she reminded him of his wife. Later they separated but he was often heard to say that he would kill her if it was the last thing he did. On the night he went to the nurses' hostel he was under the influence of both drink and drugs and it may be that he intended only robbery, not murder. Corazon Amurao remembered him gazing at Gloria Davy all the time he was talking about money, as though fascinated by her, and his family later confirmed that she looked very much like his wife. It may be that the sight of her triggered some deep desire for revenge and he went berserk; it is significant that he left Gloria until last (or so he thought) and that she was the only girl to be raped.

After his frenzy of killing, Speck began a further round of hard drinking, drug-taking and visiting prostitutes. Having spent all the money he had taken from his victims, he registered in a seedy backstreet hotel where he annoyed his neighbours by begging for dollars or drink. Then, on the night of 16 July, he staggered out of his room with blood streaming from his slashed wrists. He was taken to hospital, where the doctor recognized him by his tattoo. As the doctor told the nurse to ring the police, Speck whispered: 'Do you collect the $10,000 reward, doc?'

Speck's trial lasted for eight weeks but it took the jury less than an hour to convict him of multiple murder. He was sentenced to death but was saved when the US Supreme Court ruled that capital punishment was unconstitutional – a decision that was later reversed. Instead he received eight consecutive life sentences and though he did come up for parole several times this was always refused. A difficult prisoner at first, he eventually settled down to life in gaol and was put to good use painting the prison walls. He died of a heart attack in 1991 at the age of 49.

Norman Collins

IN 1967, some teenage boys exploring a ruined farmhouse near the town of Ypsilanti in Michigan, USA, stumbled across a decomposing body thrown on a rubbish heap. The remains were identified as those of Mary Fleszar, who had been missing for a month; she had been stabbed and her hands and feet had been hacked off. As her body lay in the funeral parlour a young man claiming to be a friend of the family arrived and wanted to take photographs.

A year later Joan Schell, like Mary Fleszar a student at Eastern Michigan University, went missing five days before her body was found with 47 stab wounds. Her clothes were bunched up around her neck and she had been raped. Friends reported that she had been seen with a fellow student, 21-year-old Norman Collins, on the night of her disappearance. Collins was a good-looking young man with plenty of charm and when he explained that he had been at home with his family on the day in question, the police had no reason to disbelieve him.

In March 1969 the body of a third university student, Jan Mixer, was found in a cemetery, shot and strangled. Fellow students knew that she had advertised on the noticeboard for someone to give her a lift to her home in Muskegon, so it seemed possible that she had been killed by the driver who had offered a ride. In the next three weeks two more bodies were found: 16-year-old Maralynn Skelton, who had been flogged with a belt before she was bludgeoned to death, and 13-year-old Dawn Basom, who was found half-naked, with the black electric cord used to strangle her still wound round her neck.

The 'Michigan Murderer' struck again in June, this time apparently in a frenzy of rage and excitement, for he stabbed Alice Kalom over and over again, cut her throat, then shot her through the head. She was found lying in a field covered in blood; she was naked from the waist down and had been raped.

So far the police had no major clues, but in July the case began to break. The last victim was 18-year-old Karen Bieneman, who had been savagely beaten, sexually assaulted and strangled. Her breasts and stomach had been scalded by some corrosive liquid and her briefs had been stuffed into her vagina. On the day she disappeared she had been shopping in town and the manageress of one of the shops remembered that a dark-haired young man had been waiting outside on a motorbike – Karen had even mentioned that she had accepted a lift from a stranger. The description given by the manageress sounded remarkably like Norman Collins.

Meanwhile Collins's uncle, State Police Corporal David Leik, returned home to Ypsilanti after a holiday to find splashes of black paint on his basement floor, which he could only assume had been left by his nephew, who had a key to the house so that he could feed the family dog. When he scraped up some of the paint, he uncovered suspicious brown stains underneath and notified the police. Tests showed that the stains were nothing more gruesome than varnish, but in the course of their investigations the forensic team gathered hair clippings (Mrs Leik had trimmed her son's hair before the holiday) which matched those found on Karen Bieneman's briefs. It seemed that Collins might well have taken Karen back to his uncle's basement to torture and kill her, then, thinking that the varnish stains were blood, he had attempted to cover them with paint, inadvertently leading the police to evidence that would incriminate him.

Collins's alibi for the day that Karen Bieneman disappeared did not stand up and, according to his roommate, he had carried a cardboard box containing various items of women's clothing out to his car on the day in question and had returned without it. The description the roommate gave of some of the items he had seen sounded like clothes belonging to the murder victims.

Collins was an attractive young man who always had plenty of girlfriends, but those who knew him reported that he was oversexed and subject to violent rages if he could not get what he wanted from a girl. He had been seen to chase a girl fitting the description of Alice Kalom down the stairs, angrily accusing her of being a tease. He was interested in bondage and found any contact with menstruation revolting. This was interesting to the police, because several of the girls had been menstruating at the time they were killed and they had been assaulted but not raped. Yet another interesting fact was that Collins had used a dud cheque to rent a trailer from a local firm in June 1969 and had never returned it. The trailer had eventually been found in California, near the site of another unsolved rape and murder, that of 17-year-old Roxie Phillips, who had disappeared while Collins was on holiday in California. However, Collins denied all knowledge of the girl and nothing could be proved.

Collins was tried only for the murder of Karen Bieneman and, apart from the identification by the shop manageress, most of the evidence was forensic. It was enough to result in conviction and Collins was sentenced to 20 years in gaol.

Wayne Boden

THEY called him the 'Vampire Rapist', the weird sadistic killer who murdered one girl after another, leaving deep bite marks all over the breasts of each victim. The first warning that there was a killer with an obsession with breasts on the loose was when a 21-year-old teacher, Norma Vaillancourt, was found strangled in her apartment in Montreal, Canada, on 23 July 1968. She was naked and her breasts were covered with human bite marks but, surprisingly enough, there were no signs of a struggle and the girl's face, far from displaying fright, bore the signs of a faint smile.

Almost a year later the body of Shirley Audette was found dumped in the yard behind her apartment block in West Montreal. She was fully clothed but had been raped and strangled and there were vicious bite marks all over her breasts. Once again there had been no apparent struggle so it seemed likely that she had known her killer and had been willing to indulge in some rough foreplay before he lost control. She had told friends that she was scared that she was 'getting into something dangerous with a new boyfriend' but no one knew who she was dating at the time.

When the jewellery store where Marielle Archambault worked as a clerk closed on 23 November 1969 she left on the arm of a young man she called 'Bill', smiling happily and obviously looking forward to her date. The next day when she failed to report for work the manager phoned her landlady to find out if she was sick. The landlady entered Marielle's apartment to find her naked body lying on the floor, partly covered by a blanket. This time there had been a violent struggle and the killer had ripped her clothes in order to rape her and savage her breasts. A crumpled photograph found on the floor of the flat was identified by Marielle's workmates as the man named Bill but though sketches appeared on the front page of the city's newspaper under the headline 'Montreal Vampire', the identity of the killer remained a mystery.

He struck again two months later, when 24-year-old Jean Way died in her Montreal apartment. On 16 January she had a date with her boyfriend but he turned up early and received no answer to his knock. He went away and returned later, this time finding the door unlocked and his girlfriend dead, her breasts bloody and covered with teeth marks. The police thought that the murderer had probably been with Jean when her boyfriend knocked the first time. In spite of the violence her body had suffered, her expression was tranquil.

Perhaps the Vampire Rapist felt that the police were getting too close, for he moved his scene of operations to Calgary, 4000 km (2500 miles) away, where schoolteacher Elizabeth Porteous failed to arrive for work on 18 May 1971 and was later found dead on her bedroom floor. She had struggled hard against her attacker, her clothes were torn, she had been raped and strangled and her breasts showed the all-too-familiar bite marks. A broken cufflink lay on the floor near the body. Friends from school said that she had a new boyfriend called Bill and they had seen her riding with a young man in a blue Mercedes on the night of the murder. They recalled that the car had a sticker advertising beef in the window. The description of Elizabeth's companion – the neat hairstyle and trendy clothes – matched that given by Marielle Archambault's colleagues.

The following day police found a blue Mercedes with a beef advertisement sticker parked near Elizabeth Porteous's home and they kept a watch on it until the driver returned. He was obviously the man in the photograph from Marielle's apartment and when police approached him he put up no resistance and went quietly with them to the station. He identified himself as Wayne Clifford Boden and said he had lived in Calgary for a year since moving from Montreal; he admitted that he had been with Elizabeth Porteous in her apartment the previous night, and that the cufflink belonged to him, but he insisted that Elizabeth had been alive and unharmed when he left her.

However, his account did not hold up against the evidence of the dental expert who compared a cast of Boden's teeth with the bite marks on the body and found 29 points of similarity. Boden was sentenced to life imprisonment for the murder of Elizabeth Porteous, then sent to Montreal for trial on three other murders, for which he received three more life sentences. Oddly enough, he always denied killing Norma Vaillancourt and was never charged with this early murder.

Boden was obviously attractive to women and able to convince them to go along with some of his strange inclinations. Perhaps he sought out girls with a masochistic streak who would submit to a certain amount of painful 'experiments' in lovemaking, little knowing that his overpowering sexual urges would lead to death. In two cases he may have misjudged his target, for both Marielle Archambault and Elizabeth Porteous tried to fight him off, but in the other cases, where girls were found with serene faces, he may well have strangled them into unconsciousness before they realized what was happening to them, then indulged his overwhelming need to rape them and worry their breasts with his teeth like a wild animal.

George Putt

LONG before George Putt committed his first murder, he was entangled with violence and criminality. At the beginning the violence was directed against him; when he was only three months old his father was arrested for child cruelty after he had thrashed his baby with a strap. By the time he was eight both his parents were in prison and George and his brothers were living with their grandparents in Virginia, USA. When George and one of his brothers got into trouble with the police after stealing an air rifle and shooting at a neighbour's windows, his grandparents sent him to an orphanage where every misdeed was punished by a beating.

At the age of 15 he attacked two young girls, forcing one of them to practise oral sex, and was considered for committal to a mental institution. While awaiting trial for sodomy later the same year he escaped from custody. Once on the run he robbed and raped a 30-year-old Richmond woman at knife-point, then fled to Texas where he broke into an apartment in Laredo and forced a woman to drive him out of town by threatening the lives of her children. After a police chase he crashed the car and escaped on foot, only to be arrested the next day.

He spent some time in secure schools and was entered into various assessment and treatment programmes. By 1965, when he was 19, doctors had described him as psychotic and referred to the 'almost unbelievable physical and emotional deprivation' he had suffered. Nevertheless, he was automatically released from custody on his twenty-first birthday in 1967 and drifted from place to place, usually moving on when he was caught stealing.

By 1969 he was married and living in Memphis. Soon after he arrived in the city a middle-aged couple, Roy and Bernalyn Dumas, were found beaten and strangled. Mrs Dumas was spread out on the bed, her wrists and ankles tied to the bedposts. She had been raped and her sex organs had been mutilated with knife cuts. Later he was to claim that all he had planned was a robbery, but that he had been carried away by a wave of sadistic violence.

Only 11 days later, on 25 August, an 80-year-old widow, Leila Jackson, was found dead in her apartment; she had been strangled with a stocking and her genitals had been mutilated with a kitchen knife. It seemed that once Putt had tasted the thrill of murder he was unable to stop, for he claimed another victim four days after Mrs Jackson. This time the dead woman was 21-year-old Glenda Harden, whose body was found in a park; she had been tied up, then stabbed 14 times.

Putt's wife was pregnant at this time and on the night of 10 August he had a nightmare and woke her with his cries. The following day tenants in an apartment block heard screams from 59-year-old Mary Pickens and saw a young man running away, a bloody knife in his hand. Police officers found Mary Pickens lying dead with 19 stab wounds. They radioed ahead to squad-car colleagues and after a chase, Putt was caught breathless and bloodstained. When questioned at the station, he admitted, 'I killed them all.'

Putt was found guilty of murdering Mary Pickens in October 1970 and sentenced to death, but his appeals were still continuing when a US Supreme Court ruling set aside the death penalty. It was not until 1973 that he was tried and convicted for the murders of Mr and Mrs Dumas. His sentences added up to a total of 497 years.

Dean Corll

ON THE morning of 8 August 1973, Pasadena police received a call from 18-year-old Wayne Henley, claiming he had just shot a man. When officers arrived the young man led them to the body of 33-year-old electrician Dean Corll, who was lying face down in the hallway of his house with six bullets from a .22 calibre pistol in his body.

Corll was known locally as a 'good neighbour and a real good guy', a lover of children who generously handed out candy and gave neighbourhood youngsters rides in his van. Meanwhile, he was paying Henley and another young man, David Brooks, to procure boys for him to torture and kill. Henley took the officers to a boatshed where Corll had rented a stall and they had only dug down about 15 cm (6 inches) when they unearthed a large parcel wrapped in clear plastic and saw a boy's dead face looking up at them. There was no doubt about the way he had died; the rope was still embedded deep in his neck. After that they made a thorough search of the shed and dug up 16 more bodies. Henley then directed them to two other sites where bodies had been buried and in all 27 were recovered, though Henley insisted there were at least four others that were never found.

Henley had been introduced to Corll by David Brooks two years before. Corll and Brooks had known one another since their schooldays and had been roommates from time to time, when Corll would pay Brooks for sex acts. The latter told how he had once surprised Corll in his apartment molesting two naked boys who were tied to boards; Corll had bought his silence with the gift of a car.

Corll was, on the face of it, an ordinary young man, with nothing in his background to suggest that he was a sadistic killer. As a child he was oversensitive and sickly, tied to his mother's apron-strings. Later he had two serious relationships with women and considered marriage; it was only when he joined the army at the age of 25 that he realized he was a homosexual and became more introverted and touchy, imagining slights where none were intended. According to Brooks he committed his first murder in 1970, killing a student hitchhiker named Jeffrey Konen.

With his two young accomplices he organized glue-sniffing parties to pick out potential victims, then the boy selected would be asked round alone and plied with drinks and drugs until he lost consciousness. Then Corll would take him to his 'torture room', strip him and handcuff him to a plank of wood. Sodomy was routine and Corll had plenty more sadistic games to play, such as plucking out his victim's body hairs one by one and sexually assaulting him with various objects. One of the boys found in the boatshed had had his sex organs removed and buried in a separate plastic bag and another had bite marks on his genitals. Sometimes Corll would amuse himself with the boys for several days before he shot or strangled them. Most of the boys were aged between 13 and 17, with the youngest – the son of a shopkeeper living opposite Corll's home – only 9, and on at least three occasions he killed two youngsters in one day.

Eventually, Corll pushed his luck too far. In the early hours of the morning of 8 August Henley brought 16-year-old Timothy Kerley and 15-year-old Rhonda Williams round to Corll's apartment for a glue-sniffing session and within an hour all three teenagers had passed out. When Henley came round he found that Corll, angry because he had ruined his plans by bringing a girl along, was threatening to shoot him. He had to beg and plead for his life, only persuading Corll to free him by promising to rape and kill Rhonda while Corll did the same to Timothy. Both youngsters were stripped and handcuffed to the 'torture boards'. Henley then attempted to rape Rhonda but was unable to perform and a heated argument broke out between the two men. Somewhere in the midst of the shouting, Henley seized the gun and threatened Corll, who mocked him, saying, 'Go on, kill me if you dare.' At the end of his tether, Henley pumped six bullets into him. He then released Rhonda and Timothy, who were still only half-conscious, and called the police.

At first Henley maintained that he had not been directly involved in the murders but Brooks had. Brooks, on the other hand, said that he knew nothing about murder but that Henley, who enjoyed inflicting pain, had been closely involved. Both were tried for murder: Brooks was sentenced to life imprisonment and Henley was given six 99-year terms.

John Wayne Gacy

JOHN WAYNE GACY'S parents called their son after their screen idol in the hope that he might one day make his mark on the world, but they could never have envisaged that the name would be remembered with horror by millions of Americans as one of the country's most sadistic mass murderers, the 'Killer Clown'.

Young John's father was disappointed in his son, who was over-weight and frequently ill. Gacy senior was a natural bully who drank too much and beat his son at the slightest excuse, calling him 'sissy' and 'stupid'. The boy never came to terms with his father's rejection and grew up longing to win his love and respect. He had various careers; during his first marriage he was a successful restaurant manager, showing himself adept at building up the business, and later he did well as a building contractor.

In the late 1970s he was a resident of a prosperous suburb of Chicago and was active in Democratic politics. Every year he organized the town's political summer fête, which was attended by all the local dignitaries and raised funds for President Jimmy Carter's re-election fund. Gacy treasured the photograph in which he was seen shaking hands with the President's wife. He desperately needed to be liked and to that end he became 'Pogo the Clown', designing his costumes himself and performing in full make-up at children's parties, hospitals and benefits.

Gacy was now 36 but, unknown to his fellow townsfolk in Chicago, he had a record for sex crimes dating back ten years. At the time of the first incident, in 1968, he was running a fried-chicken restaurant in Iowa, was active in the Junior Chamber of Commerce and was hotly tipped as a future mayor. He was charged with coercing two boys,

John Wayne Gacy in full clown costume outside his home

aged 16 and 15, into homosexual acts and then with hiring a young thug to beat up one of the prosecution witnesses. The judge rejected the defence submission that Gacy was simply experimenting with homosexuality and needed no more than parole supervision. Recognizing a sadistic streak in the defendant, he sentenced him to 10 years' imprisonment. Gacy's first wife, the mother of two children, divorced him while he was in prison, though he protested his innocence so vigorously that many of his friends believed that he had been framed by political opponents. He was such a model prisoner that he was freed in 18 months.

He moved to Chicago, started his construction business and began courting a young divorcee with two children, Carole Hoff. In 1971 a homosexual youth complained to the police that Gacy had picked him up at the Greyhound bus terminal and attempted to rape him. The boy failed to attend court for the hearing and the charges were dropped. The following year Gacy married Carole Hoff but the marriage was not a success: Gacy was little interested in sex with his bride and she soon realized that, though he assured her that he was bisexual not homosexual, he preferred boys. There was his violent temper, too – not to mention the bad smell that always seemed to hang about the house and which he said was all in her imagination.

In January 1978 Gacy came to the attention of the police again when a 26-year-old homosexual, Jeffrey Rignall, told them that he had been brutally assaulted. He had accepted an invitation to smoke a joint in Gacy's car, but Gacy had suddenly clapped a chloroform-soaked pad over his face and when he woke up he was confined in a basement room, where Gacy had alternately raped and chloroformed him. The next morning he regained consciousness in Lincoln Park in the snow. Though Rignall, who suffered permanent liver damage from the effects of the chloroform, spent weeks watching the major roads of the city until he spotted Gacy's car and identified him to the police, they decided there was too little evidence for an arrest.

Then, in December, 15-year-old Robert Piest went missing. Robert, who worked after school at a pharmacy because he was saving to buy a car, had said that he might be a bit late home because he had to talk to a local contractor about a summer job. It was his mother's birthday and the family were waiting for Robert's return to start her party, but Robert never did come home. At 11.30 pm the Piests reported his disappearance to the police, who discovered that the interior of the pharmacy where Robert worked had been remodelled recently by Gacy's firm, so it seemed likely that he might be the contractor the boy had mentioned.

When the police, now aware of Gacy's previous record, called at his bungalow to interview him, they immediately noticed a pungent odour and recognized it as the smell of decaying flesh. They opened a trapdoor leading to the crawl space under the house and found themselves gazing at the rotting remains of a number of bodies. Under the appalled gaze of the neighbours seven bodies were found under the house, all in various stages of decomposition, and eight more in lime pits about the house – there seemed no end to the horror as body after body was carried out. The investigating officers wore disposable overalls and gas masks and bathed in disinfectant at the end of each shift.

Gacy, meanwhile, was confessing to 32 murders of teenage boys in seven years – though in fact he had miscounted and there were 33. When he ran out of space to bury the bodies around the house he began throwing them into the Des Plaines River, and this had been the fate of Robert Piest. His favourite method was to lure the young man to his home then produce a pair of handcuffs and offer to show his guest a 'handcuff trick'. Once he had his victim firmly cuffed, Gacy would subject him to savage homosexual rape. 'The real trick in getting out of the handcuffs is to have the key,' he would taunt him. When he had finished, Gacy would throw a piece of cord around the young man's neck and tie two knots in it. Then he would push a piece of wood through the loop and slowly turn. Within seconds the victim was unconscious, a few seconds more and he was dead.

It was early in 1972, a few months before he married Carole Hoff, that Gacy committed his first murder, though he insisted that he was acting in self-defence. He had taken home an 18-year-old youth he had met at the Greyhound bus station and they had enjoyed oral sex together, but in the early hours of the morning he awoke to find his guest standing over him with a knife. They fought and the young man fell on the knife but Gacy was afraid that in view of his past record the police would not believe his version of events, so he buried the body in the crawl space.

Some of his victims were homosexual, others were not. Occasionally a male prostitute was well paid for sex and allowed to go free. Gacy used the construction business to contact teenagers. One of them was John Butkovich, who had argued with him over wages and was assumed to be a runaway when he disappeared in 1975. After his divorce from Carole the following year, Gacy was able to speed up his activities: Darrell Samson disappeared in April 1976 and a month later Randall Reffett and Samuel Stapleton were killed on the same day. In June, Billy Carroll joined the others in the crawl space, and so the killings continued.

Under questioning, Gacy denied being a homosexual and insisted that he hated homosexuals, which perhaps went some way towards explaining why he wanted to kill those with whom he had participated in homosexual acts. He claimed that the killings were performed by a wicked alter ego called Jack, who took over his personality when he had been drinking. It was Jack who drove him out to search for boys, then later in the night he would come to his senses to find a corpse stretched in front of him and know that Jack had been at work again. His defence lawyers argued that Gacy was insane; University of Chicago psychiatrist Lawrence Freedman decided that he was psychotic and reported that he was one of the most complex personalities he had ever encountered. However, the prosecution considered that it was incredible that a man could have committed all of 33 murders over so many years in periods of temporary insanity. Two psychiatrists testified that Gacy's insanity was feigned and that he had known quite well what he was doing. The jury accepted their opinion and in March 1980 they convicted him on all counts of murder and he was sentenced to death.

David Carpenter

THE BODY of 44-year-old Edda Kane was found on a hiking trail in Mount Tamalpais State Park near San Francisco, USA, in August 1979. She was naked and had been raped and then shot through the head while kneeling, as though she had been begging for her life. Seven months later another hiker, 23-year-old Barbara Swartz, was murdered in the park, stabbed in the chest while on her knees. The third victim of the 'Trailside Killer' was Anne Alderson, who had been jogging in the park and was found with three bullets in her head. She, too, had been kneeling.

In November 1980, 25-year-old Shauna May went missing in Point Reyes Park, near the same city, where she had gone to meet a boyfriend. After a two-day search her body was found in a shallow grave alongside that of 22-year-old Diane O'Connell, who had been missing for several weeks. Both had been killed by bullets in the head. The decomposing bodies of two missing teenagers, who had been killed in the same manner were also discovered.

On 29 March 1981, hikers Gene Blake and Ellen Hansen were accosted by a gunman who threatened Ellen with rape, then shot her when she resisted, killing her instantly. Her companion was also shot but, bleeding from wounds on his face and neck, he was able to drag himself back along the path, leaving a trail of blood. He was able to

Randall Woodfield

FROM December 1980 the police found themselves investigating a series of robberies, often coupled with sexual assaults, in the vicinity of the Interstate 5 highway in Oregon and Washington, USA. A gunman, often wearing an obviously fake beard as a disguise, was holding up restaurants, ice-cream parlours, petrol stations and grocery stores, some of them more than once. At a garage he forced a female member of staff to bare her breasts before making off with the money; at a fast-food restaurant he made a waitress masturbate him and during other robberies he committed minor sexual assaults on staff and customers alike.

In mid-January 1981, in Corvallis, Oregon, two girls aged eight and ten were stripped and made to perform oral sex in their own bedroom by an intruder whose description fitted that of the bandit down to the false beard. Only a few days later the 'I-5 bandit' became the 'I-5 killer' when two Salem office workers, Shari Hull and Lisa Garcia, were held at gunpoint, stripped and sexually assaulted, then shot in the head as they were lying on the floor. Neither was killed and Lisa managed to struggle to the telephone and call for help. When she described her assailant, police realized that their robber was ruthless and dangerous. Shari Hull died in hospital and the enquiry turned into a murder hunt.

The bandit's sexual appetite seemed to be increasing, for on 3 February 1981 a young woman was raped and sodomized after a robbery in Redding, California, and on the same day, in the same town, a 37-year-old woman and her young teenage daughter were sodomized and shot dead in their own home. There was another rape the following day and several more robberies and assaults over the next week.

Then came the shooting of a teenage girl, Julie Reitz, in her home in Portland, Oregon. A routine check on all Julie's friends led the police to Randall Woodfield, a 30-year-old bartender who had a record for robbery and sex offences. Woodfield had been a promising student at high school and had shown great promise as a footballer, with hopes of a successful professional career. He was given a tryout with a well-known team but was turned out because of his hobby of exposing himself, which had already earned him two suspended sentences. In 1975 he had been imprisoned for robbing women at knife-point and forcing his victims to perform oral sex before he would release them. He was released shortly before the spate of I-5 robberies began.

Lisa Garcia identified Woodfield as her attacker and Shari Hull's murderer and several other witnesses picked him out of identification parades as the bandit. Further investigations suggested that Woodfield might be linked to more than a dozen murders, but most of them never came to trial. In June 1981 he was tried for the murder of Shari Hull and the attempted murder of her friend and was sentenced to life imprisonment plus 90 years. Later he was to collect a further 35 years for rape and sodomy.

Andrei Chikatilo

IN 1992 the West was shocked by the trial of Andrei Romanovich Chikatilo, a man who was charged with 53 murders plus numerous sexual assaults over a 12-year period. He was nicknamed the 'Rostov Ripper', and admitted to a liking for chewing parts of his victims' bodies.

Chikatilo was born on 16 October 1936 in Yablochnoye, in the Ukraine. When he was five his mother told him the story of his cousin, who had disappeared from the village two years before Chikatilo's birth. The rumour in the village was that the boy had been kidnapped, killed and eaten, such was the level of hunger at the time. After his eventual arrest, Chikatilo was to say that the story both repelled and fascinated him, and may have been the seed of what became an obsession with death and cannibalism.

Chikatilo was a weakly boy who was bullied at school. He was so shortsighted that he could not read the blackboard, yet he was not to own a pair of spectacles until he was 30. Nevertheless, he qualified in communications engineering at a technical college, did his military service and, in 1960, began work as a telephone engineer in a little town 32 km (20 miles) north of Rostov, where his parents and sister joined him. In 1963 he married and, although his pathological shyness made sexual relations between him and his wife difficult, they had first a daughter and then a son. In 1971 he gained a degree in philosophy and literature and began teaching in Novoshakhtinsk, a few kilometres further north.

Chikatilo's new job placed him in an authoritative position over young girls, and he soon began to fantasize about his students. However, his shyness made it impossible for him to control his classes, and he was a poor teacher who was disliked by his pupils. This fed a desire to dominate, which increased as his sex life with his wife diminished. He became a peeping tom hanging around the dormitories and, in 1973, he molested a 15-year-old girl while they swam in a river on a school outing. He was once aroused to sexual excitement by beating a girl with a ruler.

Outside school, Chikatilo was in the habit of brushing against young women in buses and public places. He also molested his wife's six-year-old niece. Finally, in 1974, when his activities at school could no longer be ignored, he was asked to resign. He worked at two more schools, and it was while teaching at the nearby town of Shakhti that he committed his first murder in December 1978.

On that day Chikatilo met a pretty nine-year-old, Lina Zakotnova, hurrying home after playing with a friend after school. He fell in step and chatted, and she told him she needed to go to the toilet. They were near a lane called Mezhevoi Pereulok, where unbeknown to his wife he had bought a little house to use for his sexual escapades, and he said Lina could use his facilities. As they approached the house, Chikatilo became more and more excited and, as soon as they were indoors, he literally threw himself upon her. Stopping her screams with his large hand, he ripped off her clothes and attempted to rape her.

Chikatilo's frustrations persisted, however. He was unable to get an erection. Nevertheless, he made the little girl bleed, and the sight of the blood gave him the greatest thrill of his life. He reached for a knife he carried and began stabbing and tearing at her. In a moment his life was changed.

Afterwards he carried the dead girl, her clothes and bag to the nearby Grushevka River and threw them in. He threw the bag too hard; it landed on the opposite bank and was to pinpoint the place. Then he went back to his room in the school and cleaned himself up before his wife arrived home.

When the body was found two days later, the Shakhti police made enquiries in Mezhevoi Pereulok. A neighbour, already suspicious of him, told them that on the night of Lina's disappearance his light had been on all night (a simple mistake on his part in the excitement of the killing) although he rarely slept there.

When the police noticed a bloodstain in the snow outside his door they questioned him and discovered his record. They suspected him of the murder, but his wife gave him an alibi, innocently believing he had been indoors all evening. With incredible luck for Chikatilo, another man living in the street had a previous conviction for such a killing and had dodged the death penalty because he was only 17 at the time. The man's wife, for reasons of her own, told police he had confessed to her. He was convicted and shot, and Chikatilo had escaped.

Despite the horror of his situation Chikatilo realized that, given the chance, he would kill again. In 1981 his continuing misdemeanours forced the school to dispense with his services and he took a menial job as a clerk in the offices of a factory. This entailed travelling to suppliers and signing for components, which gave him the maximum opportunity to kill and get away.

Chikatilo acted like a madman on his second killing, that of a 17-year-old girl. For several minutes he ran round and round the body in ecstasy, throwing her clothes as far as he could. Only later did the need for concealment and escape impress itself on him.

In the next few months the rate of killings increased. In 1982 there were seven victims; in 1983 eight died; and in 1984 he killed no fewer than 18 people. He usually chose poor young women who would go with him on the promise of a meal, or naive girls or boys; as the killings increased, the proportion of boys grew larger. Often he would find the victims near railway stations, or on trains. They would alight at unmanned stations with woods nearby, where Chikatilo would attack them – on one occasion killing a mother and daughter. He became more expert at carving up the bodies, and would remove nipples or genitals. Sometimes they would be bitten off and chewed, although he was not strictly a cannibal. His main obsession was with uteruses, and he described the sensation of chewing them. There was one distinctive trademark, which was that victims were always cut around the eyes, as if he could not bear them looking at him. Often the attacks would come after an attempt at intercourse had been followed by scorn on the part of the victim.

The best minds in the police concentrated on the problem as his killings spread over a wider area, reflecting the distances he travelled by rail or air in his job. Several suspects were held by local police – usually subnormal men who confessed – but the killings continued. The clothing of several victims was examined minutely and the traces of semen found in nine murders was analysed. This revealed the killer's blood type to be AB. Apart from that and his shoe size – discovered from a footprint – not much was known of him.

In September 1984 Chikatilo was detained after an inspector had followed him all night for nine hours as he crossed and recrossed Rostov trying to pick up a victim. In his bag were knives and a length of rope. His shoe size fitted. The card index which now ran to thousands of entries revealed he had been questioned back in 1978 for the very first killing. He fitted rough descriptions, and the police were sure they had their man. A blood sample was taken; it was type A, so he was released. Only four years later did scientists discover that in rare cases – one in thousands – a man's sperm could be of a different group to his blood. Chikatilo had escaped again.

The narrow escape sobered Chikatilo and the number of killings was reduced – only five in the next three years, and those in far-flung regions. This control of his emotions was a powerful argument against his plea of insanity at his trial. However, in 1989 the rate of killing began to return to its previous level.

Police had now identified the role of the railway in the killings and hundreds of men were deployed on usually unmanned stations to check all passengers. On 17 October 1990 Chikatilo killed a boy near Donleshkov station without being noticed. On 6 November he murdered a woman there, but this time a sergeant saw him emerge

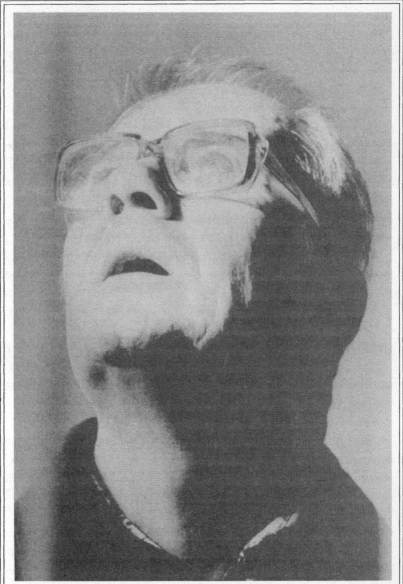

Andrei Chikatilo looks at the sun through a window in court, while the judge delivers his verdict

from the woods at 4 pm and wash his hands at a water hydrant. He had a red mark on his cheek which might have been blood, and a bandaged finger. The sergeant examined his passport, and put his name into a report.

A few days later a senior policeman came to Donleshkov to inspect the site where the boy's body had been found. A piece of blue nylon fabric was hanging from a tree. One of the local prosecutors swore it was new, saying he had been there when all the clothing from the murder was removed. The only explanation, if he was right, was that the murderer had returned and killed again. An army of men and dogs began a search, and soon the body of the woman was found. The sergeant's report was read and its contents noted. The head of the regional crime squad, who was about to attend a funeral nearby, instead called in at the local police station on hearing of the latest body; he read the report and remembered Chikatilo's name from 1984. Once more Chikatilo's card was produced from the 20,000 or so now on file. Everything except his blood group pointed in his direction, and it was decided to put him under constant surveillance, in the hope of catching him with his next victim.

Over the next few days his method of operating became clear as the police watched him try to pick up several potential victims. If there was any resistance he would give up and patiently try another, a precaution which had made him so difficult to catch. Finally, aware of the terrible risk they were running of another murder being committed, the police stepped in and quietly arrested him as he stood outside a café. His bag contained a mirror, rope and knife.

This time tests were taken on other bodily samples as well as blood. The sperm group was AB. However, several days of police questioning failed to draw any admissions from Chikatilo. It was only when he was interviewed by a Rostov psychiatrist that he began to confess to the killings.

He was charged at first with 36 murders and various rapes and assaults. As he detailed others of which the police had no knowledge, the number rose to 53. He took the police to sites where bodies were found and demonstrated with dummies what he had done to the victims. For the first time the police discovered that they had shot the wrong man for Chikatilo's first murder in 1978.

None of Chikatilo's associates during his life had suspected he was other than ordinary. His wife, who knew of his sexual problems, was hardly able to believe he was a murderer; he had been a loving father and grandfather. The knives he had used to mutilate his victims were in many cases from her kitchen drawer. She and her daughter were sent to another part of the country so they could begin a new life and escape any reprisals.

Chikatilo was judged sane, and his trial began on 14 April 1992. It took three days to read the charges, and doctors had to stand by to treat the relatives of the victims as the terrible story was told. As the trial wore on Chikatilo himself behaved outrageously, shouting, arguing and, on one occasion, stripping to wave his penis which be described as the useless cause of his problem. As the trial descended to near farce, the judge, the counsel, the police, the psychiatrists all argued with each other. The judge took weeks to write his verdict and days to read it. Finally, on 15 October 1992, while Chikatilo screamed from the cage which was necessary to protect him from witnesses, he was found guilty of 52 murders and sentenced to death. The hundreds of spectators applauded.

Ivan Millat
The Australian Backpacker Killer

One of the most famous cases in Australian criminal history was that involving Ivan Milat, the notorious 'Backpack Killer'. During September and October 1992 no less than seven bodies were discovered in the most horrendous circumstances in the Belangalo State Forest National Park, not far from Sydney, beginning with those of two young British travellers, Caroline Clark and Joanne Walters, who had last been seen over five months before.

The decomposing corpses were found by a pair of trail runners, Ken Seily and Keith Caldwell, buried under sticks and leaves, and the gruesome find was soon followed by that of the remains of hitchhikers James Gibson and Deborah Everlist, who had last been seen near the forest three years before. Less than a month later it was hitchhiker Simone Schmidl, who had disappeared in January 1991, whose body was uncovered in similar circumstances. A pair of jeans located near Schmidl's corpse were found to belong to another missing person, German backpacker Anja Habschied, and the search intensified. Her body was subsequently unearthed along with that of her boyfriend, Gabor Neugebauer, both of whom had been missing since December 1991.

There was clearly a link between the crimes. Not only had all the bodies been disposed of in an identical manner, but every body carried a stab wound to the upper back that severed the victim's spinal cord and would have rendered them helpless. As well as this grim similarity, most bodies displayed evidence of crude bondage and strangulation, many being in a state of partial undress.

Additionally, there were differences in the detail of the murders. Caroline Clark had been stabbed in the chest, while her friend Joanne Walters had been stabbed and shot in the head a number of times; Gibson had been stabbed repeatedly, and his companion Deborah

Everlist had been stabbed all over her body and across her face. Simone Schmidl had also been stabbed. Even more horrifically, Anja Habschied was found decapitated, and her companion Neugebauer was found to have been shot five times in the head, with the weapon that was used to kill Joanne Walters.

The Australian police were not getting far with the case until 1993, when a British backpacker named Paul Onions came forward with some crucial information. Onions described how, three years before, he had been hitchhiking in New South Wales, not far from the Belangalo State Forest, when a car drew up. The driver subsequently drew a gun and attacked Onions, who managed to escape and flag down another vehicle. The hitchhiker had managed to get a good description of the man, and the registration of the attacker's car.

Onions' description was identified from mugshots to be that of 40-year-old Ivan Milat, who had already been on a list of suspects with his brother Richard. A police surveillance operation of Milat's house, in which they found belongings of the victims and the weapons used to kill them, led to his arrest in May 1994, when he was charged with the murder of all seven backpackers.

At his trial, faced with overwhelming evidence against himself, Milat attempted to move the blame to his own family, who he claimed had set him up – why they should do this was never made clear. Not surprisingly, he was found guilty on all counts on 27 July 1995, and sentenced to life imprisonment.

Always insisting he was innocent, Milat declared his intention to escape, but has never followed up his threat, except for a foiled escape attempt that was masterminded by George Savvas, after which Savvas was found hanged in his cell. To this date, Ivan Milat has not been charged for his part in the escape attempt. He has, however, made attempts on his own life on at least two occasions after swallowing various sharp items including staples and razor blades.

Police later linked Milat to another four murder victims in the same area outside Sydney, though no charges have transpired. Sinisterly, when pressmen tracked down one of the killer's brothers, Boris, and asked him if he thought Ivan was guilty, he replied 'If Ivan's done these murders, I

reckon he's done a hell of a lot more.' When asked how many, he
answered 'About twenty eight.'

The Columbine High School Massacre

Nowhere could represent better the archetypal small town of middle America than Littleton, Colorado, and equally typical were the middle class teenagers Eric Harris and Dylan Klebold who resided there. However, on 20 April 1999, Harris and Klebold were to reveal a dark side to their characters that would shake the peaceful community to its roots, when they went on a highly-planned shooting spree in the Columbine High School that left 13 fellow students dead and another two dozen injured, many seriously.

The two arrived at the school parking lot that morning, entering through the back cafeteria door. They were wearing long black trench coats, a 'uniform' a number of the students, known around the school as the 'Trench Coat Mafia', had adopted as a harmless fashion statement, a minor teenage cult. However, the coats had a more sinister function on this particular day; concealed beneath them Harris and Klebold had semi-automatic weapons, with which they opened fire once they entered the school building.

So started a killing rampage through Columbine High, as the two marched through the corridors towards the library, firing at everyone and everything as they went. Students and teachers fled in all directions, some hiding in storage closets or bathrooms, some under furniture, others rushing out of the nearest exit. The alarm was raised immediately by phone, and while the killers were still shooting their way through the school the police and SWAT force were on their way.

As distraught and injured pupils poured out of the school into the arms of the emergency medical services, the SWAT teams entered carefully, not knowing at this stage what to expect. The first major cause for concern – as well as the gunfire still echoing round the building, now from the second floor – were the homemade bombs and explosive devices they discovered planted around the building.

The gunfire finally ceased at 12.30pm, just under an hour after it had started, but at this stage neither the SWAT personnel nor the police had a definite idea of how many killers were involved, and whether they were still lying in wait for them. They moved slowly through the silent school, defusing each bomb device as they found it, tending to more and more injured students, checking and removing bodies, interviewing – and searching for possible weapons – those who had escaped. They eventually found the two teenage gunmen, killed by their own hand, with more explosive devices hidden under their coats. The building was finally declared secure at 4.00pm, with a death toll (including Harris and Klebold) of 15.

The people of Littleton were traumatised, the town's calm shattered forever. The unthinkable had happened, and at the hands of two seemingly normal young people in their own midst. But what emerged in the subsequent investigations was a picture of two young men whose concerns and motivations were far from normal.

Both boys were from comfortable and stable middle class families, and when they struck up a friendship, one thing they had in common was a passion for computer games. However, what the post-massacre inquiries revealed was that they both harboured grudges – why is not very clear – against those around them, especially teachers and fellow students at Columbine High. Eric Harris had set up a website in which he expressed this irrational anger, with threats to kill people and even 'blow up and shoot everything I can' in 'some big city'. Also on the site the two posted the results of experiments they had conducted with pipe bombs and other explosive devices.

Even more sinisterly, a school video project they collaborated on showed them swaggering through the school corridors wielding guns, killing at random as they went. Some of their teachers had voiced concerns about this and other behavioural tendencies with the two; their depression, their anger, their apparent admiration of Nazism. But none of these concerns, according to the boys' parents, were communicated outside school, they claimed to have had no idea of their sons' possible problems.

The aftermath of the killings initially involved more suspects, members of the 'Trench Coat Mafia' who police thought might have been accomplices in some way or another. Although no other teenagers were eventually charged, police were convinced that other students may have had prior knowledge of the shootings.

And crucially, the crimes once again highlighted the gun law debate in the United States. Although the two killers acquired their weapons illegally, being under 21, it was the fact that guns are sold openly at all, via regular gunshops, that made them available so easily. Indeed, the 2002 anti-gun documentary movie by radical filmmaker Michael Moore made direct reference to the massacre in its title, 'Bowling For Columbine'.

Perhaps the most chilling note of the case, in retrospect, is in the journal found in Eric Harris' bedroom, in which he chronicles in detail their intended plan for their rampage. The intention stated in the journal was to kill at least 500 people, with the assault on the school being followed by continuing slaughter in neighbouring homes. After that they would hijack a plane, which they planned to crash into New York City. The date chosen was also very deliberate – it was the 110th anniversary of Adolph Hitler's birthday.

Robert Lee Yates:
The Spokane Serial Killer

The citizens of the north-west American state of Washington were well-used to the trauma of a serial killer in their midst after the horrors unleashed by both the notorious Ted Bundy and the Green River Killer, and when a number of prostitutes were found dead from the early 1990s, it was clear there was another mass murderer on the loose. In the eyes of the police, what linked the victims to one assailant from the start was the similarity of their deaths. Each body was found with a plastic grocery bag tied over the head, which in every case bore the wounds of a gun fired from a close distance.

The first body to be found was that of a known prostitute, Yolanda Sapp, whose naked remains were lying over the embankment of the Spokane River on Spokane's East Upriver Drive in February 1990. Apart from the fact that she had been shot a number of times with a small calibre pistol, the police had absolutely nothing to go on. There were no clothes or personal items to be found, and not even any bullets or empty shell casings. Unless he was an ultra-tidy killer, meticulously cleaning up after his crime, it seemed likely that he had brought the body from another location and dumped it by the river.

A month or so later another body was found in Spokane, this time a prostitute called Nickie Lowe, similarly killed with a small calibre gun. Although the police were fairly certain there was a common perpetrator of the two crimes, they had made little progress by the time a third victim was discovered. This time it was another prostitute – Kathleen Brisbois – who had been shot and beaten by her killer. As with the previous victims, the corpse was naked apart from the rings on her fingers, but this time there were articles of her clothing scattered about nearby. The fact that each victim's body had shown signs of drug intake, that they were all prostitutes and all killed with a small calibre gun convinced the police that they were dealing with a serial killer.

The serial, however, looked like it had come to an end when no more bodies were found for two years. The case had been effectively put on hold by the investigators, until in 1992 another body was found in the Spokane area, again with gunshot wounds, and shoes and other items nearby, with a plastic bag tied over the head. But another three years were to pass without any success for the police before yet another victim, bearing all the same signs of being killed elsewhere and dumped, was found.

It was then that the true horror of the Spokane Serial Killer, as he came to be dubbed, unfolded, when between June 1996 and the end of 1997 no less than eight more prostitutes were found murdered in similar circumstances. And it was one of these murders, that of 16-year-old Jennifer Joseph, that provided police with the first real lead in the case.

Joseph was last seen alive on 16 August 1997, ten days before her body was found, travelling with a white male (presumed to be a customer) in a car believed to be a white Corvette. While the police investigation was swinging into heightened action, Robert L. Yates Jr was given a ticket by a Spokane traffic cop for a minor offence in his white 1977 Corvette. Initially there was no connection made, as the cop mistakenly wrote in the booking report that the car involved was a Camaro rather than a Corvette. It was only later when the registration matched that of a Corvette, that it became significant.

Meanwhile, bodies continued to be found throughout 1998. The discovery of the remains of 35-year-old Connie L. Ellis in the October brought the count of murders attributed to the Spokane Serial Killer to 17. Like the rest Ellis was a prostitute, was shot at close range by a small calibre gun and her body was found with three plastic bags placed over the head. Another weird feature of these grisly crimes was that every corpse had been covered with waste vegetation and garden debris, but not from the immediate locale of where it was found.

Not long after the Connie Ellis murder the police had their first big breakthrough in the case. While keeping surveillance in a Spokane district known to be frequented by prostitutes, officers noted a man driving a silver Honda Civic pull over and pick up a known local 'working girl' Jennifer Robinson. The driver identified himself as Robert

L.Yates Jnr, explaining he had been sent to the area by the girl's father to find his daughter and bring her home. Not wanting further trouble with the police, Robinson concurred that she knew Yates and everything was OK, so there was little more the police could do, but their report did make its way to the task force assigned to the serial killer case.

Another report that found its way to the task force was of an assault on a prostitute, Christine Smith, by a man who paid for her services, then turned on her in the back of his van with a series of vicious blows to the head. She managed to escape, and told police what had happened, with a description of the man who, she said, had told her prior to the assault that he was a father of five and a helicopter pilot with the National Guard.

The description fitted that of Yates, and looking into his car registration details they found that as well as the Honda Civic, he also drove a white Corvette. Furthermore, he was a member of the Washington National Guard who had served as a helicopter pilot.

Yates' life history was, on the surface, one to be commended. After graduating from High School he first had a job as a guard in the Washington State Penitentiary at Walla Walla, before joining the Army where he served 19 years as a helicopter pilot. He served in Germany, took part in Operation Desert Storm (the Gulf War), and flew in the UN peacekeeping mission to Somalia. After an honourable discharge he joined the National Guard.

From there on in the noose gradually tightened. Taking Yates in for questioning, although he denied ever having associated with prostitutes, police suspicions were aroused further when he refused – as was his right – to give a blood sample.

Yates' wife Linda, with whom he was indeed the father of five, then came forward with the stunning information that her husband often came home after being out most of the night, and on one occasion (which coincided with the attack on Christine Smith) she found the rear of his van (which contained a fold-down bed) to be covered in blood. Yates told her that a dog had run in front of the van, and he had taken the bleeding animal to a veterinary surgery.

Detectives then got in touch with Jennifer Robinson, who admitted she told Yates to come up with the story about her father when the police stopped them, a device often used by prostitutes and their 'johns' to avoid arrest.

Tracking down the friend to whom Yates had sold his white Corvette, examination proved that in the year prior to the sale, the suspect had changed the car's carpeting at least twice – highly unusual, unless the carpet was radically damaged or stained. Further examination revealed forensic evidence of fabric material similar to that found on the body of Jennifer Joseph, and minute blood samples found on the passenger seat belts were found to match the DNA profile of Joseph.

Robert Yates was arrested on 18 April 2000 for the murder of Jennifer Joseph. On his arrest he was obliged to give a blood sample, DNA analysis of which revealed a match with the DNA profiles of sperm samples taken from eight more victims of the Spokane serial killer. Examination of previous vehicles owned by Yates revealed more evidence linking him to victims, and he was charged with 8 counts of first-degree murder, the attempted murder of Christine Smith and he was also suspected of the deaths of at least 18 other women in the Spokane area.

In October 2000, in a plea-bargaining offer Yates said he would plead guilty to 13 counts of murder and lead them to the body of another murdered prostitute, Melody Murfin. It transpired to be buried in a shallow grave in the backyard of Yates' former home. The eventual toll, the exact number of which may never be ascertained, even linked him to murders early in his life as a prison guard and later a soldier.

The Spokane Serial Killer was eventually sentenced to 408 years in prison by Spokane County Court, followed by another judgement in nearby Pierce County in October 2002 imposing the death penalty.
Appeals against the latter could take several years, meanwhile Yates languishes in Washington State Penitentiary in Walla Walla, where he once worked as a guard.

Albert Fish

ON 28 May 1928 a white-haired, mild-mannered man arrived at the basement apartment of Albert and Delia Budd in Manhattan, USA. He had come in answer to an advertisement that 18-year-old Edward Budd had placed in a New York newspaper, asking for a job in the country. The visitor was well-dressed and seemed to have plenty of money; Edward could hardly believe his luck when the old man, who introduced himself as Frank Howard, offered him a job on his farm on Long Island at a good wage. Moreover, when Edward asked if there might be a job for his friend Willie as well, Mr Howard agreed to take on both boys. He would return to collect them the following weekend, he told the family.

When he came back the next week he arrived early and the boys were not ready so he passed the time with the Budd's 10-year-old daughter Grace, who took to the kindly old man immediately. Mr Howard had a suggestion to make: his niece was giving a birthday party and Grace would love it – why didn't he take her along? Delia Budd hesitated but her husband thought it was a splendid idea, so Grace went off in her white confirmation dress, holding Mr Howard's hand. She was never seen alive again. The party was supposed to be at 137th Street and Columbus Avenue, an address that did not exist, and there was no farmer named Frank Howard on Long Island.

The headlines shrieked about the missing child while the police organized a widespread search and followed endless leads that led nowhere. The whereabouts of Grace, alive or dead, remained undiscovered. It was to be six years before the Budds heard of their daughter again. Then, on 11 November 1934, Grace Budd received a letter that left her – and the detectives who read it – appalled and sickened.

The writer reminded the Budds of the day he had called at their house and Grace had sat trustingly on his knee. He said that he had taken her to a deserted house in Westchester and while she was still picking flowers in the garden he had gone inside and taken off all his clothes, not wanting to get blood on them. When Grace came inside and saw him she tried to run away but he grabbed her. He gave a horrifying description of what happened next:

'First I stripped her naked. How she did kick and bite and scratch. I choked her to death, then cut her in small pieces so I could take my meat to my rooms . . . how sweet and tender her little ass was roasted in the oven. It took me nine days to eat her entire body. I did not fuck her though I could of had I wished. She died a virgin.'

Detective Will King of the Missing Persons Bureau, who had been deeply involved in the original investigation, was determined that this time the kidnapper would not escape. The envelope containing the letter bore the initials of a chauffeur's benevolent association and he spent a good deal of time investigating the members, with no result. He then questioned anyone who might have taken away any of the stationery for their own use and one of the chauffeurs admitted that he had left some of the envelopes at a previous address. This turned out to be a rooming house where one of the tenants fitted the description of Frank Howard. When the tenant returned to his room he was taken to the station for questioning.

His real name turned out to be Albert Fish and he admitted to killing Grace Budd. He had gone to the Budd's apartment intending to murder Edward, but when pretty little Grace had sat on his knee and smiled at him, he had decided to eat her. After he had strangled her he cut off her head, then cut her body in half and sliced it into pieces. He had cooked her flesh with onions, carrots and strips of

Albert Fish

bacon and for the whole nine days he was eating her he was in a high state of sexual excitement. He took the police to the Westchester house where he had committed the murder and they found the child's skeletal remains buried in the garden. Meanwhile, Fish had confessed to sexually assaulting several hundred children over the past 20 years and killing perhaps a dozen of them.

Fish was born in 1870 to a respectable Washington family but there was already a history of mental instability running through the past two generations and two relatives had died in institutions. His father died when he was five years old and he was sent to an orphanage, where discipline was rigorous and beatings commonplace. Fish, who was a persistent runaway and who wet his bed regularly up to the age of 11, came in for plenty of beatings and his leanings towards sadism and masochism began at this time, for he gained a sexual thrill from being flogged on his bare bottom, and from watching punishment administered to other boys.

At the age of 15 he was apprenticed as a painter and decorator and in 1898 he married a woman nine years younger than himself. They had six children before she ran off with another man and it was at that time that his children noticed his behaviour becoming strange and erratic. He heard voices, experienced hallucinations and became obsessed by sin, sacrifice and pain. Fish himself said that he committed his first murder, of a homosexual, in Wilmington, Delaware, in 1910. In 1917 he tortured and murdered a mentally retarded homosexual.

He felt that God had ordered him to castrate young boys and he abused both girls and boys 'in every state' of the USA, according to his own claims. He was always changing jobs and his work gave him access to basements, attics and other quiet spots suitable for abusing a child. He usually chose children from poor families, black children especially, as he said there was no great fuss if they disappeared or were hurt. He wore no clothes under his overalls, so that when he had persuaded a child to accompany him by coaxing him or her with gifts of sweets or money, he could undress in seconds to carry out his assault.

The police knew him as a minor offender; over the years he was arrested eight times for theft, passing dud cheques and violating probation. He was also arrested after sending obscene letters – one of his favourite hobbies – and sent to a psychiatric ward for observation, but released soon afterwards. The nearest he had come to being identified as a murderer was when a bus conductor identified him as the man he had seen with a tearful small boy who had since disappeared. Fish was taken in for questioning but released because no one could suspect such a mild, gentle man of indulging in violence.

If he enjoyed inflicting pain on his victims, Fish was just as eager to hurt and mutilate himself. He soaked balls of cotton wool in alcohol, then pushed them into his rectum and set fire to them. He regularly stuck needles into his groin and genital area, inserting some of them so deeply that they never came out – a prison X-ray was to reveal 29 needles, some of them eroded over time so that only fragments remained. When he tried to stick needles under his fingernails he could not stand the agony: 'If only pain were not so painful!' he exclaimed.

According to psychiatrist Dr Frederick Wertham, 'there was no known perversion which he did not practise and practise regularly'. The list included caprophagia – eating human excrement – which he had indulged in since the age of 12. Wertham maintained that Fish was insane, though Fish himself reasoned, 'I'm not insane! I'm just queer.' However, the prosecution was set on the death penalty, even bringing doctors to argue that caprophagia 'is a common sort of thing. We don't call people who do that mentally sick – socially they are perfectly all right.' It seems quite possible that the jury cared little whether he was legally sane or not and believed that he deserved the death penalty anyway.

Fish, sentenced to die in the electric chair, said that it would be 'the supreme thrill of my life'. Dr Wertham did his best to obtain a reprieve, insisting that executing a man so mentally sick was like burning witches. 'This man is not only incurable but unpunishable,' he said. 'In his own distorted mind he is looking forward to the electric chair as the final experience of true pain.'

Albert Fish had his final experience at Sing Sing on 16 January 1936.

Howard Unruh

HOWARD UNRUH was a quiet, reclusive Bible student who went berserk in a small American town on 6 September 1949 and gunned
down 13 people in 12 minutes. He was never brought to trial but was
committed to a mental institution and he expressed no remorse for his
actions. 'I'd have killed a thousand if I'd had bullets enough,' he said
simply.

He had an unremarkable childhood in Camden, New Jersey, and
wanted to become a pharmacist. However, World War II intervened
and he enlisted in the army, soon showing great proficiency with a
rifle. He fought in Italy and France and distinguished himself in
combat but he never mixed socially with the other soldiers, preferring
to divide his spare time between reading the Bible and cleaning his
rifle with loving care. Every day he made a careful entry in his diary
and one day a roommate, overcome with curiosity, took a peep, only to
find that Unruh had recorded the details of every German he had
killed: the date, the circumstances and exactly how his enemy
had looked at the moment of death.

When he was demobbed in 1945 he enrolled at Temple University
but he soon dropped out and took a succession of jobs, unable to settle
to anything. He became silent and withdrawn, scarcely speaking to his
parents and spending most of his time practising marksmanship in the
shooting gallery he had set up in the basement. He began keeping a
diary again, listing all his fancied grievances against his neighbours,
with notes about planned times for retaliation. There were plenty of
entries about the Cohens next door, who had rebuked him for taking a
short cut to his door across their yard.

He built a high fence all round the yard of his father's house to shut out the world but on 25 September his hatred of his neighbours came to a head when he found that someone had taken away the gate, leaving the yard exposed to passers-by. Perhaps he lay seething with fury in his locked room all night and rose next morning determined to exact vengeance on all and sundry. Whatever the case, in the morning he emerged with a powerful German Luger, a second pistol and a pocketful of spare clips.

He walked down River Avenue and into John Pilarchi's little shoe shop, a few yards from his home. Without saying a word he shot the cobbler dead, with a single bullet through the head. He walked out with the gun still in his hand and turned into the barber's shop next door, where Clark Hoover was cutting the hair of six-year-old Orris Smith. Unruh shot first Hoover then the child, leaving Mrs Smith hysterical as she cradled her dead son in her arms. Her screams followed him down the road on his way to the drugstore owned by his principal enemy, Maurice Cohen.

In the doorway of Cohen's store he met James Hutton, an insurance agent who had been on good terms with the Unruh family for years. He fired and Hutton fell to the pavement, dying instantly. Inside the store, Maurice Cohen screamed at his family to hide; his wife Rose shut herself in a cupboard while 12-year-old Charlie, followed by his father, scrambled through the window on to the roof. Unruh reached the top of the stairs just in time to see the cupboard door closing. He fired three shots and the door fell open as Mrs Cohen's body collapsed on to the floor. Leaning out of the window, he fired twice into Cohen's retreating back then, when the storekeeper fell to the street below, he fired a third shot into his head. Hearing a noise from the next room, he threw open the door and, finding Cohen's elderly mother trying to phone for help, he shot her too. Only young Charlie managed to reach safety and escape the carnage.

As Unruh walked out into River Avenue again, he saw a stranger who had stopped to try to help the insurance agent and immediately shot him dead at point blank range. He strolled on down the street

Police move in and overpower Harold Unruh

with no sign of hurry, as panic raged on all sides with people scream-ing and yelling, running for cover and barricading themselves into shops, frantically phoning for the police. Unruh was unmoved and even when café owner Fred Engel shot at him, hitting him in the leg, he did not pause. Among those who died in the next few moments were a three-year-old boy who was gazing out of his window and two women and a young boy whose car had stopped at a red traffic light. He missed the driver of a bakery van but wounded a lorry driver who was just climbing into his cab. He tried to shoot his way into the grocery store but the lock held and he passed on.

Unruh next walked into a house where Mrs Madeline Harris had forgotten to lock the door and found her hiding in the kitchen with her two sons. Seventeen-year-old Armond threw himself at the gunman, whose shots went awry, one wounding the boy in the leg, the other hitting his mother in the shoulder. The younger boy was left unhurt, one of the luckiest participants in the morning's horrific drama.

At last Unruh had run out of ammunition and headed home to reload, but by now the police were arriving and he was pinned down in his house by a ring of police marksmen. In the gun battle that followed Unruh rained bullets from the upstairs window. Amazingly enough, a reporter from the local newspaper rang the house and found the phone answered by Unruh himself. Asked how many people he had killed, Unruh replied: 'I haven't counted. It looks like a pretty good score, though.'

When tear-gas canisters came flying through the windows Unruh was forced to surrender, walking out with his hands up under the aim of over 50 police guns. Under questioning, his only explanation for his actions was that people were picking on him and he had to get his own back. Experts judged him to be a schizophrenic with violent paranoid tendencies. Unruh himself insisted, 'I'm no psycho. I have a good mind.'

Hans van Zon

IT COULD be argued that many serial killers are unbalanced whether or not they are legally judged insane, and a good example is the Dutch killer Hans van Zon, who lived in his own world of fantasy and had no apparent motive for most of his crimes.

He was born in Utrecht in 1942 and brought up by his mother with a completely unfounded idea of his own importance. He was quiet and introverted, only playing with children younger than himself, and was deferential towards adults. He did poorly in school and later was unable to keep a job because of his light fingers. At 16 he took off for Amsterdam, where he lived on his wits and enjoyed a number of sexual liaisons with both men and women. The real world scarcely impinged on him as he played the roles of private detective, wealthy entrepreneur, film star, fashion designer or ace pilot in his head.

In July 1964 he committed his first murder. He had been on a date with a young woman called Elly Hager-Segov and at the end of the evening he pretended that he had missed his last train home and was invited to spend the night in her apartment. They went to bed together, but when she would not let him have sex with her for a second time he was overcome with a sudden urge to kill her. He strangled her until she lost consciousness, then cut her throat with a breadknife.

He confessed to murdering homosexual film director Claude Berkely in 1965. This may have been another facet of his fantasy life, for he later withdrew the confession, saying that he had only seen the murder in a psychic vision. Soon afterwards he married an Italian chambermaid, Caroline Gigli, and lived off her income while he pursued affairs with other women. In 1967 she complained to the police that he was trying to kill her and, as he was already on probation for another offence, he spent several weeks in custody.

However, it was not his wife that he murdered later the same year but his mistress, Coby van der Voort. He gave her what he said was an aphrodisiac but was really a powerful barbiturate, then while she was drugged he battered her with a lead pipe and stabbed her with a breadknife. He stripped her body and tried, unsuccessfully, to have intercourse with the corpse.

In a drunken moment he bragged about the murder in front of an ex-convict known as Oude Nol who proceeded to half-persuade, half-blackmail him into a rash of further crimes, which gave him the chance to put his favoured lead piping to good use. Oude Nol may have instigated the robberies but van Zon certainly went overboard with his methods. In May 1967 he battered 80-year-old Jan Donse to death in his firework shop and robbed the till, dividing the takings with Oude Nol. Two months later he smashed the skull of Reyer de Bruin, a farmer, and cut his throat into the bargain.

His last victim was an elderly widow, once a girlfriend of Oude Nol, but this time van Zon's murderous touch deserted him – he did not hit Mrs Woortmeyer hard enough to kill her. When she came round she raised the alarm and later identified him as the man who had attacked and robbed her.

Once in custody, van Zon did his best to put the blame on Oude Nol and he too was arrested. Oude Nol was sent to prison for seven years while van Zon received a sentence of life imprisonment. It was recommended that he should serve no less than 20 years, so he had plenty of opportunity to retreat into his beloved world of fantasy.

Lucian Staniak

THE KILLER known as 'Red Spider' stalked the blonde young women of Poland for three years between 1964 and 1967, raping and murdering them in a twisted scheme for revenge. Most of the murders took place on public holidays, when victims would be least on their guard, and the bodies were horribly mutilated, often completely disembowelled.

The murderer taunted the police in a series of letters, sometimes giving directions to the latest body, and sent strange messages to the newspapers, all written in red ink, in the thin, spidery writing that earned him his nickname. The first letter read: 'There is no happiness without tears, no life without death. Beware! I am going to make you weep.'

The Spider struck for the first time at Olsztyn, raping and mutilating a 17-year-old girl on the anniversary of Polish liberation from Nazi occupation. The killer wrote to the police with a sinister threat: 'I picked a juicy flower in Olsztyn and I shall do it again somewhere else, for there is no holiday without a funeral.'

A letter to the police described the whereabouts of the next body, a 16-year-old who had caught the killer's attention when she led a student parade. The girl's remains lay in a factory basement, with a spike hammered through the genitals. Next the killer used a screwdriver to mutilate the sex organs of a young hotel receptionist murdered on All Saints Day and wrote to the newspapers saying: 'Only tears of sorrow can wash away the stain of shame: only the pangs of suffering can cancel out the fires of lust.'

On May Day 1966 a 17-year-old was raped and killed, her body left in the toolshed behind her home, the entrails removed and piled beside it. Then on Christmas Eve the body of 17-year-old Janina

Kozielska was found on a train; she had been raped and mutilated. The killer wrote to the press stating proudly: 'I have done it again.' Janina's sister Aniela had been killed two years before, so enquiries concentrated on anyone who had known them both. This included members of the Art Lovers' Club in Krakow, to which both girls belonged.

One of the members of the club was 26-year-old Lucian Staniak and as soon as detectives saw his paintings, with huge blood-red splashes and pictures of disembowelled women, they decided that they had found a likely suspect. When they arrested him on 1 February 1967 he was only too willing to confess: he was just on his way home from his latest killing, he said. He had murdered Bozena Raczkiewicz at a railway station because he was disappointed at the level of publicity his crimes were receiving at the time.

Staniak's life had been changed when his parents and sister were killed in a car accident and the driver responsible, a serviceman's wife, had escaped conviction, so he was determined to revenge himself on any young blonde woman who bore a passing resemblance to her. He admitted to 20 murders and was tried for six of them. Judged insane, he was committed to an asylum.

Charles Whitman

IN MARCH 1966 Charles Whitman, a 25-year-old student of architec-
tural engineering at the University of Texas, USA, went to see the
campus psychiatrist. His mother had recently left his father, a brutal
and domineering man who had frequently beaten her and his children.
Mrs Whitman had moved to Austin, Texas, to be near her son and his
wife and Mr Whitman was always involving Charles in his marital
difficulties, trying to persuade him to act as a go-between. Young
Whitman, who loved his mother and hated his father, was full of anger
and hostility, which sometimes erupted into violence, resulting in him
assaulting his wife Kathleen. He confided this to the psychiatrist but
decided not to return for a second visit. He could work things out
alone, he said. Four months later Charles Whitman was standing on
top of the university observation tower, firing indiscriminately at the
people below.

There was nothing in Whitman's past record to indicate that he was
a mass murderer in the making: as a youngster he had been an Eagle
Scout and an altar boy, he was no trouble in school, he served in the
Marines and was now attending university on a Marine scholarship.

Yet, on the night of 31 July, he began writing a 'to whom it may
concern' note. 'I am prepared to die,' it read. 'After my death I wish an
autopsy on me to be performed to see if there is any mental disorder.'
He then went to his mother's apartment and stabbed her to death. In
the early hours of the following morning he returned home and stabbed, then shot, his wife, a high-school science teacher. He then
finished his letter, noting first: '12.00 am – Mother already dead, 3
o'clock, both dead.' He then said that he loved both his mother and

his wife and had no idea why he had killed them and went on to rail against his father. He concluded with: 'Life is not worth living.'

He then began collecting together his weapons, including several high-powered rifles and hundreds of rounds of ammunition. He packed them into a box along with a clock, binoculars, nylon rope, a transistor radio, a thermos of coffee and toilet paper. He loaded the box on to a three-wheeler trolley he had hired, pushed it to the observation tower and took it up in the lift.

On the twenty-seventh floor he met the 51-year-old receptionist Edna Townsley, who was there to monitor anyone who went up to the observation deck. He smashed her skull with his gun butt, then dragged her body behind the desk. Just afterwards a young couple, Don Walden and Cheryl Batts, came down from the deck and greeted Whitman pleasantly. They must have been the luckiest people in Austin that day, for Whitman returned their greeting and let them walk out unharmed.

The next people to arrive at the twenty-seventh floor were 19-year-old Mark Gabour and his family. As Mark opened the reception-room door he was killed with a shotgun blast. His aunt, following behind him, was also killed and his mother was wounded. The husbands of the two women, bringing up the rear, quickly dragged the bodies into another room and locked themselves in. Whitman barricaded the reception-room door and took his box out to the observation deck.

At 11.48 he started to fire from the tower, the highest point in Austin. It was a splendid vantage point for a sharpshooter and he fired on men, women and children alike. At first no one could believe what was happening and even as bodies dropped to the ground, those who were still standing were too shocked to run for cover and made perfect targets. Claire Wilson, eight months pregnant, took a bullet in the stomach which killed her baby. As 19-year-old Thomas Eckman tried to help her, he was shot dead. A law student was standing with a policeman, Billy Speed, behind some pillars when a bullet ricocheted and killed the officer.

Police rained bullets on the tower but had little hope of hitting Whitman. An armoured car toured the area, trying to pick up the wounded, while a light plane circled the tower carrying a sharpshooter who attempted to take out the murderer. The plane was driven off by Whitman's bullets.

Eventually a group of policemen led by officer Romero Martinez managed to get into the tower along underground conduits. They took the elevator to the twenty-seventh floor, keeping in constant touch with colleagues outside by walkie-talkie, so that the latter could give warning if the gunman left his vantage point on the tower. They eased their way into the reception room, pushing the furniture barricade out of the way a centimetre at a time, then finally burst out on to the deck, riddling Whitman with bullets. Martinez then waved a green flag to tell the policemen waiting below that they had succeeded. An hour and a half after Whitman entered the tower, his blood-soaked body was carried out.

A postmortem revealed a malignant tumour the size of a walnut in Charles Whitman's brain. At first it seemed as though this might be the cause of his sudden rages and his final mad act, but eventually doctors decided that the location of the tumour made this unlikely.

The tower still stands dominating the town of Austin. After the massacre on that hot August day it attracted many sensation-seekers and also a number of suicides. As a result, it was closed to the public. No other gunman will even use its height to terrorize the town.

THE WORLD'S MOST INFAMOUS KILLERS

Carroll Edward Cole

FROM his earliest childhood, Carroll Cole's mother planted the seeds of hatred deep within him and throughout his troubled adult years he looked for ways of revenging himself for those early experiences, killing women he regarded as promiscuous because it was the nearest he could come to killing her.

He was only five years old when his mother started taking him along when she met her lovers, using various painful means to make him promise not to tell his father. She would ask the women of the neighbourhood round for coffee parties where young Cole was forced to serve them, dressed in skirts and frilly blouses, which made the guests scream with laughter. Word got round among his schoolmates, who made his life a misery, making fun of his Christian name and forcing him to sit with the girls. Mockery sent him wild: once he retaliated by crushing another boy's hand while they were playing on some road-mending machinery, another time he managed to drown a nine-year-old tormentor, but it was regarded as an accident resulting from natural horseplay.

As he grew to adulthood his impulses became darker and more dangerous: he was haunted by daydreams about raping and strangling women. At this point he was still fighting to keep himself under control and he begged doctors for psychiatric treatment. The result was that he spent three years in mental hospitals, where he was considered 'anti-social' but no danger to society. He proved the doctors wrong in 1966 when he tried to strangle an 11-year-old girl.

Four years later he was in Nevada, USA, when the murderous urge came over him again and he once more appealed for psychiatric help. This time doctors refused to take him seriously and were anxious to get rid of him as soon as possible. His case notes read: 'Condition on release: same as on admittance. Treatment: express bus ticket to San Diego, California.'

It was a disastrous decision that led to the death of up to three dozen women, for it was at this point that Cole tipped over the edge. He would pick up girls in bars or on the street and the very fact that they were willing to have sex with him on first meeting branded them in his sick mind as 'loose women' who 'deserved all they got'. In 1971 in San Diego he strangled Essie Buck, and though the police knew that he had had contact with her they had no proof to enable them to bring charges. He killed again in 1975 in Casper, Wyoming, and then, on a week-long drunken binge in Oklahoma in 1976, he carved up the body of a victim in the bath and fried a couple of steaks of human flesh for supper. In 1977 he strangled a Las Vegas prostitute and in 1979 Bonnie O'Neill was killed in the street in San Diego; Cole then stripped her and had sex with the dead body.

He had married an alcoholic prostitute, a combination that could only feed his growing compulsion, and he threatened to kill her a number of times before carrying out his threat, afterwards wrapping her body in a blanket and hiding it in a cupboard. He was found by police trying to dig a grave, but he was so obviously drunk and his wife's alcoholism had been so advanced that her death was accepted as accidental. There must have been something about Cole that made it impossible for police or doctors to admit that he was capable of doing anyone serious harm.

In November 1980, Cole was really busy: Dorothy King took him home to her apartment and he strangled her there, then the next night he met Wanda Roberts in a bar and proceeded to strangle her in the parking lot. He then went back to Dorothy King's apartment, where she still lay undiscovered, and had sex with the corpse. Even though Cole had been seen drinking with Wanda Roberts shortly before her death, the police failed to find him. The third November victim was Sally Thompson, strangled in her own apartment, but she put up enough of a struggle to alert the neighbours, who called the police to report the strange thuds and thumps. The police arrived to find Cole standing over the body but they were still not wholly convinced that he was the murderer until, once in custody, he began confessing to a series of homicides, some of which had been written off as accidents. Once he started talking he seemed unable to stop and admitted to 35 murders, even apologizing for not being able to provide all the details because he had been too drunk to remember.

At his trial in 1981 he pleaded guilty to the three Texas murders and was given three life sentences, two of them to be served consecutively. He was then extradited to Nevada to stand trial for two murders committed in that state. He pleaded guilty again, requesting a non-jury trial because he felt that judges would be more likely to use the ultimate sanction and sentence him to death. Sure enough, they imposed the death penalty and Cole thanked them sincerely.

There were a number of organizations eager to take up Cole's cause but he steadfastly refused to appeal against his sentence, apparently welcoming the thought of death. His life was ended by lethal injection on 6 December 1985.

David Berkowitz

ON A HOT night in July 1976 two girls, 18-year-old medical technician Donna Lauria and 19-year-old student nurse Jody Valenti, were sitting talking in a car outside Donna's New York home when a young man walked over to them. He pulled a gun out of a brown paper bag and fired five shots. Donna, who was just opening the car door, was hit in the neck and killed and Jody was hit in the thigh.

Three months later 18-year-old student Rosemary Keenan and her boyfriend Carl Denaro were parked in a secluded spot when a gunman fired through the back window of their red Volkswagen. Fortunately for Carl Denaro the path of the bullet was deflected by the glass; instead of penetrating his brain it took a piece out of the back of his skull and he recovered after surgery.

The two incidents took place in different parts of the city and there was no reason to connect them. Then, in November, 18-year-old Joanne Lomino was sitting on her porch chatting with her schoolfriend Donna De Masi shortly after midnight when a man walked up to them. He began to ask directions but stopped in the middle of a sentence, produced a gun and fired. Both girls were wounded: Donna recovered in a few weeks but a bullet had hit Joanne in the spine, leaving her paralysed for life.

Bullets from the same .44 revolver had been used in all three shootings and detectives realized that they had a random killer on their hands, someone who would shoot at complete strangers for no other purpose than the enjoyment of maiming and murdering. He seemed to choose girls with long dark hair and the theory was that Carl Denaro had been targeted by mistake – he had shoulder-length hair and was sitting in the passenger seat, so the gunman might well have mistaken him for a woman in the dark.

In 1977 the attacks continued. Panic spread through the city until young women and courting couples were reluctant to venture out after dark, for fear that a homicidal maniac was watching them from the shadows. On 30 January 26-year-old Christine Freund and her boyfriend John Diel were kissing goodnight in their car after an evening at the cinema when a bullet shattered the windscreen and ploughed into Christine's head. She died a few hours later in hospital. On 8 March an Armenian student, Virginia Voskerichian, was on her way home at 7.30 pm when a young man about to pass her on the footpath aimed a revolver at her. Virginia tried to shield herself with the books she was carrying but the bullet went straight through them into her mouth, shattering her teeth and killing her instantly.

At the next shooting the killer left the perplexed detectives a letter. This time he had claimed two victims: 18-year-old Valentina Suriana and 20-year-old Alexander Esau, killed as they embraced in the front seats of a parked car. When the police reached the scene they found a letter lying in the road, a few metres from the bodies of the dead lovers. It was addressed to Captain Joseph Borelli of the New York Police, the officer in charge of the investigation, and ran: 'I am deeply hurt by your calling me a woman-hater. I am not. But I am a monster. I am the Son of Sam . . . I love to hunt. Prowling the streets looking for fair game – tasty meat.'

Soon afterwards 'Son of Sam' sent another letter to journalist Jimmy Breslin, who had been covering the story. This letter was as rambling and incoherent as the first, apparently the babblings of a madman, but it hinted at further killings and fuelled the growing hysteria in New York.

In the summer there were more attacks: on 26 June Salvatore Lupo and his girlfriend Judy Placido escaped without lasting injury when they were wounded by bullets which shattered the car windscreen, on 31 July Stacy Moskowitz was killed by a shot in the head and her boyfriend Robert Violante was blinded for life after they had parked their car near a playground. After each murder the police switchboards were flooded with calls from members of the public who thought they had seen something suspicious, and all had to be checked out as a matter of routine. After the last shooting, the police were contacted by 49-year-old widow Mrs Cacilia Davis, who had been returning home in the early hours of the morning, at around the time of the murder. A couple of blocks from the playground she had seen two traffic officers fixing a ticket to the windscreen of a yellow car illegally parked near a fire hydrant. Then, only moments after the officers had left, she saw a young man walk up to the car, screw up the ticket then jump into the car and pull away so fast that the tyres screeched.

Police enquiries revealed that only four tickets had been issued in that area on the morning in question and only one of the four cars fitted Mrs Davis's description. It was registered to David Berkowitz at 35 Pine Street, Yonkers. When the police arrived at the address they found the car parked outside and in the back a duffle bag with a rifle butt sticking out of it. When the glove compartment was searched they discovered a letter addressed to one of the officers heading the murder hunt; it was written in the distinctive style of 'Son of Sam'.

Six hours later a pudgy young man with a round face and short dark hair came out of the apartment block and climbed into the car. The police moved in, trained their guns on him and asked who he was. He beamed at them and said: 'I'm Sam!' At first the officers took him to be retarded; even when two guns were pressed against his head he was still grinning. Detective John Falotico remembered: 'He had that stupid smile on his face, like it was a kid's game.' At the time of his arrest his apartment walls were covered with strange messages like 'I kill for my Master' and 'In this hole lives the wicked king'.

David Berkowitz was a loner, spoilt and shy as a boy, who grew up resentful and frustrated because girls never showed any interest in him. He was an illegitimate child, born of an affair between his mother and a married man, and was given up for adoption at birth. His adoptive parents were a Jewish couple, Nathan and Pearl Berkowitz, who had been unable to have children of their own. As David turned 14 Pearl died, and when Nathan Berkowitz remarried in 1971 his adopted son was hurt and angry. He joined the army to get away from home and further alienated himself from the family by becoming a Baptist. In 1974 he returned to New York but by then his father had decided to move to Florida. Nat Berkowitz realized from his son's letters, which grew strange and gloomy, that he had psychiatric problems. A month before Donna Lauria's murder he wrote to his father: 'Dad, the world is getting darker now, I can feel it more and more . . . The girls call me ugly and they bother me the most.'

Several of Berkowitz's neighbours knew him as 'a nutter' and had reported his activities to the police on more than one occasion. Sam Carr had received odd letters complaining about his labrador dog, Harvey, and shortly afterwards Harvey had been shot, though not fatally. The German shepherd dog belonging to another neighbour was shot through the window and killed, after a string of anonymous telephone calls. Craig Glassman, who occupied the apartment below Berkowitz, received letters accusing him of being part of a black magic group run by Sam Carr. All were convinced that the perpetrator of these incidents was Berkowitz but without proof the police could take no action.

After his arrest, Berkowitz happily confessed to the Son of Sam killings. He claimed that since 1975 he had been hearing voices telling him to kill and the commands were transmitted through Sam Carr's dog, who was possessed by demons. He had tried to kill Harvey but the demons had protected the dog and after that the voices had been louder and more clamorous.

His first attempts at murder had been made with a knife. On Christmas Eve 1975 he followed a woman as she left a supermarket and stabbed her in the back. Instead of falling down she turned and tried to grab hold of him, so he ran away. On the same night he tried a

David Berkowitz, 'Son of Sam'

second time, stabbing 15-year-old Michelle Forman in the head and back outside her apartment building. She fell to the ground screaming and, as Berkowitz made off, she dragged herself into the building before losing consciousness. She was discharged from hospital after a week.

After that, Berkowitz obtained a gun and a few months later he was using it on the streets. After his first successful killing, he would drive around the New York streets looking for promising victims. Of his first murder, that of Donna Lauria, he said: 'I never thought I could kill her. I couldn't believe it. I just fired the gun, you know, at the car.' He liked to return to the scene of the murders. One night, after shooting a courting couple, he drove on a few blocks to catch a glimpse of the apartment block were Donna had lived, instead of getting away as soon as possible. After the fourth shooting, he remembered: 'I imagine I didn't care much any more: I had finally convinced myself that it was good to do it . . . and that the public wanted me to do it.' He told police that after a murder he felt 'flushed with power' and it was his habit to celebrate by going to a café to eat his favourite meal, hamburger followed by chocolate icecream.

Several psychiatrists considered that Berkowitz was a paranoid schizophrenic but another, Dr David Abrahamson, was convinced that it was all an act, that the story of the 'voices' was invented to provide a defence of insanity. The court considered him capable of taking responsibility for his actions and he was sentenced to 365 years' imprisonment.

Since the trial there have been claims that Berkowitz was only one of a number of 'Son of Sam' murderers. The eye-witness descriptions of the gunman varied markedly in height and looks and none of the police sketches of the murderer looked much like Berkowitz. Some investigators have drawn attention to the strange events surrounding the Carr family: Carr's two sons, John and Michael, both died in suspicious circumstances after Berkowitz was arrested. John Carr was found shot to death with a rifle in his girlfriend's apartment; at the time it looked like suicide but later it was judged to be murder. Michael Carr died in a car crash and was shown to have a high level of alcohol in his blood, though he was known as a non-drinker. These strange events led some people to believe that Berkowitz was only one member of a killer cult whose other members have never been brought to justice.

Herbert Mullin

'SATAN gets into people and makes them do things they don't want to,' said Herbert Mullin after he had murdered eight people. Voices inside his head convinced him that he was the saviour of the world, that it was up to him to save the people of California from flood, fire and earthquake by regular killings.

Mullin was brought up in a devoutly religious Roman Catholic household. He always seemed a well-balanced boy, doing well at school and shaping up as a promising athlete, even voted 'most likely to succeed' by his classmates. By the age of 17 he was engaged and a happy future seemed assured, but it all began to fall apart when his best friend Dean Richardson was killed in a road accident in 1965. He turned his bedroom into a shrine for his dead friend and spent hours brooding in front of his picture. He began worrying that he might be homosexual and when he became eligible for conscription to military service he announced that he was a conscientious objector. His girlfriend, deciding that he was no longer the boy she had loved, broke off the engagement.

His family saw him becoming stranger and stranger, developing odd religious ideas and cutting himself off from the real world. They were sure that he needed psychiatric help and persuaded him to go into a mental hospital, but he refused to cooperate with the staff and was discharged after six weeks with no improvement in his condition. He became addicted to hallucinogenic drugs and began obeying voices which commanded him to stand on his head, shave off his hair or stub out cigarettes on his body. It was soon obvious that he was suffering from paranoid schizophrenia and over the next three years he alternated between spells of treatment in various institutions, trouble with the police and lying low in cheap San Francisco hotels. He was going downhill all the time and by 1972 his voices were telling him that he must kill.

In October he was driving along a quiet road through the Santa Cruz mountains when he saw an old tramp, Lawrence White. He stopped the car, got out and opened the bonnet. When 'old Whitey' drew level, Mullin invited him to have a look at the cause of his breakdown. As the tramp bent to peer into the engine, Mullin hit him a mighty blow with a baseball bat. He drove off, leaving the body lying by the roadside.

Eleven days later he gave a lift to Mary Guilfoyle, a student at the university in Santa Cruz, then drove her to a deserted spot and stabbed her. He cut open the body and ripped out her internal organs, scattering them as a meal for birds of prey. It was four months before her skeleton was found. A few days afterwards Mullin's Catholic upbringing reasserted itself temporarily and he went to confession in St Mary's Church. However, immediately afterwards he regretted what he had said and, afraid that the priest might betray him, he stabbed Father Henri Tomei to death.

At this time, Mullin's voices underwent a subtle change and he now heard people asking him to kill them. He bought a gun and no one who came in contact with him was safe. In his disturbed mind he blamed the man who had first introduced him to drugs, Jim Gianera, for all his problems, convinced that he had deliberately set out to scramble his head. He went looking for Gianera at an old address where the new tenant, 29-year-old Kathy Francis, gave him another address in Santa Cruz. He found Gianera there, shot him and stabbed his wife as she bent over his body. His voices still active, Mullin went back to Kathy Francis' home, and, finding her sharing a bed with her two small sons, he shot all three of them.

Twelve days later he was on the prowl again in Cowell State Park, where he found four teenage boys camping in a tent. He chatted to them for a few moments, then pulled a gun and shot all four of them dead.

On 13 February 1973, less than a week after the multiple murder, Mullin was driving towards his parents' home when his head was once more filled with voices, demanding another victim. He stopped and gunned down an elderly man called Fred Perez, who was tidying up his garden. A neighbour heard the shot and, looking out of the window, saw Perez fall and managed to note the number on the licence plate as Mullin's van drove off. A patrol car spotted him a few minutes later and Mullin was taken into custody.

He confessed to 13 murders, insisting that he had prevented thousands of deaths that would have followed the natural disasters that his actions had averted. He was tried in Santa Cruz in July 1973, when his defence was insanity – reasonable enough, considering the diagnosis of paranoid schizophrenia. However, it was decided that he was sane by legal standards and he was charged with ten of the 13 killings. He was convicted on two counts of first-degree murder and eight counts of second-degree murder and sentenced to life imprisonment.

James Ruppert

ON THE evening of Easter Sunday, 1975, James Ruppert rang the police in Hamilton, Ohio, to tell them that his entire family, 11 people in all, had been shot. When officers arrived they found six bodies in the kitchen and four more in the living room: all had been shot at close range, all but one in the head, so that they had died instantly. Ruppert admitted that he was the murderer and was arrested and held for trial.

Ruppert, who was 41, was a deeply paranoid personality. He had always felt himself persecuted by his mother and his brother Leonard – with it seems, good reason. The family was always very poor, but after his father died of tuberculosis, leaving a woman and two teenage boys to work the small, subsistence-level farm, things became even worse. James was undersized and suffered from asthma, while his brother was bigger and stronger and always his mother's favourite; Charity Ruppert constantly praised Leonard and held him up as an example while denigrating everything James tried to do and putting him down at every opportunity. She encouraged Leonard to ill-treat his younger brother and did nothing to intervene when the former tied the latter up and locked him in a cupboard, or whipped him with the garden hose. By the time he was 16 James felt so miserable and worthless that he attempted suicide, trying to hang himself with the sheets from his bed.

He failed to graduate from college and was unable to keep a job, so in 1975 he was still living with his mother and Leonard, who now had a wife and eight children and a well-paid job. His paranoia was growing, for he believed that his family were making false reports about him to the police and the FBI and that Leonard was damaging his car, breaking off the wipers, loosening the bumper or punching holes in the exhaust. It was probably the last straw when, just before Easter, his mother told him that if he did not start contributing to the household expenses he would have to leave. He saw that as the final rejection, the proof that the family was out to get him, so he concluded that he had to get them first.

The night before the shootings he had been out drinking; he returned home in the early hours, then slept half the morning. When he came downstairs he carried a rifle and three handguns but this was not particularly unusual as his hobby was guns and marksmanship and he often spent part of the weekend target-shooting. As he appeared, Leonard made a disastrous remark: 'How's your car going?' he asked. James Ruppert exploded and began shooting. In the kitchen he killed his mother, Leonard and his wife Alma, 13-year-old Carol, 11-year-old David and 9-year-old Teresa. In the living room he killed the other children – John, Ann, Thomas, Michael and Leonard, their ages ranging from 4 to 15. Except for Alma, who tried to make a grab for the gun, they were all so shocked that they had no chance to resist.

The trial revolved round Ruppert's sanity, the prosecution maintaining that he had known exactly what he was doing and that he knew full well that if he was found insane he could inherit a healthy sum from his family (which would not be possible if he was found guilty and sane) and would be free to enjoy his inheritance after a spell in a mental hospital. The final verdict was that he was guilty of murdering his mother and brother but that the first two killings had tipped the balance of his mind and he had no longer been responsible for his actions. He was given two life sentences, to run consecutively.

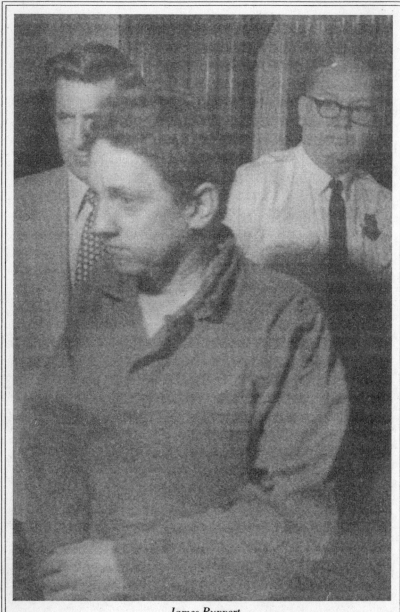

James Ruppert

Henry Lee Lucas

HENRY LEE LUCAS confessed to several hundred murders during the 18 months following his arrest in Texas, USA, in June 1983. Later he was to change his story more then once. Some of the confessions were obviously false and a major newspaper series claimed that the whole thing was a gigantic hoax, but the law enforcement agencies still believe that he was responsible for an enormous number of killings. From various states he collected a death sentence, six life sentences and several other long prison terms.

Lucas had the sort of childhood that might leave anyone unbalanced and he grew up hating the world. His family lived in a primitive cabin in the backwoods of Virginia, where his parents ran an illegal whisky still. His alcoholic father had lost both legs to a freight train as he lay drunk on the railway line and pulled himself around the floor as best he could. His mother, Viola, part Cherokee Indian, seems to have been a complete sadist. She beat him unmercifully, belabouring his head so that later X-rays were to reveal brain damage, and once left him lying semi-conscious for three days after stunning him with a wooden bar. She sent him to school dressed as a girl with his long hair curled into ringlets so that the other children would find him an object of ridicule, and gave him so little to eat that he searched through neighbours' rubbish bins for discarded food. When she was earning a little extra as the local prostitute, she forced both her young son and her husband to watch her activities. One night when Lucas senior could bear it no longer, he dragged himself out into the snow and lay there all night. He contracted pneumonia and died a week later. Lucas was not exaggerating when he said later: 'I was brought up like a dog. No human being should have to be put through what I was.'

227

Henry Lee Lucas

Lucas claimed to have committed his first murder at the age of 15, when he strangled a girl who refused his advances. After that he left home and embarked on a career of petty crime, eventually being imprisoned for six years after a series of burglaries. Soon after his release, he stabbed his mother to death in a fight and afterwards boasted of having sex with her corpse. He was committed to a psychiatric hospital, where he was diagnosed as a psychopath and sexual deviant; when he was paroled in 1970 he told the doctors, 'I'm not ready to go.' He asked them to keep him inside for he was certain that he would kill again, but they paroled him anyway and within hours of his release he apparently murdered a young woman a few blocks from the hospital.

He then apparently embarked on a murder spree that lasted for 13 years across a number of states, though his favourite venue was the 800 km (500 mile) interstate highway between Laredo and Gainesville in Texas. Scores of bodies were found here over the years, killed in a variety of ways – shot, strangled, bludgeoned – sexually assaulted and sometimes dismembered. Lucas eventually laid claim to most of them and police nicknamed the road the 'Henry Lee Lucas Memorial Highway'. He met up with another serial killer, Ottis Toole, and each recognized a kindred spirit. Over the next few years they often travelled together, raping, killing and dismembering. Lucas preferred to have sex with his victims after death: 'I like peace and quiet,' he explained. Toole was an arsonist who often liked to barbecue and eat his prey, though Lucas claimed that he never joined in that part of the proceedings. 'I don't like barbecue sauce,' was his reason.

Toole's teenage niece Becky and nephew Frank travelled with them and Frank was to be driven into a mental hospital in 1983 by memories of the deeds he had witnessed. When Toole went his own way in 1982 Lucas and Becky settled together in Stoneburg, Texas, where they earned their keep by doing odd jobs for 80-year-old Kate Rich. Both Becky and Mrs Rich disappeared at around the same time. Becky had quarrelled with Lucas and tried to hit him, whereupon he stabbed her to death then chopped her body into small pieces and distributed them in various parts of the desert. He pretended that Becky had gone off with a lorry driver but when Kate Rich also went missing, the police became suspicious and Lucas was forced to flee. When he was finally taken into custody he admitted that he had stabbed Mrs Rich and burned her body in the church store.

Lucas was first arrested for illegal possession of a handgun, but on his fourth night in custody, on 14 June 1983, he called a prison officer to his cell and told him: 'I've done some bad things.' This was the beginning of a confession that amazed law officers and caused a nationwide sensation. In October more than 80 detectives from 20 states gathered in Louisiana to view 48 hours of tapes in which Lucas recounted his long lists of crimes, with names, dates and details. Officers came from all over the States to interview him and he revisited the scenes of many crimes in the company of detectives.

Perhaps the police, anxious to close the file on troublesome murder enquiries, were sometimes a little too eager to believe that Lucas had the answer, but on many occasions he recounted details that had never been publicized and would be known only to the killer; he was able to lead the police to the exact location of many murders without any guidance. However, only Lucas can ever know how many killings he perpetrated, either alone or in company with Toole. He is currently appealing against conviction, saying that he was never a serial killer and only made up the stories because he enjoyed being in the lime-light following his arrest.

James Huberty

'I'M GOING hunting humans,' James Huberty told his wife as he left their apartment on the afternoon of 18 July 1984. He was dressed in khaki camouflage trousers and a black T-shirt and carried with him a Uzi machine gun, a 9.9 Browning automatic and a shotgun. Over his shoulder he had slung a bag filled with ammunition. He was about to turn the McDonald's restaurant in the Southern border town of San Ysidro, USA, into a slaughterhouse and become one of the worst mass murderers in American history.

Huberty was an angry man and it was an anger that he carried with him constantly, lashing out at the slightest opportunity. He came from a broken home, growing up mainly under the care of his grandmother, and he was always a loner. When his father remarried in 1971, Huberty hated his stepmother and from then on became estranged from his father. However, he married and was able to provide his family with a comfortable three-storey house in a good area of Massillon, Ohio, the town where he had grown up. Then he lost his job as a welder, failed to find another, and things began to fall apart. He was forced to sell the house and move to San Ysidro, where he worked as a security guard.

The Hubertys had never been liked by their neighbours. Back in Massillon they had been reported to the police several times for their anti-social behaviour and both had been arrested as a result of angry confrontations. In their new home they made no friends and Huberty was known for his bad temper and the way he was always shouting at children – his own and other people's. Once his daughter had to take refuge with a neighbour because her father had been hitting her. No one will ever know what finally tipped Huberty over the edge, but when he once more lost his job, his behaviour became even more strange and he began hearing voices.

What is known is that he walked into a branch of McDonald's a few metres from the Mexican border, loaded down with weapons. As he started firing, one customer said that he yelled: 'I killed thousands in Vietnam and I want to kill more.' Another reported him as saying: 'I'm going to kill you all.' He fired indiscriminately, mowing down men, women and children, even including a six-month-old baby. One survivor, Mrs Griselda Diaz, could scarcely believe what she was seeing: 'He just came in and started shooting at everyone. I dived on the floor with my boy and we crawled behind a counter.'

Huberty fired round after round at the customers, and occasionally sprayed passers-by outside with bullets. When one weapon was empty he used another, disregarding the screams of the living and the moans of the dying. When all his weapons were empty, he calmly reloaded and circled the restaurant, firing at those who had taken cover the first time and finishing off some of the wounded.

The police had been called and a team of sharpshooters was positioned in the post office across the street. Some of those wounded in the street managed to crawl into the office for safety. The police delayed firing because there were reports that the gunman was holding a dozen or more hostages, but as the killing continued the order was given to shoot to kill. Three minutes later Huberty was dead, killed by a marksman from the post-office roof. He had killed 20 people and wounded 30 more.

There was an attempt on the part of Mrs Huberty to sue McDonald's, claiming that chemicals used in their food had caused her husband's mental breakdown but, of course, it came to nothing. The restaurant, where the walls and floor had run with blood, was pulled down.

The Dunblane Massacre

School mass killings have become associated in the public mind with notorious high school shoot-outs in the United States like that which took place at Columbine in 1999. But perhaps the most poignant of all, by virtue of the age of its tiny victims, was the mowing down of five- and six-year-olds in the small Scottish town of Dunblane, near Stirling, in 1996.

On the morning of 14 March, a lone gunman simply wandered into the playground of Dunblane Primary School not long after lessons had begun, and began firing from a small arsenal of firearms. He forced his way into the building past two members of staff, and found his way to the gym where 29 children were in a class with their teacher, 45-year-old Gwen Mayor. He continued shooting for nearly three minutes, after which fifteen children and Mrs Mayor lay dead. Another child was to die in hospital later that day, and only one pupil in the gym escaped without injury.

With the sound of the gunfire shaking the small school, teachers led by the headmaster Ronald Taylor ushered panic-stricken and traumatised children to safety, as the gunman turned one of the four weapons he was carrying on himself.

One of the first members of staff to get to the gym after the shooting was Stuart McCombie, who could do nothing but comfort dying children in a scene that could only be described as a nightmare.

One of the first doctors to arrive described it as the worst scene of carnage he had experienced in nearly twenty years as a medic;

'We saw a large number of dead and injured children when we arrived in the gymnasium. There were a number of teachers comforting the children who were still alive and ambulance staff who had arrived before us. The children were very quiet. They were in shock both because of the injuries and because of the psychological shock.'

One of the pupils, eleven-year-old Steven Hopper, gave a graphic account to reporters of how he saw the gunman from the classroom next to the gym; 'He was coming towards me, so I just dived under my desk when he turned and fired at us. It was pretty scary when he started firing at our classroom window because all the glass smashed in and I got hit by a piece.'

Even as parents and other townsfolk congregated at the school gates, those believed receiving counselling, the others relieved that their children were unharmed, it began to emerge who it was that committed such a horrendous act, the worst multiple murder Scotland had ever experienced.

The killer was a 43-year-old local man, Thomas Hamilton, a former scout master who was obsessed by small boys. He had been a scout leader at the age of 20, but was asked to leave the organisation after just a year because of complaints about his behaviour towards some of the boys in his care. After various failed attempts to reinlist in the Scouts, he set up and ran a boys' club, which apparently at one stage met in the gym in the Primary School. Not taking rejection well, it seems he was especially embittered when turned down as a voluntary worker at the school.

No accurate assessment of Hamilton's twisted motive could ever be achieved, but as a result of the tragedy a government inquiry was held, led by Lord Cullen. The Cullen Report that was subsequently published and acted upon led to restrictions on centre-fire hand-guns in the United Kingdom, though the legislation angered both the pro-gun lobby – who opposed any restrictions – and the anti-gun lobby, who felt the restrictions were too weak.

With the consent of Bob Dylan, who had never before given permission for someone to modify one of his compositions, a Dunblane musician named Ted Christopher wrote a new verse for 'Knockin' On Heaven's Door' in memory of the Dunblane school children and their teacher. The recording of the revised version of the song, which included surviving school children singing the chorus and Mark Knopfler on guitar, was released on 9 December 1996 in the U.K. The proceeds went to charities for children.

Wayne Williams

BY THE LATE spring of 1981, the number of 'Atlanta Child Murders' had risen to 26. Over the past two years black children had disappeared one after another in the American city and it was sometimes months before their bodies were found, hidden in undergrowth or dumped in the river. Death was usually due to strangulation and police believed that the killer normally approached his victims from behind, locking his arm around their necks and choking them to death.

The first victims were two black teenagers, Edward Smith and Alfred Evans, whose bodies were found in July 1979. Their deaths passed as unremarkable and when a third youth, Milton Harvey, disappeared in September there was no reason to connect the two incidents. In October nine-year-old Yusef Bell, the son of an ex-civil rights leader, went on an errand for a neighbour and failed to return home. After ten days his body was found stuffed into the crawl space of an abandoned school building but he had been strangled only about five days before. This time there was a great deal of media interest, as his mother, Camille Bell, was well-known for her civil rights work. Also, the decomposed body of Milton Harvey had recently been found and people were becoming uneasy.

A year after the first murders a total of seven black children had been murdered and three more were missing. Many parents were convinced that a white killer was stalking their children on a macabre mission of assassination, but the police thought this unlikely: most of the children had been snatched in black neighbourhoods where a white person would be noticeable immediately. Some of those concerned, led by Camille Bell, called a press conference to complain of police inaction: if their children had come from white middle-class neighbourhoods, they argued, far more resources would have been devoted to the case.

As the killings continued, more manpower was drafted in to swell the special police task force. There was a rumour that the killer himself might be a policeman, who would find it easy to approach trusting youngsters. The sum of $100,000 was raised by local people as a reward for information leading to the arrest of the killer. As the hunt intensified, a grisly pattern began to emerge: all the children were aged between seven and 14, all but two were boys and except for one girl, whose murder was thought by some officers to be unrelated to the rest, they had not been sexually assaulted.

Feelings among the townsfolk were running so high that 35 FBI officers were sent to Atlanta to assist the local police chief, who was the target of almost universal criticism. The hunt for the killer became one of the biggest police operations ever mounted in the United States. Face-to-face interviews were conducted with over 20,000 citizens and a further 150,000 were questioned by telephone. Police talked to tens of thousands of children, reasoning that the killer must have been unsuccessful in some of his attempted abductions and that the children involved might be able to provide some valuable clues.

On 22 May 1981 there came a dramatic breakthrough in the investigation. Police on a routine patrol near the South Drive Bridge over the Chattahooch River heard a splash and identified the nearest vehicle as a station wagon. They radioed ahead and a patrol car stopped the vehicle as it left the bridge. The driver was a 23-year-old black man named Wayne Williams and after checking his documents the police allowed him to go on his way. Two days later the body of Nathaniel Cater, aged 27, was fished out of the river. If the same killer was again responsible, then he had varied his pattern by selecting an adult victim. Forensic tests showed that dog hairs found in the rear of Wayne Williams' car matched those on the body of Nathaniel Cater and he was questioned further.

All those who knew Williams were astonished to learn that he was a suspect. He was 23, the only child of two elderly schoolteachers, and lived with his parents in a modest single-storey house in west Atlanta. He had been a gifted child who spent his spare time studying the stars through his telescope and by the age of 14 he had set up his own radio station, selling advertising time and giving interviews to magazines and on television. When he left school he became fascinated by police work and would tune his shortwave radio to police frequencies so that he could arrive first on the scene, taking photographs that he sold to the highest bidder. The only time he had been in trouble was when he was arrested for impersonating a police officer. Now he was pursuing a new career as a music promoter and was inviting young men to audition for possible inclusion in pop groups.

On 3 June Williams was given a 12-hour grilling by the police and the next day he called a press conference to announce his innocence. The police, he said, considered him the prime suspect: 'One cop told me "You killed Nathaniel Cater. It's just a matter of time before we get you." He insisted, 'I never killed anybody and I never threw anything from the bridge.'

In January 1982 Williams was put on trial, charged with the murder of Nathaniel Cater and of Jimmy Payne, who had been seen in his company before being found in the river. The prosecution case was weak: no link could be proved between Williams and either of the dead men. There was no motive, though the prosecution argued that he was 'a frustrated man driven by a desire to purify the black race by murdering poor young blacks'. It was suggested that he had contacted potential victims through his musical scouting work. The trial took a remarkable turn when the judge acceded to a plea from the prosecution to allow them to introduce evidence linking Williams with the death of ten other victims. District Attorney Anthony Joseph Drolet said: 'He has not been formally charged with the killings but the cases will reveal a pattern and bend of mind.'

Forensic evidence showed that the hairs found in Williams' car and

Wayne Williams (centre), being escorted from Fulton County Gaol en route to court

home were similar to those found on all ten bodies. A 15-year-old boy said that he had been fondled by Williams and had later seen him with Lubie Geter, who disappeared from a shopping mall in January 1981 and whose body was found a month later. Another teenager testified that Williams had offered him money for oral sex.

When Williams gave evidence he denied everything. He had not stopped his car on the bridge; he had not thrown Cater's body into the river and doubted if he would have had the strength to lift it; he was not and never had been a homosexual. 'I never met any of the victims,' he told the court. 'I feel just as sorry for them as anybody else in the world. I am 23 years old and I could have been one of the people killed out there.' When cross-examined he accused the prosecutor of being a fool and described the two FBI men who had questioned him as 'goons'.

The jury, consisting of eight blacks and four whites, found him guilty and he was sentenced to two consecutive life terms. He was led away with tears streaming down his face, still protesting his innocence.

Since the conviction, there has been much argument over the Williams case and the quality of the evidence. There have been suggestions that evidence linking the Ku-Klux-Klan with the Atlanta deaths was suppressed at the time of the trial and further developments in the case are quite possible.

Ted Bundy

TED BUNDY was just about as far from the popular idea of a homicidal maniac as it is possible to be. To all outward appearances he was the all-American boy: good-looking, well-educated, self-assured and ambitious, successful with girls and with an old-fashioned courtesy that appealed to their parents. But beneath the easy charm lay the raging sex drive, the immaturity and the suppressed resentment that turned him into one of America's most notorious serial killers. His victims may have numbered as many as 40 and they were raped, strangled and beaten to death.

The bloody trail of murders that was to follow Bundy for four years began in Seattle with the disappearance of six attractive and strikingly similar young women. In January 1974, 21-year-old Lynda Ann Healy, a psychology student, vanished from her apartment, leaving blood-stained sheets on the bed and a bloody nightdress hanging tidily in the wardrobe. It was not the first attack on girls in the area: a week before Sharon Clarke had been found battered into unconsciousness with a metal bar wrenched from the bed frame rammed into her vagina, though she had not been raped.

In the two months following Lynda Healy's disappearance 19-year-old Donna Manson vanished on her way to a concert and Susan Rancourt, a biology student, never arrived at the cinema, where she was due to meet a friend. Roberta Parkes, Brenda Ball and Georgann Hawkins all disappeared during May and June. Their abductor was choosing his victims with care: all the girls were intelligent and attractive, all in the same age group, all with long dark hair parted in the middle.

July was sunny and hot and Lake Sammamish State Park, outside

Seattle, was crowded with young people who had come to picnic and enjoy water sports. On 14 July 23-year-old Janice Ott was lying by the lake when a young man with his arm in a sling sat down beside her and began chatting. Those nearby heard him introduce himself as 'Ted' and noticed that after a while she got up and strolled off with him. She was never seen again. The same afternoon Denise Naslund left her friends to visit the lavatory and never returned. Enquiries showed that the man called Ted had approached two other girls, asking them to help him put his sailboat on to his car because he could only use one arm. One had refused but another had gone with him to his small Volkswagen, only to become suspicious and return to the beach when there was no sign of a sailboat.

Newspapers printed descriptions and artists' sketches of Ted, with the result that over 3000 calls were received, all naming possible suspects. One of them was from Ted Bundy's girlfriend, Meg Anders, who was worried about his strange sexual behaviour and had noticed that he was never with her on the days the girls disappeared. Police gave Bundy a routine screening but the respectable law student, active in law-and-order politics, was never considered a serious suspect.

In September a group of forestry students found a shallow grave containing human bones in a wood a few kilometres from Lake Sammamish. They were the remains of Janice Ott and Denise Naslund. Three months later the remains of four more missing girls were found 16 km (10 miles) away.

As autumn progressed the girls of Seattle began to relax; no more murders were reported and it seemed that the terror was over. At the same time, a wave of killings was beginning in Salt Lake City, Utah, where Ted Bundy had enrolled as a student. Nancy Wilcox disappeared on 2 October after accepting a lift in a Volkswagen; on 18 October Melissa Smith, daughter of a police chief, vanished while hitchhiking home from a restaurant; on 31 October Laura Aime failed to arrive at a Halloween party. The bodies of Melissa and Laura were later found: they had both been raped and beaten.

In November, 17-year-old Carol DaRonch was walking through a shopping mall when a young man approached her, identified himself as a police officer and told her that someone had been seen trying to break into her car in the parking lot. He accompanied her to her car, which proved to be still locked with none of her property missing. He then asked her to go with him to the station and, though his battered Volkswagen did not look much like a police car, she agreed. It was only when she realized that the supposed officer was driving the opposite way from the station that Carol panicked. There was a scuffle, with her captor threatening her with an iron bar and trying to snap handcuffs on her wrists, but she managed to escape, screaming for help. That same evening 17-year-old Debbie Kent was abducted from a high-school car park.

Over the winter the scene of action moved to the ski resorts of Colorado, where five more girls went missing, but the police made no further strides in identifying the killer until August 1975, when a highway patrolman noticed a Volkswagen shoot down the street when the driver saw a police car. When he stopped the Volkswagen and looked inside he found a stocking mask, an iron bar and a pair of handcuffs. At first the driver, Ted Bundy, was suspected as a burglar but detectives soon made the link between the items in Bundy's car and the abduction of Carol DaRonch. Her testimony was sufficient to convict him of attempted kidnapping, but by this time graver charges were on the horizon. A search of his flat had produced brochures and maps of the Colorado ski resorts, as well as credit card receipts that showed that he had been in several of the areas where girls had disappeared, only to be found violated and murdered. Bundy was sent to Colorado to face murder charges.

He escaped for the first time by jumping through the window of a courthouse but was rearrested a week later. A few months later he broke out of Garfield County Gaol by unscrewing a metal plate around

Ted Bundy

the light fitting, crawling along the roof space and dropping down into a room in the gaoler's house. A few days later a student calling himself Chris Hagen took a room on the outskirts of Florida State University in Tallahassee and no one connected the quiet, polite young man with escapee Ted Bundy.

On the night of 15 January 1978 a student returning to the Chi Omega sorority residence saw a man with dark clothes, cap and some sort of wooden club hurrying out of the door. As she went inside one of the sorority members, Karen Chandler, staggered from her room, blood streaming from her head. Inside, her roommate, Kathy Kleiner, was sitting on the bed holding her bloodsoaked head. Worse was to come. In another room Margaret Bowman lay dead; she had been strangled with a stocking, pulled round her neck with such ferocity that it looked as though she had been decapitated. A fourth victim, Lisa Levy, was already dying when she was found; the killer had been in such a frenzy that he had sunk his teeth into her buttocks and almost bitten off one of her nipples.

An hour and a half later, in a house six blocks away, a young woman heard cries and moans and sounds of rhythmic thumping from the next room, occupied by Cheryl Thomas. She dialled Cheryl's phone number and as the telephone rang next door she heard the sound of running feet and a door banging. When the police arrived they found Cheryl badly beaten but still alive. The weapon, a length of board, lay on the floor where the attacker had dropped it: he had been rhythmically beating Cheryl over the head while masturbating with his other hand.

On 9 February 12-year-old Kimberly Leach disappeared from a school yard and her body was found two months later in an abandoned cabin. She was Bundy's youngest victim and was also to be his last. In the early hours of the morning on 15 February a patrolman pulled over a car he believed to be stolen, and when the driver tried to run for it he was overpowered and arrested.

Bundy denied everything. When his defence lawyers wanted him to enter into a plea-bargain, pleading guilty to three murders in return for a guarantee that he would avoid the death penalty, he sacked them and decided to represent himself. The sensational trial that followed was broadcast to the nation on television and attracted newsmen from all over the world. Much of the evidence against Bundy was circumstantial but the young woman who had seen the killer leaving the Chi Omega sorority house was able to identify him. Even more damaging was the forensic evidence which proved that the bite marks on Lisa Levy's body had been made by Ted Bundy's teeth. He was found guilty on the two Chi Omega murders in July 1979 and sentenced to die in the electric chair. When he was asked if he had anything to say, he answered: 'I find it somewhat absurd to ask for mercy for something I did not do.' Later a third conviction and death sentence were obtained in the case of Kimberly Leach.

His current girlfriend, Carol Boone, remained convinced of his innocence and married him in a hurried ceremony in a Florida court just before he was given the third death sentence. 'Ted is not vicious or a savage mass murderer,' she insisted. 'The charges were the result of snowballing hysteria on the part of law enforcement people looking for a fall guy on whom they could pin all their unsolved crimes.'

To many people who watched his courtroom battles, it seemed incredible that this could be the same man who ravaged and battered women in frenzied sprees of violence and his personality remains a mystery. He was born to an unmarried mother and brought up believing that she was his sister; his grandparents treated him as their own son. His mother later married John Bundy, an ex-navy man who worked as a cook, and though young Ted was never close to his stepfather there was never any sign of hostility. To his mother he was 'the best son in the world,' who never forgot her on Mother's Day, however busy he might be. However, he was a lifelong liar and thief – he distinguished himself as a skier, but stole most of his equipment – and had an overpowering sex drive which no 'normal' behaviour with his girlfriends could satisfy. He was embittered by a failed relationship with a girl he yearned to impress: Stephanie Brooks, beautiful, clever and from a rich family, was taken in for a while by Bundy's undoubted charm and they became engaged, but she eventually jilted him because of his emotional immaturity. He was devastated, and some family members believed that he never recovered from the rejection. It was perhaps a deep resentment against women, allied to his overwhelming sexual urges for complete control over them, that led him to commit rape and murder.

Donald Harvey

WHEN John Powell died in hospital in Cincinnati, USA, after lying in a coma for eight months following a motorcycle accident, a routine postmortem was carried out. The pathologist was amazed when he detected the telltale odour of bitter almonds which indicated the presence of cyanide. Once he had decided that the patient had been murdered, dozens of members of the hospital staff, as well as Powell's friends and relatives, came under suspicion.

Among those interviewed by the murder squad was nurse's aide Donald Harvey, a good-looking, smiling 35-year-old. Everyone at the hospital spoke well of him: he was always cheerful, always willing to help out. But when enquiries were made into his background, detectives unearthed facts that made them wonder if the real Donald Harvey might be rather different. It appeared that while in his previous job, as a mortuary attendant in the Cincinnati Veterans' Administration Medical Center, he had been suspected of stealing tissue samples from the morgue. Then, in July 1985, he was stopped by security guards when leaving work and found to be carrying a revolver as well as hypodermic needles, surgical scissors and gloves and anatomy textbooks. No charges were brought and he was allowed to resign.

Under rigorous questioning, Harvey admitted to poisoning John Powell by administering cyanide through a gastric tube. While he awaited trial a local television station reported on 23 other mysterious deaths in the hospital which had all taken place since Harvey joined the staff. Harvey's trial, scheduled for July 1987, was postponed until January 1988 to allow further investigations to take place. Complicated legal negotiations began behind the scenes to strike a deal: if Harvey gave details of all the crimes he had committed, pleaded guilty and agreed never to appeal his sentence, he could avoid the death penalty. As Harvey began his confession, it was soon obvious that the death toll was higher then anyone had imagined.

Harvey grew up in Kentucky, in a farmhouse surrounded by tobacco fields. His family were ordinary, hardworking people who went to church regularly and got on well with their neighbours. There seemed no reason why young Donald should grow up with major hang-ups; he was remembered as a winning child, well-liked by everyone. At the age of 19 he joined the Air Force and, stationed near San Francisco, he became involved in the gay community. A year later he was honourably discharged from the service and made a suicide attempt, followed by psychiatric treatment. He then took jobs in various hospitals, joining the staff of the Drake Memorial Hospital in Cincinnati in February 1986.

Most of the murders of patients that followed were accomplished by injecting cyanide into gastric tubes or with arsenic added to orange juice. Occasionally Harvey used petroleum distillate – a substance normally used to clean tubes – and once he tried to kill by injecting the victim with HIV-infected blood, but this was unsuccessful and he had to resort to cyanide after all. 'I got another one today,' he would tell colleagues each time a patient died on the ward and they would smile with him, never dreaming that there was any meaning behind the cheery young man's jokes.

Detectives listening to Harvey as he reeled off his list of victims were chilled by the matter-of-fact way that he talked about murder, as though he was discussing what to have for lunch. He claimed that he had killed the hospital patients because he felt sorry for them.

He made the same claim over some of those he killed, or attempted to kill, outside the hospital. In 1983 he poisoned Helen Metzger, an elderly woman in the flat above that occupied by Harvey and his homosexual lover Carl Hoeweler. She had been ailing for some time and Harvey often called in with shopping or an extra treat; this time it was a piece of pie, its whipped topping full of arsenic. Harvey was one of the pallbearers at her funeral. When his lover's father went into hospital, he used a visit as an opportunity to sprinkle arsenic on the old man's pudding. He also fed Mrs Hoeweler arsenic over a long period but she survived his ministrations. There were other murders too, where there could be no suggestion of 'mercy killings'. Various neighbours were murdered after minor disputes and Harvey even gave arsenic to his lover after a quarrel, relenting later and nursing him back to health.

At his trial, the prosecutor argued; 'He's no mercy killer and he's not insane. He killed because he *liked* killing.' A psychiatric expert pointed out that the motive, like that of many serial killers, was power: 'Donald Harvey could kill these people – watch them die – and they couldn't do a thing.' When Harvey appeared in court a huge board listed the names of 28 victims and the dates of their death. He pleaded guilty to 24 murders and four attempted murders and received a life sentence on each count, the first three to be served consecutively.

This was only the beginning: in Kentucky Harvey pleaded guilty to eight counts of murder and one of manslaughter, then back in Ohio he pleaded guilty to three more murders, collecting in all 11 more life sentences and various other terms ranging from 7 to 25 years.

Jeffrey Feltner

NURSE'S aide Jeffrey Feltner spent four months in a Florida gaol in 1988 for filing false reports and making harassing phone calls. The police were glad to see the case closed; it had already taken up far too much of their time since Feltner had made the first phone call, hinting that several patients at a Putnam County nursing home had been murdered.

He had begun by ringing a local television station pretending that a man he met in a bar had bragged about killing five nursing-home patients, but refusing to give a name. On the same day he called a crisis intervention centre, announcing himself as 'Jeff' and saying that he had already killed five patients at the nursing home and had planned to kill a sixth, only to have his attempt foiled at the last moment, after he had used a chair to climb in through the window of a sleeping female patient. He had been about to carry out his purpose when he heard a knock at the door and hastily retreated the way he had come. The police decided that the calls needed investigation, especially as the second caller had named all the patients he claimed to have killed.

Detectives who visited the nursing home discovered that there was a Jeff on the staff – Jeffrey Feltner – and the deaths mentioned had all taken place since his arrival. However, the idea that Feltner might be a murderer seemed laughable: he was a small, slight young man of 26, gentle and kindly, with a real feeling for the patients in his charge. He had been given the job on the recommendation of a relative who had worked at the home for years and no one had any criticisms of him. Moreover, there was no reason to suspect foul play in any of the deaths; all the patients had been old and ill and their demise had been no surprise. When investigations were made into 'Jeff's' claim that he had just attempted another murder, a chair was found outside the window in question, but detectives were able to demonstrate that no one had stood on the chair and there was no sign that the window had been opened.

In due course Jeffrey Feltner admitted to making both phone calls but said that he had made up the murder story in order to draw public attention to the inferior standards of care provided for patients in nursing homes. The police took the view that he was more concerned with drawing attention to himself.

The authorities considered the matter closed with Feltner's gaol sentence but they were mistaken. The following year various agencies received phone calls – one of them purporting to come from Jeffrey Feltner's homosexual lover – saying that Feltner had killed two patients at nursing homes in Volusia County, as well as those already reported to the police in Putnam County.

Once again, Jeffrey Feltner admitted making the calls, for the same reasons as before. Detectives recommended that he should obtain psychiatric help and he committed himself to a mental-health treatment centre as a voluntary patient.

This time the police were not prepared to close the case so easily and under intensive questioning, Feltner confessed to seven murders. His method had been suffocation in every case: he would wait until the patients were asleep, then climb on top of them so that they could not move. Wearing surgical gloves to give him a better grip, he would place one hand over their mouths, then pinch their noses with the other. Within five minutes, they were dead. His only motive, he said, had been the relief of suffering: his chosen victims had been ill and in pain and this was the only way he could help them. He felt guilty about what he was doing but it was worth it to see the look of pain leaving their faces.

Proving a case against Feltner was not easy, as four of the seven patients he had named had been cremated, but the authorities in

Putnam County decided to exhume the body of one of the remaining three patients: Sarah Abrams, aged 75, who died on 10 February 1988. Of all the patients on the list, her death had been the greatest surprise and her family were anxious to help with an investigation. Examination of the body showed that she had been asphyxiated.

Feltner was charged with first-degree murder but his lawyers announced that he was planning to plead not guilty: 'He seems to have some kind of mental disorder that drives him to compulsive confessions to acts he has not committed' they announced. On the morning of the arraignment, Feltner was found lying in his cell with blood oozing from his slashed wrists. Doctors who treated him decided that the cuts were superficial and that his attempt at suicide had not been serious. Back in prison he lay curled up on his bunk, refusing to speak and taking nothing to eat or drink for five days.

He was examined by a psychiatrist and a clinical psychologist and both decided that he was unfit to stand trial, but at a competency hearing the judge preferred to accept the word of prison officers who considered that Feltner's depressed state was not abnormal among prisoners. He declared that Feltner had proved his own competence by his alert demeanour throughout the hearing.

As the trial approached Feltner was still announcing that he intended to plead not guilty but at the last moment his lawyers arranged a plea-bargain.

Feltner pleaded guilty to the first-degree murder of Sarah Abrams in return for an agreement that the prosecution would not request the death penalty. He would also plead guilty to the second-degree murder of 88-year-old Doris Moriarty at a Volusia County nursing home on 11 July 1989. He was given a life sentence, which in Florida meant a minimum 25 years, for the murder of Sarah Abrams and 17 years to run concurrently for the killing of Doris Moriarty.

Even after the conviction, Feltner's family and friends refused to believe that he was guilty. They always maintained that he had invented the story to highlight the poor care given to elderly patients in nursing homes. Two years before he had been diagnosed as an AIDS sufferer and they believed he wanted to achieve something useful in the time he had left, something that his family would be able to remember with pride. .

Dr Harold Shipman
a.k.a. "Doctor Death"

Harold Shipman has gone down in history as Britain's most prolific serial killer, with over 250 victims, all but one of them middle-aged or elderly women. But the villain in this case was no axe-wielding monster or deranged sex fiend; on the contrary, his appearance and demeanour as an intelligent and respected member of the community, a family doctor no less, belied the evil that lurked beneath his comforting façade.

For, like with any doctor of medicine who has the trust of his patients, it was comfort his victims anticipated when he came to visit them, or they him. But in a staggering amount of cases what they got instead was a lethal injection of diamorphine – commonly known as heroin – that sent them to their final resting place in a matter of minutes.

Harold Shipman – who was always known as Fred – was born in the British midland town of Nottingham in 1946. He passed the '11-plus' entrance exam into Grammar School, and it was while he was completing his studies there that his mother Vera died of cancer aged only 42. Although her death undoubtedly traumatised him, he didn't let it show for too long, and moved from Nottingham to Leeds University where he studied medicine.

Unlike most students, Harold got married while still at college, to his then-pregnant girlfriend Primrose Oxtoby, so fellow students saw little of him, and those that remember him just recall a very 'average' sort of person; one later commented 'The thing I remember as remarkable about Fred was that he was unremarkable.'

After graduating in 1970 he began his career in the general hospital in nearby Pontefract, before going into general practice in 1974 at a medical centre in the town of Todmordon, in a pretty Pennine valley between Lancashire and Yorkshire. His reputation quickly blossomed in the district; colleagues were impressed by his skill and knowledge, patients by his care and attention. He was well-liked, and comfortably settled into the social life of the town, joining the local Conservative Party, and his wife the choral society.

But a darker side to his character was emerging even then. In November 1975 he was charged with three offences of obtaining a controlled drug by deception, three of unlawful possession of the same drug, and two of forging prescription charge exemption certificates. The reason for these crimes was simple – Shipman was addicted to the drug in question, pethedine, and had been injecting himself for six months with large amounts of it. He was prescribing some of his patients with the drug, but keeping some (or sometimes all) for himself.

He was fined £600 and suspended from his practice in 1976, but by 1977 was able to work as a doctor again and joined the Donnebrook House medical practice in Hyde, near Manchester. And it was in Hyde, after he set up his own one-man practice at 21 Market Street in 1991, that the most notorious killing spree in British criminal history was to take place.

Four years after moving into Market Street, in March 1995, he was to kill his first victim, 81-year-old Marie West, injecting her with a massive dose of diamorphine as she sat in her own front room. It was a horrific pattern of murder he was to repeat again and again over the next three years.

When Shipman was eventually arrested on suspicion of the murder of his final victim, Kathleen Grundy, the townsfolk of Hyde simply thought the police had got it wrong. How could a gentle, reliable doctor like Shipman do such a thing? His life was dedicated to saving lives, not taking them.

But gradually the doubts started to spread, as people who had lost relatives under the care of the doctor began comparing notes. There emerged stories of his being unnaturally cool when announcing a sudden death 'from natural causes', even though he had just witnessed it. There was the case of his telling a woman her mother had died, only to change it to mother-in-law after the distraught daughter had found her mother alive and well. Five of his patients had actually died in his surgery. Tongues were wagging now, and the good doctor didn't seem so good after all.

What finally raised the alarm in the case of Kathleen Grundy's death was of Shipman's own making, and perhaps deliberately so.

When the 81-year-old, who was fit and well for her age, failed to turn up at her senior citizen's luncheon club on 24 June 1998, two concerned friends went to her unlocked house, only to find her fully-clothed body on the sofa in the sitting room. They called her doctor, the trusted Shipman, who gave the corpse a very brief examination before declaring her dead, later certifying the cause of death as old age. In fact he had visited the house earlier that morning, a pre-arranged appointment to take a routine blood test. Instead he took her life.

What happened next was to be the start of the doctor's undoing. Shipman advised Mrs Grundy's grieving friends to contact a firm of local solicitors who, he said, handled the deceased's affairs including her will; he knew they held her will, because he had forged it himself.

A couple of weeks earlier, Mrs Grundy had visited his surgery asking whether she need treatment on her ears; on the pretext that it was a permission form, Shipman got her to sign a folded over piece of paper, asking two patients in the waiting room to also provide their signatures as witnesses. With these he forged signatures on a blank Last Will and Testament form, in which he untidily typed Kathleen Grundy's 'wish' to bequeath all her property and money to her doctor: 'I give all my estate, money and house to my doctor. My family are not in need and I want to reward him for all the care he has given to me and the people of Hyde.'

This immediately raised alarms bells with Mrs Grundy's daughter, Angela Woodruff, herself a solicitor living in Leamington Spa, Warwickshire. She had a will signed by her mother, leaving everything to her. When she saw the document held by the Hyde solicitors, she was convinced it was a forgery. And when she took it to the police, they were too.

The detective who led the subsequent murder inquiry described the 'will', and the letter purporting to be from Kathleen Grundy that accompanied it, as 'a cack-handed attempt at forgery'. Shipman had typed the documents (all in upper case) on an old manual typewriter he kept in his surgery, and there were letters missing in them where the machine was failing to make contact with the paper properly. It didn't take the police long to match the typewriter with the forgery, on which forensic experts were later to find Shipman's fingerprints.

The victim's body was exhumed and found to contain morphine. With this in mind, Shipman had even altered her medical records as a contingency measure, suggesting in them that she was abusing codeine, which can break down into morphine after death.

But the game was up, and while he was being questioned and charged over the autumn of 1998, another twelve bodies linked to Doctor Shipman were exhumed before the end of the year. After due process, in January 2000 'Doctor Death' as the tabloid newspapers dubbed him was sentenced to life fifteen times for murdering fifteen of his patients. He showed no signs of regret during the trial, arrogantly refusing to cooperate with the police at every stage of the investigation, and has been in solitary confinement in Frankland Prison near Durham ever since.

Harold Shipman's motives have never been clearly established. It seems likely that the pathetic attempt at forgery was a deliberate mechanism to end the ritual of murder, and various theories have been put forward to explain why that history of homicide happened in the first place. Some suggest he was avenging the premature death of his mother when he was only 17 – that would explain why he only killed older women. Others see his motives as being about personal power over his victims, the very power of life and death, in contrast to an otherwise humdrum life in a small provincial town.

Whatever, the fifteen murders were just the tip of a horrific iceberg. When the official results of the Shipman inquiry were finally released on July 2002, the positive death toll was put at 215, with 45 more 'suspicious' deaths putting the possible total at 260. But a further trial has been ruled out, on the grounds that Shipman couldn't expect to get a fair procedure in the light of his earlier conviction, his name now forever established in the history books as one of the most prolific serial killers of all time.

Jack the Ripper

JACK THE RIPPER is Britain's best-known criminal. The terror he created in the country in 1886 was such that part of his name has been adapted for numerous more recent killers – the Yorkshire Ripper, Jack the Stripper, even the Rostov Ripper.

The original Ripper's first victim is taken to be Mary Ann Nichols, who was killed in Buck's Row, Whitechapel, on 31 August 1888. A prostitute living in a slum in London's notorious East End, she had been strangled, her throat had been cut and her stomach slashed. 'No murder was ever more ferociously or brutally done', said a report.

In this poverty-stricken area of London, with its alleys, gaslights, drinking dens and crime, it was not uncommon for prostitutes to be killed, violently or otherwise, and indeed the vicious stabbing of Martha Turner on 7 August in Commercial Street, Stepney, is some-times thought to be the Ripper's first murder. Not much notice was taken at first of these two killings.

It was different, however, on 8 September, when the body of 'Dark Annie' Chapman, with her entrails hanging out, was discovered in Hanbury Street, Whitechapel. A fresh touch was that coins and brass rings had been laid round her feet as if in sacrifice. *The Lancet* reported: 'The intestines had been lifted out of the body and placed on the shoulder of the corpse', and the coroner declared that 'an unskilled person could not have done this'.

The newspapers were now wild with the story of the latest horrible murder, and there was speculation that perhaps a surgeon was res-ponsible. Reference to this speculation was made in a letter the Ripper sent to 'the Boss' of the Central News Agency on 27 Septem-ber, in which he said he wanted to be getting to work again right away

A hawker discovers the body of Elizabeth Stride (contemporary engraving)

and promised he would send the police a human ear. He signed the letter 'Jack the Ripper', with the added: 'Don't mind me giving the trade name'. He also asked that the letter be kept back until he 'do a bit more work', and this came immediately.

On 30 September Elizabeth Stride, known as 'Long Liz', was found in Berners Street. Her throat had been cut and an attempt had indeed been made to remove an ear. Her killer had been disturbed. Less than an hour later the Ripper had reached Mitre Square, in the Houndsditch area of London, and killed Catherine Eddowes. Despite the short time he had – the local policeman patrolled the square every 15 minutes – he slashed her from ribs to pubic area and removed an ear and a kidney. He washed his hands in a communal sink, and chalked a message on a wall: 'The Juwes are not the men who will be blamed for nothing.' The Police Commissioner, Sir Charles Warren, who was under pressure to resign over the affair, had the message rubbed out before it could be photographed apparently because he feared a wave of anti-semitic attacks.

The Ripper wrote again to Central News, apologizing for not having time to get the ears for the police. He also sent half a kidney in a box to George Lusk, Chairman of the Whitechapel Vigilance Committee, saying he had fried and eaten the other half and 'it was very nice'.

On 9 November the Ripper performed his most spectacular murder. Mary Kelly's body was found in her room in Miller's Court off Dorset Street. This time the Ripper had obviously had all the time he wanted. The head had been removed and the legs skinned. The intestines were hung round a picture frame and one hand was in the empty stomach. The heart was on the pillow.

This brutal murder caused a sensation. Even Queen Victoria voiced her opinions and Sir Charles Warren finally resigned. However, it was the last of the Ripper murders. A lawyer, Montague John Druitt, who drowned himself in the Thames in December, was claimed by Scotland Yard to be the murderer. Yet there was no evidence, and over the years there have been numerous other theories. The most striking is that the Ripper was Queen Victoria's grandson, the Duke of Clarence, who died in the flu epidemic of 1892. Another is that he was James Stephen, a homosexual friend of Clarence and man-about-town, who also died in 1892. Sir William Gull, Queen Victoria's physician and also connected with Clarence, is another whose name is put forward. Over a hundred years after the crimes, there is still no definitive solution.

The Mad Axeman of New Orleans

ON 25 May 1918, brothers Jake and Andrew Maggio, a cobbler and a barber who lived with another brother, Joe, and his wife at their grocery store in New Orleans, heard groans from their brother's bedroom. Investigating, they found Mrs Maggio in a pool of blood, her head almost off her body, and Joe groaning on the bed with his throat cut. While awaiting the police they discovered that an intruder had entered the house by chiselling a panel from the back door. In the yard was a bloodstained axe and razor.

The New Orleans police, who seem to have been singularly incompetent, arrested the two brothers for murder. But two streets away, a message had been chalked on a pavement: 'Mrs Maggio is going to sit up tonight, just like Mrs Toney.' It was recalled that seven years earlier three other Italian grocers and their wives had been similarly attacked: their names were Cruti, Rosetti and Schiambra, and Schiambra's Christian name was Tony. Was his wife Mrs Toney? The Maggio brothers were released while New Orleans, and particularly Italian grocers, wondered if there was to be another spate of murders.

Five weeks later, on 28 June, a baker went round the back of the grocery store of Louis Besumer. Most people lived in wooden-framed buildings with back yards, and the baker was horrified to see a panel chiselled from the back door. He knocked, and Louis Besumer, his head pouring blood from an axe wound, opened it. Inside, Mrs Harriet Lowe, who lived with him as his wife, was similarly injured. Besumer was Polish rather than Italian, but many locals thought he was German, and therefore probably a spy. When Mrs Lowe died, apparently saying Besumer was the axeman, he was arrested for murder.

On 5 August, however, the day Besumer was charged, the axeman struck again: Edward Schneider arrived home to find his pregnant wife covered with blood. She was able to tell police she had been attacked by a man with an axe. She recovered, a week later giving birth to a girl, and this time the police showed unusual restraint in not arresting the husband.

It was only another five days until the next attack. Two nieces of Joseph Romano, a barber, heard noises from their uncle's room. They crept to the door, and saw a man holding an axe by their uncle's bed. They screamed and he vanished. Two days later Romano died. The method of entry had been the usual one through a panel of the door, and the axe was found in the yard.

By now panic reigned in New Orleans, especially among Italians; many claimed sightings of the axeman, and there were numerous reports of panels chiselled from doors. However, there were no more attacks until March. Then a grocer, Iorlando Jordano, heard screams from over the road where a rival grocer, Charles Cortimiglia, lived. He dashed across, and found Cortimiglia on the floor, with blood pouring from wounds. His wife Rosie, with her head spurting blood, was sitting on the floor holding their dead and bloody two-year-old daughter. The back door had the familiar missing panel, and the bloody axe was outside. Mrs Cortimiglia was two days in shock – then she accused 69-year-old Iorlando Jordano and his son Frank of the crime. Despite the heated assertions of husband Charles, who recovered, that the Jordanos were not involved, the two men were arrested.

The axeman then sent a letter to the *Times-Picayune*, the local paper, saying that he would attack next on 19 March, St Joseph's Night, and that he would avoid any houses with a jazz band in full swing, as he liked jazz. Students invited him through a newspaper advertisement to join their party, and it is reported that New Orleans that night was noisy with music. There was even a tune composed: 'The Mysterious Axeman's Jazz, or Don't Scare Me Papa'.

It was not so funny for Louis Besumer, who stood trial in April. The evidence against him, however, was weak to non-existent, and he was acquitted. In May, however, the Jordanos were convicted solely on Mrs Cortimiglia's assertion – all the other evidence, including that of her husband, was against conviction. The young Jordano was sentenced to hang, his father to life imprisonment.

On 10 August 1919 an Italian grocer, Frank Genusa, opened his door to find his friend, neighbour and fellow grocer Steve Boca outside, blood pouring from a head wound. He had been attacked by the axeman. Naturally the police arrested Genusa, but released him on Boca's insistence.

On 2 September a man heard scratching at his back door and, after shouting a warning, fired a revolver through it. Chisel marks were found on the door. Next day a 19-year-old girl was badly injured by an axe attack. She eventually recovered, but could not remember the attack.

Mike Pepitone, another grocer, was attacked on 27 October. His wife, who slept in a separate room, heard noises and saw the axeman disappearing. Her husband was dead, attacked so violently that blood had stained the wall and ceiling.

There were now no attacks for over a year, but the *Times-Picayune* had another exclusive when, in December 1920, Mrs Cortimiglia burst into the office and confessed that it was untrue that the Jordanos, whom she disliked, had attacked her husband. In the past year she had been ravaged by smallpox, her husband had left her and she believed God was punishing her for her sins. The Jordanos were released.

The incompetent New Orleans police heard of the last act in the mystery of the axeman when their counterparts in Los Angeles told them that, on 2 December 1920, a man from New Orleans named Joseph Mumfre had been shot dead in the street by a veiled woman dressed heavily in black who had stepped from a doorway and emptied a revolver into him. The mystery woman was caught and, after lengthy questioning said she was Mrs Pepitone, and that Mumfre was the axeman she had seen running from her husband's bedroom when he committed his last murder. She had followed him to Los Angeles to exact revenge. The New Orleans police checked Mumfre's record. He was a criminal who had been in and out of prison and the axe murders tallied neatly with his periods of freedom. Mrs Pepitone was sentenced to ten years but served only three. Had she solved the identity of the axeman?

The Mystery of Birdhurst Rise

ON 23 April 1928 59-year-old Edmund Duff set out from his house at 16 South Park Hill Road, Croydon, for a fishing holiday with an old friend in Fordingbridge, Hampshire. When he returned a week later, he was feeling ill. The family doctor, Dr Robert Elwell, could find little wrong with him, but during the night and following morning he got worse and late that night he died. Elwell and his partner Dr Binning, who had also been present at the death, could not issue a death certificate and an inquest was held. Duff's wife Grace, much younger than him at 41, told of a flask of whisky he had taken with him on his holiday and then finished when he got home, although the flask was never produced. Dr Bronte, the pathologist who carried out a postmortem, said there was no poison in the body, and the verdict was death from natural causes.

Mrs Grace Duff took her three children to live a few streets away at 59 Birdhurst Rise, to be nearer to her widowed mother Mrs Violet Sidney and sister Vera Sidney, who lived at number 29. Mrs Duff's brother Tom and his wife and family also lived nearby, at 6 South Park Hill Road. They were a close-knit family, always in each other's homes.

On 11 February 1929 Vera Sidney became ill. This was attributed to some soup made up by Kate Noakes, the servant, from vegetables and a powdered base, as Mrs Noakes and Bingo the cat, who also took a little, were also ill. Vera, usually the only one in the house who took soup, recovered a little and, on 13 February, was well enough to have lunch with the family and an aunt, Mrs Greenwell, who was visiting from Newcastle. Vera was not pleased to see some fresh soup of the same kind as before, but drank some, only to find that she was immediately very ill again with sickness and diarrhoea. So was Mrs Greenwell, who had also sampled the soup.

Next day Vera was considerably worse, and Dr Elwell was called. A specialist was summoned but, at just past midnight on 15 February, Vera died. Mrs Greenwell lay ill in her London hotel for days before recovering. Dr Elwell issued a death certificate stating natural causes and Vera was buried near her brother-in-law.

Vera's mother, Violet, took the death badly. Dr Elwell gave her a tonic called Metatone, and her other children, Grace and Tom, were always calling round. On 5 March Violet felt very ill near the end of lunch and announced she had been poisoned. Dr Binning and Dr Elwell called, and another specialist was sent for, but at 7.30 pm Violet Sidney died. Again there had to be a postmortem, and Violet's major organs were sent away for analysis. The CID were called in and a number of bottles, including Violet's medicine bottle, were removed. After Violet's burial arsenic was discovered in her medicine bottle and organs, and on 22 March 1929, in the middle of the night in a futile attempt to avoid publicity, the bodies of Violet and Vera Sidney were exhumed from Queen's Road Cemetery, Croydon.

While separate inquests were proceeding on Vera and Violet, Edmund Duff's body was exhumed on 18 May 1929 and a second inquest on him opened in July. All three inquests overlapped, and the same principal witnesses were at each. It was now announced that Edmund Duff had also died of acute arsenic poisoning. Dr Bronte was strongly suspected of having mixed up Edmund Duff's organs with those of another person when performing his original autopsy, although he denied this. The verdicts reached in the inquests on Vera Sidney and Edmund Duff were 'murder by poison administered by person or persons unknown'. In Violet's case the verdict was much the same, although the jury would not rule out the possibility that she had poisoned herself.

Who was the triple killer? There were only two serious possibilities: Grace Duff or her brother Tom Sidney, despite an anonymous letter to the coroner which claimed that Tom's wife was guilty. Grace benefited financially by all three deaths and Tom by two of them, although not by a great amount. After the inquests, Tom, who was by profession an entertainer, took his family to New Orleans, where he eventually became an antique dealer. Grace moved to the south coast and opened a boarding house. Despite their previous closeness, they did not see each other again. At the inquests, Grace made the better impression: quiet, considerate, apparently grieving. Tom was more irritable, and had exchanges with a coroner, particularly at the suggestion in the latter's summing-up that Tom had not always taken the proceedings seriously and, as opposed to Grace, was not the most truthful witness. The maidservant made the point that Tom was hanging about strangely at the times of his mother's and sister's poisonings, while the detective-inspector reported that Tom had claimed he was indoors with flu at one of the crucial times. On the other hand, there were those who thought Grace's calm and dignity were part of an act.

Detective-Inspector Fred Hedges wanted to charge Grace, partly in view of Tom's suggestion that there was something between her and Dr Elwell, but the Director of Public Prosecutions thought the evidence too thin. Tom also alleged that Grace was behind the anonymous letter, a copy of which Grace said she had herself received but destroyed. An interesting fact to emerge later was that the Duffs had had a paying guest from 1924, a Miss Anna Kelvey, but that soon after they moved to South Park Hill Road she had died of a stroke aged 76. On her deathbed she was alleged (by Tom) to have said: 'Mrs Duff, you are a wicked woman.' There was much speculation during the inquests that her body would be exhumed too, but police suspicions about it were left at that.

In the 1960s Richard Whittington-Egan interviewed many of the principals, including the doctors and main suspects, for his book *The Riddle of Birdhurst Rise*. He pointed the finger of suspicion at Grace Duff and the book could not be published until after her death in 1973.

The Mad Butcher of Kingsbury Run

KINGSBURY RUN is an old creek running through Cleveland, Ohio, which now carries several railway lines. The waste ground either side of the lines was popular in the 1930s as camping ground for tramps, and a dangerous play area for children.

On 23 September 1935 children found two headless and castrated male bodies. The missing parts were found nearby. Decapitation was the cause of death, and only one victim was identified – Edward Andrassy, 29, a bisexual with numerous convictions. A reddish tinge on the other body, as if it had been treated with a chemical, recalled half of a woman's torso found a year before at Euclid Beach, a few kilometres to the east, with similar staining.

On 26 January 1936 a Cleveland butcher, told by a customer that there was some meat behind his shop, found a basket which contained parts of a woman's body. The remaining parts were discovered two weeks later behind a nearby empty house, but the head was never found. The body was identified as that of Florence Polillo, a prostitute.

During the rest of 1936 further heads and bodies – usually unidentifiable – were found in Kingsbury Run or nearby, and when the total of victims reached seven, a special 'torso squad' of detectives was formed to find the killer. However, over the course of 1937 and 1938, when numerous other body parts were discovered in the region, the squad had no success at all.

Then, in 1939, a letter addressed to the Cleveland chief of police was received from Los Angeles. This purported to come from the killer, a man who was going to 'astound the medical profession' after

Frank Dolezal, at the time of his confession to the Kingsbury Run murders

his experiments on his 'laboratory guinea pigs'. He promised that Cleveland could 'rest easy now' as he proposed to carry on his work in Los Angeles, and pinpointed where a head was buried on Century Boulevard in the latter city. However, no heads were found in Los Angeles.

In 1939 a private detective helping the Cleveland police discovered that Florence Polillo and one or two other Kingsbury Run victims had all used a particular tavern. Police arrested another customer, Frank Dolezal, and extracted a confession from him. But Dolezal hanged himself in his cell (or perhaps was murdered) and he is not seriously considered to have been a killer.

In May 1940 three male corpses were discovered in abandoned rail trucks outside Pittsburgh. All were decapitated, and bore the mark of the Kingsbury Butcher. They had met their deaths between three and six months earlier, possibly when the trucks were in Youngstown, Ohio. One victim was identified as a homosexual ex-convict.

A possible final victim of the killer was discovered over ten years later. On 23 July 1950 a headless, castrated male body was found in a timber yard a few kilometres from the Kingsbury Run. The head was found and identified four days later, and the coroner pointed out the resemblance of the crime to the torso murders.

It is unknown how many victims the Kingsbury Run Butcher claimed. Between 1925 and 1939 there were several decapitations near New Castle, Pennsylvania, near the railway line which runs to Cleveland; none of the victims were identified and no murderer was found. However, the Butcher killed at least 16 times, and eight of his heads were never traced.

The Moonlight Murderer

TEXARKANA, a small town right on the border of Texas and Arkansas, hit the headlines of the American newspapers in May 1946 as the story broke of a serial killer who murdered when the moon was full. The 'Moonlight Murderer' spread terror among the townsfolk.

The killer's first attack occurred on 23 February 1946. A couple were parked by the side of a lonely road just outside the town when a tall man wearing a mask approached their car. Jimmy Hollis, aged 24, was ordered from the car at the point of a gun and clubbed to the ground. The man now turned his attention to 19-year-old Mary Lacey and inflicted such serious sexual assaults on her, using the barrel of his gun, that she asked him to kill her to end her ordeal. Instead the man clubbed her to the ground and began assaulting her companion, not bothering when the girl stumbled off to seek help. On this occasion both victims were allowed to live.

The next couple were not so lucky. On 23 March 29-year-old Richard Griffin and 17-year-old Polly Ann Moore parked their car on another lonely road in Texarkana. Both were found next morning in the car, shot dead through the back of the head. Blood found 6 m (20 ft) away from the car suggested that they had been killed there and their fully clothed bodies taken to the car, where the girl's body was sprawled on the back seat, the man's stuffed between the dashboard and the front seat. Immediately locals linked the crime to the one before, and the papers added to the horror by reporting, wrongly, that the sexual assaults of the first attack had been repeated and, indeed, exceeded in the second.

Exactly three weeks later two youngsters who had been last seen entering Spring Lake Park following a local dance were killed. The body of 17-year-old Paul Martin was found the following morning,

271

14 April, beside a road leading out of Texarkana. He had been shot four times. The body of his friend, 15-year-old Betty Jo Booker, was found 1.6 km (1 mile) away a few hours later; she had been shot in the heart, and also in the face. There was more colourful reporting about the 'Moonlight Murderer' and locals firmly believed that there was at large a sex-fiend whose lust for torture and killing was prompted by the sight of a full moon. The Texas Rangers patrolled the lovers' lanes and detectives were planted as decoys to try to attract the killer. Needless to say, several innocent people were challenged and, in some cases, subjected to violence by over-zealous citizens by mistake.

Three weeks later, perhaps in order to foil all this attention, the killer changed his style. On 4 May, 36-year-old Virgil Starks was reading the paper after supper in his farmhouse 17 km (10 miles) outside Texarkarna when he was shot through the window. His wife, entering the room at the noise, was hit by two shots before managing to get out and summon help. While she was away the killer roamed through the house, leaving footprints from the blood of his victim. Tracker dogs were brought and a flashlight was found outside, but the killer had escaped by car.

With every adult man in Texarkarna a suspect in a highly charged atmosphere, there was particular excitement when a man's body was found two days later on the railway line to the north of Texarkarna, towards the town of Hope. He was Earl McSpadden, and the coroner found that he had been stabbed before his body was placed on the line to be run over by the 5.30 am train. It is possible that McSpadden was the last victim of the Moonlight Murderer, the killing designed to look like a suicide in the hope that the manhunt would be called off on the assumption that he had been the murderer. Some reporters did indeed claim the killer had committed suicide, ignoring the stab wounds.

It is true that the murders stopped. There have been claims since that the killer's identity has been discovered, or at least suspected, but there have been no charges or convincing evidence. The case remains a mystery.

Dr John Bodkin Adams

IN 1956 Fleet Street editors felt that they were on the edge of one of the greatest criminal stories of all time. It seemed that in the respectable seaside resort of Eastbourne a prosperous doctor had been collecting large legacies from wealthy widows whom he had been easing into the next world. The *Daily Mail* suggested that the wills of more than 400 of the doctor's patients were being examined, and anticipated a sensational murder trial.

The doctor in question fitted the role perfectly. Dr John Bodkin Adams was only 1.65 m (5 ft 5in) tall yet weighed 114 kg (18 stone); he was bald, and his fleshy round face supported round spectacles. He was either an old buffoon or, as the *Mail* suggested, a sinister maniac.

Bodkin Adams at times seemed to be his own worst enemy, and helped precipitate rumours into something more serious by his own impetuous and odd notes to coroners. When energetic, 49-year-old 'Bobbie' Hullett died soon after giving him a cheque for £1000 and leaving him a Rolls-Royce, such a note prompted the suspicious coroner to hold three postmortems in an effort to ensure the death was not foul play. The eventual verdict was suicide by means of an overdose of drugs. Twenty years before, a Mrs Whitton had left Adams £3000, at that time a huge sum, and made him her executor, a curious arrangement which led the family to challenge the will, without success. Soon afterwards the doctor received an anonymous note in his mail: 'Keep your fingers crossed and don't bump off any more wealthy widows.'

So many rumours had circulated in Eastbourne over 20 or more years that after Mrs Hullett's death Scotland Yard were asked to investigate, and Superintendent Hallam went to the town. It was

Dr John Bodkin Adams

quickly established that during these years Dr Adams had benefited from 132 wills of his patients to the tune of £45,000. Further, in many cases he had authorized the cremation of the bodies without declaring his interest – thus avoiding an obligatory postmortem. Witnesses were found to attest to a rapid decline of patients after they had made out a will – often with Dr Adams 'guiding their hands'. He was found not to keep a poisons register, as required by law. Superintendent Hallam's final dossier was a thick one. He reported that in his view Adams had killed 14 people in just the previous few years. Adams's case seemed a lost cause, and foreign newspapers, outside the reach of the British libel laws, freely described him as a 'Bluebeard'.

Adams was arrested on 18 December 1956 and charged with the murder in 1950 of Mrs Edith Morrell, who had left Adams a Rolls-Royce and her collection of silver. The crown was given permission to link the deaths of both Mr and Mrs Hullett in 1956 to show systematic poisoning. The prosecution at the committal proceedings explained the pattern: rich patient receives heavy drugging, leading to a fatal final dose; the patient is kept under the influence of the doctor who benefits under the will; his impatience and desire for money is not kept in check. In the event the prosecution decided to keep the Hullett case in reserve and proceed with the Morrell charge.

The trial opened at the Old Bailey on 18 March 1957, with the prosecution led by the Attorney General, the unpopular old Etonian Sir Reginald Manningham-Buller, who was widely known as Bullying-Manner. The basic prosecution case was simple. Mrs Morrell, who was 81, was half-paralysed and irritable, but not in pain. Four nurses attended her round the clock, with Adams always on call. He dosed her with huge amounts of morphia and heroin to make her an addict. He called her solicitor so that she could change her will, and she bequeathed him her Georgian silver. A little later he instructed the solicitor to prepare a codicil in which Mrs Morrell also left him her Rolls-Royce and jewellery, the codicil to be destroyed later if Mrs Morrell did not approve. The solicitor called on Mrs Morrell and she executed the codicil. Adams immediately increased the drugs alarmingly: in her last few days she was in a coma and given massive overdoses.

The prosecution's star witnesses were the nurses who, on Dr Adams's instructions, had helped to deliver the drugs. Nurse Helen Stronach described Mrs Morrell in those last days as 'rambling and semi-conscious'. She referred to injections given by herself and Dr Adams. The defence counsel, Geoffrey Lawrence, asked her in cross-examination if she had kept a written account of events at the time, as was the practice. Nurse Stronach agreed that everything had been entered in a book and signed. She agreed that the book would be absolutely accurate. Lawrence innocently put it to her that if only the records were available they would all know exactly what was given to Mrs Morrell. 'Yes, but you have our word for it,' was the reply.

Lawrence then produced the sort of stroke familiar to all viewers of the television series *Perry Mason*. He produced eight exercise books containing all the nurses' notes for the last months of Mrs Morrell's life; the police had missed them at Adams's home, where they had been behind a desk. Nurse Stronach now had to face her own notes which proved that her memory was utterly at fault regarding the injections. The patient, on a day when evidence had said she had been semi-conscious, had actually eaten a lunch of partridge, with a pudding and brandy to follow. The nurse was also forced to admit that her notes showed that on one occasion the patient had called her a nasty, common woman.

The other nurses fared no better than Nurse Stronach. In their discomfort they made the mistake of discussing their evidence amongst themselves on the train to Eastbourne one morning, contrary to the orders given to all witnesses, and an eavesdropper passed on remarks to Mr Lawrence. Thus Sister Helen Mason-Ellis was forced to admit that Nurse Stronach's testimony that Mrs Morrell's drugs were kept in a locked cupboard was a lie – they had been in an unlocked drawer. On the last evening of Mrs Morrell's life Dr Adams was alleged to have given her a huge injection of heroin, and to have left Nurse Randall a repeat injection which he instructed her to give later. The exercise books showed that no such injection was made. The trial lasted for 13 more days after the nurses' evidence, with points scored by both sides, but in reality the exercise books settled it. The judge pointed out that not all fraudulent rogues were murderers and it took the jury only 44 minutes to bring a verdict of not guilty. The prosecution saw no point in proceeding with its 'reserve' case on the Hullett deaths.

Later Adams pleaded guilty to 14 charges of professional misconduct and was fined £2400 and struck off the medical register. However, he continued his pleasant life in Eastbourne, retaining many of has friends, and in 1961 he was reinstated to the medical register. He won huge libel damages from newspapers who had rashly and too early presumed his guilt. He died in 1982, aged 83, whereupon some of the papers immediately returned to the attack with headlines such as, 'Did this man get away with murder?'

After Adams's death, the prosecution let it be known that they had plenty of evidence against him, and some think that his counsel's decision that he should not go into the witness box himself possibly saved him. He was certainly greedy, and he no doubt 'eased' the last hours of old people. In 1985 his judge, who by then was Lord Devlin, gave his opinion that Adams 'sold' an easy death to his clients.

The Sign of the Zodiac

ON 20 December 1968 a woman driving past a lovers' lane near Vallejo, California, saw what appeared to be bodies near a parked estate car. She drove on and alerted police. The bodies turned out to be of 17-year-old David Faraday, shot in the head near the car, and his girlfriend Bettilou Jensen, shot in the back a few yards off, probably as she tried to run away. There was no sexual interference or robbery, and no other apparent motive for the killings.

On 5 July 1969 the Vallejo police received a call from a man with a gruff voice, who reported a double murder, describing a car in a car park 3 km (2 miles) from where the earlier murder took place. He ended by saying: 'I also killed those kids last year.' Police found 19-year-old Michael Mageau, seriously injured with gunshot wounds, and a 22-year-old waitress, Darlene Ferrin, who was dead. Mageau later told how a car pulled up beside them and a man got out, shone a blinding light at them and began shooting. Mageau provided a description as best he could.

Nearly four weeks later, on 1 August, three evening newspapers received letters from the killer threatening to go on a 'kill rampage' if the letters weren't published that day. Each paper was sent part of a coded message which the murderer said would reveal his identity when put together. The letter was signed with the symbol of the zodiac, a circle with a cross superimposed, so that each arm of the cross breaks the circle. The three papers – the *Vallejo Times-Herald* and two in San Francisco, the *Chronicle* and *Examiner* – printed the letters, and the fragments of code. When the code was cracked the message was found to read:

'I like killing people because it is more fun than killing wild game in the forest because man is the most dangerous animal of all to kill something gives one the most thrilling experience it is even better than getting your rock off with a girl the best part of it is when I die I will be reborn in paradise and all I have killed will become my slaves I will not give you my name because you will try to slow down or stop me collecting slaves for my afterlife.'

The message ended with a jumble of letters. Over a thousand readers offered leads, but all proved fruitless. Then, on 27 September, the gruff voice reported another killing. On the shore of Lake Berryessa police found another couple of students, both stabbed. Bryan Hartnell, aged 20, survived and told how a hooded figure had approached from the trees. On his chest was the zodiac sign. He had a pistol and a knife and said he was an escapee from the Deer Lodge state prison and needed money and their car. It sounded plausible and they allowed him to tie them up with clothesline. Then he said that he was going to have to stab them. He repeatedly stabbed Hartnell in the back, then turned to his companion, 22-year-old Cecilia Shepard, a strikingly beautiful blonde girl. He stabbed her in a frenzy, first in the back and then several times in the stomach, on which he carved a cross with his knife; Cecilia was to die two days later in hospital. Before he left, the killer wrote his sign with a black marker pen on the door of their white car, with the dates of his previous assaults. Hartnell gave police a description of what he could see of his assailant through the hood, but it was not much.

Two weeks later, on 11 October, Zodiac struck again. Two youths saw a taxi pull up in San Francisco and heard a shot. The passenger got out of the back, tore some cloth from the driver's cab, wiped the cab with it, and hurried off when he saw the youths. The driver was 29-year-old student Paul Stine, and he had been shot dead through the head; it was part of his shirt that had been ripped off. The youths were able to give the police the best description yet of Zodiac: 1.72 m (5 ft 8 in) tall, fortyish, with reddish-brown hair in a crew cut and thick horn-rimmed glasses.

Zodiac sent a piece of bloodstained shirt to the San Francisco *Chronicle* with a letter criticizing the inefficiency of the police and threatening to wipe out a school bus next. A few days later, however, he rang the police, offering to give himself up if he could have a famous lawyer and talk on a television show. Police arranged it and lawyer Melvin Belli stood by on the Jim Dunbar morning talk show, which drew a record audience. At 7.41 am a caller with a soft voice identified himself as the Zodiac killer. Those who had heard the gruff voice shook their heads. The caller, who asked to be addressed as 'Sam' rang back 15 times and spoke to Belli, who tried in vain to persuade him to give himself up. When they were off the air, 'Zodiac' arranged to meet Belli, but he failed to keep the appointment, where armed police were on hand. Experts are divided as to whether the caller really was Zodiac.

Just before Christmas, Belli received a letter asking for help from Zodiac (another piece of shirt was enclosed as proof of identity). The letter claimed eight victims and threatened a ninth, causing the San Francisco police urgently to search the files for the missing eighth victim.

There were no more 'official' Zodiac killings after this, but the Los Angeles *Times* received a letter in March 1971 intimating that the total had reached 17 and, amid several hoax letters, the San Francisco police received what seemed a genuine one in 1974 claiming the total was now 37. An officer using a computer and details of unsolved murders found this a possibility, but nothing has been heard of the Zodiac since. Police opinion is that he is dead or perhaps is in a mental institution.

The Babysitter Murders

IT WAS snowing in Bloomfield Township, near Detroit, on the morning of 15 January 1976. Lying by a road was the naked body of Cynthia Cadieux, aged 16, who had disappeared in Roseville the previous day. She had been raped and killed by a blow from a blunt instrument. Her clothing was in a neat pile a few metres from the body, and tracks could be seen where the body had been dragged for some way along the pavement.

Four days later police were investigating an incident in nearby Birmingham, where John McAuliffe had been bound and robbed by an intruder in his house, when they discovered that 14-year-old Sheila Schrock had been raped and shot in her home two blocks away.

Three weeks passed and then 12-year-old Mark Stebbins disappeared in Ferndale. His body was found six days later, on 19 February, in the car park of an office building. He had been sexually assaulted and smothered. An odd point was that his body had been carefully cleaned and manicured before he was laid out in the snow as if in a coffin. It was estimated that the body had been there for a day and a half before discovery.

It was August before the killer made his next strike. A 13-year-old, Jane Allan, disappeared while hitchhiking in Royal Oak, on the outskirts of Detroit. Her body was found in Miamisburg, Ohio, three days later. Three days before Christmas 12-year-old Jill Robinson disappeared, also from Royal Oak. Her body was found on Boxing Day, near Troy, laid out neatly on a bank of snow by the side of a road. She was the victim of a shotgun, and her body had been scrubbed before she died. The similarity between the way that her body and that of Mark Stebbins had been laid out suggested a link in these two killings and awoke the citizens of Oakland County, Michigan, to the fact that a serial child-killer might be at work in their area.

This seemed to be confirmed on 21 January 1977. Kristine Mihelich, aged ten had disappeared in Berkley nearly three weeks previously, and her body was now discovered not far from where Cynthia Cadieux had been found almost exactly a year earlier. She had been suffocated and her body had been washed and laid out in the manner of the two previous victims.

At least three victims now seemed certainly to be linked, and there was a fourth on 23 March, when the body was found of 11-year-old Timothy King, who had disappeared on 11 March in Birmingham. Timothy's mother had pleaded on television for the return of her child, and said she would have his favourite chicken dinner waiting for him. Examination of his body showed that Timothy had indeed been given a chicken dinner by his killer before he had been suffocated. After he died he had been scrubbed and his clothing had been cleaned and pressed.

The care with which the killer treated his victims led the papers to call him the 'Babysitter'. Despite the striking similarities it is not certain that all the deaths were linked, since there were variations in the circumstances – the use of the shotgun, for example, and the fact that some were sexually assaulted and others not. After the discovery of the last body, an open letter to the killer from a psychiatrist inviting him to seek help was published in the newspapers. One caller phoned with the message, 'You'd better hope it doesn't snow any more', thus emphasizing another link between some of the crimes. Another caller who wrote and telephoned often claimed to be the roommate of the killer, a Vietnam veteran with a grudge against soft-living well-off Americans.

When the snow returned late in 1977 the frightened citizens of Oakland County were at their most vigilant, but the Babysitter did not strike again.

The Ann Arbor Hospital Murders

IN THE summer of 1975 the administrators of Ann Arbor Veterans Administration Hospital in Michigan, USA, were forced to admit that there was a killer loose on the wards. On 15 August the FBI was called in to investigate the astonishing number of respiratory arrests occurring over the past few weeks, for no apparent reason. Since 1 July there had been 56, while the usual number for that period would have been between eight and ten.

The majority of the unexpected breathing failures occurred on the 3 pm to 11 pm shift and though most of them were in the intensive care unit, some patients suffering arrests had undergone only minor surgery and were otherwise regarded as fit and healthy. In the first four weeks of July there were 22 breathing failures, on 28 July alone there were three and after that the number went on rising steadily. On the nightmare night of 12 August there were eight respiratory arrests between 6 pm and 9 pm. Prompt intervention by nursing staff saved all but one patient, an elderly man who was recovering from an operation for a broken hip. Internal investigations indicated that the victims had been given a dose of the muscle relaxant Pavulon, a drug derived from the South American poison curare and normally used before surgery. As no needle marks were found on the patient's arms it seemed likely that it was being added to the intravenous drips.

The doctors still hesitated over calling in outside help but when one of the patients, a 49-year-old man who had suffered two respiratory arrests since undergoing open heart surgery, confided that a Filipino nurse called Filipina Narcissco had left the room immediately before one of his attacks, it was obvious that action must be taken and taken quickly.

The last two surprise respiratory arrests happened on the day the FBI arrived. A fortnight later one of the patients who had suffered three arrests died, probably from the delayed effects of his breathing problems. Two more of the victims died on 29 August. In all, the deaths of eight patients were probably caused by induced respiratory arrests. The hospital was closed to all but emergency admissions.

The FBI agents questioned every patient in the hospital and as a result of their enquiries two experienced Filipino nurses, 30-year-old Filipina Narcissco and 31-year-old Leonora Perez, came under suspicion. No one could suggest any reason why they should want to injure patients, but they had been on duty in the vicinity of victims shortly before the respiratory arrests took place. Both were transferred to non-nursing duties, Miss Narcissco at the same hospital and Mrs Perez to a Veterans Administration hospital in Detroit. Steps were also taken to make sure that Pavulon could only be obtained on an anaesthetist's authority.

Psychiatrists who worked on the case to compile a profile of the killer decided that he, or she, must have a grudge against the hospital or the medical profession in general and, perhaps, wanted to bring about such a lack of confidence in the hospital that it would be forced to close. There were fears at one time that this might happen, but once the doors were open again the excellent reputation of the hospital soon reasserted itself. Some psychiatrists favoured the theory that the killer might be a Vietnam veteran who was trying to draw attention to the plight of ex-soldiers who were poorly treated by their country; others thought it more likely to be a nurse with a hatred of men in general and her medical superiors in particular.

The long-running investigation turned up little in the way of hard evidence. In 1976 a former supervisor of the hospital committed suicide after writing a letter confessing responsibility for the deaths but she had been in a mental hospital for some time, suffering from acute depression and hallucinations as well as terminal cancer, and the confession was discounted because of her state of mind. At the end of the day, the prime suspects were still Miss Narcissco and Mrs Perez and they went on trial in March 1977 on eight charges including murder, poisoning and conspiracy.

The prosecution called a number of patients and relations to testify that they had seen one or other of the nurses in the patients' rooms at or near the time of the respiratory arrests and made much of the fact that from the moment the nurses had been transferred to other duties, not a single unexpected seizure had been reported. However, they could produce no evidence to link either woman with the unauthorized use of Pavulon and no witness who had seen either of them tampering with the intravenous lines.

Halfway through the trial the murder charge against Perez was dismissed on instructions from the judge and after 13 weeks of evidence Narcissco was found not guilty of murder, though both nurses were convicted of poisoning and conspiracy. Both were freed on bonds of $70,000 each while appeals were lodged and both were ordered to undergo psychiatric testing before sentence was decided. The convictions were set aside on appeal and a new trial was ordered; meanwhile the psychiatric testing showed that the behaviour patterns of both women were normal. A second trial took place in February 1978 and all charges were dismissed. The mystery of the Ann Arbor killings remains unsolved.

Jack the Stripper

On 2 February 1964 the body of a prostitute, Hannah Tailford, was found in the water by Hammersmith Reach on the Thames. She was naked except for her rolled-down stockings, and fabric from her briefs was stuffed in her mouth. An open verdict was recorded, although murder was the probability.

On 9 April the naked body of another prostitute, Irene Lockwood, was found only 270 m (300 yd) from the first, tangled among weeds by Dukes Meadow. Neither the clothes nor the handbags of either girl could be found, and the police faced the possibility that a cunning serial killer had begun work. They recalled the death of another prostitute, Gwynneth Rees, whose body was found by the Thames in November 1963, and wondered if her death could be linked with the other two.

There was little doubt that a serial killer was operating when the body of Helen Barthelemy, another prostitute, was found dumped on garden rubbish in an alley in Brentford on 24 April. She had been stripped and had had three teeth removed after her death. Tyre marks suggested she had been murdered elsewhere and her body brought to the alleyway. Three days later Kenneth Archibald, a caretaker at Holland Park Tennis Club who lived at Hammersmith, confessed in Notting Hill police station to the murder of Irene Lockwood. However, at his trial in June he withdrew his confession and was acquitted.

Meanwhile, in May, examination of Barthelemy's body proved fruitful. Traces of paint spray of various colours were found, suggesting that the body had been kept in the spray shop of a factory using many colours. Commander Hatherill, head of the CID, appealed for prostitutes to come forward in absolute secrecy to help the police

Bridie O'Hara, the last victim of Jack the Stripper

catch the killer. By now the papers had seized on the story of a maniac sex killer, and the name of 'Jack the Stripper' was coined. The response from prostitutes was good but, on 14 July, the killer struck again.

At 5.30 that morning painters working all night had heard a van door shut and seen a man standing by a van in a cul-de-sac. The man drove out of the cul-de-sac so fast he nearly collided with a car in Acton Lane whose incensed driver informed the police. Shortly afterwards the naked body of prostitute Mary Fleming was found sitting against a wall outside the garage door of the end house in the cul-de-sac. She had been missing for three days and the same paint was found on her body. Unfortunately, the irate car driver had not been able to take the number of the van.

On 25 November the naked body of prostitute Margaret McGowan was found hidden by rubble in a car park near Kensington High Street. It had been there a week and she had died much earlier than that. A tooth was missing, and the paint was present.

The final known victim of Jack the Stripper was Bridie O'Hara, whose bright red toenails were noticed by a man walking to work along Westfield Road, Acton, on 16 February 1965. Her naked body was lying on bracken behind a store shed, and was partly mummified, suggesting it had been kept where it might have dried out.

Detective Chief Superintendent John Du Rose, head of the Yard's murder squad, was now put in charge of the hunt, with a 300-strong special patrol group reporting to him. They were helped by 200 CID officers and 100 uniformed police. Various facts suggested a possible picture of the killer and his operation. All the murdered prostitutes were small, between 1.52 m (5 ft) and 1.6 m (5 ft 3 in) suggesting the killer might be a small man. They were picked up in the Notting Hill area, probably between 11 am and 1 pm. Most had had teeth removed and semen was found in the throat, suggesting that the killer had insisted on fellatio and after death had performed further acts of oral sex on the body after removing the teeth. The bodies were stripped and kept at a paint-spray shop before being dumped by van in the early morning near the Thames. The killer was probably a night-worker.

The biggest find the hours of police checking produced was a disused warehouse by a paint-spray shop on the Heron Factory Estate, Acton. Globules of paint exactly matched those on the bodies. Du Rose decided to frighten the killer by hinting to the press that the number of suspects was diminishing – he finally reduced it to three – and that an arrest was approaching.

Then suddenly the murders stopped, and gradually the police operation was wound down, public interest faded and there were rumours that the police knew the identity of Jack the Stripper.

Du Rose told the rest of the story on his retirement in 1970. In March 1965 an unmarried man committed suicide in South London, leaving a note saying he was 'unable to stand the strain any longer'. The man was a security guard on the Heron Factory Estate, and his hours fitted in with police theories about the Stripper. There was other circumstantial evidence to suggest the hunt had ended. Du Rose stated in 1970 that the man, whose identity was not revealed, was indeed the Stripper.

Bible John

GLASGOW'S Barrowland dance hall was very popular in the late 1960s, particularly for its Thursday 'Over-25s' night, when the dating was necessarily more furtive since many patrons were without their spouses and used false names.

On such a Thursday, on 22 February 1968, 25-year-old Patricia Docker, separated and with a son, went out dancing and didn't return to her parents' home. Next morning her naked body was found outside a lock-up garage; she had been strangled. Her handbag was missing and her body was not identified until Friday evening. She had said she was going to the Majestic ballroom, and police enquiries therefore started in the wrong place. No one amoung the clientele who were eventually questioned at the Barrowland was prepared to say anything at all.

Over a year later, another mother from a single-parent family, 32-year-old Jemima McDonald – a regular at the Thursday night Barrowland dances – failed to return home from a Saturday night dance. She wasn't missed at first, and her sister, Mrs Margaret O'Brien, only became worried when she was still not home on Monday morning. On the Sunday Mrs O'Brien had heard children talking of a body where they played in derelict flats nearby – childish chatter which nobody had taken notice of. She decided to search, and found her sister's partly clothed body. Jemima had been strangled with her own tights.

Police linked the deaths of the two women because of the Barrowland connection, the strangling and, despite a huge search by corporation dustmen, the disappearance of their handbags. There was another link, which might be coincidence – both women were menstruating when they died.

This time police did better with clues, as Jemima had been seen with a man both outside the dance hall and later near her home. An artist's impression of a man was shown on Scottish television and published in the papers. He was aged 25–35, between 1.82 m (6 ft) and 1.88 m (6 ft 2 in), slim, neatly dressed, and with fair, reddish hair worn in a then unfashionable style for the Barrowland, neat and short. However, nothing came of the police enquiries, and, in October the police stopped their surveillance at the Barrowland – which, to the disgust of the management, had caused attendances to drop dramatically.

It was an unfortunate decision. On 30 October 29-year-old Helen Puttock went dancing there, as she often did, with her sister Jeannie Williams who lived nearby. Helen's husband, George, was happy to babysit, and he gave the two women the cab-fare home, as the buses would not be running. They met two other girlfriends as arranged, and had a few drinks before entering the dance hall around 10 pm. Jeannie soon met a man, John from Castlemilk, who was as good a dancer as herself, and they stayed together all evening. Helen also met a man called John, and the couples made a foursome for the night. Soon after 11.30 pm the dancing ended and the four went to a cab rank where Jeannie's partner, whom she suspected was married, left them to catch a bus. The two girls and John took a cab.

Jeannie sensed that John was not happy with her playing gooseberry, and he insisted she be dropped off first. It was the last she saw of her sister alive. Early next morning a neighbour found Helen's body at the back of a tenement block. She had been strangled with one of her stockings and her handbag was missing. While police were still trying to establish who she could be, George Puttock, who had seen the activity from his flat just up the road, arrived to tell them his wife hadn't come home. He had assumed she was at her sister's, but when he was shown the body he immediately identified it. There was one other fact to link this death with the others. Helen Puttock also was menstruating and, although she was fully clothed, her sanitary pad had been removed and tucked under her armpit. Was the killer a man who killed in rage at being denied sex because his intended partner was at the 'wrong time of the month'? Or was he a peculiar sexual deviate? Or was it just an odd coincidence?

Jeannie Williams was an observant woman with a good memory and she provided police with plenty of clues. John didn't drink. He was tall, about 1.78 m (5 ft 10 in), and aged between 25 and 35. His short, sandy, reddish hair was neatly cut and rounded at the back. He had a tooth missing, and one front tooth slightly overlapped the other. She helped in the drawing of an identikit picture.

John had been so polite, well-mannered and soft-spoken in the dance hall – even pulling out a chair for his partner to sit down – that he stood out from the usual clientele. In the taxi, however, his chivalry had vanished, and he was broody and aloof. He spoke of the 'adulterous' women at the dance halls, places which his father had told him were dens of iniquity. He said he prayed rather than drank at Hogmanay, and talked a lot about the Bible and its laws, and about the woman taken in adultery who was stoned. When these facts were publicized, the man immediately became tagged by the papers as 'Bible John'. When Jeannie saw the drawing of the Jemima McDonald suspect, she immediately recognized the likeness.

The police also had a clue in that a passenger had seen what was probably the killer on a night service bus at about 2 am, and had remembered where he alighted. But despite many calls from the public, hundreds of police visits to hairdressers and dentists and a half-hour BBC documentary on the case in 1970, 'Bible John' was never found.

The Monster of Florence

EVERY summer tourists flock to Florence, one of the cultural centres of Italy and indeed the world. The countryside around also has its attractions, especially in the summer, and is popular with hikers, nature-lovers and courting couples. Since 1968 it has also gained a reputation as the territory of a sadistic killer, who seemed to settle into a routine which required the annual sacrifice of a loving couple to keep him happy.

On 21 August 1968 Barbara Locci and her lover Antonio lo Bianco were shot dead as they lay together on the front seats of their car, parked in a lovers' lane. The woman's six-year-old son was in the back of the car and seemed to have slept throughout, suggesting that the murderer used a silencer. Perhaps the killer noticed the boy for the first time after he had committed the crime, and crept away. The woman's husband was arrested, charged with murder, and convicted. Sentenced to 13 years' imprisonment in 1970, the poor man had to wait another four years before the murderer struck again and proved his innocence.

It was on 14 September 1974 when the second couple were killed, again in their parked car. Forensic tests showed the same .22-calibre Beretta pistol had been used as in the first killing; the distinctive copper-jacketed bullets were manufactured in Australia during the 1950s. The bodies were naked and the female victim, Carmela de Nuccio, had had her genitals removed by a scalpel.

There was another long break, and then the killer struck twice in 1981. On 6 June the female victim, Stefani Pettini, was stabbed more than 300 times and was violated with a stalk from a grape vine, and on 23 October Susanna Cambi had her genitals removed.

From 1981 the killer found victims each year to 1985, all within 32 km (20 miles) of Florence. His established method was to approach a couple in a car, always on a moonless night between the hours of 10 pm and midnight. The man was shot first and then the woman, on whose body he practised his sadism, mutilating the body with his scalpel. From 1984 this mutilation included the removal of the left breast, as well as the genitals. No fingerprints were ever found, and it was suspected that the killer used surgical rubber gloves. The killer probably made a mistake in 1983, when two homosexual West German men were shot while sleeping in a van. Perhaps the fact that one had long blond hair misled him.

The newspapers, who as usual needed a convenient label for the attacker, called him the 'Monster of Florence'. All the murders occurred in the holiday season from June to October, with the first two weeks in September being the favourite time.

On 8 September 1985 a French couple who were touring with a tent were murdered. The woman's body had suffered over 100 slashes, with the genitalia and left breast removed. This time one of the familiar cooper-jacketed bullets was found outside a nearby hospital. Coupling this fact with the killer's use of a scalpel and possibly surgical gloves, the police made a through investigation of the hospital staff. It provided no more results than anything else, and the police seemed to be mocked when an envelope was delivered to them. The address had been formed with letters cut from a newspaper to prevent discovery of the sender, and it contained a part of the genitalia of the murdered woman. However, this was the last of these distinctive killings.

Belle Gunness

BELLE GUNNESS, a personable Norwegian widow living in La Porte, Indiana, USA had a novel way of attracting the victims she killed for their money: she advertised. Her carefully worded advertisements, carried in selected local papers circulated in areas where numbers of Scandinavian immigrants had settled, were tempting, though the wary might have taken warning from the emphasis on money. One read:

> Wanted – A woman who owns a beautifully located and valuable farm in first-class condition wants a good and reliable man as partner in the same. Some little cash is required for which will be furnished first-class security.

And another:

> Personal – Comely widow, who owns large farm in one of the finest districts of La Porte County, Indiana, desires to make the acquaintance of a gentleman unusually well provided, with a view to joining fortunes. No replies by letter will be considered unless the sender is willing to follow an answer with a personal visit.

A stream of men arrived at Belle's door, impressed to find that the farm was so well-kept and charmed by the large blonde with clear blue eyes who could lay on a delicious meal and was not averse to a kiss and a cuddle. The townsfolk occasionally remarked that Belle's visitors never seemed to stay for long but she explained that they were acquaintances from the old country, men who had to return to their homes and families. In fact, few of them ever left.

On the night of 27 April 1908, the farmhouse caught fire and by morning the building was completely gutted. When a party of townsfolk, under the supervision of two local deputies, began searching the charred ruin they found the remains of Belle's three children, 11-year-old Myrtle, 9-year-old Lucy and 5-year-old Philip. Nearby was the body of a woman without a head. The authorities decided that all four had been killed before the fire started and the most likely perpetrator was a labourer named Ray Lamphere, who had been seen nearby at the time the fire started. He had once worked for Belle and there had been talk of a more intimate relationship, but then there had been a complete split; at one point Belle had prosecuted him for trespassing and made other spiteful allegations. Lamphere had often hinted that he 'had enough' on Belle to keep her under his thumb but his listeners could only guess at what he meant. Belle had always been independent and no one knew much about her affairs.

Belle had arrived in America in 1883, joining her sister and brother-in-law in Chicago. Within a year she had married Mads Sorenson, a security guard. Financially they never did more than scrape by and the first time Belle had money to spend was after her husband died – suddenly, with convulsions that could well have been due to poison – when she benefited from two handsome insurance policies. With her two daughters Myrtle and Lucy and her foster-daughter Jenny, she moved to the farm at La Porte. She married a widower, Peter Gunness, who died nine months later when, according to Belle, a sausage grinder fell on him from a great height. He, too, was well insured. For a while after that she ran the farm with the help of a succession of hired men. One of them was Ray Lamphere, who shared her bed for a time but was given his marching orders when the well-dressed strangers began arriving for brief visits.

One of the visitors was Andrew Helgelein from South Dakota, who had corresponded with the understanding Scandinavian widow for 16 months before setting off to meet her at last. In December 1907 she had written to him:

'To the dearest friend in all the world – I know you have now only to

Belle Gunness

come to me and be my own. The king will be no happier than you when you get here. As for the queen, her joy will be small when compared with mine. You will love my farm, sweetheart. In all La Porte county, there's none will compare with it. It is on a nice green slope near two lakes. When I hear your name mentioned, my heart beats in wild rapture for you. My Andrew, I love you!

'Be sure and bring the three thousand dollars you are going to invest in the farm with you and, for safety's sake, sew them up in your clothes, dearest.'

The last time Andrew Helgelein was seen was when Belle drove him towards the farm in her pony and trap. When his brother Axel began to make enquiries about him Belle insisted that he had left her home happy and never returned, leaving her grief-stricken. If only Axel would sell all his brother's possessions and bring plenty of money they could mount a search together. Axel, less credulous than his brother, left his money safely behind but came to investigate. He arrived to find men sifting through the remains of the farmhouse in search of anything that could identify the dead woman as Belle. As they began digging in the yard they found Andrew, his limbs and head hacked from his torso and the pieces neatly wrapped in sacking. The diggers redoubled their efforts, unearthing the remains of four people under the rubbish dump and several more in the chicken pen. Most had been cut into pieces and sprinkled with quicklime so that there was little left to identify but one body was that of Belle's foster-daughter Jenny, who was supposed to have left home 18 months before at the age of 16.

As reports of the finds were published, the relatives of missing men began arriving in the town, all telling a similar story: their brothers, sons or fathers had journeyed to Indiana to marry a rich widow. The bodies of 10 men were recovered but when all the reports were in, another dozen were still unaccounted for. John Moo, a farmer from Wisconsin last seen drawing $1100 dollars from the bank, and Tonnes Peter Lien, who had sold his farm in Minnesota and brought with him

$1000, were both identified by their watches; Olaf Lindboe, who had arrived at the bank in the company of Belle to draw out $1800, was identified by his teeth. The others were thought to include George Berry, who travelled with $1500, Christian Hinkley with $2000 and Herman Konitzer with $5000.

It was estimated that Belle had netted herself at least $30,000 but the balance in her bank account was modest, leading many people to believe that Belle, far from dying in the fire, was enjoying her ill-gotten gains on her travels. The head belonging to the burnt corpse had never been found (though a section of Belle's bridgework had been recovered from the ashes), and the body itself seemed too small for Belle's large bulk. Belle had been seen driving to the farm with a smaller companion the day before the fire and, given her past history, it would have been easy enough for Belle to kill an unknown woman along with the children and render her unidentifiable by removing her head. Then she could have decamped with her money, charging Lamphere to set the fire and leaving behind her false teeth to allay suspicion. The doubts cast on Belle's death were enough to acquit Lamphere on the murder charge, though he was found guilty of arson and sentenced to 20 years in prison. From his cell, he always insisted that Belle was still alive. After his death the prison chaplain revealed that Lamphere had confessed to chloroforming Belle's three children and setting fire to the house while she made her escape. However, by this time he had told several different stories and it is impossible to know whether he was telling the truth.

Dorothea Waddingham

WHEN Dorothea Waddingham decided to call herself Nurse Waddingham and open a nursing home for 'aged and chronic cases' she may have only had an eye to a lucrative business which would bring in far more money than her menial job. However, she soon became greedy and decided that disposing of her patients would bring better returns. Dorothea had never been too particular about how she obtained what she wanted – in the past she had twice been given probation by the English courts for false pretences and she had served a three-month prison term for theft. She was a thin, dour woman with a far from winning personality and it is difficult to see why anyone would put themselves in her care, but presumably she could be persuasive when she chose.

She never obtained any nursing qualifications but she had worked as a ward maid in a workhouse infirmary, so she had a good idea of how nurses worked and could put on a convincing performance. When her husband, Tom Leech, died leaving her almost penniless, she fixed her eye on his easy-going friend, Ronald Sullivan, who had his own house in Devon Drive, Nottingham. She convinced him that she had all the expertise necessary to run a nursing home which would bring in a good income for both of them. Reverting to her married name, she advertised for patients who could look forward to care from an 'unregistered nurse'.

In January 1935 89-year-old Mrs Baguley saw the advertisement and decided that the nursing home might be just what she needed. She had been caring alone for her daughter Ada, who was 52 and suffering from disseminated sclerosis, but Ada was now confined to a wheelchair and Mrs Baguley was too frail to look after her properly.

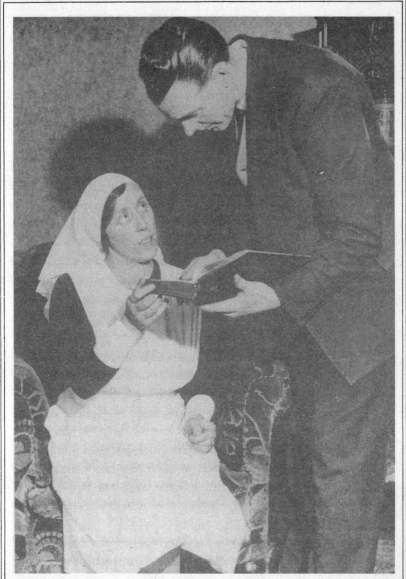

Dorothea Waddingham giving instructions for the day to Ronald Sullivan at the nursing home in Devon Drive, Nottingham

Dorothea, now Nurse Waddingham, agreed to take both women for the sum of £3 a week, which was the most they could afford. Dorothea's only other patient, Mrs Kemp, had died so she needed the money – but she soon found that looking after Ada was hard work, for the latter was a large, fat woman, scarcely able to move by herself. However, she put herself out to satisfy the Baguleys and must have succeeded, for on 6 May Ada made out a new will revoking a previous will in which she left her £1600 to her relatives and leaving it instead to Dorothea Waddingham and Ronald Sullivan. In return, the weekly payments would cease and the Baguleys would be looked after for the rest of their lives. It must have seemed like an advantageous arrangement to Ada and her mother at the time but in signing the will, Ada was signing their death warrants.

Little over a week later Mrs Baguley breathed her last, but there was no reason for the doctor to suspect that it was anything but the natural death of a very old lady. Four months later Ada died quite suddenly but again the doctor was quite happy and had no hesitation in issuing a death certificate, giving the cause of death as cerebral haemorrhage. Dorothea, anxious for a cremation to be arranged as soon as possible, dispatched to the medical officer in health a note (supposedly written by Ada and witnessed by Sullivan), expressing Ada's desire to be cremated and requesting that 'my relatives shall not know of my death'. It was never certain whether the letter was forged or obtained by Dorothea from the helpless Ada, but the last sentence was enough to ring alarm bells. Moreover, Dorothea made the mistake of giving her address as 'The Nursing Home, 32 Devon Drive' and Dr Cyril Banks, the health officer, knew that no nursing home was registered at that address.

Dr Banks contacted the coroner and a postmortem was ordered. It showed that there was no question of a cerebral haemorrhage; Ada had died from an overdose of morphine. When Mrs Baguley's body was exhumed sufficient traces of morphine were found to suggest that she had died in the same way. 'Nurse' Waddingham and Ronald

Sullivan were both charged with murder but Sullivan was discharged for lack of evidence at the beginning of the trial, leaving Dorothea alone to face the charge of murder.

Her defence was that she had only given her patient medicine as intimated by the doctor and that he had prescribed morphine for Ada, who was suffering from severe stomach pain, in five doses of two tablets at a time. Dr Manfield, who had attended the residents in Devon Drive, said that he had prescribed morphine for Dorothea's patients in the past but that Ada had never been in sufficient pain to warrant its use. She was found guilty but, for some unaccountable reason, the jury added a strong recommendation for mercy. This was disregarded by the judicial authorities. Dorothea's appeal was turned down and she was hanged at Winson Green prison, Birmingham, on 16 April 1936.

The Baby Farmers

THE NOTORIOUS baby farmers of the late 19th century plied a revolting trade. These women took illegitimate or unwanted babies for a fee, promising to provide foster care or find new homes. Then they quietly 'disposed' of the infants. Their terrible business was permitted by almost non-existent child protection laws in England at the time and encouraged by a moral code that left unmarried mothers as the outcasts of society.

The grim work of Amelia Elizabeth Dyer came to light in 1896, when she had already killed an unknown number of children. One day in March a bargeman hauled a brown paper parcel out of the Thames near Caversham. As the wet paper fell away, he found that he was holding the body of a baby girl. She had been strangled with a bootlace, which was still around her neck. A few days later a carpet bag was fished out of the river near Reading and this time there were two murdered infants inside. A search of the river bed turned up several tiny bodies, in various stages of decomposition.

The first find had yielded an important clue, for one of the layers of brown paper bore the name and address of a Mrs Harding. Though Mrs Harding had moved from that address, neighbours revealed that she was always taking foster children and she was soon traced to a house where she had been living with her daughter and son-in-law, Polly and Arthur Palmer. The police set a trap, whereby a young woman posed as an unmarried mother wanting her baby adopted. She met Mrs Harding, a fat, elderly woman with an ingratiating manner, who agreed to take the imaginary child for £100 with a guarantee of no further problems for the mother. Instead of receiving the expected child she received a visit from a police inspector and his sergeant, who found a pile of baby clothes in a cupboard under the stairs, together with an unpleasant smell, which led them to believe that a decomposing body had been left there for some time. Mrs Harding, when questioned, admitted that her real name was Amelia Elizabeth Dyer.

Meanwhile, some of the dead infants had been identified and linked to Amelia Dyer. Evelina Marmon was a barmaid in Cheltenham, Gloucestershire, who had found it impossible to look after her illegitimate baby and keep her job. Consequently, she had answered a newspaper advertisement offering a caring home in return for a small payment. She was contacted by Amelia, posing as Mrs Harding, who said that she was thrilled at the idea of having 'a dear little baby girl' to bring up as her own. She assured Evelina that 'a child with me will have a good home and a mother's loving care'. On 31 March Evelina handed over baby Doris to her new 'mother', along with a payment of £10, and saw them off at Cheltenham railway station. Doris was one of the infants found in the waterlogged carpet bag with a knotted bootlace round her throat. Another of the bodies recovered from the river was that of Elizabeth Goulding's 10-month-old baby, who had been left with Amelia and a young man matching the description of Arthur Palmer.

Amelia had made a good business out of baby farming, always charging £10 or more for taking a baby and seldom keeping the child more than 24 hours. She operated under several names and from various addresses, always moving on before neighbours became suspicious or a parent started making enquiries about the welfare of a particular child. She had spent several short spells in lunatic asylums but it was suggested that sometimes she found this a convenient way of avoiding detection, knowing that she could demonstrate her sanity as soon as she was ready to resume her calling once more.

While awaiting trial, Amelia tried twice to kill herself, once with scissors and once with bootlaces, but she found suicide more difficult than killing babies and she was revived each time. Arthur Palmer was charged along with her but at the last moment Amelia wrote a confession in which she declared that, though her own days were numbered, she could not bear the thought of 'drawing innocent people into trouble' and that Arthur knew nothing of her crimes and had nothing to do with her wickedness. The authorities accepted her statement and released him.

The only possible defence was insanity and doctors testified that she suffered from extreme depression and delusions and was not responsible for her actions. For the prosecution, an eminent specialist in mental illness considered that there was no evidence of insanity and Dr James Scott, the medical officer of Holloway Prison, where he had seen Amelia on a daily basis, gave his opinion that her so-called delusions were all pretence. The jury rejected the plea of insanity and the judge, sentencing Amelia to hang, voiced the pious hope that the Lord would show more mercy to her than she had shown 'to these poor, innocent, unprotected infants'.

In 1902 another thriving baby-farming business was discovered. Amelia Sach, a personable 29-year-old redhead who ran a discreet nursing home in East Finchley, London, and Annie Walters, aged 54 and a great deal less personable, had a cosy little arrangement between them. Mrs Sach advertised her nursing services to expectant mothers with the tempting extra offer 'Baby can remain', thus attracting many young women desperate to leave the consequences of their little indiscretion behind and avoid the disgrace of admitting to an illegitimate baby. Whenever one of these young women gave birth Mrs Sach contacted Annie, who had lodgings in Islington, and Annie took away the baby.

Annie, who lodged with a policeman's family, told her landlady that she acted as a short-term foster mother, arranging suitable adoptions for the babies placed with her. She spoke so warmly of her charges and put up such a good pretence of doting on her 'little darlings' that her landlady was taken in for a while. However, she began to watch her lodger more closely after Annie, called away unexpectedly to collect another child, asked her to mind a baby girl for an hour, during which time the baby needed a nappy change and turned out to be a boy. At the same time, the landlady's policeman husband had begun to wonder about the speed with which Annie seemed able to arrange adoptions. No prospective parents ever came to the house, yet every baby disappeared with amazing rapidity. If questioned, Annie told highly coloured tales of the wealthy families with whom she placed the babies, handing them over to fine ladies in luxurious carriages, en route for their country estates.

On 15 November, a Miss Galley gave birth to a boy in Mrs Sach's nursing home and paid £25 to have the child adopted. Later that day, Annie Walters arrived to collect the baby and her share of the payment. The baby remained with her for two days, then on the third morning she was seen leaving the house carrying a well-wrapped bundle. This time she was followed and caught trying to dispose of the Galley baby's body. Among her baby-feeding equipment was found a supply of deadly chlorodyne, suggesting that the babies had met their end quickly once in the hands of their kindly foster-mother. Annie denied everything, repeating stories of rich but nameless adoptive parents and claiming that she had only used chlorodyne to keep her charges quiet, so that they would not disturb the household – but the more she talked, the more unlikely her story sounded.

She soon led the police to Mrs Sach of the Claymore House Nursing Home, who said that her only contact with Annie was when she had employed her for domestic work; there was no question of her being allowed to remove any babies from the nursing home. Her listeners remained unconvinced: it seemed far more likely that Mrs Sach was the brains behind the lucrative operation and that, though she might never have enquired about the method of disposing of the babies, she knew full well that they were going to their death.

The women went on trial before Mr Justice Darling at the Old Bailey on 15 January 1903. Both were sentenced to death and hanged at Holloway Prison less than three weeks later.

Euphrasie Mercier

IN THE spring of 1883 Elodie Ménétret confided in a neighbour that she was a little scared of her new companion, Euphrasie Mercier. She had known Euphrasie for a short time before engaging her, as she had been a customer in Euphrasie's shoe shop. The business had been failing fast and Euphrasie, who was nearing 60, had been looking for another job; meanwhile Elodie was feeling lonely and nervous, alone in her house near Paris. The arrangement had seemed perfect for both of them at the time but Elodie now felt she had made a mistake. She had asked Euphrasie to leave but her companion had flatly refused.

Following that conversation, the neighbour never saw Elodie again. When she enquired about her, Euphrasie told her that her employer had entered a convent and did not wish anyone to know the place chosen for her retreat. She told the same story to Elodie's family, adding significantly 'She is dead to the world.' A week later, Euphrasie made a trip to Luxembourg and went to a lawyer, introducing herself as Elodie Ménétret and saying that she had moved to Luxembourg and wanted to draw up a power of attorney in favour of her friend Euphrasie Mercier, who would be looking after her affairs in France. When she was told that two witnesses had to swear to her identity she brought in two strangers from the street and bribed them to vouch for her.

Back in France, she lost no time in installing her three sisters in the house: all of them were mentally deranged, suffering from religious mania, and she had been looking after them for years. The household remained undisturbed until 1885 when Alphonse Chateauneuf, son of one of the unbalanced sisters, moved in. Euphrasie doted on her shiftless nephew, who was too self-centred to return her devotion.

From the beginning, Alphonse sensed that his aunt had a guilty secret. When he questioned her about Elodie her answers were evasive and he found the story of her employer suddenly vanishing into a convent without a word to anyone unconvincing, to say the least. Then there was his aunt's extraordinary behaviour. More than once he saw her throw open the window and cry out 'Back, phantoms of the garden!' or 'Rest in peace, family of Ménétret!' At first he wondered if she was going the same way as her sisters but her strange obsession over the dahlia bed convinced him that her worries were not imaginary. The gardener was not allowed to touch that particular part of the garden and Euphrasie kept a close watch on it, making sure that she could see it from the dining table or from her armchair. Once, when a stray dog got into the garden and started digging in the dahlia bed, she ran out of the house screaming hysterically and belabouring it with her hoe.

Alphonse listened, too, to the strange mutterings of his mother and her two mad sisters who were always talking about the dead coming to life and 'misfortune' coming from the garden. He scoured the house for clues and eventually came up with the theory that Euphrasie had murdered Elodie, burned her body, then buried the remains in the dahlia bed. It was at this time that Alphonse asked his aunt for a substantial loan. When she turned him down he threatened to reveal a family secret, but still she refused. He then wrote to the police, outlining his suspicions and enclosing a plan of the garden, and to Elodie's uncle, claiming that she had been murdered by his aunt and even identifying the room in which the killing had taken place.

When the police dug up the dahlia bed they found charred human bones as well as several teeth. One of them had been filled with gold and was identified by Elodie's dentist as his work. A botanical expert was brought in to examine the bulbs and he concluded that they had been disturbed in the spring of 1883, at about the time of Elodie's disappearance. In the chimney of one of the bedrooms there was a greasy substance of the kind found in restaurant chimneys where meat had been cooked.

Though it was not possible to conclude how Elodie had met her death, Euphrasie was charged with murder and put on trial in April 1886. Alphonse, her beloved nephew, testified against her and a sad collection of her dead friend's bones stood in a jar on the courtroom table. She still insisted that Elodie was alive and living in a convent and, when she was told that investigators had contacted every religious house in the country and none of them had ever heard of Elodie, she countered by saying that the confusion could have arisen because her friend had changed convents frequently and that she had seen her several times. She said that the house had been bought with her money, not Elodie's, and she had nothing to gain from her death.

Euphrasie failed to convince the court and was sentenced to 20 years' imprisonment which, at her age, was to be a genuine life sentence. Alphonse, having failed to raise his loan, managed to make money out of her downfall by selling his account of the murder.

Barbara Graham

BARBARA GRAHAM'S path to the gas chamber of San Quentin began in childhood. When she was two years old her teenage mother was sent to a reformatory and she was left in the care of neighbours. A difficult and unhappy child, she was judged incorrigible at the age of nine and packed off to the same reformatory as her mother.

She married the first of four husbands in 1941 and subsequently had three children. She gathered convictions for vagrancy, disorderly conduct and prostitution and by 1947 was one of the call girls employed by Sally Stanford, San Francisco's most notorious madam. Her fourth husband, Harry Graham, introduced her to drugs and she became involved with a group of criminals headed by Jack Santos.

The Santos gang was made up of robbers who were ready to commit murder whenever it seemed expedient: in 1951 they tortured and robbed gold buyer Andrew Colner and his wife and in 1952 they murdered a gold miner, then a grocer and his two children. Barbara Graham could only be linked with certainty to the murder in 1953 of Mabel Monahan, a 63-year-old cripple who was reputed to keep a lot of valuable jewellery in her home.

The plan was for Barbara to trick her way into the widow's home by pretending an emergency and asking to use the phone. Then her three companions would crowd in, overpower Mrs Monahan and ransack the house. According to John True, a gang member who later turned state's evidence to convict Barbara, the idea was to leave the elderly woman unharmed – though on the past evidence of the gang's methods, this could be doubted. In fact, Barbara lost her temper and hit Mrs Monahan over the head with her gun butt. As the woman fell to the floor, crying 'Oh, no, no, no!', one of the men egged Barbara on, urging: 'Give her more.' Barbara seized the woman's hair and laid about her again, cracking her skull. After that the gang turned the house upside down in search of valuables but were eventually forced to leave empty-handed. They had killed for nothing.

When arrested, Barbara came up with two different alibis in turn but both were easily proved false. While she was awaiting trial an undercover agent posing as another prisoner offered to provide her with an alibi for the right price and she agreed to pay $25,000. When a tape recording of the deal was played in court she cried out: 'Haven't you ever been desperate? Do you know what it means not to know what to do?' The tape recording weighed heavily against her, for the prosecution argued that only a guilty person would be willing to go to any lengths to furnish a false alibi.

The press called her 'Bloody Babs' and the prosecutor at her trial told the jury that the victim had looked 'as if she had been hit by a heavy truck travelling at high speed. The savage brutality of the attack is like nothing I have seen in my 20 years' experience. I can scarcely believe that human beings could do that to an elderly woman against whom they had nothing, merely because they wanted money.'

Barbara, now 32, and two of her male companions were sentenced to death; John True had saved his life by testifying against the others. For two years Barbara's lawyers battled for a reprieve and newspapers carried pictures of the tearful mother with her 19-month-old son, but it was in vain. As she was led into the gas chamber on 3 June 1955, she asked for a blindfold. 'I don't want to have to look at people,' she said.

*Barbara Graham holds her son Tommy in Los Angeles Jail, 14 October 1953,
the day after she was sentenced to die in the gas chamber*

Anna Hahn

ANNA HAHN, a German immigrant who had arrived in the USA in 1929, managed to make a lucrative business out of caring for the lonely and elderly in the German community of Ohio. Whenever a grateful patient died, Anna seemed to end up with extra money in her bank account. She had engineered a very comfortable lifestyle by the time the law caught up with her.

She first came to America as a housekeeper to her uncle, Max Doeschel, in Cincinnati. He had sent her the money for the fare but soon felt that he had made a bad bargain; Anna cared far more about her social life than about looking after the house. They soon came to a parting of the ways and she moved on to stay with a distant relative, Karl Osswald. Recently widowed, he was more interested in a wife than a housekeeper and within a few weeks he proposed. Anna explained that she had an illegitimate son, Oscar, who was living with her parents in Germany and that she would only consider marriage if she could bring him to join them in America. Osswald duly lent her the money for the fare but while she was still making plans for the journey she met a young telegraph operator, Philip Hahn, and decided to marry him instead. She used Osswald's cash to go back to Germany and collect Oscar but came back to Philip, with whom she opened a bakery.

Anna soon tired of the hard work of running a shop and looked around for a way out. She had become friendly with an elderly and reputedly well-off customer, Ernst Koch, and when he offered her a job looking after him she liked the idea. Philip objected but was soon too ill to enforce his objections – so ill that his mother had him taken into hospital. When he came out, he found that Anna had already moved in with Koch. It was only much later that anyone associated Philip's illness with the large quantity of croton oil, a fierce purgative, that Anna had bought from the chemist.

When Ernst Koch died, leaving a will naming Anna as chief beneficiary, his family contested the will and voiced strong suspicions over his death. A postmortem showed that the old man had died from cancer rather than from Anna's ministrations, but the episode must have shown Anna the way to easy money. She went to look after Albert Palmer, a retired railway worker in his seventies, and borrowed $2000 from him, supposedly to pay doctor's bills for her son. When Palmer died suddenly, early in 1937, Anna tore up her IOUs and moved on.

Her next patient was less cooperative. She managed to charm George Heiss into lending her money but he had serious doubts about his new housekeeper when he saw the flies that perched on the edge of his beer glass for a sip keeling over and waving their legs frantically in their death throes. He demanded that Anna should take a drink from the glass and when she refused, ordered her out of the house. Undeterred, she moved in with Jacob Wagner, who died very soon afterwards, leaving her $17,000.

Her next patient was George Opendorfer, a retired shoemaker, to whom she represented herself as the owner of a substantial ranch in Colorado. She persuaded him to take a trip there, in the course of which they travelled as man and wife, but when they got to Denver he fell ill. After a couple of days the hotel manager became worried and tried to persuade Anna to take him to hospital but when he became too pressing Anna took the sick man and boarded a train to Colorado Springs. At the other end, Opendorfer collapsed on the platform. He was taken to hospital and died a few days later. Anna refused to pay for his funeral, saying that she had met him on the train and had posed as his wife at his suggestion.

The authorities decided to investigate when they found that she had managed to draw several thousand dollars from the bank while pretending to be Mrs Opendorfer. Quantities of both croton oil and

arsenic were found in Opendorfer's system and when the bodies of
Jacob Wagner and Albert Palmer were exhumed, the cause of death
was shown to be just as unnatural. When Anna was arrested, substantial quantities of both croton oil and arsenic were found among her
possessions.

According to the prosecution at her trial, her ministrations had
netted her as much as $70,000. Even the defence admitted that she
had looted the bank accounts of her patients and even stolen jewellery
belonging to their dead wives, but that was as far as it went: Anna had
never harmed any of them, much less committed murder. 'I am as
innocent as a new-born babe,' Anna announced to the court. The
evidence of the pathologists, of George Heiss and his lucky escape
and of Philip Hahn, who had been taken ill with stomach pains and
vomiting as soon as he tried to cross Anna, weighed too heavily on the
other side. Anna Hahn became the first woman to be executed in
the electric chair in the state of Ohio.

Ulrike Meinhof

IN THE early 1970s Ulrike Meinhof was regarded as the most dangerous woman in Europe. With her partner Andreas Baader, she led a fearsome terrorist group whose aim was to achieve world revolution and establish Marxism in place of capitalism. They committed so many crimes that by the time they were arrested the list ran to over 350 pages. Though Andreas Baader was the charismatic leader of the group Ulrike was the brains, the driving force behind it.

Ulrike was an attractive red-haired girl from an intellectual upper-middle-class family in Lower Saxony, Germany. By the time she was 14 both her parents were dead and she was fostered by a woman professor, a formidable intellectual with radical views. At university she proved to be an outstanding scholar and a natural leader, campaigning against the atom bomb and the American presence in Vietnam. She went to work on a left-wing literary magazine, *Konkret*, and married the editor. She gave birth to twin girls, then returned to work and established a reputation as a brilliant writer and a television personality. In 1968 she divorced her husband on the grounds of adultery.

It was when she interviewed Gudrun Ensslin who, with Andreas Baader and Thorwall Proll, had planted bombs in a Frankfurt department store as a protest against American activities in Vietnam that she decided to do more than write in favour of the cause. Though Ensslin and Proll had escaped, Baader was serving a prison sentence for his part in the bombing and in May 1970 Ulrike led a daring raid to free him. The leaders of the raid then fled to the Middle East to train with the Palestine National Liberation Front, but the Arabs thought the

Germans cold and arrogant and summed them up as rebels without a true cause.

When Ulrike returned to Germany she decided to send her two nine-year-old daughters to Jordan, where they would be trained along with Palestinian children to fight against Israel. Her plans were foiled when her ex-husband, who had engaged private detectives to find his daughters, heard that they were being kept in a gang hideout in Palermo, and arranged to have them snatched back in the nick of time. The children had been brainwashed into hating their father but he eventually managed to win back their trust and affection and give them a normal family life.

The gang was now some 150 strong, most of its members being from prosperous backgrounds. They had large stocks of small firearms, submachine guns, handgrenades and bombs and set out on a series of bank raids to fund the movement. In one particularly violent robbery, at the Bavarian Mortgage and Exchange Bank in Kaiserslauten in December 1971, a police officer was shot dead. It was only when the gang reckoned that their finances were healthy enough that they turned their attention to political targets and had a set of explosive devices manufactured to order, including bombs designed to be worn under a woman's clothing so that she looked pregnant.

A reign of urban terror ensued. In a single month in 1972 bombs planted in a US army headquarters in Frankfurt killed a lieutenant-colonel and injured 13 others; 5 policemen were injured by a bomb at police headquarters in Augsburg; 17 employees were hurt in explosions in a Hamburg publishing house; bombs planted in cars driven into the US army headquarters in Heidelberg killed three Americans and wounded several others. Ulrike Meinhof now displayed a complete disregard for human life, dismissing the police and US soldiers as 'pigs'.

The German public was horrified and the government intensified security precautions while the police concentrated their manpower in an all-out effort to smash the gang. Their first big break came early in 1972 when an anonymous tip-off sent them to a garage in a quiet Frankfurt street which was used by the gang as a bomb factory. Bomb-disposal experts worked to neutralize every device while marksmen took up their positions at strategic points and the whole area was surrounded. Early on the morning of 1 June 1972 a lilac Porsche drove up to the garage with Andreas Baader at the wheel, in the company of two other terrorists. Carl Raspe, Ulrike's lover, realized that they had walked into an ambush and fired on the police before making a run for it, but he was quickly arrested. Baader and another gang member, Holger Meins, barricaded themselves in the garage but after a long, tense siege, Baader was shot in the thigh and both men were forced to surrender.

A few days later Gudrun Ensslin was arrested in a Hamburg dress shop. She had taken off her jacket in order to try on a sweater and a shop assistant had found a gun in the pocket. Ulrike was now the only gang leader left at large and even her former friends began to shy away, feeling that she was too dangerous to know. She planned a getaway from Hanover airport, arranging through friends to stay overnight with a teacher in the suburban village of Langenhagen, near the airport. The teacher had left-wing leanings but had a respected position as Federal President of the Teachers' Union and was appalled to realize that his houseguest was a wanted terrorist. He phoned the police and on the evening of 15 June a band of officers entered the flat and overpowered her. Her suitcase, packed ready for the flight, contained three pistols, two hand grenades, a submachine gun and a 4.5 kg (10lb) bomb.

The remainder of Ulrike's life was to be spent in prison. The trial of the Baader-Meinhof gang began at Stammheim on 21 May 1975. The terrorists were confined in the nearby top-security prison, where special cells had been constructed. Such was the fear of rescue attempts or terrorist reprisals that armed guards with attack dogs patrolled the perimeter of the goal, anti-bomb netting was fixed on the roof and machine gunners were ready to counter any helicopter attack from above. The courtroom, where Ulrike screamed abuse and shouted political slogans at her judges, was also heavily fortified.

In the prison, the gang members turned against one another and Ulrike began to feel increasingly isolated. When Gudrun Ensslin eventually admitted that the gang had carried out several of the bombings, it was obvious that there was no hope of acquittal. It must have been the last straw for Ulrike, and on the morning of 6 May 1976, she was found hanging in her cell; she had been dead for several hours. Her followers refused to believe that she had committed suicide and were convinced that she had been murdered with the connivance of the authorities. Revenge attacks followed and in the most serious the Chief Federal Prosecutor was killed. Four thousand sympathizers marched in her funeral procession in Berlin, many of them masked to prevent identification.

A priest who had known Ulrike Meinhof when she was still a deeply religious young woman said after her death: 'I think she finally decided that she had come to the end of the wrong road.'

Charlotte Corday

CHARLOTTE CORDAY saw herself as a new Joan of Arc, a sort of avenging angel who could remove from the earth a wicked tyrant who daily condemned innocent men and women to the guillotine. When she plunged a knife into the breast of Jean Paul Marat, one of the leaders of the French Revolution, on 13 July 1793 she thought she was committing a noble act for the sake of the country. In fact, by disposing of Marat, a notable scientist turned politician, she may well have unleashed a wave of indiscriminate killing that cost hundreds more French lives, for following Marat's death Robespierre could proceed with his brutal reign of terror. Marat, who had always eschewed power and opposed those who craved it, was the one man who might have held him in check.

The undoubted beauty of the young woman from Normandy probably played a part in the near-worship with which she was regarded in the last century. Her hair was red-gold, her figure curvaceous and her eyes were grey and deepset. She was an intelligent, well-educated girl from a poor but aristocratic family in the town of Caen, where support for the Girondists, a middle-class party who opposed any idea of power for the people, was passionate. When the Girondists were routed in Paris and forced to flee into the country they blamed Marat, the 'friend of the people', for their downfall. They raised a force of volunteers and as Charlotte watched them marching through Caen she began hatching her own plan of revenge. She decided that it was wrong for so many brave men to risk their lives to defeat the tyrant. 'He did not deserve the honour,' she wrote later. 'A woman's hand was enough!'

Without telling anyone of her plan she set off by coach for Paris, taking with her a single change of clothes, and took a room at a hotel. She had hoped to get into the Convention and kill Marat there, in public, but when she found that he was unwell and remaining at home she decided that she would have to bluff her way into his house. First she bought a kitchen knife with a long, razor-sharp blade and an ebony handle from a shop in what is now the Palais Royal. Then she took a horse-drawn cab to No. 20 Rue des Cordeliers, where Marat lived with his mistress Simone Evrard, and asked to see him. She did not manage to get further than the doorstep, where she was told that Marat was too ill to see anyone, now or in the immediate future.

She returned to her hotel and penned a letter to Marat which read:

'I come from Caen. Your love of your country must make you wish to know the plots that are hatching there. I await your reply.

Charlotte de Corday, Hôtel de la Providence.'

She had no intention of awaiting his reply, for as soon as she was sure that the letter would have been delivered, she made ready to call on him again. She dressed in her best clothes – an Indian muslin gown and a hat with a black cockade and green ribbons – and carried gloves and fan, probably thinking that the smarter she looked, the more likely she was to get into the house without arousing suspicion.

She arrived at the house at 7 pm and at first was no more successful than before. This time she stood her ground, protesting that she had to see Monsieur Marat, it was a matter of life and death. Marat, on hearing the argument and being told that it was the lady from Caen who had written to him, decided that her mission must be important and asked her inside. A strange sight met her eyes. Marat was seated in a slipper bath – bathing for hours on end was the only way of relieving his painful skin complaint – with a dressing gown round his shoulders and a board across the bath so that he could work on his papers. A towel soaked in vinegar was wrapped round his head to soothe his headache.

He questioned Charlotte about the plots among the Girondists in Caen and asked for the names of the ringleaders. When she supplied a

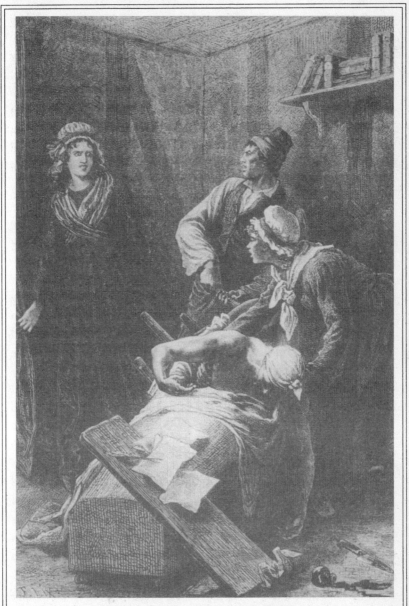

Charlotte Corday and the death of Marat

list of fictitious names he wrote them down and promised that they would be rounded up and sent to the guillotine. While he was still absorbed in making his death list Charlotte drew the knife from her bodice and lunged at him, plunging it into his body up to the hilt. Marat's scream brought Simone running and she tried to stop the blood with her hands but it was too late; by the time Marat was lifted from the bath, he was dead.

Two servants knocked Charlotte to the floor and bound her hands. Soon the house was full of police and soldiers and the news of the killing spread quickly through Paris. A mob of furious citizens gathered outside the house, ready to tear the assassin to pieces, but Charlotte remained calm and self-possessed. Four members of the Convention were sent to question her and spent several hours doing so, as they could not believe that she had acted alone and were determined to discover the names of her accomplices. How was it, they asked her, that she had managed to kill her victim with a single blow if she had not been taught how to kill. Charlotte replied: 'The anger in my own heart showed me the way to his.'

At last she was driven away to the Abbaye Prison through the jeering crowds. Four days later she was put on trial, a mere formality with the verdict never in doubt. At the tribunal she remained clear-headed and defiant and, when asked what she had hoped to gain by killing Marat, she replied: 'Peace for my country. . . . I know that he was perverting France. I killed one man in order to save a hundred thousand.' The defence lawyer had been instructed to put in a plea of insanity, on the grounds that the young woman's judgement had been impaired by her political fanaticism. By portraying her as a mad-woman, the revolutionaries hoped to prevent her from becoming a martyr.

She was condemned to death on the guillotine that same day. As she waited for the appointed time the artist Jean Jacques Hauer made a sketch for a portrait, so overcome by the tragedy of the situation that he could hardly see through his tears to complete his work. She also wrote a final letter, saying: 'I have hated only one person in my life and I have proved the strength of my hatred.'

As she made ready for execution her beautiful hair was cut off and she gave a lock to Hauer, who burst into tears as he took her last gift. She put on the simple red shift that all condemned murderers had to wear and calmly mounted the cart that was to take her through the streets to the Palace de la Revolution.

During the journey a thunderstorm broke, with great rolls of thunder and flashes of lightning adding a special drama to the scene. Rain poured down, plastering her shift to her voluptuous body, but she stood with her head held high, showing no sign of fear. As she mounted the scaffold, some members of the crowd cheered her and one young man even threw a rose at her feet.

When the guillotine had done its work the executioner's assistant held up the head for all to see, punching it gleefully, but the crowd booed and hissed so angrily that he quickly dropped it into the basket. The romantic martyrdom of Charlotte Corday was already under way.

The Price Sisters

IN 1973, after the British government had decided to hold a referendum in Northern Ireland on the future of the Province, the IRA launched a bombing campaign on the British mainland. On 8 March bombs exploded outside the Central Criminal Court at the Old Bailey and the army recruiting office in Whitehall. One man was killed in the blast and over 200 people were injured. Several other bombs were traced and defused after an anonymous phone call gave clues to their locations.

The bombers, a group of IRA stalwarts led by two sisters, Dolours and Marian Price, were arrested as they tried to board a plane to Dublin. Their plan had been simple: they had driven several stolen cars loaded with explosives to London, parked them outside pre-arranged targets and primed the bombs. Their task completed by 8.30 am, they immediately caught the coach to Heathrow airport in the hope of being on their way back to Ireland before the security authorities were alerted.

The terrorists were unaware that warnings from Belfast had alerted Scotland Yard to a possible outbreak of bombings and security at airports had already been stepped up. Policemen on the beat were also extra-vigilant and at 9 am two officers stopped to check a car parked in Victoria because the numberplate did not match the year of manufacture. A bomb was found under the back seat, its clock already ticking, and explosives experts were called to defuse it. The word went out immediately to all airports and Special Branch detectives began checking every passenger on a domestic flight. The nine suspects were held because they had given false names and addresses and had consecutively numbered tickets showing that, though they denied any connection with one another, all the tickets had been bought at the same time.

From the beginning Dolours Price, an intelligent and articulate 22-year-old, stood out as the leader of the group. Her 19-year-old sister Marian was second in command. Both girls were students at one of Belfast's leading teacher training colleges; Marian was in her first year and Dolours was completing her Bachelor of Education thesis. They had been steeped in the Republican cause since childhood, for their father had spent 10 years in internment for his IRA activities, and by 1972 Dolours was already a brigade courier. She was thought to have had a hand in planning the Bloody Friday bombings when 20 devices exploded in Belfast and she had spent the previous summer in Italy, whipping up support for the IRA at meetings organized by Marxist groups. Marian was just as committed to the cause and had a reputation as a first-rate marksman, earning her the nickname of the 'Armalite Widow.'

At the trial, when Dolours and Marian were accused along with seven other defendants, counsel for the sisters argued that they were the type of people to engage in reasoned arguments to promote their cause, rather than resorting to bombings. He accused the police of planting incriminating evidence: a strip of Green Shield stamps obtained from a garage in Liverpool on the night before the bombings, a list of names and initials, including those of the other defendants, and a J-cloth identical to one found in the timing mechanism of a bomb defused outside New Scotland Yard. The prosecution firmly denied any such interference with the course of justice and said that the defendants were all officers or volunteers in one of the Provisional IRA's three Belfast battalions.

The trial lasted for 44 days and when the jury was ready to return a verdict the already stringent security precautions in the court were stepped up even further. Everyone entering was searched and once the court was in session the doors were locked. The defendants were surrounded by police officers and four rows of plain-clothes detectives sat behind the dock.

One of the defendants, the only one to deny on oath being a member of the IRA, was found not guilty and the rest expressed their feelings by humming the dead march from *Saul* in unison. The other eight were found guilty, with the Price sisters and another student teacher, Hugh McFeeney, held to be the ringleaders.

The judge, preparing to pronounce sentence on the two women, began by calling their actions evil and wicked, whereupon Dolours Price called out: 'May we be removed from the dock? We don't want to listen to a lecture.' The judge told her to stay where she was and sentenced her to life imprisonment, a sentence greeted by shouts of 'Up the Provos' and clenched fist salutes from her supporters in the gallery. Dolours simply remarked: 'That's a death sentence.'

When Marian was sentenced she announced: 'I stand before you as a volunteer of the IRA. I consider myself a prisoner of war. From this moment on I shall be on hunger strike until I am sent home to Ireland.'

Even in the face of the verdict the Price sisters remained as cheerful as they had been throughout the trial and their months on remand. Their supporters explained that they had no reason to be unhappy: they had made history for their cause and they had done right by their lights. Moreover, they did not believe they would be in prison for long; either their friends would find a way to free them or they would be granted an amnesty.

The Price sisters made good their threat to stage a hunger strike in support of their right to serve their sentences in Ireland and in March 1975 they were transferred to Armagh prison. After seven years Marian was freed on licence, as she was suffering from physical and psychological illness which could be life-threatening if she remained in prison. Dolours has also been released on licence.

The Sadistic Nazis

THE NAZI creed, as propagated by Hitler and his followers, promoted the belief that certain races and groups of people were inferior beings who could be persecuted and killed by members of the master race, and gave many sadistic monsters an outlet for their own perverted sexual tastes in torturing and killing their helpless prisoners. Most were men, but among them were a handful of loathsome women who found no difficulty in equalling the cruelty of their male colleagues. Among them were the 'beast of Belsen', Irma Grese, and the 'witch of Buchenwald', Ilse Koch.

Irma Grese, born in 1923, came from a family with little sympathy for Hitler's ideals, but she was subjected to Nazi brainwashing in her formative years. Her father opposed her participation in the Hitler Youth and gave her a severe beating when he found that she had volunteered for work in the concentration camps but he had no influence over the determined young woman. She learned her trade at Ravensbruck, then in 1943 she was moved to Auschwitz and later to Belsen. In these camps, whose names are synonymous with horror, she was free to indulge every sadistic whim. She would patrol the camp with two vicious German shepherd dogs, who were set on inmates at the slightest excuse. Once the dogs had brought them down, she would kick them to death with her heavy boots. She always carried a whip and delighted in slashing the breasts of large-bosomed women, then watched with pleasure while the camp doctor sewed up the cuts without anaesthetic.

When she was in charge of the work detail she would deliberately leave a tool just outside the barbed wire enclosure and order one of the Jewish women prisoners to fetch it, laughing when the woman was mown down by machine-gun fire from one of the watchtowers. When she was rounding up prisoners to be sent to the gas chambers she would taunt them, pretending to select those whose names were not on the list, then telling others that they had a few weeks of life left, only to change her mind at the last moment and send them off to their deaths. Witnesses at her trial had seen her shoot those who tried to hide when their time came to join the gas chamber lines with her pistol, though she claimed that the weapon was only for show and was never loaded.

At the end of the war her main defence to the charges against her was that it was Himmler, who had set up the camps, who was responsible for all that went on in them and that anything she did was to maintain discipline when she was responsible for several thousand women at a time.

Ilse Koch was more robust in her own defence: her husband might have been commandant of Buchenwald, she said, but she was nothing more than a wife and mother. She had seen no atrocities in the camp and she had certainly never committed any: witnesses who told a different story were enemy stooges, engaged to play a part. She even pretended to have a fit in the witness box, to convince the court that she was a sick woman, not fully responsible for her actions.

Ilse Koch may have looked the part of a typical German wife – plump, blonde and blue-eyed, with a pleasant smile – but, not content with holding sex orgies with the young SS officers of the camp, she had taken advantage of her position to satisfy her sadistic urges. One of her 'games' was to sunbathe naked in full view of the male inmates, then if any of them dared to look at her she had them beaten to death. She thought up the novel idea of having the skin of dead prisoners made into gloves and lampshades for her home. Her mantelpiece was also decorated by the shrunken heads of camp inmates.

When the guards indulged in a killing spree, setting a crowd of prisoners loose in the compound and taking pot shots at them as they ran desperately to and fro, Ilse took part gleefully, managing to shoot several men herself. At her eventual trial she was charged with murdering 45 people as well as being an accessory to scores of other killings, but unlike Irma Grese she was spared the noose and died in prison in 1971.

Elizabeth Brownrigg

THE BRUTISH women of the concentration camps may have refined the art of cruelty but they were not the first to find that having complete power over a helpless human being brought out all their sadistic urges. In the 18th century young apprentices were delivered into the hands of a master and mistress who would have control over their lives from then onwards, with no outside supervision or inspection; consequently, they were at the mercy of any man or woman with a twisted personality.

Elizabeth Brownrigg and her husband James were both upstanding members of the community, with a substantial house in the City of London and a second home in Islington, used as a weekend retreat. James was a prosperous plumber and Elizabeth was a midwife who had been appointed by the parish of St Dunstan's to look after the female inmates of the workhouse. More fortunate women were looked after in her own home and she had a high reputation for kindly care of both mothers and infants.

In 1765, needing help with the private cases she took into her home, Elizabeth took her first apprentice, 14-year-old Mary Mitchell, a child from the workhouse. Shortly afterwards she took another teenager, Mary Jones, from the Foundling Hospital. For each child she paid £5 and in return received the services of an unpaid servant who would, in theory, be taught a trade. Elizabeth's idea of training her apprentices was to work them for 18 hours a day, dress them in rags and feed them on scraps, and beat them regularly until the blood ran down their backs.

Mary Jones tried to escape from her miserable existence but was caught and brought back. As a punishment she was stripped naked and laid across two chairs in the kitchen then viciously whipped by Elizabeth, who only gave up when she was faint from exhaustion. After a whipping, Elizabeth would revive the child by dipping her head in a pail of water and, finding that Mary had a special fear of drowning, she devised a new game, shared by her husband and son, whereby one of them would hold the girl up by her ankles with her head in the bucket of water while she fought for breath.

In spite of her fear of the Brownriggs, Mary Jones made a second bid for freedom and this time she succeeded in stealing out of the house, wandering the streets for hours until she found her way to the Foundling Hospital. Here she poured out her story and showed the terrible wounds she had received from the savage beatings. The hospital authorities wrote to the Brownriggs, threatening prosecution unless they received an explanation and financial compensation for the treatment handed out to Mary Jones. The Brownriggs ignored the letter, probably confident that the hospital authorities would not want to court a scandal by making the matter public, and no action was taken, beyond the termination of the apprenticeship.

Meanwhile, Elizabeth had applied to a workhouse in a different parish for another apprentice and 14-year-old Mary Clifford joined the Brownrigg household. Poor Mary Clifford was a dim girl with a slight physical infirmity and instead of giving her a bed, Elizabeth made her sleep on a mat in the coal-hole with a collar and chain round her neck so that she would have no chance of escaping like her predecessor. Throughout the day she was repeatedly punched, kicked and beaten about the shoulders with a cane. Elizabeth had found a splendid new way of whipping her apprentices: she tied their hands with cord which was strung over a waterpipe that ran across the kitchen ceiling, then as they dangled there naked, their feet swinging in mid-air, she would horsewhip them for the entertainment of Brownrigg father and son. When the waterpipe broke through over-use, James fixed a stout hook in the ceiling so that the whippings could continue.

A Frenchwoman who was spending her confinement in the house

took pity on the ill-treated Mary Clifford, who sobbed out her story and begged her for help. But her intervention, when she reproved Elizabeth for her brutality, only made matters worse: Elizabeth held Mary down while she slashed her tongue with scissors, threatening to cut it out if she told tales again.

One morning in July 1767, an aunt of Mary Clifford had called to see her niece, having been given the address by the parish. Elizabeth denied that any apprentices lived in the house and shut the door in her face. However, when the aunt made enquiries among the neighbours, a Mrs Deacon told her that the Brownriggs did have young apprentices and that she had been worried about them for some time. At weekends, when the Brownriggs went to Islington, the girls were left behind in the cellar and she had heard them crying. When the family was in residence she had often heard the children screaming in pain. A servant girl was set to watch for the girls through a skylight in the Brownrigg house and she saw the naked, bleeding body of Mary Clifford, but she was unable to rouse her.

At last the parish officials were forced to take notice and Mr Grundy, an overseer of the parish, arrived at the Brownrigg door with the police, demanding to see the girls. They found James Brownrigg alone in the house and at first he maintained that they had only one apprentice, Mary Mitchell. When the girl was brought forward, the rags of her dress were stuck fast to her shoulders by dried blood; they later had to be soaked from her body in hospital. A full-scale search of the house followed and Mary Clifford was found hidden in a cupboard, scarcely conscious, her body covered with cuts, bruises and festering sores. She died of her injuries in St Bartholomew's Hospital a few days later.

James Brownrigg was taken into custody, protesting all the time that he had never ill-treated the girls, it was all his wife's doing. Elizabeth and her son John had taken all the money they could find and fled, disguising themselves in second-hand clothes. After moving lodgings several times, they registered under assumed names at an inn in

Elizabeth Brownrigg awaiting trial

Wandsworth. Public feeling against Elizabeth was running high and newspapers carried her description prominently: a woman of medium size, around 50 years old, with a swarthy complexion and 'remarkably smooth of speech'. Her landlord, who had noticed that his new guests had not left their room and were exceptionally nervous, reported them to the police and both were arrested. At the subsequent trial, where Mary Mitchell gave evidence, James and his son John escaped with a mere six months in prison but the loathsome Elizabeth was sentenced to death.

Vast crowds assembled to see her executed and the hangman did the job as quickly as possible, afraid that the angry mob might snatch the prisoner and tear her limb from limb. Her corpse was taken to the Surgeon's Hall in the Old Bailey, where the bodies of all murderers were dissected at that time. Afterwards her skeleton was displayed for all to see.

Jean Harris

JEAN HARRIS was known as a refined and dignified woman, highly educated and the headmistress of a well-known girls' school in Virginia, USA, where she was a strict disciplinarian who laid so much emphasis on integrity that her pupils nicknamed her 'integrity Jean'. When she was tried for murder, her defence counsel described her as 'a very fine lady, of the kind you don't see much any more'. Yet she had another side – the jealous mistress about to be pushed aside, who pumped four bullets into her lover of 14 years.

Her lover was the world-famous Dr Herman Tarnower, known as 'Hi', the originator of the Scarsdale diet, which was followed by millions. The doctor, who lived in a fashionable section of New York's Westchester suburb, had helped to found the highly successful Scarsdale Medical Center and in 1979 had published an expanded version of the diet he had long recommended to his overweight patients under the title *The Complete Scarsdale Medical Diet*. The book quickly became a best-seller.

At 69, the doctor was physically active and enjoyed a good life: golfing, fishing, shooting, exotic foreign travel and, above all, women. He had first met Jean Harris in 1966 and the following year gave her a large diamond ring and asked her to marry him. Later, when she asked about setting a date, he told her that he could not go through with it. By then she was so much in love with him that all she cared about was continuing the affair, and the idea of marriage was allowed to lapse. Over the years she was aware that he had casual affairs with other women but she turned a blind eye, confident that they were unimportant. She was content to be the hostess at his intimate dinner parties and his companion on foreign trips. She had helped him with his book and was enjoying her share of his new celebrity status.

Then Lynne Tryforos, the doctor's nurse-secretary at the clinic, came on the scene and things began to change. It became obvious that the doctor was planning to trade in his long-standing mistress for a newer model. He began spending more and more time with Lynne, who was 19 years younger than Jean, and in the year before the killing he took two winter holidays: one at Palm Beach with Jean, the other in Jamaica with Lynne. New Year saw him in Florida with the head-mistress, but the nurse made her feelings clear by putting an advert in the *New York Times* which read: 'Happy New Year, Hi T. Love always, Lynne.'

Jean's love for the doctor was as strong as ever but she feared that she was about to be jilted. An important dinner was to be held at the Westchester Heart Association on 19 April 1980 to honour Dr Herman Tarnower and Jean assumed that she would accompany him – only to find that he was proposing to take Lynne. This came at a time when Jean was facing problems at school. A consultant hired to report on the school had recommended that she should be dismissed and though a second study had supported her it was made clear to her that she was on probation.

The basic facts of what happened on 10 March 1980 were never in dispute. On that stormy evening Jean Harris drove from Virginia to New York, a five-hour journey, arriving at the doctor's home at around 11 pm. She had with her a .32 calibre revolver, bought 18 months earlier, with five of its six chambers loaded and she carried another five rounds. She let herself into the house and went to the doctor's bedroom, where he was already asleep. During the scene that followed several shots were fired and the doctor received four bullet wounds from which he died within the hour.

Suzanne van der Vreken, the doctor's cook, was watching television when she heard the buzzer from his room. When she picked up the intercom phone she could hear shouting and banging, then Jean

Harris's recognizable voice, then a gun shot. Suzanne woke her husband and called the police. Upstairs she found the doctor slumped on the bedroom floor, his pyjamas drenched in blood and his pulse scarcely detectable. Meanwhile Jean had left the house, driving off without attempting to summon help, but when she saw the police car approaching she did a U-turn in the road and returned to the house. She told the police detective that she had driven to the doctor's home with the intention of killing herself. There had been a struggle and the gun had gone off several times, but she did not know who had control of the gun at the time. 'I've been through so much hell with him,' she said. 'I loved him very much, he slept with every woman he could and I had had it.'

At her trial for murder Jean, now 57, pleaded not guilty and the defence counsel pointed out that they were not asking for sympathy because of the defendant's age or sex and that they were not claiming mitigation on the grounds of diminished responsibility. Their contention was that she had intended to shoot herself and that the doctor had died as the result of a 'tragic accident'. There were basic problems with this line of defence: a woman intent on killing herself might well carry a loaded gun but why would she take along extra rounds of ammunition? It was also difficult to explain why the doctor sustained four bullet wounds while the would-be suicide escaped without a single wound.

Complex ballistics evidence referred to ricochet points and bullet trajectories and experts contradicted one another over whether or not the wounds were consistent with Jean Harris's account of a struggle between herself and the doctor. Dr Louis Roh, Deputy Medical Examiner for Westchester County, even produced a life-size plaster model of a man to illustrate where the bullets entered the body.

The case would obviously turn on the jury's opinion of Jean Harris when she gave evidence. The defence portrayed her as a victim: exhausted, lonely, frail, vulnerable. Unfortunately for this line of defence, the defendant came over as a woman with a strong personality and a quick mind. She frequently passed notes of instruction to her counsel, spoke contemptuously to the prosecutor and even once appealed angrily to the judge, who had to remind her that she had a lawyer to make objections on her behalf. It was difficult to picture this woman as a victim.

All the same, the defence mustered a good deal of evidence to show that Jean had been in a suicidal state before the killing. She had been taking antidepressants prescribed by the doctor and shortly before the killing she had made her will and written farewell notes to friends and colleagues. One read 'I wish to be immediately cremated and thrown away', while another said 'There are so many enemies and so few friends . . . I was a person and no one ever knew.' Asked in court what she had meant by this, she said, 'I wasn't sure who I was and it didn't seem to matter. I was a person sitting in an empty chair . . . I can't describe it any more.'

Jean said that she had chosen the spot where she planned to kill herself, near Herman Tarnower's pond, where the daffodils were thick in the spring. She had rung the doctor on the afternoon of 10 March, telling him that she wanted to come to talk to him for a few minutes. She had intended to see him one last time without telling him her intentions. When she arrived, she found the house in darkness and the doctor asleep. When she woke him and tried to talk to him he told her, 'I'm not going to talk to anybody in the middle of the night.' Jean went into the bathroom where she found a satin negligée belonging to Lynne. She threw it on the floor and, angry and frustrated, she then hurled a box of curlers at the window, breaking it. The doctor hit her across the face. She threw another box and he hit her a second time.

She sat on the edge of the spare bed and lifted her face to him, saying, 'Hit me again, Hi. Make it hard enough to kill.' When he walked away without touching her, she took her gun from her handbag and put it to her head, saying, 'Never mind, I'll do it myself.' The doctor grabbed for the gun and it went off, putting a bullet through his hand. 'Jesus Christ, look what you did,' he exclaimed. As he made for the bathroom, she went down on her knees to retrieve the gun. The doctor lunged across the bed and seized the gun in his right hand, pressing the buzzer with the left. In the struggle that followed she had felt what she thought was the muzzle of the gun pressing into her stomach and had pulled the trigger, but it was the doctor who fell back. Another bullet had ricocheted into the cupboard but she did not remember any more shots. She had put the gun to her head again 'and I shot and I shot and I shot' but it just went on clicking. Afterwards she had banged the gun on the edge of the bath until it broke. The doctor was still conscious and she did not realize that he was dying when, discovering that the bedroom phone seemed to be broken, she ran out to get help. She was driving to find a phone box when she saw the police car and turned back. When her defence counsel asked if she had meant the doctor harm she said, 'Never in 14 years and certainly not that night.'

Perhaps the jury might have accepted the picture of a dignified and sensitive woman, so distressed by the doctor's callous behaviour that life no longer seemed worth living, if it had not been for one damning piece of evidence which came to be known as the 'Scarsdale letter', written on the morning of the fateful day. Jean had sent it to the doctor by registered post and it had been recovered from the mail. It was an agonized shriek of a letter, full of anger and violent emotion, railing against the wrongs she had suffered. She wrote 'distraught' because he proposed taking Lynne to the dinner on 19 April. She was determined to be there 'even if the slut comes – indeed, I don't care if she pops naked out of a cake with her tits frosted with chocolate'. Hatred of her rival raged through the letter as she accused Lynne – 'your psychotic whore' – of ripping up her clothes, stealing her jewellery and making obscene phone calls. She had received a copy of the doctor's will with Lynne's name substituted for hers. She had grown poor loving him, she said, while 'a self-serving, ignorant slut has grown very rich'.

The letter, with its ugly language, undermined the 'fine lady' image presented by the defence. It also revealed the jealousy and rage she

A policeman reacts to the pushing and shoving as Jean Harris arrives at court shortly before the jury delivers its murder verdict

was feeling. In cross-examination she had answered 'No' when the prosecution asked if she had ever felt publicly humiliated by the fact that the doctor was seeing Lynne Tryforos in public. Yet, in the letter, she had written: 'I have been publicly humiliated again and again.'

The prosecution described a phone call between the victim and the defendant on the morning of the killing. 'Goddammit, Jean, stop bothering me,' he had said. This, they alleged, was the trigger that had caused Jean to take her revolver and the extra ammunition and head for the doctor's home. She may well have planned to kill herself but she planned to kill the doctor first.

The jury agreed and found her guilty, a verdict carrying a mandatory sentence of 15 years to life. In a final flash of spirit, Jean Harris told the judge: 'I want to say that I did not murder Dr Herman Tarnower, that I loved him very much and did not wish him ill. For you or for Mr Bolen [the prosecutor] to arrange my life so that I will be in a cage for the rest of it . . . is not justice; it is a travesty of justice.'

Christiana Edmunds

EVEN unrequited love can become a powerful motive for murder, as the case of Christiana Edmunds proved. Christiana, not content with attempting to poison the woman she saw as her rival, was prepared to poison complete strangers to disguise her crime. She was a spinster of 42, who always claimed to be 10 years younger, living with her widowed mother in Brighton, England. The two women took a walk along the seafront every day and it was there that Christiana first saw Dr Beard, a well-known local physician. Perhaps he cast admiring glances at the tall woman with eye-catching fair hair or perhaps it was all in Christiana's mind, but for her it was love at first sight.

The fact that Dr Beard was a married man with a family did not discourage her for a moment. She began to invent headaches and vague stomach pains as excuses to call in the doctor, who found her reclining gracefully, her hair spread across the pillow. He found little wrong with her, but was quite happy to accept a new patient from a well-off family. In his presence Christiana sparkled and he found her obvious admiration flattering. He introduced her to his wife and Christiana put herself out to be charming, so she was soon accepted as a friend of the family. She began writing long letters to Dr Beard and these were far more than friendly: they began 'Caro Mio', referred dismissively to Mrs Beard as 'La Sposa' and were signed 'Dorothea'. A sensible man would have stamped on the correspondence from the beginning but Dr Beard kept all the letters and even replied to them, in friendly but restrained terms, all without telling his wife.

Mrs Beard, then, had no reason to be wary of Christiana when she made an unexpected visit one afternoon in March 1871, bringing a box of chocolates as a gift. She insisted that Mrs Beard should try one, selecting one she claimed to be her favourite and popping it in her hostess's mouth before she had a chance to refuse. Finding it unpleasantly bitter, Mrs Beard delicately removed most of it into her handkerchief and refused the pressing offer of a second. Later in the afternoon she had sharp stomach pains and accompanying nausea which she traced to the offensive chocolate. Perplexed, she told her husband that she thought she had been poisoned. Dr Beard immediately put two and two together, at last realizing that Christiana's attentions went far beyond harmless flirtation, and he told her in no uncertain terms that he no longer wished to see her, either privately or professionally.

Christiana was beside herself with fury at the disastrous outcome of her plan and she immediately hatched a new one, a way of convincing Dr Beard that his suspicions were unfounded. If he could be made to believe that a maniac poisoner was at work in the town, he would see how wrong he had been to accuse his 'Dorothea'. If other people developed the same symptoms as Mrs Beard after eating chocolates, she reasoned, she herself would be beyond blame.

She stopped a small boy playing in the street and paid him to collect a bag of chocolate creams from the fashionable shop run by John Maynard. When he returned, she said that they were the wrong type of chocolates and sent him back to change them, but the chocolates she sent back had already been laced with strychnine. She did the same thing several times over the next few months, until poisoned chocolates must have been in circulation all over the town. Later, many people complained that the chocolates had made them ill but, surprisingly, no complaints reached the authorities until tragedy struck and four-year-old Sidney Barker died in early June after a kind uncle had given him a bag of chocolates.

Several people came forward to say that they had experienced unpleasant symptoms after buying sweets from the same shop. One of them was Christiana Edmunds, who reported that she had noticed a metallic flavour in chocolates bought from Mr Maynard and that after eating one she had had a violent burning sensation in her throat. The verdict was accidental death but over the next few days the dead boy's father received several anonymous letters, signed only 'seeker after justice' or 'indignant tradesman' – later shown to be in Christiana's handwriting – urging him to start proceedings against Mr Maynard.

To Christiana's disappointment no further action was taken and the whole affair seemed to be dying down. She could no longer target the sweetshop, so she hit on a new scheme and began sending parcels of fruit or cakes to well-known Brighton residents, always with a cryptic note suggesting that they were a surprise gift from a close friend, saying things like: 'You will guess who this is from. I cannot mystify you, I fear.' Though the recipients *were* mystified they would eat the contents of the parcels with pleasure, only to find themselves becoming sick or doubled up with pain. Several children were ill after a stranger gave them chocolates on their way home from school and a shopkeeper who found a bag of sweets on the counter, left by a customer, had tried one and become sick: later, they were all to identify Christiana Edmunds.

It was when Dr Beard at last came forward that attention focused on Christiana. The boys who had run errands to and from the sweetshop were questioned and her writing was analysed. A chemist, Isaac Garrett, remembered selling her strychnine on more than one occasion; she said it was to dispose of some cats that were causing havoc in her garden and had signed the poison register in an assumed name. When she was arrested she protested that it was all a mistake: after all, was she not one of the people who had suffered at the hands of the poisoner?

She was due to be tried at Lewes Assizes but feelings against her ran so high in Sussex that it was obvious that she would not get a fair trial and the case was transferred to the Old Bailey. On 15 January 1872 she was tried for the murder of Sidney Barker. The most surprising witness was her mother, Mrs Ann Edmunds, who told a sad story of insanity on both sides of the family. Her husband had been confined in an asylum for two years before his death in 1847, her father had lost his mind while still a comparatively young man and had died in a fit at the age of 43. Christiana's brother had died after spending six years in an asylum and her sister, who died at the age of 36, had also suffered from mental instability. Mrs Edmunds had always dreaded that Christiana would go the same way. In spite of this testimony, the jury decided that Christiana was in full possession of her faculties, quite sane enough to know what she was doing, and she was sentenced to death. When asked if she had anything to say, Christiana spoke out clearly and rationally. It was because of her treatment by Dr Beard that she found herself in this position, she said: 'I wish the jury had known the intimacy and his affection for me, and the way I have been treated.'

Following the trial the Home Secretary commuted the sentence to life imprisonment and Christiana was confined in Broadmoor, an institution for the criminally insane, where she died in 1907.

Simone Deschamps

IT WAS love that impelled Simone Deschamps to stab and slash to death a helpless woman – albeit a twisted and horrifying form of love. She was a middle-aged woman, not an impressionable young girl, when she met physician Yves Evenou in 1953 but he was to transform her life, filling it with the excitement of sadistic sexual pleasure.

Simone was thin and plain, a dressmaker leading a humdrum existence, but there must have been something about her that attracted the doctor immediately, for they first met when she came to his surgery as a patient. Perhaps he sensed in her a kindred spirit, for though he was a married man and, by all accounts, a devoted father, he needed a woman he could subjugate and use as he pleased. Simone happily became that woman, not protesting when he insulted her in public, treating her like a doormat and calling her lewd names in front of embarrassed waitresses. They indulged in flagellation and in sex orgies involving groups of men Yves recruited on the streets. As their perverted relationship progressed, Yves installed her in an apartment on the ground floor of the Paris block where he lived with his wife and family, so that she would be easily available at all times. Simone was besotted with him, revelling in the unbridled orgies, a willing pupil for the sado-masochistic indulgences he suggested.

When he told her that she was to kill his wife, Simone seems to have accepted it without demur, obediently going out to buy a heavy clasp-knife with a horn handle. On the appointed night, Simone sat alone in her apartment, patiently waiting for her lover's call that would tell her everything was ready. Upstairs, Yves had eaten the meal his wife Marie-Claire had cooked for him then gone out for a stroll while the sleeping pill he had given his wife took effect. Then he summoned Simone.

She put on her fur coat to walk upstairs to the Evenou apartment, for she was naked except for red high-heeled shoes and black gloves. It was what Yves had ordered her to do. When she entered the flat she removed her coat, took the knife from the pocket and advanced on the drugged woman in the bedroom. Yves pulled aside the bedclothes and pointed to his wife's heart. 'Stab, stab!' he commanded.

Simone brought down the knife again and again, stabbing Marie-Claire's defenceless body 11 times. At her trial, the defence was to claim that she was totally bewitched by Yves Evenou so that she was not responsible for her actions, but the prosecution was to point out that after the murder she had washed the blood from her knife and gloves and sewn them neatly into her mattress, indicating that she was fully aware of her guilt and the consequences if she was caught.

When the police came for the lovers each tried to put the blame on the other but Yves, his health destroyed after years of heavy drinking, died in prison while awaiting trial, leaving Simone to answer for both of them. For the most part she listened impassively to the evidence throughout the three-day trial in October 1958, though at one stage she did say that she would always feel remorse for what she had done. Yves had been everything to her: she had loved him, she had obeyed him.

Perhaps it counted in her favour that Yves Evenou was not there to speak for himself for the jury found that, though she was guilty, there were extenuating circumstances, as she had been under the control of a sadistic brute. In spite of her bloody and horrific crime, Simone escaped the guillotine.

Simone Deschamps after her arrest

Denise Labbé

DENISE LABBÉ murdered her two-and-a-half-year-old daughter because her lover ordered it as proof of her love for him. If she killed the child he would marry her; if she refused he would leave her. She called it a 'ritual murder'.

The Labbé family came from a small French village near Rennes. They were always poor and things became even harder after Denise's father committed suicide when she was 14. She worked in a factory to help the family finances but, ambitious and determined to rise in the world, she spent all her spare time studying for a university degree. By the time she was 20 she was working as a secretary with the National Institute of Statistics. By this time she had discovered sex, moving quickly from one affair to another, sometimes taking more than one lover at a time, enjoying the excitement of lies and secret meetings. She had no interest in settling down to marriage and a family, but an affair with a married doctor left an unwelcome legacy: her illegitimate daughter Catherine.

She left Catherine with her mother and sister when she moved to the headquarters of the Institute in Paris but she visited frequently and it was at a May Day dance in Rennes that she met 24-year-old Jacques Algarron, an officer-cadet at the famous Saint-Cyr military school. Jacques had a brilliant but strangely twisted mind. He was a follower of the 19th-century philosopher Nietzsche and thought of himself as a 'superman' in Nietzsche's terms, so that his actions could not be judged by normal moral standards. Women, he considered, existed only to become the slaves of men.

Denise was soon completely under his spell. The perversions he taught her satisfied her strong sexual urges and she took pleasure in

Denise Labbé is taken into custody

grovelling at his feet while he used and humiliated her in every possible way. One of his requirements was that she should bring young men to the flat and seduce them while he watched unseen. Afterwards she would have to spend hours begging his forgiveness for her 'betrayal' on her knees.

Jacques' desire for complete power over his mistress knew no bounds and he required more and more extravagant proofs of her devotion. In the autumn of 1954 the situation came to a head when he demanded that she should kill her daughter. Denise made several abortive attempts at carrying out the murder, but drew back at the last moment. She wrote to Jacques with a keen sense of drama: 'If it were not for our great love, I would give up. Will my love be stronger than fear? Will the devil triumph over God?'

Then, on 8 November, she took the child out into the yard of her mother's house for a wash in the stone basin and pushed her head under water, holding it there, in spite of her struggles, until she drowned. Her mother, returning from the shops, almost caught her in the act but by then all attempts to revive the child failed. Neither her mother nor the police believed Denise's story that Catherine had fallen into the basin by accident and that her mother had passed out from shock, coming round only after her daughter had drowned.

Under prolonged questioning, Denise told the police the whole story and both lovers were arrested. When they appeared before the magistrate Denise was hysterical, accusing Jacques of being a devil who forced her to kill her daughter. He had told her: 'Kill for me. There can be no great love without sacrifice and the price of our love must be your daughter's death.' Jacques was cold and sneering; he had tired of Denise and her 'sacrifice' was a matter of complete indifference to him. 'The woman is mad,' he shrugged.

Denise was tried for murder while her lover was charged with provoking the crime. Her lawyer asked the court to recognize that the young woman had been a puppet in the hands of a cruel and immoral man who had dominated her every action. The jury could hardly avoid

finding her guilty but added that there were extenuating circumstances for the crime, so that instead of the death penalty Denise was
given a sentence of life imprisonment. Jacques Algarron, the architect
of the murder, was sentenced to 20 years' penal servitude.

Aileen Wuornos

In the public mind – and the media – since the days of Jack The Ripper the stereotypical serial killer is male, his victims female, and often those victims are prostitutes. While this model has proven true in a large number of cases, it in no way applies to the cases of homosexual serial slayings, mass killings with no gender-bias whatsoever, child murderers and so on. And it is certainly the complete opposite of the tragic case of Aileen Wuornos, a prostitute who went on a slaughter spree, the victims being her male customers.

Late in 1989, the body of a middle-aged man, Richard Mallory, was discovered in woods in Ormond Beach, Florida, not far from a main highway. He had been shot four times with a .22 handgun, robbed of money and valuables, and his car stolen and found shortly afterwards. But what alerted the media to a state of frenzy over the following year was when this pattern was repeated no less than six times, with all the victims middle-aged males, but with no sign of homosexual activity involved. It became apparent that this was a female serial killer, almost certainly a prostitute assaulting and killing her 'johns'. Whether this was plain robbery or some kind of revenge killing was not clear, or indeed self-defence as the accused was to claim in her trial.

The history of the woman who would become something of a media monster makes disturbing reading. Born Aileen Pittman in Rochester, Michigan in 1956, her teenage parents separated months before she was born, her father eventually being committed to mental hospitals as a child molester. Her mother somewhat coldly described Aileen and her brother Keith as 'crying, unhappy babies', and was to leave them with her parents, Lauri and Britta Wuornos, when Aileen was just four years old. It seems likely she was beaten by her grandfather, and by the time she was fourteen she had become pregnant, giving birth to a son in a Detroit maternity hospital in March 1971. Her grandmother died three months later, and although her death was attributed to liver failure

Aileen's mother believed it was at the hand of her father, who apparently had threatened to kill Aileen and Keith if they did not leave his home.

The siblings became wards of court, and before long Aileen had dropped out of school to work as a hooker, moving from state to state, and committing various felonies, ranging from drunken driving to assaulting a bar tender with a well-aimed cue ball.

Moving down to Florida, she continued to break the law in increasingly serious incidents. In 1981 she was arrested for armed robbery, serving a year in prison, and in 1986 – perhaps heralding the style of the serial killings – she was accused by a male companion of pulling a gun on him in his car and demanding $200.

A matter of days after this, she met lesbian Tyria Moore in a Daytona gay bar, and they soon became lovers. Under the assumed name of 'Susan Blahovec' she and Moore (as 'Tina Moore') were involved in a series of violent altercations with bus drivers, landlords, shop assistants and so on. Aileen's personal attitude was increasingly belligerent, she provoked confrontations and was seldom without a loaded pistol in her purse. Tellingly, she talked at length to Moore about her troubled life.

So it was that she took to prostitution more and more as her main source of income, but with an obvious sense of resentment. Six months after the Mallory murder, the naked body of David Spears was found 40 miles north of Tampa, and by the time it was identified a third victim had been found. Throughout 1990 the list grew, all the male victims having been shot with a .22 pistol.

By now she was using a number of aliases including 'Lee Blahovec', 'Lauri Grody' and 'Cammie Marsh Greene'. However, fingerprints left at the scene of the crimes, plus the same found on various stolen items being sold or pawned by 'Blahovec', 'Grody' and 'Greene', led inexorably to Wuornos, the police already having her on their files under her own and various assumed names.

Once arrested, she immediately claimed – as her defence lawyers would throughout her trial – that she killed the six customers in self-defence after being raped and assaulted by them, a risk always run by prostitutes. She denied one murder, where the body was yet to be found. Sensing something of a cause celebre in the making, within two weeks she and her attorney had sold the movie rights to her story, while at the same time three of the main investigators also 'put themselves on the market' with their version of events.

Continually protesting that she was not getting a fair trial, and with two TV films covering the case in the pipeline, Wuornos became more and more flamboyant in her behaviour, now under the media spotlight. She and her advocate quoted the Bible in court, and when the guilty verdict (for the first murder) was announced she screamed (by way of contrast) 'I'm innocent! I was raped! I hope you get raped! Scumbags of America!'. Three months after she was sentenced to death, however, she pleaded guilty to three of the subsequent murders, and a second death penalty was imposed.

Despite substantial evidence to the contrary, many women's groups clung to the notion that the Wuornos slayings were in self-defence. Though it was true to say she had certainly been abused (and raped) by men during her lifetime, particularly by her grandfather, these were revenge killings rather than acts of self-defence.

After last-minute pleas and a psychiatric test which found her 'mentally competent' to be executed, on October 9th 2002 Aileen Wournos was put to death by lethal injection, becoming the 10th woman to be executed in the United States since the death penalty resumed in 1976. Just before her execution she uttered these words: 'I'd just like to say I'm sailing with the Rock and I'll be back like Independence Day with Jesus, June 6, like the movie, big mothership and all. I'll be back.'

Marie Lafarge

MARIE LAFARGE, sentenced to life imprisonment at the age of 24 for the murder of her husband in 1840, was probably the victim of her own romanticism. In her daydreams she was the adored and petted wife of a rich husband and the centre of an admiring family, presiding over a magnificent French château. The reality was so bitterly different that she could only see one way out of an unbearable situation. A few years earlier a clever defence might have enabled her to hide her crime by exploiting disagreements between doctors over the presence or absence of arsenic in the body, but the new science of toxicology was coming into its own and the foremost chemist in France was able to demonstrate to the satisfaction of the court that Charles Lafarge died from arsenical poisoning.

Though Marie had royal blood her descent was illegitimate, so she was always left on the fringes of aristocratic society; she never had the security and expectations of the well-born girls at the fashionable Paris school she attended. By the time she was 18 both her parents were dead and she went to live with an aunt and uncle who had little genuine affection for her and regarded her as a liability. Though she had various admirers she considered them too far below her socially, so her guardians, anxious to marry her off, applied to the De Foy matrimonial agency. This specialized in advertising for suitable husbands for respectable young ladies with equally respectable dowries, and the candidate who was produced seemed eminently suitable: a wealthy young ironmaster from the south of France with a large and prosperous estate. Though Marie found him boorish and uninteresting at their first meeting she was pressured by her guardians, who insisted of publishing the marriage banns three days later, and tempted by the position she would hold as mistress of the great château of Le Glandier. Charles had brought watercolours showing the house of her dreams, a beautiful converted monastery oozing history and romance from every stone.

If Marie's uncle had taken the trouble to make further enquiries, he would have discovered that Charles was not what he seemed. His iron foundry was bankrupt and he was deeply in debt. He had married before for the sake of a dowry but by the time his first wife died all her money had been used up. As for Le Glandier, Marie arrived to find it filthy, dilapidated and infested with rats, the surrounding estate hopelessly run down. The horrified bride locked herself in her room, issuing a note to Charles, saying that their marriage had been a terrible mistake and begging to be allowed to leave him. Marie gave her imagination full rein and invented a lover who had supposedly followed them and was waiting for her to join him. She then added a paragraph that would be used against her later:

'Get two horses ready. I will ride to Bordeaux and then take a ship to Smyrna. I will leave you all my possessions . . . turn them to your advantage . . . you deserve it. If this does not satisfy you, I will take arsenic – I have some. Spare me, be the guardian angel of a poor orphan girl or, if you choose, slay me and say I have killed myself.'

Eventually Marie was persuaded to leave her room and admit that the lover was a fabrication. Charles made some effort to pacify her, promising that Le Glandier would be thoroughly renovated according to her wishes and that he would be content to live with her like a brother, rather than a husband, until everything met with her approval. At the time, Marie decided to make the best of things, making endless plans for restoring the estate to its former glory and imagining a time when she and Charles could spend six months a year in Paris and the rest at the château. She wrote letters to her Parisian friends that painted a picture of married life as she wished it to be, rather than as it was. She described Charles as hiding a noble heart 'beneath a wild and uncultured exterior' and her new family as 'delightful and kind'. She was, she said, 'admired . . . adored . . . always in the right . . . a spoilt and happy person'. In fact, she met nothing but hostility from her new family, particularly her dour and critical mother-in-law.

Four months after the marriage, in December, Charles made a journey to Paris to raise money for his business and instructed Marie to write letters to all her influential acquaintances asking for their help – a task she found unpleasant and embarrassing. Before he left, husband and wife made wills leaving all their property to one another but Charles, who had years of practice in confidence trickery, secretly made a second will, cancelling the first and leaving everything to his mother.

Marie, having obtained arsenic from the chemist, ostensibly to deal with the rat population of Le Glandier, suggested that Madame Lafarge should make some of Charles's favourite cakes for him to enjoy over Christmas, a reminder of his loved ones at home. In Paris, one of the hotel staff watched Charles open a box containing a single cake: he ate only a small piece then, complaining that the flavour was poor, threw the rest away, thus foiling Marie's plan that he should die hundreds of kilometres from home. As it was, he suffered agonizing stomach cramps and severe vomiting, which went on for days.

It was a fortnight before he was strong enough to travel home. On the day of his return, Marie ordered more arsenic. She was all solicitude, cooking special dishes for her ailing husband and mixing his drinks herself, while Charles grew worse day by day. Several members of the household saw Marie mixing a white powder, taken from a box in her pocket, into his drinks but she reassured them that it was only gum arabic, to soothe his stomach. Once, in front of Madame Lafarge, Marie drank down a whole glass of milk that had been meant for Charles in order to allay her mother-in-law's well-justified suspicions. When Charles died, on the early morning of 14 February 1840, Madame Lafarge accused Marie openly of poisoning her son. At first, when Alfred the groom supported Marie's story that she had given all

Marie Lafarge denounced to her dying husband by his mother

the arsenic to him and that he had made it into paste and laid it down for rats, it seemed as though Madame Lafarge would have to take back her accusation – but when the rat-paste as examined it was found to contain nothing but bicarbonate of soda. However, arsenic was found in the remains of an eggnog prepared by Marie for her husband, in some of his vomit, carefully preserved by his mother, and in the box Marie carried with her.

In spite of an impassioned defence by Charles Lachaud, a young lawyer who was infatuated with her and believed her completely innocent, Marie was sentenced to life imprisonment. For a time she basked in her notoriety as she was showered with letters from thousands of admirers and well-wishers sympathetic to her story; for once in her life, she was getting the attention she had always craved. She wrote her memoirs, portraying herself as little loved and much maligned, but she never confessed her crime.

Mary Ann Cotton

MARY ANN COTTON, Britain's most active mass murderess, must rank among the foremost of the world's poisoners. She seems to have disposed of anything up to 21 people: husbands with tempting life insurance, children who were too expensive or troublesome to keep, relatives or friends who were in the way of her plans. By the time she was arrested in 1872 40-year-old Mary Ann already had many years of killing behind her, but it was the death of her stepson Charlie that aroused the suspicion that led to her downfall.

There had already been several deaths in the Cotton family since they arrived in the village of West Auckland, Co. Durham, less than two years earlier. The first to go was Frederick, Mary Ann's husband (though the marriage was bigamous), who doubled up with stomach pains at work, just a few weeks after Mary Ann had met an old lover, Joseph Nattrass, and reopened her affair with him. At the time she planned to marry Nattrass but that was before she found another lover with more to offer: an excise officer called Quick-Manning. Now she saw Nattrass, her two stepsons and her own baby by Cotton as obstacles to a good marriage and a boost in society. Within three weeks Nattrass and two of the children were dead, supposedly from gastric fever, which was prevalent at the time. Only Charlie was left and Mary Ann tried to put him in the local workhouse. She failed and when he died a few days afterwards tongues began to wag. The keeper of the general store remembered Mary Ann complaining that it was hard on her to keep a boy who was not even her own and adding: 'But I won't be troubled long. Charlie will go like all the Cotton family.' The chemist remembered Mary Ann sending the boy for two-pennyworth of arsenic and soft soap to dispose of bed-bugs.

Dr Kilburn, who had seen Charlie the day before his unexpected death, insisted on a postmortem and an inquest was held at the Rose and Crown, next door to Mary Ann's house. The doctor's examination revealed no poison, though he was still suspicious and took away some of the stomach contents in case of further questions. The inquest returned a verdict of death by natural causes and Mary Ann promptly collected the £4 10s due on Charlie's insurance policy. All the same, the gossip about the doomed Cotton family spread and reporters began enquiring into Mary Ann's past. The result was an article in the *Newcastle Journal*, pointing out that the Cotton deaths were only the latest in a series of suspicious fatalities associated with Mary Ann.

Her first husband had been William Mowbray who died of 'gastric fever', leaving her with the handsome sum of £35 insurance money. Six of her eight children had already succumbed to 'gastric fever' and another died a few months later. The only survivor was Isabella, who was sent to live with her grandmother. This left Mary Ann free to take a job nursing a 32-year-old engineer, George Ward, who became her second husband. George lasted only a short time after he lost his job, leaving the couple poverty-stricken.

Mary Ann then went as housekeeper to James Robinson, a Sunderland widower with five children. She soon became his mistress and looked forward to a third wedding but, just at the wrong moment, her mother fell ill and Mary Ann was summoned to look after her. It was only a temporary inconvenience. Mary Ann was not prepared to test Robinson's affections by staying away too long and within nine days of her arrival her mother was dead. Mary Ann went back to Sunderland with nine-year-old Isabella and very soon Isabella was dead, along with three of the Robinson children. Though the children's aunts were uneasy about their deaths, suspecting that Mary Ann's ministrations had something to do with their violent symptoms, Robinson was besotted with Mary Ann and determined to marry her. At first all went well, but Mary Ann's extravagance soon began to cause problems. When Robinson found that she was keeping back for herself some of the money he gave her to pay the building society as well as trying to take out loans behind his back there was a scene and Mary Ann walked out. When she tried to return later she found that Robinson had gone to live with one of his sisters, who shut the door against her. Robinson was the only one of Mary Ann's husbands to survive; he was the only one who had refused to take out insurance.

As the rumours about Mary Ann's terrible past grew, Dr Kilburn decided to put the contents of Charlie Cotton's stomach through a more rigorous examination. This time he found traces of arsenic; Mary Ann was arrested and the authorities decided to make further enquiries. They exhumed the corpse of Joseph Nattrass, who had died immediately after making a will in Mary Ann's favour and when they found a considerable amount of arsenic in his body they decided to exhume the rest of the Cotton family. At the time paupers were buried in a special section of the churchyard, the graves unmarked and crowded together and though one grave after another was opened the only bodies found of the Cotton family were those of 14-month-old Robert and 10-year-old Frederick. It was enough: examination showed that both had died from arsenical poisoning.

Mary Ann's committal hearing was postponed for several months for she was pregnant with Quick-Manning's child but after the birth she was committed to stand trial at Durham Assizes for the murder of Charles Cotton. If she were acquitted other murder charges would follow but, though Mary Ann pleaded not guilty, there was little chance of acquittal. The defence counsel did his best to demonstrate that Charlie could have ingested arsenic in various ways – from particles dropping from the mixture pasted over the bedstead to get rid of bed-bugs or from the peeling wallpaper, which had arsenic in its green colouring – but evidence about the long string of accidental deaths that attended Mary Ann made nonsense of the idea of accidental poisoning; the jury took only an hour to reach the expected verdict. When the judge donned the black cap to read the death sentence, Mary Ann fell into a faint and was carried out by two wardresses.

Mary Ann maintained her innocence to the end, trying to organize a petition for a reprieve, while the *Newcastle Journal* described her as 'a monster in human shape' and the *Durham County Advertiser* talked about her 'diabolical inhumanity'. Five days before the hanging her baby, Margaret, was taken from her. She had chosen new parents for the child herself but at the last minute she clung to her and wardresses had to tear the baby from her arms. Tears of sympathy were pouring down the wardresses' faces as, for the moment, they forgot that Mary Ann was probably the most dangerous mother in the world. For many years after her death, Durham mothers used to discipline their children with the threat; 'If you're naughty, Mary Ann Cotton will get you.'

Sarah Jane Robinson

SARAH JANE ROBINSON was another of the '19th-century Borgias' who managed to put most of her family under the ground before anyone suspected that the constant illness and death that surrounded her was anything more than bad luck. In most cases the motive was the insurance money, that mainstay of the hard-up poisoner of the time, but once she had become accustomed to dispensing arsenic-laced drinks this became a convenient way of ridding herself of any family member who was proving a nuisance.

The first murder may well have been committed to cover up a theft, though it only came to light five years later, when Sarah Jane's other crimes were discovered, and there was no proof one way or the other. Sarah Jane was 42 at the time, the mother of five children and a resident of Massachusetts, USA. She had married Moses Robinson at the age of 19 and, since his wage as a factory worker had never been enough to support the family, she worked as a dressmaker, a trade she had learned back home in Ireland. Even then they were forever in debt, with loans taken out on the very chairs they sat on and rent always owing. When the bills added up to more than they could ever hope to pay the Robinsons would organize a 'moonlight flit' and start again in another dismal tenement building, stacking up a whole new set of debts.

It seems that Sarah Jane found a new way out of her financial problems in 1881. Her elderly landlord Oliver Sleeper became ill and she volunteered to nurse him. When his death had been hastened by arsenic she sent a hefty bill to his executors and denied all knowledge of the $3000 missing from the premises since Sleeper had fallen sick. Any money Sarah Jane had acquired from her landlord's death afforded the Robinsons only a temporary respite, for 12 months later they were being threatened with eviction. The rent problem should have been solved in July for Moses Robinson died, his system full of arsenic, leaving life insurance of $2000. Unfortunately there was a dispute over the payment records and no immediate payment could be made, so that left Sarah Jane casting around for another source of funds.

She saw her opportunity when her sister Annie Freeman fell ill. Annie had pneumonia but was mending nicely under the care of a nurse her husband Prince had called in. Then Sarah Jane decided that only her personal care would suffice and immediately Annie took a turn for the worse. Sarah Jane began hinting to Prince that if Annie did not recover he should bring his two children to live with her. Annie died soon afterwards and Prince moved into Sarah Jane's three-bedroomed flat, which was soon bursting at the seams. That didn't worry Sarah Jane, for she knew that the overcrowding would not last for long.

The first to go was 12-month-old Elizabeth Freeman; looking after a baby was far too much trouble for Sarah Jane. She made no secret of her dislike of Prince, either: she told a number of people that he was idle and shiftless and would be better off dead. Those words were to count heavily against her in the future. Prince died in June 1885, but not before Sarah Jane had checked whether his insurance policy was fully paid up and, finding that a premium was still outstanding, had borrowed the money to pay it. When Prince first moved in she had persuaded him to name her as the beneficiary, so that she would have enough money to look after his children.

Most of the $2000 insurance went on paying off her ever-mounting debts, but she kept enough to pay for an insurance policy on her daughter Lizzie. In February 1886 Lizzie died and Prince's seven-year-old son Thomas followed her in July. The next victim was her 23-year-old son William, whose death would bring another healthy $2000 payout. The perfect opportunity presented itself only a few weeks after Thomas's death when William had an accident at work and Sarah Jane was solicitous in making him rest and plying him with tea. When he began vomiting she blamed it on the after-effects of the accident but she confided to a friend that she had had a dream in which Lizzie came back to tell her that William would soon be joining her. The friend remembered that a similar dream had warned her of Prince's death, though that time it had been Moses who thoughtfully warned her of the forthcoming demise.

Before he died, William told the doctor: 'The old woman dosed me.' His words, together with the unusual number of deaths in the family, were enough to launch an enquiry. When arsenic was found in William's system, Sarah Jane was charged with murder. The subsequent trial was a hurried affair with badly presented evidence and the jury were not allowed to hear incriminating facts about the surprising list of deaths in the family, with the result that they were unable to agree on a verdict.

Meanwhile, the insurance company had pressed for a full investigation of the demise of anyone close to Sarah Jane Robinson over the past five years. The superintendent of the local cemetery, who had buried them all, now 'took them pretty much all up', he later told the court. The authorities decided that their best chance of obtaining a conviction was to charge her with murdering Prince Freeman, because in so doing they could also bring evidence about the murder of her sister Annie, who had been removed as part of the plot to dispose of Prince and obtain his insurance money.

At her second trial, Sarah Jane's lawyers maintained that she was a harmless victim of circumstances, an unlucky woman who had lost many of those near and dear to her. They tried to suggest that William had been poisoned, not by arsenic, but by noxious fumes at the ironworks where he was employed. When the scientific evidence made this claim look ridiculous, they tried to find someone else to take the lion's share of the blame, casting suspicion on old Dr Beers, a known admirer of Sarah Jane, who peddled a patent medicine said to cure a whole range of ills. This medicine, it was claimed, could make the recipients so sick that those with weak constitutions could well die, worn out from vomiting. It would be easy enough to add poison to such a concoction.

Dr Beers appeared in the witness box, so doddering and confused that he seemed incapable of such a crime and the jury had no hesitation in putting the full blame where it belonged. When the verdict of guilty was announced and the death penalty given, Sarah Jane remained as self-possessed and unruffled as she had been throughout the trial.

Anjette Lyles

THE ANONYMOUS letter received by Mrs Bagley of the small Georgia town of Cochran, USA, read: 'Please come at once. Little Marcia is getting the same doses as the others. Please come at once.' Marcia was her nine-year-old niece, the daughter of Anjette Lyles, who ran a restaurant in the nearby town of Macon.

The letter was passed to the county sheriff, who had only just begun to make enquiries when little Marcia died. She was the fourth member of Anjette Lyles' close family to die in the past seven years. The first was her husband, Ben F. Lyles Jnr. They had been married for four years, had two daughters, Marcia and Carla, and they had opened a successful restaurant in partnership with Ben's mother. Early in 1951 Ben fell ill with severe stomach pains and was taken to hospital, where he lapsed into a coma and died soon afterwards. Anjette collected more than $12,000 in insurance money.

Four years later, Anjette opened another restaurant and among her regulars was Joseph Gabbart, an airline pilot. Though he was more than 10 years younger than Anjette, he fell in love with the attractive widow and within two months of meeting they were married. Anjette saw to it that her new husband took out more than adequate life insurance, with two policies of around $10,000. Five months after the wedding Joseph went into hospital for a minor operation and everyone noticed how devoted his new wife was, always at his bedside, bringing him fresh fruit juices to build up his strength. However, far from getting better, Joseph got worse, developing intense abdominal pains and a bad case of dermatitis. In spite of all that the puzzled doctors could do, he died on 2 December 1955. Once again, the grieving

371

widow collected the insurance money and promptly changed her name back to Lyles.

In the summer of 1957, Anjette's mother-in-law ate a meal in her restaurant and was taken ill with stomach pains afterwards. Her daughter-in-law visited her frequently in hospital, where she developed the same symptoms as her son. The nurses noticed that Anjette was always convinced that her mother-in-law would die and that. even though she was so attentive to Mrs Lyles, she admitted to the hospital attendants that she hated the woman. After Mrs Lyles died in September, a will was found, leaving two-thirds of her property to Anjette and her daughters, while the remaining third went to her second son. There was talk in the hospital: the will was dated four weeks before Mrs Lyles died, when they were certain that she was incapable of holding a pen, let alone writing a legible signature. There was talk among the restaurant staff, too: while Mrs Lyles was eating in the restaurant Anjette had been seen with a bottle of ant poison in one hand and a glass of buttermilk meant for her mother-in-law in the other.

It was Carrie Jackson, a cook at the restaurant, who wrote the anonymous letter in March 1958. She knew that Anjette kept a bottle of ant poison in her big black handbag and more than once she saw her disappearing into the cloakroom carrying drinks meant for Marcia, with her black handbag over her arm. Anjette had made plenty of unkind comments about her elder daughter, who took after the Lyles family rather than her mother and constantly reminded her of people she would rather forget. She had even made remarks to the effect that she would have done away with her long ago if little Carla had not been so attached to her. When Marcia fell ill in March, Carrie Jackson was convinced that she was being poisoned.

When Marcia was taken to hospital her mother regularly brought her grape juice and more than once she was seen taking it into the cloakroom just before she gave it to Marcia – and, of course, she had her black handbag with her. At one point, when Marcia's doctor told her that the child was getting better, she flatly contradicted him. No, she said, Marcia was sure to take a turn for the worse. She was proved right and Marcia died on 5 April.

By now the authorities were thoroughly alerted and a postmortem was ordered. When a large amount of arsenic was found in Marcia's body, exhumations were ordered on Anjette's two husbands and her mother-in-law. In each case, arsenical poisoning was found to be the cause of death. Anjette was arrested but declared: 'I have committed no crime. I have done nothing wrong.' When her house was searched detectives were amazed to find it a 'witch's lair,' with a wide stock of ingredients for love potions and a strong smell of incense. There were also several bottles of ant poison which contained arsenic as one of its main ingredients.

At the trial a number of people, both from the restaurant and the hospital, reported seeing Anjette carrying drinks into the cloakroom before giving them to her relatives. Several of them knew that she carried ant poison in the handbag that was constantly on her arm. When her maid had queried this Anjette had told her that the restaurant was plagued by ants, but the pest exterminator firm that regularly serviced the restaurant gave evidence that there had never been a problem with ants in the building.

A nurse recalled a conversation with Anjette, who told her that Marcia had swallowed some ant poison while playing doctors and nurses because she liked the sweet taste. After Marcia died, her younger sister Carla had said she wanted the same drink as Marcia, so that she could go and join her in heaven. A neighbour, Mrs Leo Hutchinson, remembered an even more sinister conversation when Anjette had talked seriously about getting rid of Marcia, saying 'I'll kill her if it's the last thing I ever do.'

Handwriting experts gave evidence about the will supposedly signed by Anjette's mother-in-law shortly before her death: the signature had been forged with the aid of tracing paper. A letter received by Joseph Gabbart's insurance company shortly before his death, purporting to come from him and asking questions about his policy, was also a forgery.

Anjette claimed that she was innocent and had never administered arsenic to anyone, but no one believed her and she was sentenced to die in the electric chair. Though her appeals failed, doctors observing her over the months that followed eventually decided that she had lost her reason and she was confined to an asylum.

Mary Elizabeth Wilson

MARY ELIZABETH WILSON, who has gone down in history as the 'widow of Windy Nook', became a murderess in her mid-sixties and managed to rid herself of four unwanted men in a three-year period before she was eventually brought to justice.

A working-class girl from the industrial north of England, Mary went into service with a builder's family at the age of 14 and married the eldest son of the house, John Knowles, in 1914. At the time it must have seemed a good match for her but John never rose any higher than labouring work and though the couple stayed together for more than 40 years, they ceased to share a bed or communicate over anything but the basic necessities of life. They took in a lodger, a chimney sweep named John George Russell, who soon became Mary's lover while her husband looked the other way, not caring where his wife found her pleasures so long as it did not disrupt his comfortable routine. For several years all three of them seemed content with the arrangement but then in July 1955 John Knowles, who had always been strong and fit, was taken ill and within a fortnight was dead.

Mary told her neighbours that it was time for a change – something she had been discussing with her husband before he died, she said – and she made arrangements to move to a larger, more modern house in Windy Nook, taking her lodger with her. Perhaps she had expected him to marry her, only to find that the lack of any ties or responsibilities suited him too well, or perhaps she found that her new life did not provide enough of a change from the past. Whatever the reason, she must have decided that John Russell must go the way of John Knowles. Just before Christmas 1955, the lodger fell ill with stomach cramps and vomiting. Mary made him plenty of hot soup to warm him

Mary Elizabeth Wilson

in the bitter winter weather and his condition deteriorated day by day until his death in January. John left Mary £46 and no sooner had the doctor signed the death certificate than she set about redecorating his room.

In the summer a new lodger moved in. He was retired estate agent Oliver James Leonard, aged 76, and Mary had reason to believe that he had a comfortable nest-egg. On 21 September they were married but either Mary found the marriage a great disappointment or she could not wait to lay her hands on Oliver's savings, for her new husband did not last very long. Thirteen days after the wedding Mary came knocking frantically on the door of a neighbour, Ellen Russell, to say that her husband was ill. Oliver Leonard was lying on the bedroom floor, doubled up in pain. The women helped him into bed and Mary brewed a pot of tea but when Mrs Russell brought him a cup, Oliver knocked it out of her hand. Later this was brought up as evidence that he knew that his wife was poisoning him.

Mary did not call in the doctor – she reckoned there was no point, as he was obviously going to die anyway – but next day she went to report that her husband had died in the night. The doctor recalled that Mr Leonard had been to him a few days before with a bad cold and had seemed very feeble and tottery, so he signed the death certificate without a second thought and Mary collected her late husband's modest savings and the payment on his insurance policy. Everyone in Windy Nook felt for the new bride in her sad loss.

Mary waited just over a year before marrying again, this time a 75-year-old retired engineer, Ernest George Lawrence Wilson, with £100 in savings. This husband, too, lasted only a fortnight. The doctor was called in when the old man had a slight stomach upset then, a few days later, he answered a second call, only to find that his patient had already been dead for several hours. This time there was talk, especially when people remembered that at the wedding reception, when someone mentioned that there was a good deal of cake left over, Mary had laughed, 'Well, we can always keep it for the funeral.'

So far, Mary had escaped detection because it was hard to believe that an elderly woman would suddenly turn to murder and take such risks for such meagre rewards. After all, none of her men were well off, none had much in the way of possessions or property, and she had taken out no new insurance policies for them. However, so many deaths in a single household in such a short time, coupled with stories of Mary's behaviour, which was unsuitable to a grieving widow, led to a police investigation and the exhumation of the four bodies.

All four corpses were found to contain both phosphorus and wheat-germ, ingredients of a popular rat poison called Rodine. John Knowles and John Russell had been in the ground too long for any positive conclusions to be drawn and the inquests returned open verdicts on both of them. The other two bodies still contained lethal quantities of phosphorus and, as a result, Mary found herself standing trial for two murders.

The doctors who had written death certificates for Oliver and Ernest both admitted that they had no experience of phosphorus poisoning and had no reason to suspect that the deaths were due to anything but the natural processes of old age. One had written the death certificate without actually seeing the body; the other had been called only after the patient had died. There was a long discussion about the means by which Rodine could have been administered to the two victims, as it has a strong smell and an extremely unpleasant taste. Tests in previous cases had shown that it could not be disguised in a cup of tea but that the taste could be concealed in strongly flavoured jam – though in this case it was more likely to have been given in the cough mixture which was taken by both men. No container of Rodine was found at Mrs Wilson's home, but this was used by the prosecution as proof that suicide and accident could both be ruled out.

The defence lawyer produced a bottle of pills, freely available from the chemist, which contained phosphorus and were recognized for use as an aphrodisiac. 'What more natural,' she said, 'that these old men, finding a wife in the evening of their lives, should purchase these pills? It was a brave try, but no such pills were found in the house and an expert pointed out that to obtain a lethal dose of phosphorus, it would be necessary to take three whole bottles full. On the advice of her counsel, Mary chose not to give evidence so many questions remained unanswered, but she was found guilty of both murders. Though she was sentenced to death she was reprieved five days later by the Home Secretary, probably because of her age. She died in prison at the age of 70.

Edith Carew

A MYSTERIOUS 'woman in black' flitted in and out of the enquiry into the death by arsenical poisoning of Walter Carew. She was an insubstantial, shadowy figure who could have been a murderess – but was far more likely to have been the figment of a murderess's imagination.

Walter Carew's death, and the events that followed it, shocked the comfortable European community in Yokohama, Japan, where Walter was engaged in the import–export business. He had brought his bride Edith to Japan seven years before, in 1889, and they enjoyed the elegant expatriate lifestyle, with Walter the secretary of the British club and Edith a popular and successful hostess. When Walter fell ill in October 1896 it seemed to Dr Wheeler, who attended the British families, like an ordinary bilious attack. When he suffered another, more serious attack a few days later Dr Wheeler called in a second opinion, but both doctors were mystified. The patient was sent to the naval hospital, where he died within two hours of arrival.

Meanwhile, a strange note had been pushed under Dr Wheeler's door saying: 'Three bottles of arsenic in one week!' It added the name of a local chemist, Maruya, and when the doctor made enquiries he found that three orders of arsenic had been supplied to Edith. She admitted that she had bought the poison, but only at her husband's request. He used it to treat a painful, longstanding complaint which he had never mentioned to the doctor, she said.

At the inquest Edith told a dramatic story about a Miss Annie Luke, with whom her husband had had a brief affair in his bachelor days and who had appeared at the house asking to see him only two weeks before his death. She had been dressed in black and so heavily veiled that Edith did not see her face, but she had left a calling card with the initials 'AL'. Edith produced a letter, also supposedly from Annie Luke, which had been found among Walter's papers:

'I must see you . . . I cannot meet her again. She makes me mad when I think of what I might have done for you. I cannot give you any address. I am living wherever I can find shelter; but you can find me and help me if you will, as I know you will for the sake of old times.'

Another letter, written by the same person, had been sent to the lawyer advising Edith:

'Dead men tell no tales; no, nor dead women either, for I am going to join him. Do you know what it means, waiting for eight long weary years? I have watched and waited. Waited until I knew he would grow tired of that silly little fool, and then I came to him. What is the result? We, between us, electrify Japan. I have never pretended to be a good woman but, for the sake of a few lines, I do not see why I should let a silly, innocent woman be condemned for what she knows nothing about.'

Another witness, a young bank clerk called Henry Dickinson, gave evidence that he had seen a veiled woman in black hanging about the club at the time when Annie Luke was supposed to be asking for Walter. He was the only person apart from Edith to have seen this oddly dressed woman, which was quite remarkable, as any European stranger would have stood out and become an object of speculation. However, it was enough to suggest that Edith was not the only possible suspect and the jury decided that Walter had died from arsenical poisoning but that there was 'no direct evidence to show by whom it had been administered'.

A week later Edith Carew was arrested and charged with murder. There had been another sensational development in the Carew household for the children's nurse-governess, Mary Jacob, who was on poor terms with her employer and suspected that letters addressed to her were being intercepted by Edith, had been checking through the waste-paper basket in search of them when she came across some torn-up love-letters. They had been written to Edith by Henry Dickinson, the only person to substantiate her story about a 'woman in black'.

At the trial the letters were read out and Henry Dickinson confessed to his infatuation for Edith (though there was no evidence that adultery had ever taken place) and that they had discussed the possibility of the Carews' divorce. There were references to Walter's cruelty and Henry revealed that Edith had painted a picture of her husband's ill-treatment, which she claimed made her life a misery. He now knew that this account was false.

A handwriting expert for the prosecution gave evidence that Edith had probably written the Annie Luke letters herself, but this was contradicted by experts on the other side. The defence tried to suggest that it was Mary Jacob who had written the letters and that she had developed a relationship with Walter. At one point the young governess was arrested, but there was no real evidence against her and she was quickly released. Needless to say, no new evidence of the existence of a real Annie Luke was produced, though Edith had publicized a £500 reward for information.

Edith's counsel reasoned that she had no convincing motive for killing Walter: he was a cheerful, kind husband, she was an affectionate wife and mother and their life together was comfortable. The jury did not accept his summation and they found Edith guilty. She was sentenced to death, though this was later commuted to life imprisonment and she was returned to England to serve her sentence.

Mary Blandy

THE POISON Mary Blandy used to kill her father came through the post, in little packets labelled 'powders to clean Scotch pebbles'. These pebbles were fashionable ornaments of the time, but the white powder that accompanied them was destined for a far less innocent purpose – for Mary saw her father as an obstacle to her union with her beloved, the Honourable William Henry Cranstoun, the fifth son of a Scottish peer.

Mr Francis Blandy was a prosperous English lawyer and town clerk of Henley-on-Thames and his daughter Mary was a charming, attractive young woman with a £10,000 fortune of her own and expectations of a respectable inheritance in the future. She was a 'good catch' and could be expected to marry well but, though there was no shortage of suitors, no young man had yet managed to please both Mary and her father.

Mary was 26 when she first met Willy Cranstoun, a captain with the recruitment service, at a ball given by his uncle, Lord Mark Kerr. He was some 20 years her senior and by all accounts a rather unattractive fellow, but his military bearing and city sophistication proved irresistible to Mary. She was soon deeply in love and had no hesitation over accepting his proposal of marriage. Her father, who was less impressed by his prospective son-in-law, was appalled to receive a letter from Lord Mark Kerr which tactfully pointed out that his nephew already had a wife and child in Scotland; he had married a Miss Anne Murray two years before but his father had disapproved of the match and, as he depended on parental generosity for his standard of living, he soon left her behind and returned to London, leaving his wife and child dependent on her family.

Willy, faced with the letter and Mr Blandy's indignation, chose to deny everything. It was all a misunderstanding, he said: he had at one time promised to marry Miss Murray but the marriage had never taken place, though Miss Murray had been posing as his wife, to his considerable embarrassment. Meanwhile, he was persuading Anne Murray that he had no chance of rising in the ranks of the army as a married man with a family but that if she agreed to deny the marriage and say that she had only been his mistress, he would soon achieve promotion which would provide him with sufficient money to support her properly. Eventually Anne gave in and provided him with a letter 'disowning' the marriage, which he used to try to get it anulled. He failed and the marriage was confirmed as legal.

Mary, her heart still set on marriage to Willy Cranstoun, wanted to hear none of it and the more that her father tried to make her understand the realities of the situation, the more she resented his interference. It was then that Willy started sending the powders. Later, she was to claim that he told her that they were potions that would change her father's temper, leaving him well-disposed towards Willy, and that he had obtained them from a fortune-teller called Mrs Morgan, who provided love potions to the best families. At first Mary gave her father a good helping in his tea, but it was so bitter that he refused to drink it, so instead she began mixing it in his food.

Mr Blandy soon took to his bed, weak and in pain, with his devoted daughter ministering to him, his decline perplexing his doctors. When a kitchen maid, Susan Gunnel, became ill after tasting some food destined for the invalid, Mary forbade the servants, on pain of instant dismissal, from touching anything she prepared for her father. They became suspicious, and one even suggested the possibility of poisoning to Mr Blandy, but he could not believe his daughter capable of such a thing. He was even shown a letter in which Mary warned Willy to be careful what he wrote, but all he said was, 'Poor, lovesick girl! What a woman will do for the man she loves.' Susan, remembering how sick she had been after tasting Mr Blandy's gruel, felt less

Mary Blandy

charitable towards her mistress and when she found traces of white scum on a saucepan which had contained the latest batch of gruel, she took a sample which was passed on to the doctor.

It was too late to save the sick man, for Mary, acting on Willy's instructions, had increased the dose and her weakened father had no chance of survival. As he was dying, Mary was suddenly overcome with remorse and flung her arms round him, confessing her guilt and asking for his blessing.

Mary was tried at Oxford Assizes in March 1752 and the servants were able to describe all her suspicious actions during her father's illness. At one point, in a panic that she might be discovered, she had tried to burn Willy's letters and a packet of 'pebble powder'. The packet had been rescued from the fire by the cook and was produced in evidence, identified by several doctors as arsenic. The jury took only five minutes to find her guilty of poisoning her father. Mary went to the gallows in a smart black dress with a prayerbook in her hand, and requested that she should not be hung too high 'for the sake of decency'. William Cranstoun escaped justice by taking refuge in France, where he died six months later, still maintaining that the poisoning was entirely Mary's idea.

Daisy de Melker

IN 1932, 20-year-old Rhodes Cowle was living with his mother Daisy, an ex-nurse, and her third husband, rugby player Clarence de Melker, in Johannesburg, South Africa. The atmosphere in the house was highly charged, for Rhodes was a bad-tempered young man with a grievance. His father had died nine years earlier and Rhodes, who was unable to find a job, thought that when he reached the age of 21 he should inherit his father's estate. His mother, with the financial reins firmly in her hands, was not willing to concede and they had many bitter arguments, with Rhodes alternately threatening to commit suicide and resorting to violence.

In March, Rhodes died suddenly after a four-day illness diagnosed as malaria and the house became peaceful again – but there were those who could not believe that yet another of Daisy's relatives had died of natural causes. Daisy had had five children by her first husband, William Cowle, and none had lived to attain their majority. William himself had died in 1923 after 14 years of marriage, apparently of a cerebral haemorrhage, leaving her with an insurance policy worth £1700.

When Daisy married her second husband, Robert Sproat, three years later he had already drawn up a will leaving his £4000 savings to his mother, but Daisy had soon convinced him that it was only proper to leave it to his new wife. In November 1926, Robert died, just as unexpectedly as his predecessor. Robert's brother, Albert Sproat, was worried about the circumstances of his death but was never able to find any proof of wrongdoing. He had not spoken to Daisy for years and it was the news of the death of Daisy's last remaining child, a fit young man, that prompted him to contact the authorities.

Preliminary enquiries showed that the number of surprise deaths in Daisy's family went far beyond the bounds of coincidence or ill-fortune. Rhodes's body was exhumed and found to contain arsenic. The bodies of Daisy's first and second husbands were also examined and both contained traces of strychnine. Their doctors, when contacted, admitted that their symptoms could have indicated poison, though they had no cause to look for it at the time.

Daisy was arrested and the police began enquiries among the local chemists but at first they drew a blank: there was no evidence that she had ever purchased poison. However, widespread newspaper publicity eventually produced a chemist from the other side of the city who remembered Daisy buying arsenic a few days before Rhodes Cowle became sick. She had told him that she wanted to get rid of stray cats that were ruining her garden.

The trial of Daisy de Melker lasted 30 days; at that time it was the longest-ever trial of a white person in South Africa. In the witness box the defendant was an unsympathetic figure, giving the impression that she was a cold and emotionless woman who might well be capable of causing a painful death in an unwanted family member.

On the day the verdict was to be announced, police officers from Rhodesia stood ready to take Daisy into custody if she was acquitted on the current charges; they had reason to believe that she had been involved in several deaths there before coming to South Africa. Their presence was unnecessary. Daisy was convicted and hanged at Pretoria Central Prison on 30 September 1932. She never admitted her guilt.

Mary Bateman

MARY BATEMAN was well-known as a witch in the Leeds area of northern England in the late 18th century but her success owed more to trickery, a lying tongue and a grasping nature than to the supernatural. As a child she was hired out as a servant but in every household she joined small items went missing and were soon traced to Mary, so she never kept a job for long. Later she turned to dress-making and managed to make extra money on the side by fortune-telling for her customers.

She married a wheelwright, John Bateman, who was to stick to her through thick and thin, even when her thieving meant that they were turned out of their lodgings, and when she made up a story to get him out of the way for a couple of days and sold off every stick of furniture they owned.

Over the years, Mary managed to build up a thriving little business in charms and love potions and a stream of gullible clients came to her for marriage predictions or to have a fancied curse lifted. She invented two 'wise women', Mrs Moore and Mrs Blythe, who gave her messages from the world of the supernatural, so that when her prophecies proved wrong, she could put the blame on them. It also protected her from direct accusations of witchcraft, for she could always claim to be merely a go-between. Even so, most of her clients were too frightened of her powers to attempt to denounce her.

She became more and more daring in her trickery. She told one of her customers that her husband had been kidnapped and that unless she produced several gold coins to be melted down by Mary as part of a spell to ensure his release he would certainly be killed. Sure enough, the husband returned home safe and sound a few days later –

hardly surprising, as he had never been in the hands of kidnappers. Another woman was told that her husband was having an affair and the only way to stop it was to pay Mary three half-crowns for a special spell to restore her husband's affections. Later she was told that this had been successful and that she had nothing more to worry about. She only began to doubt Mary's honesty when her husband, a soldier, came home on leave and convinced her that infidelity had never crossed his mind.

In 1806 Rebecca Perigo came to consult her, complaining of pains in the chest, which she attributed to the curse of a neighbour. Mary, after apparently consulting the reclusive Mrs Blythe, confirmed that it was a strong curse and that strong measures must be taken to counter it. She told Rebecca and her husband William to bring her four guinea notes which she sewed into a pillowcase, keeping the money and secretly substituting four sheets of blank paper. She then told them to take the pillowcase home and sleep on it. This was only the beginning; over the following months she invented one essential charm after another, charging so much that the Perigos had to part with their life savings and became so impoverished that they were going without food to meet Mary's demands. Eventually, when they had nothing more to offer and she felt that William was becoming critical of her methods, Mary decided that it would be simpler to dispose of them than to risk repercussions.

She produced a letter, supposedly written by Mrs Blythe, which predicted that they would both fall seriously ill in May 1808 and that they would 'seem dead but live'. Mary said that she would provide them with a special potion which they must add to a pudding which would last them for six days and they must start eating it on 15 May. They did as they were told and, after the first serving of pudding, they both started vomiting. William, who already had his doubts about Mary's potions, refused to eat any more but Rebecca, who had complete faith in the witch's brew, continued to follow her instructions. She died on 24 May.

Though Mary had told the couple that all her work would be in vain if they consulted a doctor, William called in his physician, who confirmed that both he and Rebecca had been poisoned. William immediately told his story to the authorities but when they went to arrest her Mary, in anticipation of their arrival, was vomiting and complaining of stomach pain, accusing William of giving her poison and attempting to hold him responsible for his wife's death.

It was soon obvious who was telling the truth for a variety of poisons were found at Mary's home, including mercuric chloride and arsenic, and several of the servants who had worked for her in the past gave evidence that she had included poison in her potions, especially when a client wanted to harm his enemies. Mary Bateman was sentenced to hang on 20 March 1809 but the large crowd that assembled to see sentence carried out was strangely silent, still afraid that Mary might use her witch's power to avenge herself.

Henrietta Robinson

HENRIETTA ROBINSON was a mystery woman from the moment she arrived in the town of Troy, New York, in 1852. She obviously had a wealthy lover, for a luxurious carriage appeared at her door from time to time and a richly dressed gentleman dismounted to spend an evening in Henrietta's cottage. He was said to be an important politician. Then, one night, neighbours heard raised voices and slammed doors as the top-hatted gentleman left in a hurry and for the last time.

The townsfolk were naturally curious about the newcomer and the tales told by Henrietta herself fed the rumours. She told a number of different tales about her background – she was descended from European royalty and had been brought up in a French château; she was the daughter of an Irish lord and had been turned out of his castle because she married a working man; she was the illegitimate child of an aristocrat and had been brought up in an English convent. She told her Irish gardener an involved story about being turned out by her father, an Irish admiral, when she became pregnant by a worker on his estate. Her lover had taken her to America, where he had deserted her; later she had become the mistress of an influential New York official who had installed her in the cottage in Troy but now had deserted her too.

After this last desertion her behaviour became stranger and stranger: sometimes, while talking to people, she would burst into tears, sometimes she would start laughing uncontrollably and sometimes she would break into a strange, jerky dance. She did make some attempts to join in the social life of the town but these attempts came to an abrupt end after an unpleasant incident at a dance, where a young man named Smith apparently made an improper suggestion to her. A few days later she cornered Smith in the grocery store and held a pistol to his head until he apologized. She went on to threaten him with death if he dared to insult her again but by this time the owners of the shop, Timothy Lanagan and his wife, had recovered from their initial shock and they hustled Henrietta out, scolding her vigorously for her unwarranted behaviour and threatening her with arrest if she produced the gun again.

For the next two months Henrietta was at daggers drawn with the Lanagans and it seemed that she could hardly bring herself to speak to anyone in the town. Then, one day in May, she arrived at the shop, all smiles and apologies. She hoped that they would forget the past and make friends after all and as a mark of the new beginning, she would like to buy them a beer. The Lanagans were astonished at her sudden change of heart but they knew that it was good business to encourage a well-heeled customer, so they agreed to drink a beer with her and invited her into the kitchen where one of their relatives, Catherine Lubee, was preparing a meal.

Mrs Lanagan brought beer and glasses and also powdered sugar, which Henrietta had requested, as she liked her beer sweetened. When Catherine Lubee went out into the yard for some potatoes, and Mrs Lanagan had left for a moment to attend to a customer, Henrietta announced that she was hungry and asked Mr Lanagan for one of the boiled eggs he kept in the shop. When the three returned, they found that Henrietta had poured the beer and added sugar to all four glasses. She proposed a toast and Mr Lanagan and Mrs Lubee drank with her, surprised to find how bitter the beer tasted. Mrs Lanagan had been called into the shop again and by the time she returned, Henrietta was leaving. Mrs Lanagan, who disliked sugared beer, was glad that she did not have to drink out of politeness and she poured the contents of her glass down the sink.

During the afternoon both Timothy Lanagan and Catherine Lubee were taken ill. By 5 pm Mr Lanagan was dead and Catherine Lubee died next day. From the moment her husband started vomiting

Mrs Lanagan was sure that he had been poisoned by something that Henrietta had put in his beer so she summoned the police immediately and Henrietta was arrested. Arsenic was found in both bodies and a packet of arsenic was found concealed beneath a rug in the cottage. Henrietta had bought it from the local pharmacist 10 days before.

Reporters covering her trial called her 'The Veiled Murderess', for her face was shrouded by several blue lace veils which she only lifted briefly when it was essential for a witness to identify her. The defence counsel did his best to prove her insane and doctors who interviewed her in prison testified that they thought that she was irrational and incoherent, but she was judged legally sane and sentenced to death. The sentence was commuted to life imprisonment on the day set for her execution – 3 August 1853. It was only 37 years later when she set fire to her cell in a vain suicide attempt that she was finally transferred to a hospital for the criminally insane, where she died in 1905 at the age of 89.

Louisa Merrifield

LOUISA MERRIFIELD was a plump, smiling 46-year-old, a homely and reassuring presence even as she stood in the dock, accused of poisoning her employer, Mrs Sarah Ricketts. Louisa had recently married for the third time when she answered 80-year-old Mrs Ricketts' newspaper advert for a housekeeper and, with her 71-year-old husband Alfred, moved into the old lady's bungalow in Blackpool, England.

Louisa had been running a lodging house when Alfred moved in as one of her boarders but the business was doing poorly and Louisa never had enough money to meet the bills. She borrowed money from anyone who would lend it and seldom paid them back. When she married Alfred he was shocked to find that she had not even paid the bill for her second husband's funeral. She was finally forced to leave the lodging house to keep a step ahead of her creditors.

At first, all went well in her new life. Louisa put herself out to look after her employer's every need. Mrs Ricketts thought herself very fortunate and, as an incentive to the couple to stay on as long as she might need them, she changed the will that left her house to the Salvation Army and left it to the Merrifields instead. The honeymoon period was soon over. Louisa found Mrs Ricketts bad-tempered and demanding and Mrs Ricketts found that her new housekeeper's devotion to her duties was shortlived. She considered that Louisa was extravagant with the housekeeping and rather too fond of her tot of rum. She began to think seriously about sacking her and, of course, a rethink of the will would follow.

On the night of 14 April 1953 Mrs Ricketts died, but Mrs Merrifield did not call the doctor until the next morning. She had been busy looking after the old lady, she explained, trying to make her comfortable and giving her an occasional sip of rum. She didn't want to leave her at that time of night to go in search of a doctor. At the end Mrs Ricketts had got out of bed on her own; Louisa had found her lying in the hall and had picked her up to get her back to bed. Her last words had been thanks for all that Louisa and Alfred had done for her.

Louisa hoped to arrange a quick cremation for her employer and, though the death came as no great shock, the unseemly haste made Mrs Ricketts' doctor wonder if all was in order. A postmortem was arranged and this found that Mrs Ricketts had been poisoned by yellow phosphorus, an ingredient of rat poison. Though Louisa had recently bought a rat poison containing phosphorus, none could be found at the bungalow; however, a spoon coated with a gooey substance which experts thought was probably a mixture of rat poison and rum was found in Louisa's otherwise tidy handbag. The suggestion was that she had hidden it there after feeding the deadly mixture to Mrs Ricketts and then forgotten about it.

The evidence might have been insufficient to convict but for Louisa's garrulous nature, for her chattering tongue had already betrayed her. Three weeks before Mrs Ricketts died, Louisa met a friend in the street and exclaimed: 'Oh, David, I've had a bit of real luck. Where I'm living an old lady has died and left me a bungalow worth £3000.' When visiting another friend she told her: 'I can't stay. I've got to go home and lay out an old woman,' adding quickly 'Actually she's not dead yet but she soon will be.' She confided in an astonished stranger at a bus stop that she had come home one day to find Alfred and Mrs Ricketts in bed together. If it happened again, she said angrily, 'I'll poison the old bitch and my husband as well.'

When Louisa and Alfred were both put on trial for murder in July 1953 Louisa denied that any of the incriminating conversations had ever taken place, saying that the witnesses were jealous of her legacy because they were all 'up to their necks in mortgages'. There was no question that rat poison had been fed to Mrs Ricketts, but there was some doubt whether the amount she had consumed was enough to kill

The crowd waiting outside Strangeways Prison, Manchester examines the bulletin posted after Louisa Merrifield's execution, 18 September 1953

her. If she had died of natural causes, then the defendants would only have been guilty of attempted murder and not subject to the death penalty.

Louisa was found guilty and was hanged at Strangeways Prison on 18 September. On the matter of Alfred's guilt, the jury was unable to agree a verdict and it was decided not to proceed with a second trial. As nothing had been proved against him, Alfred was able to inherit a half share in the bungalow his wife had been so determined to own and with the proceeds of the sale he bought several caravans, living in one and renting the rest. He died at the age of 80.

Gesina Gottfried

WHEN Gesina Gottfried finally appeared in the dock in 1828 she had 10 years of killing behind her and admitted to murdering at least 30 people by mixing white arsenic in their food and drink.

The first was the young man she married in her home town of Bremen, Germany, in 1815. Everyone had warned her that he was a hopeless alcoholic who could never keep a penny in his pocket but Gesina was too spoilt and wilful to listen and she married him for his good looks. She soon found that it was a mistake, for her husband was so often in a drunken stupor that he could not satisfy her sexually. Once she found a lover she decided to dispose of her husband by lacing his wine with arsenic. No one wondered at his death; they only wondered how anyone who drank so much could have lived so long.

Now Gesina was free to marry her lover, Gottfried, but he was reluctant to tie the knot. At first he said that the stumbling block was Gesina's two children, fathered by another man. This obstacle was soon removed by Gesina, who simply poisoned them. Her next problem was her parents, who were shocked at the idea that she should contemplate marriage so soon after the death of her husband and children. She asked them to lunch and fed them poisoned stew. Their painful deaths were attributed to gastric inflammation.

Though there now seemed to be nothing in the way of an immediate marriage, Gottfried still prevaricated. Soon he was ill in bed with Gesina nursing him devotedly. Realizing that he was dying and overcome with gratitude for her selfless care, he summoned a priest to conduct a bedside marriage ceremony and a lawyer to change his will, leaving everything to his new bride.

In the years that followed, Gesina managed to poison anyone she disliked or anyone she fancied had done her a bad turn. By 1825 she had overreached herself in buying a large house on which she could not afford to keep up the mortgage. When the bank foreclosed the house was sold to a wheelwright named Rumf and his family. When she lamented that she had nowhere else to go, Herr Rumf invited her to stay on as a housekeeper. It seemed like an excellent arrangement on both sides and Gesina excelled in preparing delicious meals for the family. Herr Rumf relied on her more when his wife died soon after giving birth to her latest child. When the children of the family fell ill, one after another, Gesina looked after them just as she would her own – and one by one, they died.

Perhaps, by the time only Herr Rumf was left, Gesina had grown careless, for the wheelwright began noticing a film of white powder on his meals. He took a white-speckled piece of meat to the police, who soon confirmed that the meat had been sprinkled with white arsenic. In due course Gesina was arrested and charged with the murder of Frau Rumf.

Far from trying to deny her crimes or excuse herself, Gesina openly admitted that she had killed the Rumf family and boasted of killing some 30 people, as though it was a pleasure to be able to parade her cleverness before an audience at last. Committing a murder, she said, had given her an all-enveloping rush of excitement, like a sexual climax. Only a woman with a very strong personality, she announced proudly, could accomplish what she had accomplished. When it was time to face the executioner's axe she stood just as tall and proud, apparently convinced that she had performed some feat to be admired.

Caroline Grills

CAROLINE GRILLS was a kindly little woman of 63, affectionately known as 'Aunt Carrie' around her suburban neighbourhood in Sydney, Australia, where she was always ready with tea and sympathy. But neither her age nor her harmless exterior could save her from a life sentence after she was charged with four counts of murder and two of attempted murder in the 'Aunt Thallie' poisoning case.

In 1947 Caroline called in the pest control officer to deal with an infestation of rats. The poison that he used, based on thallium, did the job in no time and he left an extra supply in case the problem recurred. Later that year Caroline's stepmother, Mrs Christiana Mickelson, died. She was 87, so no one was unduly surprised and no one expected Caroline to shed many tears; she had never liked her father's second wife.

Caroline's husband inherited a cottage when 84-year-old Mrs Angeline Thomas died. She had been fond of him since he was a boy and Caroline was jealous of their affection for one another. The following year Caroline's brother-in-law, 60-year-old John Lundberg, died. The Grills and the Lundbergs had been spending a holiday together and when he became ill he blamed the seafood he had been eating. When his hair began to fall out he could no longer blame it on a simple case of food poisoning. Nothing that his doctor could do seemed to help and he died in October, followed soon afterwards by Mary Ann Mickelson, widow of Caroline's brother, who suffered the same symptoms.

John Lundburg's widow, Eveline, had been feeling off-colour since her husband's death and Caroline was a frequent visitor. When Eveline and her daughter Christine began losing their hair and felt a spreading numbness in their limbs, Caroline was full of concern; she was round every afternoon, making pots of tea and serving it with her own home-made cake. One afternoon Christine's husband, John Downey, wandered into the kitchen just as Caroline was making tea, ready to carry it out to the verandah, where the two women were sitting, comparing symptoms. John saw 'Aunt Carrie' take something from her pocket and add it to one of the cups – the one she handed to Eveline a few seconds later. That evening Eveline was feeling much worse and John Downey was sure that he knew why. The next day he made a point of being at home during Caroline's visit. This time, when he saw her drop something into Eveline's tea he snatched the cup from her and took it straight to the police station. An analysis by the police chemist showed that it contained thallium, a deadly poison without taste or smell, so that it was easy to administer without the knowledge of the victim.

At Caroline's trial Eveline Lundberg was a star witness for the prosecution. She was a pitiful figure suffering from the permanent effects of thallium poisoning, completely blind and walking with the aid of sticks. Though there was a possible motive for the first two murders, there seemed no good reason for the rest. According to the prosecutor Caroline enjoyed the sense of power she gained from controlling the life and death of her victims. She had found murder easy, he said, and 'continued her career of poisoning out of habit'.

Martha Rendall

IT WAS a sad day for Thomas Morris's children when he took Martha Rendall into his home in Fremantle, Western Australia. Thomas, a railway worker, had turned his wife out of their home because of her slovenly ways and when Martha took over he was delighted by her careful housekeeping and high standard of cleanliness.

His five children were less delighted for though she insisted that they called her 'Mother' she had no affection for them, disciplining them harshly and beating them frequently. The neighbours noticed that the children, once healthy and happy, were now pale and listless and losing weight fast. They muttered among themselves but no one had the courage to take any action.

The children frequently caught cold and by summer 1907 Anne and Clive, both under 10, were suffering so badly from coughs and sore throats that the doctor was called in. He prescribed throat swabs and these were administered by Martha, ignoring the screaming and crying of the children, who found the process agonizing. The children grew steadily worse and in July Anne died, followed soon afterwards by Clive. The doctor who examined them noted the inflamed mucous membrane of the throat in each case and certified that the cause of death was the dreaded disease diphtheria.

Twelve months later 14-year-old Arthur also developed a severe sore throat and Martha once again produced the throat swabs and took no notice of Arthur's cries of agony. The neighbours listened to his shrieks in astonishment: surely no medicine could be effective if it caused so much pain? Still they were reluctant to report Martha's strange behaviour. Arthur died on 6 October 1908 and this time the doctor decided on an autopsy. This revealed nothing untoward and once again the death was attributed to diphtheria.

In April 1909 young George, one of the two remaining Thomas children, took a cup of tea from Martha and found that it was so hot it scalded his throat. Martha announced that throat swabs would be the perfect remedy but George had listened to the screams of his brothers and sister and he had watched them die. He was determined that he was not going to suffer the same fate, so while Martha was preparing the swabs he bolted out of the door and did not return.

His disappearance was reported to the police, who on making enquiries in the neighbourhood, soon heard from the neighbours about the ill-treated Morris children and Martha's strange idea of nursing. When George was found he said that he was afraid that 'Mother' was going to kill him, like the others.

Further enquiries revealed that over the past three years Martha had bought large quantities of hydrochloric acid from the chemist. The bodies of the three Morris children were exhumed and this time a more thorough postmortem was carried out, showing that their throats had been washed with large amounts of hydrochloric acid, producing inflammation hardly distinguishable from that caused by diphtheria.

Martha and Thomas were both charged with murder, but there was no evidence to convict Thomas. Martha, it was shown, was a sadistic murderer who had given the children acid in their tea to make their throats sore, then had used copious amounts in the swabbing procedure. She was, apparently, jealous of the attention Thomas gave to the children and wanted to have him to herself. Martha Rendall became the last woman to be hanged in Western Australia, on 6 October 1909.

Christa Lehmann

CHRISTA LEHMANN had an unhappy youth and made a miserable marriage. She grew up in Worms, Germany, in the 1920s and 1930s, a time of deep economic depression. Her mother was committed to an asylum when she was in her teens and her father drowned his sorrows in drink. Christa was caught in a number of petty thefts and put on probation.

She hoped to turn over a new leaf when she married Karl Franz Lehmann in 1944 but her happiness was short-lived when she realized that, like her father, he was a drunkard. No one expected her to be grief-striken when a ruptured stomach ulcer led to his death in 1952. After that, Christa was free to take lovers and to spend a good deal of her spare time with her closest friend, Anni Hamann.

On 12 February 1954, Christa generously offered several of her neighbours cream-filled chocolate truffles. Most of them ate and enjoyed them right away but 75-year-old Eva Ruh, Anni's mother, put hers in the fridge for later. When Anni came home from work she saw the tempting sweet and took a bite, only to grimace and spit most of it out on to the floor, where the family dog wolfed it down eagerly. Shortly afterwards Anni was doubled up with stomach pains and only minutes later she was dead. The dog, too, went into convulsions and died.

At first the police were at a loss: Anni had obviously been poisoned but the forensic examination failed to detect any of the usual poisons. It was only when a university scientist was brought in to help that the cause of death was identified as a new and lethal phosphorus compound known as E–605, developed as a chemical insecticide.

Eva Ruh had witnessed the effect of the chocolate truffle, yet it was hard for her, or the police, to believe that Christa would poison her best friend. However, they soon discovered that her husband had died suddenly, and in great pain, and that the following year her father-in-law, with whom she had been living since Karl's death, had fallen off his bicycle soon after leaving home and died in the street after several agonizing convulsions. It was obvious that Christa had some explaining to do and she was taken into custody.

Within a few days, Christa had confessed all. She admitted that she had given a poisoned sweet to Eva Ruh – she, not her daughter Anni, had been the intended victim. Christa had a grudge against her because she fancied that the old lady was trying to break up her friendship with Anni. Obviously thinking that she no longer had anything to lose, she also admitted to murdering her husband and her father-in-law. She had seen the new insecticide on the shelf at the local chemist's shop. It had been labelled 'poison', so she assumed that it would do the job.

At her trial, Christa's lawyer tried to argue that she should not be held responsible for her actions as she was a 'moral primitive' who had grown up without developing the standards by which normal people measured their actions. It was an unconvincing defence and Christa was sentenced to life imprisonment on 20 September 1954. Even then, she seemed quite cheerful about her crimes, telling newspaper reporters that she had always enjoyed a good funeral. 'I suppose I shouldn't have done it,' she was quoted as saying, 'but except for Anni, they were all nasty people.'

Christa's discovery of E–605 as an effective poison started a new fashion, with a couple of dozen murderers following her lead and more than 70 suicides using it to escape the hopelessness of the current recession.

Sharon Kinne

IN THE USA, where gun licences are easy to obtain and many ordinary families keep a revolver beside the bed or in the glove compartment of the car, deaths by the bullet are frequent and it is much easier to claim that the shooting was an accident. Police called to investigate the death of James Kinne at his home near Kansas City found James lying dead on his bed, shot in the back of the head, and a sobbing young wife, Sharon. Through her tears she told how her two-and-a-half-year-old daughter had been playing a game of cops and robbers with her father's gun, with fatal results. James was always leaving the gun around the house, she said, and the little girl often played with it.

There were those who had their suspicions, knowing that after four years of marriage the Kinnes quarrelled frequently and that Sharon wanted a divorce, but the child was obviously accustomed to handling the gun and Sharon's story was accepted. As soon as she received the money from her husband's insurance policy she bought a flashy new car from an attractive salesman, and in the weeks that followed they became more than friends. Only two months after James Kinne's death the body of Patricia Jones, the salesman's wife, was found in an area well-known as a haunt for courting couples. She had been shot four times with a .22 calibre revolver and it was Sharon Kinne and a boyfriend who discovered the body. Sharon said they had been out looking for Patricia because they thought she was seeing another man and did not want to tell her husband before they had concrete proof.

A witness came forward to say that she had seen Patricia getting into Sharon's car early on the evening of her death and a friend described buying a .22 pistol for her, which she did not want registered in her name. Sharon admitted having such a pistol but said that she had lost it some time before. Though she was charged with murder, all the evidence was circumstantial and not strong enough to convict her. The previous owner of the pistol was traced and he remembered firing bullets from it into a tree. These were dug out and examined, but they did not match the bullets in Patricia's body. Though the witness said that he had owned several guns and could well have been mistaken about the pistol used on the tree-shooting day, his mistake helped in Sharon's acquittal.

Her troubles were not yet over; she was arrested again, this time on the charge of murdering her husband. A review of the evidence, in the light of subsequent events, had revealed holes in her story and a witness gave evidence that she had once offered him $1000 to kill her husband. The court decided that a toddler would have been unable to pull the trigger and found her guilty, but a clever lawyer managed to have the verdict set aside on a technicality and the replacement jury could not reach agreement. Once again, Sharon was free.

She dropped out of sight for four years until the night of 18 April 1964 when a motel owner in Mexico City heard gunshots and, hurrying to investigate, found Sharon Kinne still with the pistol in her hand and a man lying dead on the floor. This time Sharon could not deny the shooting but said that the man, a Mexican radio presenter called Francisco Ordonez, had invited her back to his motel room because she was feeling ill. Once there, he had attacked her and tried to rape her, so she had been forced to defend herself.

It was one story too many and this time, no one believed her, especially when it was found that bullets fired from her .22 gun matched those found in the body of Patricia Jones. She was sentenced to 13 years in gaol.

Kathryn England

KATHRYN ENGLAND, living in a Tennessee farming community, had the choice of two guns: with one she practised her husband's murder, lining up her shot, so that with the other she could shoot him as he lay on his bed. The couple had been married for 25 years and, as far as those who worked with them in the tobacco fields knew, their marriage seemed happy enough – but in reality they had both begun to look outside for fulfilment.

Early one Saturday morning in March 1982, a neighbour of the Englands' scrambled into his clothes to answer the hammering on his door. Kathryn England, shaking and tearful, gasped: 'Please come. Something's happened to my husband.' At the Englands' house, he found 45-year-old Franklin lying in his own blood in the bathroom. He assumed that Franklin had committed suicide but the police had other ideas. There was a large bloodstain on the bed, which seemed to be where Franklin had been shot. Though the bullet had missed his heart, a fragment had opened an artery in his arm as he staggered from the bedroom to the bathroom. It looked far more like murder than suicide.

Above the bloody patch there was a hole in the bedroom ceiling and closer examination showed another, smaller hole which had been stopped up. Below it, a .22 bullet was found buried deep in the mattress. In the attic, near the hole in the ceiling, were two guns: a .22 rifle and a .270 weapon. Kathryn's first explanation was that she had been in the attic shooting at the blackbirds that were damaging her garden when the gun had jammed; as she tried to free the bullet it had fired while the gun was pointed at the floor, penetrating the ceiling and accidentally hitting her husband.

Her story left many questions unanswered and she told several others over the weeks that followed, including one in which she fired a shot at her husband just to wake him up. When she came to trial the prosecutor maintained that she had planned the murder carefully, testing out the angle of the shot with the lighter gun, plugging up the hole so that her husband would not notice, then using the heavier rifle to fire on Franklin.

Kathryn now told a different tale, painting a graphic picture of a violent marriage and herself as a victim, a battered wife who lived in fear of her husband. He had forced her into perverted sex acts, assaulted and ill-treated her, once causing a miscarriage. He threatened to kill her if she told anyone of his brutal treatment, which explained why no doctor could testify to the bruises she had sustained from his fists. She had considered killing herself many times but had never quite had the courage.

She had to admit, under cross-examination, that she had a male friend who had taken her away for weekends and that she had once consulted a lawyer about her financial status as a widow. All the same, she protested that she had never intended to kill Franklin, whom she had once loved, but only to stop the beatings. It was a good performance but the jury remained unconvinced: she was sentenced to life imprisonment.

Ruth Ellis

RUTH ELLIS has gone down in history as the last woman to be hanged in Britain. Ruth, a peroxide blonde who worked as a club manageress, had gunned down the lover who had tired of her, racing car driver David Blakely, in full view of passers-by in a suburban London street. She made contradictory statements about where she got the gun and it still remains something of a mystery. If someone else was involved, giving her the gun when she was obviously full of drink and jealousy, then he would have been implicated in the murder and Ruth might never have hanged.

Ruth, who was 28 when she committed murder, had led a che-quered life. She left school at 14 to work as a waitress and at 18 she had an affair with a French-Canadian soldier which resulted in an illegitimate baby. In her ambitious search for a more affluent lifestyle she became a night club hostess and at the Court Club she met dentist George Ellis, a big spender who bought her champagne, clothes and expensive presents. They married and she bore him a daughter, but George was a violent drunkard and they soon separated. Ruth moved on to work as a call-girl and nude model, then as manageress of the Little Club, an upstairs drinking room in Knightsbridge. It was at this time that she met David Blakely, who came from a far more affluent background. Born in 1929, the son of a Sheffield doctor, he was educated at a leading public school but, in spite of his upper-crust accent and suave charm, he was temperamentally incapable of hold-ing down a steady job. He had a passion for racing cars which he could indulge on the legacy left by his father but, though he raced at well-known venues like Silverton and Le Mans, mixing with the stars of the racing circuit, he was never successful. When Ruth first met

Ruth Ellis with her lover David Blakely

him he was drunk and insulting and she thought him a 'pompous ass'. Unfortunately for her, she later succumbed to his boyish charm and easy, cultivated manner.

Though David was engaged to another girl, he and Ruth became lovers and late in 1953 she found she was pregnant. She later said that David had offered to marry her but at the time she was not really in love with him and thought that she could 'get out of the mess quite easily' by having an abortion. Perhaps in an attempt to distance herself from David, Ruth began a new affair, this time choosing a more dependable lover, 33-year-old company director Desmond Cussen, who fell deeply in love with her. Predictably, this sharpened David's interest. He became jealous and began hanging around the club all the time, telling her that he had broken off his engagement.

When Ruth took a flat in Egerton Gardens, Kensington, Cussen lent her money to pay the rent but it was David who moved in with her. They lived there as Mr and Mrs Ellis but there was nothing harmonious about their relationship. David was drinking heavily at Ruth's expense – he had by now frittered away his inheritance – and had fits of violent jealousy about her continued liaison with Cussen during which he would beat her so badly that she had to use camouflage make-up to cover the bruises. Ruth was also jealous of David's growing friendship with a married couple, Carole and Anthony Findlater, and suspected him of having an affair with Carole.

Things came to a head at Easter 1955 when Ruth and David had had a bitter row, with Ruth receiving a black eye and David a superficial cut from a knife. On Friday 8 April, David told the Findlaters that he was becoming worried about what Ruth might do and that he wanted to get away from her. They invited him to spend the weekend with them in Tanza Road, Hampstead, and though he was expected home that evening he accepted. Ruth, who had had a miscarriage 10 days earlier and was feeling ill and depressed, waited all evening for David to arrive, then phoned the Findlaters at about 10.30 pm. She spoke to Anthony, who denied that David was with him. Ruth phoned several times after that but found that as soon as she spoke, the receiver was replaced. In the early hours of the morning Ruth went to Tanza Road, where she saw David's green Vanguard parked outside the Findlaters' flat. No one answered when she rang the bell, so she banged on the windows of the van until they fell in, trying to make as much noise as possible. Anthony Findlater appeared at the door in his pyjamas, still insisting that David was not there, while Ruth shouted to her lover to come down and talk to her. The police were called and though Ruth insisted that 'I shall stay here all night until he has the guts to show his face', they eventually persuaded her to go home. Too upset to sleep she paced about smoking until morning, when she went back to Tanza Road and hid in a doorway, watching David and Findlater come out of the house and drive off in the Vanguard.

On the Saturday night Ruth was back in Tanza Road, watching the flat from the road while the Findlaters held a party. She could hear David's voice and a woman she thought to be the Findlaters' nanny giggling in response. Later, when the blinds in the nanny's room went down, David's voice was no longer audible and Ruth concluded that he was 'up to his tricks' again and that the nanny was the new attraction. She spent another night sleepless, fuming and drinking. By the evening of Easter Sunday, she admitted at her trial, 'I was very upset. I had a peculiar feeling I wanted to kill him.'

Once more she went back to Hampstead but this time the Vanguard was not in Tanza Road, so she made her way to the Magdala pub at the foot of South Hill Park. When she arrived, David and a friend, car salesman Clive Gunnell, were just leaving, carrying three quarts of light ale. At first, neither of them noticed Ruth. Gunnell went round to the passenger side of the Vanguard while David, juggling the flagon of beer, fumbled for his keys. Ruth called his name, but he did not seem to hear. Again she called him, pulling a heavy Smith and Wesson .38 revolver from her handbag. As David ran for the back of the van, two shots rang out in quick succession. He slammed against the side of

the vehicle, then staggered towards the motionless Gunnell, screaming to him for help.

'Get out of the way, Clive,' shouted Ruth, firing a third shot at David
as he tried to run for safety. As David fell to the ground, Ruth stepped
up to his body and fired three more shots. The sixth bullet ricocheted
off the road and hit the hand of a woman who was on her way to the
Magdala to join her husband for a drink. Ruth stood still, unmoved by
the blood and the cries of the gathering spectators. As a customer
from the saloon bar approached her, she told him, 'Phone the police.'
PC Thompson, who had been enjoying an off-duty drink, replied, 'I am
a police officer', and took the gun gently from her.

From then onwards, Ruth remained cool and composed. Before
her trial one of her main concerns was that her hair was showing its
dark roots and arrangements were made for the right dye to be sent
into Holloway Prison. Though she pleaded not guilty, Ruth did not put
up a spirited defence. She was unwilling that too much of her past
should be revealed in court and she refused to invite the sympathy of
the jury. When answering her counsel's questions about the times
David had beaten her she made light of them, saying, 'He only used to
hit me with his fists and hands, but I bruise very easily.'

When Mr Christmas Humphreys, for the Crown, rose for cross-
questioning he asked only one question: 'Mrs Ellis, when you fired
that revolver at close range into the body of David Blakely, what did
you intend to do?'

'It is obvious', replied Ruth simply 'that when I shot him I intended
to kill him.'

With that reply, she sealed her fate. In his summing up, the judge
pointed out that it was no defence to show that the accused was
jealous, unwell and badly treated by her lover and that she was overcome with an uncontrollable urge to kill him. If the jury was satisfied
that Ruth Ellis fired the shots that killed David Blakely, the only other
question to decide was 'that at the same time she fired those shots she

had an intention to kill or do grievous bodily harm'. It was obvious that the only possible verdict was 'guilty'.

From the death cell, Ruth wrote to David's mother, saying, 'I shall die loving your son and you should feel content that his death has been repaid.' When she heard that there was to be no reprieve, she wrote to a friend about her coming execution: 'Don't worry, it's like having a tooth out and they'll give me a glass of brandy beforehand.' She was calm to the end – 'the bravest woman I ever hanged' said the official hangman, Albert Pierrepoint.

As for the gun, Ruth originally claimed that it had been given to her about three years before by a man in a club, but she did not know his name. The police did not believe the story at the time and after the trial she made a statement saying that Cussen, with whom she had been drinking, had given her the gun, ready loaded, and had even driven her to Hampstead. This was never proved and Cussen flatly denied all knowledge of the gun. 'She was a dreadful liar, you know,' he said.

Pauline Dubuisson

FOUR YEARS before Ruth Ellis's crime, Pauline Dubuisson shot her ex-lover dead in his Paris flat. In her case the jury brought in a verdict of murder without premeditation so that she was sentenced to imprisonment rather than execution. It was a surprising decision which seemed to fly in the face of all the facts.

In 1946 Pauline had enrolled as a medical student at the University of Lille, where her first report described her as very intelligent but 'not a steady worker. She is well-balanced but haughty, provoking and a flirt. Her conduct is mediocre'. At university she plunged into a stormy three-year-long affair with another student, Felix Bailly, but Pauline never managed to remain faithful to one man; she continued to sleep around and even kept a notebook recording details of the comparative performance of her various lovers. Though Felix wanted to marry her, she was enjoying herself too much to settle down and eventually Felix decided to end the relationship and continue his studies in Paris.

For 18 months there was no contact between them. Pauline had a number of lovers and it was not until she heard from a friend that Felix was engaged to be married that she decided to visit him in Paris and attempt to start up their affair again. When she found that Felix was no longer interested Pauline was furious and spent her cash birthday present from her father on a .25 calibre automatic. She left a note for her landlady in Lille to say that she planned to kill Felix and herself, so by the time she arrived in Paris in March 1951 Felix had been warned and was on his guard. He refused to let her into his flat and would only agree to meet her in a public place, with one of his friends present.

Pauline did not go to the arranged meeting-place; instead, she sat in a café opposite Felix's Left Bank flat, calmly sipping coffee as she watched the two men leave and return an hour or so later. She waited until the friend had left then made her way up to Felix's seventh-floor flat. Felix was expecting the arrival of a second friend, Bernard Mougeot, who was taking over the role of protector, so when Pauline knocked he may have opened the door expecting to find Bernard standing there. Instead it was Pauline, with pistol at the ready. She shot him three times. Any one of the three shots could have killed him but Pauline was taking no chances: the final bullet entered her ex-lover's head behind the right ear.

Pauline then turned the gun on herself but it jammed on the fourth bullet, so she disconnected the pipe leading to the gas cooker in the kitchen, put the free end in her mouth and lay down, preparing to die. Bernard Mougeot, whose taxi had been stuck in a traffic jam, arrived to find the smell of gas seeping into the corridor. Inside the flat, his friend was lying in a pool of blood on the living-room floor and Pauline was unconscious in the kitchen. He quickly removed the pipe from her mouth and called the fire brigade, who revived her to stand trial for murder.

When he heard the news Pauline's father, overcome with shame, killed himself, first taking a dose of poison and then gassing himself. On the day fixed for her trial Pauline was found unconscious in her cell, bleeding profusely from a cut wrist. Her suicide note said: 'I think my family is accursed and myself also. I only hurt those whom I love most in the world.' Once more she was revived and the trial began a month later.

It was difficult for the defence to represent Pauline's act as a 'crime of passion' when she had been separated from Felix for 18 months – and when her acid remarks about her various lovers were read out in court she could not claim to be deserted and lovelorn. Far more pitiful was Felix's fiancée, robbed of her happiness by Pauline's jealousy. Pauline's background was also against her: she had been in her early teens when the German occupation of France began but by the age of

Pauline Dubuisson at the opening session of her trial

17 she was the mistress of a 55-year-old German colonel, so that after the Allied landings she suffered the punishment reserved for collaborators and had her head publicly shaved.

The prosecutor even mocked Pauline's suicide attempt, suggesting that it was just too convenient that the gun had jammed. Perhaps she had only turned on the gas tap when she heard steps approaching the flat door. Then again, she had managed to fail when cutting her wrist. She had managed murder far more efficiently than she had managed suicide, he suggested. However, it may have been the suicide attempts that caught the sympathy of the jury, for the evidence showed that her story of the gun jamming on the fourth shot was correct, and that by the time the firemen arrived she had second-degree asphyxiation and was foaming at the mouth. By the time she was discovered bleeding in her cell, she had lost a litre (2 pints) of blood. Whatever the reason, the verdict resulted in a more lenient sentence than Pauline might have expected.

Leone Bouvier

LEONE BOUVIER was far more deserving of sympathy than Pauline Dubuisson, though she too killed her lover with a bullet. However, the French court handed down the same verdict, ignoring the extenuating circumstances of her miserable background and blighted love affair. Leone had been a victim all her life, growing up in an unloving household with a violent, alcoholic father and a bitter, hard-drinking mother. She was a plain girl of limited intelligence but with a generous nature and need for love that made her an easy prey for the local lads who laughed at her behind her back.

Her luck seemed to be changing when she met Emile Clenet, a 22-year-old garage mechanic in Nantes. They first met at a dance and made a date for the next afternoon, but on the way to the rendezvous Leone's bicycle had a puncture and by the time she got there Emile had gone. It was six months before they met again at the local Lent carnival. 'You're six months late', joked Emile. 'Never mind, we've found each other again.' After the fair Emile took her to a hotel where they made love, and Leone felt valued for the first time in her life.

Sunday was Emile's only free day and it soon became the one highspot in Leone's dreary life. The couple would ride on Emile's motorbike, go dancing sometimes, and end the day in a cheap hotel. They talked about marrying and Emile took her home to meet his parents, who were welcoming and kindly. Everything seemed to be going well but Leone seemed dogged by misfortune. A minor accident with the motorbike resulted in a bang on the head and after that she suffered from headaches and depression which got on Emile's nerves. A few months later Leone became pregnant, only to lose the baby and find her bouts of depression getting more frequent and less manageable.

In January 1952 she was sacked from her factory job, resulting in a violent row at home with her mother screaming and her father raining blows on her. Leone took off on her bicycle, riding all night to reach the garage where Emile worked. She was exhausted and tearful, he was irritable and unconcerned: she had no business bothering him at work, he had no time to listen to her and at the moment he was too busy even to meet for their regular Sundays. Leone was devastated. She had no money and nowhere to go, so she spent days wandering the streets and nights sleeping rough before drifting into prostitution to buy food and shelter. She found herself standing outside gun shops, mesmerized by the gleaming weapons in the window. She could not explain later what was going through her head – perhaps suicide, perhaps murder – but one day she had a hallucination, seeing a young man standing at her side saying: 'Don't. He is too young. He has a right to live.' Subconsciously she must have been thinking of killing Emile, even if she had not admitted it to herself yet.

Over the next few weeks she saw little of Emile but she pinned her hopes on her birthday on 15 February. Last year they had been close and happy and Emile had bought her a bicycle lamp, the only present she had received since childhood. She was thrilled when he agreed to meet her but he did not acknowledge her birthday and he stayed with her only long enough to use her body, just like the men she picked up on the docks. The next day she bought a gun. Even for an illiterate girl like Leone, there was no problem; the .22 automatic had recently been designated a 'sporting weapon' and was available to anyone.

When Emile asked her to meet him at the Lent carnival, Leone hoped that the carnival, with all its memories, would be a new beginning for them – but she must have had her secret doubts, for she carried her gun in her handbag.

At first all went well; they wandered through the gaily decked stalls and Emile spent some time at the shooting range. Then he casually told her that he was leaving for a job in North Africa and did not plan to return. When Leone asked what had happened to their marriage plans, he merely shrugged and told her to find someone else. He drove her back to where she had left her bicycle and, deaf to her entreaties, prepared to ride away. Leone asked him to kiss her one last time, drew him towards her with her left arm and kissed his cheek. At the same time she placed the barrel of the gun against his neck and fired a single bullet. Afterwards she fled to the convent where her sister was a nun, and where she was arrested the following day.

The judge at her trial was hostile, unwilling to concede that Leone's circumstances made any difference to the case. If her sister could rise above her home background and become a nun, then why should Leone have gone wrong? He found it outrageous that she should have shot her lover while she kissed him and demanded to know why she killed him.

'I loved him,' Leone answered simply, tears streaming down her face.

Middle-class women had walked free from French courts on the excuse that they had committed a 'crime of passion' but poor, dim Leone Bouvier was sentenced to penal servitude for life – a minimum of 20 years.

Dr Alice Wynekoop

DR ALICE WYNEKOOP, a frail 62-year-old widow who was highly respected in her neighbourhood of Chicago, seemed an unlikely murderer, hardly the type to shoot a young woman in cold blood. Yet not only did she commit the crime but she left the body in her basement surgery while she cooked an evening meal of pork chops and mashed potatoes for herself and Enid Hennessy, her lodger. Then the two women sat and chatted about the book Miss Hennessy had recently been reading, a volume of Galsworthy's *Forsyte Saga*.

It was late in the evening of 21 November 1933 when Alice's daughter Catherine, a doctor specializing in paediatrics, took a distraught phone call from her mother. 'It's Rheta,' she gasped. 'She's dead . . . she's been shot.' When the police arrived Dr Alice let them in, saying, 'Something terrible has happened here.' She led them down to the surgery, where they found a naked girl lying face downwards on the operating table. A revolver lay near her head and her clothes were heaped on the floor. When the police pulled away the blanket they found that she had been shot in the chest and there were burns on her face, thought to be the result of chloroform.

The dead girl was Alice's daughter-in-law Rheta, the daughter of one of the leading merchants of Indianapolis, Burdine H. Gardner. She had recently married Alice's favourite son Earle. As Earle had proved incapable of holding a steady job, the young couple had moved in with Alice but the marriage had been a disaster from the start. Earle saw no reason to curtail any of his pleasures – which mainly revolved round liquor and girls – for the sake of his young wife. Rheta, left for weeks on end in the forbidding three-storey house with only Alice and her elderly lodgers for company, soon turned into a nagging neurotic, forever complaining about her health and haunted by the fear of developing tuberculosis.

When Earle, forced to cut short his latest trip by news of Rheta's death, arrived back in Chicago, he made no pretence of grief. He told waiting reporters that his wife was 'sickly and mentally deranged', so much so that she had once tried to poison his whole family by drugging their food. The marriage, he said, was an utter failure. He supported his mother's story that Rheta was killed by a burglar who had broken into the surgery in search of drugs. Rheta, as part of her hypochondria, was in the habit of weighing herself naked in the surgery and the burglar, expecting to find the room empty, must have panicked and shot her.

To the experienced eyes of the detectives, it was obvious that this was not the work of a burglar and they subjected Alice to days of questioning. At first they trod carefully – after all, she was a doctor of some standing, known for her dedicated work among the poor. After her husband, Dr Frank Wynekoop, died she had supported her three children, enabling her daughter to study medicine and her elder son to enter the business world on a good footing. There was nothing in her life to suggest that she was anything but a fine, upstanding citizen, but as the questioning continued her interrogators became convinced that she had committed the crime. Her utter devotion to Earle was obvious and it was equally obvious that she had little time for Rheta. To the rest of the world Earle might be a wastrel who neglected his wife and refused to shoulder his obligations, but in his mother's eyes he could do no wrong. She would do anything for him – even, perhaps, taking action to rid him of a cumbersome wife.

Eventually Alice confessed that no burglar was involved, but she insisted that Rheta's death had been an accident and the gunshot had been an attempt to make it seem like the work of an outsider. The doctor said that Rheta was suffering from a recurrent pain in her side and she had offered to examine her. The pain was so bad that Rheta had asked for an anaesthetic, so the doctor had given her chloroform on a sponge. She took several deep breaths but then stopped breathing and did not revive even after 20 minutes of artificial respiration. The doctor's description of what followed was worded like a medical report, as though she were distancing herself from any possible emotion: 'wondering what method would ease the situation best of all and with the suggestion offered by the presence of a loaded revolver, further injury being impossible, with great difficulty one cartridge was exploded at a distance of some half dozen inches from the patient.' She concluded by trying to explain why she then left the body lying in the surgery while she went about her ordinary household tasks: 'The scene was so overwhelming that no action was possible for a period of several hours'.

Later Alice retracted even this guarded confession, saying that she was not in her right mind after prolonged questioning. Earle never accepted it and, in an attempt to save his mother, he confessed to the murder himself. He was arrested, but released when it was proved that he was on a train to Arizona with his latest girlfriend at the time the shot was fired.

At her trial the defence advanced the burglar theory once more, while the prosecution suggested that Alice had murdered her daughter-in-law for her insurance. Though insurance money has been sufficient motive for many murders, Alice's known character and past life suggests that it was far more likely that she saw this as the best way to liberate her beloved son from a bad marriage. Whatever her motive, she was found guilty of first-degree murder and gaoled for life. She was paroled at the age of 78 and died two years later.

Addie Mae Lemoine

THERE WAS always a gun in the Lemoine household in Louisiana, for Louis Lemoine's greatest pleasure in life was hunting in the swamps and woods he had known since boyhood. Sometimes he was gone for days at a time, usually returning with a deer slung across his shoulders to provide extra meat for the table. But when he went off on 23 April 1962 without letting anyone know where he was going, his brothers were surprised. According to his wife, Addie Mae, he had taken his .410 calibre shotgun, which would point to a regular hunting trip – but Louis always told one of his brothers where he was heading so that if he did not return they could come to his aid. It was a sensible precaution for a man who had been deaf and dumb since birth.

As the days lengthened into weeks, the sheriff began to take an interest in Louis's disappearance. Louis had a reputation as a thoroughly reliable workman, yet he had let down a logging contractor who had engaged him for a job, leaving him short-handed. It was also discovered that he had left his box of .410 shells behind in the boot of his car, where he kept them safely from the children. At this point Addie Mae arrived at the sheriff's office with a letter, supposedly written to her son by his aunt in Baton Rouge. It said that Louis had visited her a few days before and sent his love to his children. It was a bad mistake: the sheriff only had to compare the letter with an example of Addie Mae's handwriting to know that she had written it herself and put it into an envelope posted in Baton Rouge.

Addie Mae's fate was sealed when the local shopkeeper remembered selling her two .410 shotgun shells the day before her husband's disappearance. It had stuck in his mind because no one had ever bought two shells rather than a box-full. Addie Mae pretended no longer. Louis was buried under the washhouse, she said, where she had hidden his body after shooting him.

Addie Mae had married Louis 20 years before when she was only 15 years old. He was eight years older and, strong and silent, he seemed very attractive to the unsophisticated girl who had known nothing but poverty and hardship. They had seven children, so looking after them kept Addie Mae busy, but as time went on she found her marriage unsatisfying. Her husband could make himself understood at work and at home but communication was necessarily limited. Louis was a self-sufficient man, unwilling to mix with people more than necessary; he was given to dark moods and would respond to a disagreement by taking himself to the woods for a couple of days. Addie Mae was still young enough to crave company and fun and the silence weighed heavily on her.

Husband and wife grew apart and after 13 years of marriage Addie Mae obtained a divorce, only to find that living apart from Louis did not bring the freedom and happiness she wished for. The children missed their father and she insisted that it was for their sake that she decided to move back in with Louis. The resentment and anger she felt about her life did not go away: it grew and festered until she could say in her statement that she had watched her sleeping husband on the night of 22 April and 'the more I looked at him the more I hated him'.

They had had an argument the day before and the frustrating, one-sided conversation, with no relief to be had from screaming at one another like most couples, had been the last straw. Now, with the children in bed and her husband sleeping, she loaded one of her two shells into the gun, held it near his head and fired. She had bought the second shell for herself but when the moment came to kill herself she lost her nerve. Instead she rolled the bloodstained bedclothes around her husband's body and pulled it into the washhouse, where she knew it would remain undiscovered until the next day. In the morning, after the children had gone to school, she took up some boards from the washhouse floor and buried Louis in a shallow grave.

Addie Mae pleaded guilty and was sentenced to life imprisonment – an imprisonment that would probably be no more miserable than the prison of her life with Louis. She had tried living with him, she had tried living without him and neither way filled her needs. In the end she saw the only way out as death for both of them, but had lacked the courage to fulfil her intentions.

Winnie Judd

IN 1932 Winnie Judd, the wife of a doctor, was committed to a hospital for the insane in Arizona, USA. She had shot her two best friends, Helwig 'Sammy' Samuelson and Agnes Ann LeRoi, then packed their bodies into two trunks and taken them by train from Phoenix, Arizona, to Los Angeles. Her crimes became known as the 'Phoenix Trunk Murders'.

In 1924, at the age of 26, Winnie had married William Judd, 32 years her senior. His work meant frequent moves and by 1931 they were living in an apartment in North 2nd Street, Phoenix, and Winnie was employed as a doctor's secretary at the Grunow Clinic. One of their neighbours in the building, Ann LeRoi, also worked at the clinic and Winnie became firm friends with Ann and her room-mate Sammy, who was ill with tuberculosis. When William Judd moved again, this time to Los Angeles, Winnie stayed behind, living with her two friends for a time before moving to an apartment at 1130 East Brill Street.

On 17 October she rang to say that she would be late getting to work. Shortly afterwards a call came in from someone who said that she was Ann LeRoi and that she was unable to come to work that day; Sammy's brother had arrived on a visit and she had to take him to Tucson. Later the receptionist who answered the phone said that she thought that it was Winnie Judd's voice, disguised in the hope of sounding like Ann. About 15 minutes later, Winnie arrived at the clinic, looking 'as white as a sheet'.

That evening, Winnie called a delivery company and asked them to pick up a trunk from North 2nd Street. When the delivery men arrived there were no lights in the apartment and Winnie told them that the power was cut off because she was leaving and they would have to

Winnie Judd

work with the aid of matches. The men told her that the trunk was too heavy to go as baggage and suggested that they should keep it overnight and send it by express in the morning. Winnie said that she would take it to her sister's home instead and asked them to deliver it to East Brill Street.

The next day Winnie arrived at the railway station with two trunks, which were loaded on to the Los Angeles express. The porter who handled them noticed a dark liquid dripping from the larger trunk and suspected that it might contain a butchered deer. Winnie's brother Jason accompanied her on the journey and at the other end the trunks were stored in the left luggage office. When Winnie and Jason returned to collect them later in the day they were asked to open them, because station staff had noticed an unpleasant smell coming from the larger trunk. Winnie said that she would get the keys from her car and left the station hastily with her brother, but she failed to return. The police were called to the station where they broke open the trunks to find the body of Ann LeRoi in the larger one and the remains of Sammy Samuelson, cut into pieces to fit into the smaller one. Winnie's brother was quickly apprehended and admitted that Winnie had told him about the contents of the trunks and that they had planned to throw them into the sea. He said that his sister was subject to 'insane fits of anger'.

Dr Judd put out a public plea to his wife through the newspapers: 'I earnestly beg and implore her to come to me . . . If she has committed the crime with which she is charged, it means that it was done in a period of irresponsibility and an irrational state or condition. I want to assure her that if this comes to her attention, she will have every support and assistance I am able to give her.' It was several days before Winnie responded and gave herself up at a Los Angeles funeral parlour. At the time her hand was roughly bandaged and later a .25 calibre bullet was extracted from between her middle and index fingers. At her trial, it was shown that the bullets from the victims' bodies and that from the prisoner's hand all came from the same gun and that this gun, together with a set of surgical instruments, was in a hat-box carried by Winnie on her train journey.

A long, semi-incoherent letter from Winnie to her husband was found, in which she gave an account of the murders. According to her she had quarrelled with the two girls over breakfast, while they were all still in their pyjamas. Sammy had threatened her with a gun, whereupon Winnie put her hand over the muzzle and grabbed the breadknife. The gun went off, wounding Winnie in the hand but she managed to knock Sammy down and take the gun from her then, maddened by pain, she had shot both girls. Then she had panicked and packed the bodies in the trunks. 'It was horrible to pack things as I did,' she wrote. 'I kept saying "I've got to, I've got to or I'll be hung." '

For the next 39 years, until she was finally paroled in 1971, Winnie managed to remain in the news. Insane or not, she was clever enough to escape from custody seven times. The first six escapes all lasted only a few days and sometimes she gave herself up voluntarily but the seventh time she remained at liberty for over six years, making a life for herself in a California town where she worked as a housekeeper and was liked and trusted.

Claire Reymond

CLAIRE REYMOND arrived at the apartment her husband shared with his mistress, took out a revolver and shot the woman dead. In England she might well have hanged but she committed her crime in France, which had always accepted the idea that a 'crime of passion' was excusable, and a sympathetic jury discounted the apparent premeditation and the fact that she tricked her husband into leaving the apartment so that her rival was unprotected and helpless in the face of a firearm. Consequently, she was allowed to walk free.

She was 25 and had been married for four years to a prosperous businessman, her senior by 15 years. The marriage was happy enough, though the couple were disappointed that Claire had not become pregnant. After a year abroad, they returned to live in Paris in 1890. There Claire met up with a close friend from her schooldays, Yvonne Lassimone, a pretty blonde from a moneyed family who, to her great delight, asked her to become godmother to her baby daughter. Unfortunately Yvonne, a self-willed young woman who was used to getting her own way, was discontented with her own marriage, finding her young husband weak and uninteresting, and was immediately attracted to the older, more sophisticated Paul Reynard.

The two couples spent a good deal of time together but it was months before Claire began to wonder if there was more than friendship between her husband and Yvonne. One night they were returning from the theatre when their cab passed under a street lamp and, as the light came through the window, she thought for the moment that she saw Yvonne and Paul holding hands. Assuring herself that she had been mistaken, she put the incident out of her head until she found a bill for the purchase of an expensive ring. She had received no such present, but she had noticed a ring matching the description on Yvonne's finger.

In the scene that followed, with Claire in floods of tears, Paul admitted to being tempted into a brief affair but promised to put an end to it immediately. Yvonne, too, was penitent: she could not bear to lose Claire's friendship or have her daughter lose the attentions of her godmother, she said. It was just as important that she did not have to explain an estrangement between the two couples to her husband. However, despite all the promises, the affair continued and when Lassimone's work took him away from Paris Yvonne remained behind, giving the excuse that she was not well enough to face moving at the time. Lassimone had already received anonymous letters about his wife's behaviour – which might or might not have been written by Claire – and soon discovered that the couple had been meeting secretly at his mother-in-law's home. Still in love with his beautiful wife, he hung back, reluctant to risk precipitating a split, but in April 1892 there was a confrontation during which Lassimone struck Yvonne, with the result that she began divorce proceedings.

Things came to a head on 21 May, when Paul broke a lunch date with his wife. Claire, certain that he was visiting his mistress, took the opportunity to summon a locksmith to open his locked portmanteau. Inside she found several dozen love letters from Yvonne and the lease of an apartment, recently rented by Paul Reymond. For Claire it was the last straw; she took her husband's revolver, went to the address she had found on the lease and climbed up to the third-floor apartment. At first her alarmed husband refused to open the door but she slipped a note under the door saying that she had only come to warn them that Yvonne's husband had discovered their love-nest and was on his way, intent on making trouble. Paul opened the door and hurried downstairs to tell the concierge not to admit any strange men, leaving the two women alone.

Yvonne was sitting on the edge of the bed, putting on her stockings, and Claire claimed that she was 'strangled with emotion' at seeing her rival half-naked after making love with her husband. 'How could you be so shameless? It was I who was so good to you, who forgave you,' she cried. When Yvonne only replied mockingly, Claire said she lost her head. She fired five times and, though four of the bullets went wide, the fifth hit Yvonne in the stomach. Some sort of brief struggle followed, with Claire receiving scratches and Yvonne superficial cuts from a knife, then as Yvonne slumped to the floor Claire hastened from the apartment, passing her husband on the stairs.

Later in the day, Claire gave herself up at the police station. She maintained that she had gone to the apartment to catch the two lovers and confirm her suspicions. She had not intended to hurt Yvonne, much less kill her. When questioned about the gun and the knife, she insisted that she was in the habit of carrying them for protection when, as a young woman, she lived with her family in Haiti, and she had carried them ever since.

At her trial, extracts from Yvonne's letters, in which she always signed herself 'your wife', were read to the jury and were powerful tools in swinging the mood of the court Claire's way. In them the woman who professed to be her friend had told Paul that she viewed any affection shown by him to Claire as a 'profanation of my property' and ordered him: 'Stop sleeping in her bed, she disgusts me.' The jury, full of sympathy, ignored the obvious premeditation in Claire's acts – the fact that she had substituted her husband's revolver for her own tiny pistol and the way in which she had bluffed her way into the apartment – and found her not guilty. It was more a comment on the mood of the times than the merits of the case: in the early 1890s in France, more than half the women tried for crimes of passion were acquitted.

Lofie Louise Preslar

LOFIE LOUISE PRESLAR, later Peete, later still Judson, along with a handful of pseudonyms, was imprisoned for one murder and executed in the gas chamber for another. Her method was a quick bullet in the back of the neck, probably while she was chatting pleasantly to her unsuspecting victim, for Louise was an accomplished confidence trickster. She was a good-looking woman, rounded in her middle years, with luxuriant chestnut hair and a refined, ladylike manner. She gave the impression of being trustworthy and reliable but instead she was a cheat, a liar and a thief, as well as a killer. All those who came too close to her were in danger of their lives, for she was responsible for a number of deaths besides the murders she committed with her own hands.

She grew up in Louisiana, USA, and as a young teenager married Henry Bosley. The marriage lasted only two years and after their separation Bosley, still enamoured of Louise, killed himself. In 1913 she was involved in the death of a hotel desk clerk named Harry Faurote. The clerk and Louise, a guest in the hotel, were suspected of stealing a valuable diamond ring and Faurote apparently shot himself rather than face the disgrace of conviction. Louise, the only person left to give evidence, told a plausible tale and was believed. In 1915 she married a car dealer, Richard Peete, who was a steady, loving man and for a time she seemed to settle down happily, giving birth to a daughter, Betty. Five years later she was on the move again. Her husband's business was going badly and his health was declining, so she left him and went to Los Angeles. There she leased a house belonging to a wealthy mining engineer, Charles Denton, who had recently lost his wife and was planning a long trip. The arrangement was that Louise would move in immediately and Denton would stay on in the house for a short time while he made arrangements for his journey.

A few weeks later Denton disappeared and shortly afterwards Louise was displaying fine new jewellery to her admiring friends. When Denton's daughter and friends began to make more pressing enquiries, Louise came up with a colourful story: Denton had lost an arm after an infection turned septic and he had gone away for a time, too embarrassed to see anyone until he had adjusted to his disability. It was such an unlikely explanation that it was accepted for a while, but more questions were asked when it transpired that various business dealings had been left in mid-air and that no record could be found of payments made for the medical care needed by an amputee. Several months after Denton's disappearance a search was made at his house and his body was found buried in the cellar, wrapped in a quilt. Both his arms were intact but there was a bullet-hole in the back of his neck.

By this time Louise Peete had rejoined her husband in Denver, but when it was shown that she had forged Denton's name on cheques, pawned some of his property and charged clothes and jewellery to his late wife's account she was summoned back to Los Angeles for questioning. In 1921 she stood trial for murder and was sentenced to life imprisonment. Richard Peete stood by her during the trial, bringing their four-year-old daughter to court and earnestly telling reporters that Louise could never have committed such a crime. Her conviction was such a blow that he never fully recovered from it and three years later he committed suicide.

Louise was paroled in 1939, when she took the name of Anna Lee, and a few years later she went to live with two old friends, Margaret and Arthur Logan. Arthur was over 70 and fast lapsing into senility and Margaret was glad to have a friend to help with his care. It was not, of course, in Louise's nature to care for anyone. There were heated arguments as she pressed to have him sent to a sanatorium. At the beginning of May Louise married for the third time; her husband, Lee Judson, was a trusting widower, who knew nothing of her past. She invented reasons why he could not move in with her immediately and kept the marriage secret from the Logans. At the end of the month Margaret Logan disappeared and in June Arthur Logan was committed to an asylum where he died a few months later. Judson moved in with Louise, who was once more forging cheques and making free with other people's property.

It was in December that Margaret Logan's body was found, buried in her own garden. She had been shot in the back of the neck and the job had been finished by smashing the butt of the revolver into her skull. Both Judsons were promptly arrested, though the bewildered Lee was quickly cleared and released. Shortly afterwards he jumped to his death from a high-rise building, becoming yet another of Louise's victims.

In court, Louise told the mainly female jury that she had done nothing to harm Margaret Logan. Her husband had killed her in a fit of insanity and Louise had feared that she would be blamed because of her past record, so she had buried the body. The jury was unimpressed and took only a short time to decide on her guilt. She was sentenced to execution in San Quentin. Louise had remained calm and composed throughout both her trials and her demeanour did not change when she was led from the condemned cell and strapped into a chair in the gas chamber, under the gaze of several reporters.

Styllou Christofi

STYLLOU CHRISTOFI was a mother-in-law straight out of a nightmare who killed her son's wife with her own hands. She had come to England from Cyprus to live with her son Stavros, who worked as a waiter at the famous Café de Paris in London's West End. Stavros had been in England for 12 years and had married a German girl, Hella; they lived in a ground-floor flat in Hampstead with their three young children and did their best to welcome Styllou into their home. Unfortunately Styllou was a bitter, bad-tempered woman, overbearing and possessive, and from the day she arrived life in the Christofi household was thoroughly miserable. Nothing that Hella did was right for her; according to her mother-in-law she dressed like a woman of the street, she wasted money on make-up, she knew nothing about bringing up children. Styllou carped and criticized, argued and shouted and it was impossible to reason with her.

Twice Stavros found other lodgings for his mother but no landlady would tolerate her for long and she was soon back with his family. Eventually Hella put her foot down. She decided to take the children to Germany for a holiday and made it clear that, by the time she returned, Styllou must be back in Cyprus. Hella never had the chance to put her plans into effect. When the two women were alone in the kitchen Styllou set about Hella with the ashplate from the stove and battered her into insensibility, then she followed up by throttling her. She then dragged Hella's body out into the yard, soaked it with paraffin and set fire to it, stoking the blaze with newspaper, apparently hoping to make her daughter-in-law's death look like an accident. A neighbour, John Young, had taken his dog into the garden and saw the whole back of the next-door house aglow. When he saw Styllou

Styllou Christofi

tending the fire he assumed that everything was in order and as far as he could tell, as she stoked the flames, she was burning a tailor's dummy. Once she was satisfied that the fire had done its work, Styllou ran into the road, crying that her kitchen was on fire and her grand-children were in danger.

Police found bloodstains in the kitchen and burned paper and wood soaked in paraffin surrounding the charred body. Styllou told them: 'I wake up, I smell burning, go downstairs. Hella burning. Throw water, touch her face. Not move. Run out, get help.' Later, when the house was searched, they found Hella's wedding ring wrapped in paper and hidden behind an ornament in Styllou's bedroom, though Stavros said that his wife never took it off her finger. Styllou's explanation was: 'I find it on stairs. I wrap it up. I think it is a curtain ring.' In the dustbin were pieces of charred material, part of a scarf that belonged to one of the children, tied in a noose. Styllou had used it to strangle Hella, then cut it from her neck.

At her trial, her previous history was her downfall. It was revealed that as a young woman she had been accused of killing her own mother-in-law by ramming a burning torch down her throat, though for some unaccountable reason she had been acquitted. This time the jury recognized her for the vengeful, uncontrolled creature that she was and brought in a verdict of guilty. They dismissed her feeble story that she had gone to bed that evening leaving Hella doing some washing but had woken to the smell of smoke. Finding that Hella was not in her room, she said she had rushed into the kitchen to find that the back door was open and her daughter-in-law's body was lying in the yard in flames. She had thrown water on her face in an attempt to revive her but when this was unsuccessful she had run into the street for help.

If she had pleaded insanity she might well have escaped execution but she refused, saying 'I am a poor woman with no education but I am not a mad woman – never never, never'. She was hanged in 1954, a year before Ruth Ellis, who killed her lover in the same street – but while the Ellis hanging provoked a storm of protest, Styllou Christofi's execution passed with no lament. To the end she showed no feelings of sorrow or shame; her overwhelming emotion seemed to be anger that her son Stavros had found no way to protect her from her fate.

Julia Ransom

THE GARDEN of a pretty English cottage in Matfield, Kent, was the scene of a triple murder on a summer afternoon in 1940. The body of Mrs Dorothy Fisher was found in one corner of the orchard and her 19-year-old daughter Freda lay dead on the other side of the orchard. Both had been shot in the back. The third member of the household, a middle-aged maid named Charlotte Saunders, lay on the path at the side of the cottage, shot in the head. Inside, the contents of drawers and cupboards had been strewn across the floor.

Mrs Fisher was separated from her husband Walter, who lived at Piddington, Oxfordshire. The Kent police had called in the Flying Squad and Detective Chief Inspector Peter Beveridge went to interview Walter Fisher and search his farm. The most interesting thing he found was an auburn-haired woman asleep in Fisher's bedroom. Though Fisher explained that she was a friend who had been visiting when she felt ill and went to lie down, it was obvious to the detective that the two were lovers.

A little later, when she was up and dressed in blue slacks and a multi-coloured jumper, the woman was introduced as Mrs Florence Iris Ouida Ransom, for some reason known as Julia. Fisher said that his marriage to Dorothy had been over in all but name before the war started. He had begun an affair with Julia, a young widow, while Dorothy had taken a Danish lover. When the elder Fisher daughter married the family finally broke up, with Dorothy moving to Matfield and Walter to Piddington, though he claimed to have a warm regard for his wife, whom he visited frequently.

Beveridge had already checked out Dorothy's Danish friend, who lived in London. She had recently applied to the police for permission to entertain him at her home in Kent but this part of England was a sensitive area at this stage of the war, when preparations were under way to counter the expected invasion by German forces, and permission had been refused. Beveridge had satisfied himself that it would have been impossible for Dorothy's lover to have travelled down to her home and committed murder. Meanwhile, at the two Fisher homes, he was making some interesting discoveries. Among the servants at Walter's farm there was obvious resentment of Julia Ransom, who seemed to be taking over control and acting in a bossy and high-handed manner. She had engaged extra staff, a Mrs Guildford and her son Fred, but no one, including Walter, had known that these two were in reality her mother and brother. Beveridge learned that over the past fortnight, Fred had been teaching Julia to use a shotgun and to ride a bicycle. Julia acknowledged that she sometimes visited Dorothy and Freda but claimed that on the day in question she had not left home. She said that Mrs Guildford could confirm this, but under questioning Mrs Guildford wavered and seemed far from certain.

At Matfield, Dorothy Fisher's bicycle had been found lying in a ditch near the cottage, slightly damaged. In the orchard, between the two bodies, was a woman's white pigskin glove. All the victims had been shot at close range, which led Beveridge to conclude that the murderer was well-known to the Fishers. He guessed that Dorothy and her daughter, who had both been wearing gumboots, had taken their visitor into the orchard, perhaps with the idea of shooting rabbits. The maid had been preparing tea in the kitchen and had dropped the tray, smashing four cups, saucers and plates when she heard cries from the orchard and hurried out to see what was wrong.

A teenage boy from the village remembered seeing a woman with a bicycle circling the cottage on the day of the killings and stopping several times to peer through the hedge. His description of the auburn-haired woman, who wore blue slacks and a multi-coloured jumper, matched Julia Ransom exactly. The ticket collector at

Tonbridge station remembered the same woman arriving on the train from London a few minutes past midday, carrying a long thin parcel that might well have been a shotgun. A taxi-driver who drove her to Matfield agreed with the description. Four and a half hours later the woman had returned to the station and boarded the London train.

Julia Ransom was arrested and several witnesses picked her out at an identity parade as the woman seen in Matfield on the fateful day. One or two said that she had been wearing white gloves and the glove at the scene fitted her hand perfectly, though its mate was never found. A routine medical examination, performed when she was arrested, recorded abrasions on her knees that were consistent with a fall from a bicycle and detectives believed that she had taken Dorothy's bike to check out what was happening at the cottage, but had fallen off and left the bike in the ditch.

The prosecution case was that she had arrived in Matfield with the shotgun she had borrowed from her brother Fred. He admitted that he had been teaching her to use the gun and that on 8 July, the day before the murders, she had borrowed it. On 10 July she had returned it, saying that it needed cleaning. At the scene of the shooting she had reloaded the gun at least six times and had fired extra shots into the backs of both Dorothy and Freda as they lay dying. Her motive was jealousy over Walter's continued attachment to his wife and daughter.

At her trial Julia claimed that her mind was a blank, that she had no memory of what she did on 9 July. She was found guilty and sentenced to death, but was later certified insane and confined to an asylum.

Bridget Durgan

BRIDGET DURGAN was one of a number of notorious servant killers who turned to brutal murder after dismissal by their employers, using the nearest household implements to commit, or attempt to conceal, their crimes. Bridget was a 22-year-old Irish girl who had spent several years in America working for one family after another. She was quiet and unremarkable and most of her employers remembered little about her; there was certainly no hint of the horror to come when she joined the household of Dr and Mrs Coriell in New Jersey in 1866.

Bridget was very happy with her new employers. Mary Ellen Coriell, a frail little woman whose body had suffered from a number of miscarriages, was kind to her, she was well paid and the work was not too hard. Unfortunately the Coriells were not so happy with Bridget. She suffered from a type of epilepsy and had frequent fits, and she was incapacitated for several days every month with 'women's sickness'. This, combined with some unpleasant personal habits that offended Mary Ellen, made the couple decide to dispense with her services. Bridget was devastated: she had nowhere to go and knew she would never find such an agreeable household again.

The night before she was due to leave, the Reverend Little and his wife were roused from bed by a hammering on the door. There stood Bridget, thoroughly dishevelled and in her stockinged feet in the snow, holding two-year-old Mamie Coriell in her arms and babbling that two men were ransacking the house and that Mrs Coriell could be in danger of her life. Mr Little armed himself as a precaution against violent burglars, enlisted the help of neighbours and went to investigate. The first thing he saw was signs of a struggle downstairs and smoke issuing from the bedroom. Upstairs an oil lamp had been thrown at the bed, perhaps in an attempt to set fire to the house and destroy evidence, for on the floor lay Mary Ellen's dead body, soaked in blood. She had obviously fought long and hard, for her face and limbs were a mass of bruises, handfuls of her hair had been ripped out by the roots and there were several dozen knife slashes on both the back and front of the body.

Bridget's version of events was as follows: at 7.30 pm two men, complete strangers, had arrived at the house asking for the doctor, only to be told that he was out, attending a woman in labour. Three hours later they had returned and Mrs Coriell had opened the back door to them, assuming that it was her husband coming home. As the strangers pushed their way in and began menacing Mrs Coriell, Bridget had snatched up Mamie and escaped to summon help. The inconsistencies in her tale were soon apparent. She had claimed that Mrs Coriell thought that she was letting in her husband by the back door, while he pointed out that he always let himself in at the front. The only footprints found in the fresh snow outside the house were those of Bridget and the rescue party. A next-door neighbour had heard thumping and crashing coming from the Coriell house but not at the time that Bridget had described. The Reverend Little had seen a patch of blood on Bridget's skirt when she arrived at his house and she had later tried to change the clothing surreptitiously. When she was seen sneaking out to the garden shed she was followed and the household meat knife was found hidden there.

As the net closed around her, Bridget suddenly decided that she knew the two murderers after all and named two local men. When they could both prove their alibis beyond all doubt, she changed her mind and blamed another maid in the town. The maid, too, was able to show that she had been in bed at the time.

No one had the least sympathy for Bridget, least of all the judge at her trial, who was not even willing to consider the possibility that a previously quiet and inoffensive young woman who suddenly carried out such a frenzied attack, apparently without provocation, might not be responsible for her actions. No convincing motive was ever established, though it is just conceivable that Bridget thought that, with Mary Ellen out of the way, the doctor might need her services and keep her on. Alternatively, perhaps Bridget might have made a last plea to keep her position and, as a row developed and she finally faced the reality of being thrown out into the cold world, Bridget suddenly flew into a rage and attacked.

With or without a motive, she was found guilty and sentenced to death, to the delight of the courtroom spectators. On 30 August 1867 she was hanged in front of an enthusiastic crowd, all jostling for a better view.

Mary Flora Bell

MARY FLORA BELL, aged 11, was a pretty dark-haired child with intelligent blue eyes and a quick mind. She could scarcely have had less in common with such gruesome women as Kate Webster or Styllou Christofi yet she, too, strangled her victims and exhibited no remorse.

She was born to an unmarried mother of 17 in 1957. A year later her parents married and moved to the slums of Newcastle, where William Bell was seldom in work and Betty Bell was hospitalized several times because of psychiatric problems. Mary had an unsatisfactory upbringing; she could never count on affection from her mother, who frequently farmed her out to relatives or friends and once even took three-year-old Mary along to an adoption agency and tried to give her away to a woman who was leaving as she arrived. At school Mary was known for clever lying, showing-off and fighting at the least excuse.

On 25 May 1968, two boys exploring a derelict house in the Newcastle slums found the body of four-year-old Martin Brown lying in an upstairs room. Nearby lay an empty pill-bottle. At first it seemed that Martin had taken a lethal dose of pills, but later it was established that he had been asphyxiated. The following day there was a break-in at a nursery school nearby and several notes were found, obviously written by children, all referring to murder. One read: 'We did murder Martin Brown fuck off you bastard!' and another 'I murder so that I may come back.' A few days later the school's new alarm went off and police found two girls in the building: Mary Bell and 13-year-old-old Norma Bell. The girls were not related but lived next door to one another and, in spite of the difference in their ages, had been inseparable for some time. Both girls insisted that they had never

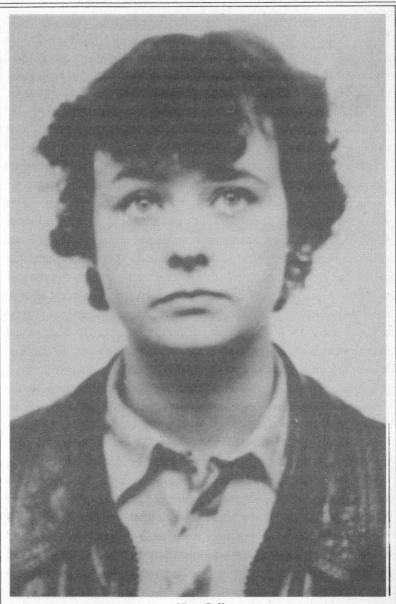

Mary Bell

been inside the school before and no action was taken against them. However, it was obvious that they had developed a morbid fascination with death. Mary called at the Brown's house, asking to see Martin, and when Mrs Brown told her that he was dead she replied cheerfully: 'Yes, I know he's dead. I wanted to see him in his coffin.' Horrified, Mrs Brown slammed the door in her face. Both girls went several times to see Martin's aunt, asking strange questions about how much she missed him and giggling at her answers.

On 31 July the body of three-year-old Brian Howe was found on a patch of waste ground in the same area of Newcastle. He had been strangled and there were cuts on his stomach and small puncture wounds on his legs. Police circulated hundreds of questionnaires to families with children, asking which of them were known to play on the waste ground where the body was found, what they were doing on the day of the murder and whether they had seen any strangers in the area. A number of children were questioned further about their answers, including Mary and Norma. Following their interviews, the two girls were asked for samples of their handwriting. Comparisons with the notes left at the nursery showed that they were the authors. When some of their clothes were sent for forensic examination, fibres from one of Mary's dresses matched with those found on both Martin Brown and Brian Howe. Fibres from Norma's skirt linked her with the second boy.

The children were taken to the police station, where Mary coolly enquired whether the interview room was bugged, demanded to see a solicitor and complained of being brainwashed. As the questioning intensified, the girls both talked about Brian Howe's murder, but each blamed the killing on the other. According to Norma, Mary had pulled the little boy down on the ground and gone 'all funny', squeezing his throat with her hands while he struggled and gasped. Mary had told her that her hands were 'getting thick' and asked her to take over but Norma had run away. Later they had gone back to the body, when Mary had punctured the boy's legs with scissors and tried to carve her initials on his stomach with a razor. Mary, in her turn, said that it was Norma who had strangled Brian while Mary tried to stop her. She had told him to lie down and then started squeezing his neck: 'She squeezed it hard, you could tell it was hard because her fingers were going white. Brian was struggling and I was pulling her shoulders but she went mad. . . . His face was all white and bluey and his eyes were open. His lips were purplish and had all like slaver on, it turned into something like fluff.' It was also Norma, she said, who had collected scissors and razor and marked the little boy's body.

On 5 December 1968 the two girls stood trial at Newcastle Assizes charged with the murders of Martin George Brown and Brian Edward Howe. The prosecuting counsel said that the girls had committed the murders entirely 'for the pleasure and excitement afforded by killing' and that Mary, though two years younger than Norma, was the dominant personality. As the trial progressed it became obvious that Mary was far more intelligent and dangerous. Norma, on the other hand, had a mental age of less than nine years and was immature and insecure.

The girls continued to blame one another for Brian Howe's death. As far as Martin Brown was concerned, Norma claimed that Mary had talked about murdering him on two occasions and had suggested writing the notes found in the nursery school though Mary, of course, said that the notes were Norma's idea. A 12-year-old-old boy testified that he had been playing with them in the nursery sandpit a week after Martin Brown's death when Mary had tripped Norma up and jumped on top of her, crying, 'I am a murderer.' She had showed him the house where Martin's body was found and told him that was where she had killed him. He hadn't believed her at the time, thinking she was just showing off. Norma's mother told the court that shortly after the first murder she had found Mary apparently trying to strangle her 11-year-old daughter Susan. Her husband had had to slap Mary to make her let go. In his summing up, the prosecutor described Norma as 'a simple, backward girl of sub-normal intelligence' and Mary as 'aggressive, vicious, cruel and incapable of remorse'.

The jury found Mary not guilty of murder, by reason of diminished responsibility, but guilty of manslaughter. They accepted the argument that Norma was completely under Mary's influence and found her not guilty. Mary was sentenced to detention for life but there seemed no suitable institution for housing a girl so young and yet so dangerous. When plans were announced to send her to a remand centre in south-east London worried local parents petitioned the authorities saying that their own children would be in danger should she escape. Shortly afterwards she was transferred to a secure unit established especially for her in an approved school for boys in Lancashire. There were protests from local people here, too, but they were reassured that she would be under strict individual supervision. Mary Bell was in the headlines again in 1977 when, with another girl, she escaped from an open prison. They were at large for three days, long enough to find men to have sex with. Mary told the tabloids that her aim was to stay out in the world long enough to prove that she was a normal young woman.

Jeanne Weber

THE 'Ogress of the Goutte d'Or' used no weapon other than her bare hands to kill over and over again. Her victims were all children and her crimes so horrifying, and so pointless, that those involved in the judicial process were unwilling to believe that she could possibly be guilty. The result was that Jeanne Weber evaded justice twice and was set free to kill again.

Jeanne was the daughter of a Breton fisherman, married at the age of 18 and living in a poor district of Paris known as the Goutte d'Or. She had three children but two died in infancy – an everyday occurrence in the slums of the 1890s – and following the deaths she became deeply depressed and turned to drink for solace. After that, strange things began happening to the children in her care. The first was when Jeanne was babysitting for her sister-in-law Mme Pierre Weber while the latter took the laundry to the public wash-house. Mme Weber was only beginning her wash when a neighbour arrived to say that 18-month-old Georgette was having a choking fit. The mother hurried home to find her baby blue in the face and gasping for air, while Jeanne was apparently massaging her chest. Georgette was revived and her mother went back to her washing, only to be summoned again an hour later to find that Georgette had died. The neighbour, Mme Pouche, tried to draw attention to marks on the baby's neck but no one took any notice and the doctor certified the death as due to convulsions. Only nine days later Mme Weber left Jeanne babysitting for her other daughter, Suzanne, and came back to find that this child too had died, again apparently of convulsions. Once again, Mme Pouche noticed marks on the child's throat; once again she was ignored.

So far, the Weber family seem to have accepted Jeanne's version of events without question and they had every sympathy when her only remaining child, seven-year-old Marcel, died in similar circumstances. They even failed to suspect her when another child from the family, seven-month-old Germaine, died in her care. However, when Mme Charles Weber, another sister-in-law, left her little son Maurice with Jeanne for a few minutes while she did some shopping, only to find Maurice choking in Jeanne's arms, it was one coincidence too many. This time the red marks on the body's throat led to a police investigation. Jeanne Weber was tried, and acquitted, in 1906. The eminent medical expert who examined Maurice and the exhumed bodies of the other children, Professor Thoinot, found no evidence of strangulation.

Jeanne Weber moved on and was not heard of again until 1907, when she had changed her name and was working as a housekeeper for the Bavouzet family in central France. When one of the Bavouzet children died, the local doctor reported the red marks found on the child's neck to the police. Meanwhile one of the older children found newspaper cuttings about the 'Ogress of the Goutte d'Or' in the housekeeper's room and put two and two together. Jeanne was arrested again. The same clever counsel defended her for a second time, insisting that an innocent woman was being hounded for no good reason. Professor Thoinot was involved once more and the medical evidence was so contradictory and inconclusive that the case was thrown out.

Once more, Jeanne changed her name. For a while she worked in a nursing home for sick children but she was sent away hastily after being caught pressing her thumbs into the throat of one of the patients. The event was not reported and so yet another family was exposed to tragedy. In May 1908 an innkeeper and his wife named Poirot were charmed by the woman guest who seemed so fond of their young son. Little Marcel seemed equally fond of his new friend, so when she pleaded loneliness and asked if he could share her bed, his

Jeanne Weber

parents agreed. In the night the guest in the room next door heard screams and rushed in to see the woman bending over Marcel. The child's face was blue and blood poured from his bitten tongue. This time there was no doubt about the cause of death and the guest's true identity was soon revealed. Jeanne Weber had committed her last murder.

Public feelings ran high against the fiend who strangled children and crowds in the streets outside the courtroom cried 'death for the ogress'. Before her first trial, when the Weber family was urging that she should be confined to an asylum, Jeanne had been examined by medical experts but though they reported that she was subject to 'nervous upsets', they had found her completely sane. This time the findings were quite different. She was declared guilty but insane and sent to a secure mental hospital. Her counsel argued that she had only committed one murder, that of Marcel Poirot, and that she had been driven out of her mind by the unjust harassment and constant accusations. Once locked away, Jeanne quickly sank into more obvious madness, suffering fits where she grasped her own throat and foamed at the mouth. She died two years later, her fingers locked tightly around her neck.

Kitty Byron

WHEN Kitty Byron's love affair turned sour and she saw herself about to be cast aside by the only man she had ever loved, she went out and bought a knife. It was this deliberate action that was to result in a verdict of murder rather than manslaughter after she stabbed her lover to death in broad daylight in front of a dozen witnesses, for everyone in court was sympathetic to her plight.

Kitty was a pretty 23-year-old who had been living for several months with stockbroker Arthur Reginald Baker in a flat in the West End, where they represented themselves as Mr and Mrs Baker. At first Kitty was happy; she was deeply in love and Reg declared that she was the only woman for him. However, as the novelty of the relationship wore off, Reg began to tire of his 'adorable Kitty'. He spent a good deal of time away from the flat, he drank heavily and often knocked Kitty about. All the same, Kitty remained loyal, telling no one of his behaviour. Then, one Friday night in November 1902, raised voices from the Baker flat could be heard all over the house. When the landlady went up to investigate she found the flat in chaos, the bedclothes flung all over the floor and, in one corner, a hat ripped to shreds. 'Oh there's nothing the matter,' Kitty told her, laughing it off before she could confront the drunken Reg. 'We've been playing milliner.' Later in the evening the quarrel broke out again and at 1.15 am the landlady went back again in an attempt to stop the noise. This time she found Kitty crouching terrified on the landing in her nightdress. Even then, Kitty insisted that nothing was wrong.

The next morning the landlady, mindful of the peace of her other tenants, gave the couple notice. Over the weekend all was quiet and by Monday morning domestic harmony seemed to have been restored.

Reg took Kitty a cup of tea before leaving for work and Kitty kissed him goodbye as usual. But on his way out Reg spoke to the landlady, asking her to reconsider and allow them to keep the flat. When she was adamant, he revealed that Kitty was not his wife and blamed all the trouble on her. She had 'no class' and he would see that she was gone by tomorrow. A maid overheard the conversation and repeated it to Kitty, who was furious. 'I'll kill him before the day is out,' she exclaimed. The landlady, surprised that any woman would stay with a man who treated her badly when not bound by matrimony, asked why she did not leave him. 'I can't because I love him so,' replied Kitty simply.

Kitty went straight to Oxford Street and bought a large knife with a spring blade that fitted into the hasp. Concealing it in her muff she made her way towards the City, where the streets were crowded with spectators waiting to see the Lord Mayor's Day parade. She arrived at Lombard Street post office at about 1 pm and sent an express letter by messenger to Reg at the Stock Exchange. It read: 'Dear Reg. Want you immediate importantly. Kitty.' The boy had to make two journeys before he found Reg and returned with him, and this meant an extra charge of twopence. Post office staff remembered that Reg flatly refused to pay and Kitty offered Reg a florin to settle up.

The couple were already arguing heatedly when they left the post office. Suddenly the knife flashed and Kitty stabbed her lover twice, once through the back and once through the breast. Though at first the witnesses saw no blood, and thought that she was hitting him with her muff, Reg died almost instantly. A workman grabbed Kitty, sending the knife clattering to the ground, but she broke free and collapsed over her lover's body, sobbing: 'Let me kiss my Reggie . . . Let me kiss my husband.'

Kitty made two separate statements to the police just after her arrest. In one she said: 'I killed him wilfully and he deserved it, and the sooner I am killed the better.' A little later she stated: 'I bought the knife to hit him; I didn't know I was killing him.' She pleaded not guilty at her trial and looked dazed and pitiful as she listened to the 20 or so witnesses called by the prosecution. When a surgeon described the stab wounds on her lover's body she broke down and sobbed. There were no defence witnesses and Kitty did not go into the witness box. Her counsel, Harry Dickens, son of the great Victorian novelist Charles Dickens, tried to show that Kitty had bought the knife to kill herself rather than Reginald Baker, but the idea was given little credence. Far more telling was his description of the prisoner's character and her ill-treatment at the hands of the murdered man.

In his summing up, even the judge admitted that 'if I had consulted my own feelings I should probably have stopped this case at the outset'. All the same, he ruled out manslaughter as a proper verdict and the jury, after deliberating for only 10 minutes, found her guilty, but with a strong recommendation for mercy. The formalities were observed and the death sentence was read out, but there was little likelihood of it being carried out. The Home Secretary quickly granted a reprieve and her sentence was commuted to penal servitude for life. Even that was later held to be too harsh a sentence and she was released in 1908.

Marguerite Diblanc

THE CASE of Marguerite Diblanc, seven years earlier, had much in common with that of Kate Webster. She too was a servant who killed her employer in a rage after being dismissed from service but her crime took place in London's fashionable Park Lane and set society tongues wagging, as her victim was the mistress of the rich and aristocratic Earl of Lucan, notorious as the man who had instigated the disastrous Charge of the Light Brigade 18 years earlier. Lord Lucan was already in his seventies when he installed his 46-year-old French mistress in Park Lane, where she lived with her actress daughter Julie.

Marie Riel was a difficult, ill-tempered woman guaranteed to make life unpleasant for any servant unfortunate enough to be in her employ. It was inevitable that there would be trouble between Mme Riel and her strong-minded Belgian cook Marguerite, a large-boned 28-year-old with a distinctly mannish look about her. Only a year before Marie had been fighting at the barricades in France, along with the Parisian revolutionaries. She had been forced to flee to England after their defeat but she was not the type of woman to submit to bullying. There were many angry exchanges and in March 1872 she was dismissed with a week's wages. Marguerite refused to go: she was paid monthly and so, she insisted, she was entitled to a month's wages. Mme Riel refused to pay her a penny more in cash but said that she could work out a month's notice instead.

On 31 March, when Julie Riel left for a short holiday before beginning a season of French comedies at St James's Theatre, she left the stage in Park Lane set for murder. The continuing rows between the two obdurate women came to a head on Sunday 7 April, when

Mme Riel was expecting a visitor and was concerned that everything should be properly prepared. In the middle of the morning she went down to the kitchen to check on preparations, only to find that Marguerite was still working upstairs. The altercation that followed soon turned violent and Mme Riel ordered Marguerite out of the house immediately. If she wanted money she could go on the streets, which were the right place for her, she said. Marguerite retorted that Mme Riel had been on the streets far longer than she was ever likely to be. For both women, these insults were too much to bear and they set about one another. At one point Marguerite tried to throttle her mistress, at another she caught her such a blow that Mme Riel fell to the floor.

As Marguerite stood over Mme Riel she heard the only other servant in the household, Eliza Watts, coming down the stairs. She hastily pushed and pulled the body into the coal cellar, then she made an excuse to get Eliza out of the house while she found a way to dispose of her mistress. Once Eliza had left, on a quickly invented errand, Marguerite slung a rope round her victim's neck and hauled the body across the kitchen and up the steps that led to the pantry. This was probably the safest hiding place in the house as it contained the safe and was always kept locked, only opened when necessary with the mistress's key. Later Marguerite was to claim that Mme Riel was already dead, killed by accident when she struck an unlucky blow, but it is probably more likely that she made sure of finishing the job with the rope. Once the body was safely in the pantry, Marguerite opened the safe, pocketed a pack of banknotes and carefully locked the pantry door.

Meanwhile Eliza had returned and, finding herself locked out, was knocking vigorously on the outside door. All through the unusual events of that day, Eliza remained unsuspecting. This was, perhaps, not surprising, for she was a slow-witted girl and, as Marguerite and Mme Riel always spoke French, she was accustomed to understanding very little of what went on in the house. Later in the day Mme Riel's expected visitor arrived but, after waiting most of the afternoon for her friend, she finally left. Marguerite then changed into her best satin dress and told Eliza she was going to church. Instead she took the boat train to Dover and travelled to Paris.

The following day Julie Riel returned and discovered her mother's body. The search for Marguerite began immediately. Her parsimonious nature and poor English had left a clear trail: a cab driver remembered an argument about the fare to Victoria and a station clerk who spoke a little French recalled the woman who had wanted an economy fare but had been forced to buy a first-class ticket in order to join the overnight boat train. Marguerite was arrested in Paris and eventually, after much reluctance on the part of the French police, was extradited to stand trial in Britain.

The main defence was that the killing had not been intentional and that Marguerite had suffered great provocation from her unpleasant mistress. The jury found her guilty, adding a recommendation for mercy. Marguerite was sentenced to hang but, eight days after the date initially set for her execution, she was reprieved.

Marybeth Tinning

IN JANUARY 1972 Marybeth Tinning gave birth to her third child, Jennifer, at Schenectady, New York. The baby was born with meningitis and was never well enough to leave St Clare's Hospital, where she died nine days later. Perhaps the shock of her new-born baby's death upset some delicate mental balance within the mother – if so, it might explain the tragedy that followed, for over the next 13 years, eight more Tinning children were to die and the police came to believe that she had killed them all.

Only a fortnight after Jennifer died, Marybeth arrived at the emergency room of Ellis Hospital with two-year-old Joseph, saying that he had suffered a seizure and stopped breathing. Doctors admitted him and kept him for 10 days, diagnosing a probable viral infection. He seemed well when he was discharged but later in the day Marybeth brought him back again and this time he was dead on arrival. Two months later Marybeth was back with four-year-old Barbara, who died soon after arrival. A postmortem showed no obvious cause of death but there seemed no reason for suspicion.

Marybeth was to give birth to several more children but none lived longer than a few months. Timothy, born in November 1973, lived less than three weeks, his unexpected demise being ascribed to cot death. Nathan was five months old when he died in September 1975. He had earlier spent a month in hospital after experiencing breathing difficulties and bleeding from the nose. He was thought to have died from pulmonary oedema. Little Mary was admitted for emergency treatment at the age of four months, then a few weeks later she died, apparently another victim of cot death.

When Marybeth and her husband Joseph applied to adopt a child, the adoption agency was sympathetic about their run of bad luck and wanted to help them. In 1979, when baby Michael joined the family, Marybeth was pregnant again and Jonathan was born in the following January. Jonathan died at the age of three months. In August 1981, Michael was rushed to St Clare's Hospital with 'breathing difficulties' but the doctors could not save him. Though they had some reservations, they certified the death as due to bronchial pneumonia.

Marybeth's last child, Tami Lynne, was born in September 1985 and at three months she was found dead in her cot, with blood staining the pillow. This time the doctors were not prepared to write this off as yet another death due to natural causes. Careful consideration of all aspects of the case led them to believe that the child had been suffocated.

Under questioning, Marybeth broke down and confessed that she had held a pillow over her daughter's face because she would not stop crying. After her arrest she admitted that she had also killed Timothy and Nathan, but she always denied doing anything to harm any of the others.

Eventually she was charged with the murder of Tami Lynne and convicted of second-degree homicide. The jury did not find her guilty of planning to kill the children but said that she had a 'depraved indifference to human life'. No motive was ever put forward; Marybeth had told the police that she had smothered the children 'Because I'm not a good mother'.

Florence Maybrick

FLORENCE MAYBRICK was convicted of poisoning her husband in 1889 at Liverpool Assizes but there was little hard evidence against her and in a different age she would undoubtedly have been acquitted. As it was, she had flown in the face of strict Victorian morality and found herself on trial as much for adultery as for murder. The press had branded her guilty in advance and the judge, his mental powers already in a decline that led to insanity a year later, was obsessed with his view of Florence as an immoral and degraded woman. Her trial left so many question marks that it was to lead to major changes in the British judicial system.

The Maybrick marriage had begun on a romantic note. Florence Elizabeth Chandler was a vivacious 17-year-old, the daughter of an Alabama banker, when she met James Maybrick on the Atlantic liner *Baltic*, on which she was sailing with her mother for a tour of Europe. She was quite a beauty, with curly golden hair, violet eyes and a curvaceous figure. He was the picture of a prosperous British businessman, tall, blond, sophisticated and self-assured – and still a bachelor at the age of 42. They walked together on deck beneath the stars, they played cards and danced and by the end of the voyage they had fallen in love.

Eventually the Maybricks settled in England, in a 20-room mansion in Aigburth, Liverpool. They had two children and five servants and entertained lavishly, but James's business did not flourish and their lifestyle was soon outstripping their means. James tried to keep up outward appearances by budgeting strictly at home but Florence was not the budgeting type and there were daily quarrels over money. Florence was always on tenterhooks in case the ring at the doorbell meant someone else asking for payment of an account and dreaded her husband's return from the office in case he had heard of another of her debts. She wrote to her mother: 'I am . . . in such a state of overstrained nervousness I am hardly fit for anything . . . my life is a continual state of fear of something or somebody.'

There were problems besides money in the Maybrick household. James was a thorough-going hypochondriac who took endless pills and potions for imaginary ills. After being successfully treated for malaria with strychnine and arsenic he took to dosing himself with both drugs and became addicted to daily pinches of arsenic, which he found particularly palatable in beef tea. It was easily available from the chemist and many a Victorian gentleman had acquired the dangerous habit. Florence worried about the strange powders her husband took so frequently, but after the birth of her second child she made a discovery that upset her even more: James was supporting another household, a long-established mistress who had several children by him. In one bitter row, James tore up his will making Florence sole legatee and settled everything on the children instead.

Undoubtedly Florence was hurt and angry and it was at this vulnerable moment that she met one of her husband's younger friends, a handsome, bearded bachelor called Alfred Brierley. They were charmed by each other and he came more and more frequently to the house – especially when James was absent. Throwing caution to the winds, Florence agreed to spend a weekend in London with him. The ill-fated weekend may well have been her idea for she made the arrangements, foolishly reserving a room at a central London hotel in the name of 'Mr and Mrs Thomas Maybrick of Manchester'. It was their first and last passionate rendezvous and, for whatever reason, they resolved to end their short affair. However, a few days later the Maybricks met Brierley at Aintree, where race-goers had gathered for the Grand National and Brierley took Florence to meet the Prince of Wales, leaving James to hear the rumours of his wife's indiscretion from 'well-wishers'. When they got home there was a furious row.

James blacked her eye and the servants heard him shouting: 'Such a scandal will be all over town tomorrow.'

About a month later, in late April, Florence bought a dozen flypapers from the chemist, saying that 'flies were beginning to be troublesome in the kitchen'. Shortly afterwards she bought two dozen more at another shop. The servants were amazed to see them soaking in a bowl on her bedroom washstand, covered by a plate and a folded towel. Florence was later to explain that she was extracting the arsenic from the flypaper for use in a face-wash mixed with lavender and elder water, and applied with a handkerchief – a recipe used by many of her friends in Germany. Though this may sound ridiculous today, it was not beyond the bounds of probability; in the 19th century many women used small amounts of arsenic to lighten their complexions.

At about the same time James had a bout of vomiting and complained of numbness in his legs. He recovered and went back to work, only to be taken ill again after eating a patent food called Du Barry's Revaleta Arabica, made up by Florence. His legs were now very painful and the doctor prescribed morphine. When his sickness increased, Fowler's solution (a mixture of arsenic and carbonate of potash) was prescribed but James's condition did not improve. Another doctor was called in and Florence engaged a nurse.

It was while her husband lay ill that Florence, with a disastrous sense of timing, began writing to Brierley. She gave her letter – written at her husband's bedside – to the children's nanny, Alice Yapp, to post. Miss Yapp, well versed in the servant's gossip about soaking flypapers, conveniently dropped the letter in the mud so that she had to bring it back for a clean envelope. In transferring it certain words caught her eye and she felt obliged to deliver it to one of Mr Maybrick's brothers. The letter began 'Dearest' and went on to say: 'Since my return I have been nursing M night and day and he is sick unto death . . . I cannot answer your letter fully today, my darling, but relieve your mind of all fear of discovery now or in the future.'

On the evening of 11 May, James Maybrick died. Several family members were at his bedside but Florence had collapsed and was lying semi-conscious in the dressing room. The servants, instructed to search the house, found a sachet of powder labelled 'Arsenic: poison for cats' in her room together with letters from Brierley and, of course, more flypapers. A bottle of meat juice, which Florence had taken to her room at one point, contained traces of arsenic. Florence claimed later that James had begged her to add some of the white powder he took every day to his food. Eventually she had given in to his entreaties and added it to the meat juice though, in the event, James never drank it. She had only realized later, she said, that it was arsenic.

A postmortem revealed a tiny amount of arsenic in James's stomach – hardly surprising when he was known to take it on a regular basis and when, quite apart from Florence's small store, enough arsenic had been found in the house to poison two dozen people. The amount of arsenic found in the body was not sufficient to cause death but none the less the doctors decided that he had been poisoned and Florence was charged with murder.

The medical evidence at the trial was shaky in the extreme; the defence called several doctors who said that James had died from gastro-enteritis and a number of witnesses who testified to his habit of taking arsenic as a pick-me-up. The moral evidence, however, was damning. Florence – an upstart American, which counted against her from the start – was guilty of betraying her husband and was therefore only too likely to be guilty of a murder 'founded upon profligacy and adultery', in the words of the prosecutor. Mr Justice Stephen took 12 hours to sum up, rambling frequently, often confusing the facts and mistaking the dates. His belief in Florence's guilt was clear enough: 'For a person to go on deliberately administering poison to a poor helpless sick man upon whom she has already inflicted a dreadful injury – an injury fatal to married life . . . must indeed be destitute of the least trace of human feeling,' he told the jury. 'You must remember the intrigue which she carried on with this man Brierley, and the incredible thought that a woman should be plotting the death of her

Florence Maybrick makes her statement in court

husband in order that she might be left at liberty to follow her own degrading vices.' Needless to say, the jury followed his lead and found her guilty.

Many of those concerned with the judicial system were worried by the unfairness of the trial and began pressing for changes in the system: this eventually led to the establishment of the Court of Appeal and the right of a person accused of murder to give evidence on his or her defence, which was not allowed at the time of the Maybrick trial. It was all too late for Florence. She served 15 years in prison and then, after a brief period as a celebrity, giving interviews and lectures, she sank into obscurity and poverty. For the last 20 years of her life she lived in a wooden shack in the woods of Connecticut, under her maiden name, feeding her many cats and collecting newspapers from dustbins for reading matter. No one connected her with the pretty, extravagant Florence Maybrick and her true identity was only revealed after her death at the age of 79.

Madeleine Smith

THE MAYBRICK case had echoes of the trial of Madeleine Smith in Edinburgh, Scotland, over 30 years earlier, on the charge of murdering her lover by poisoning him with arsenic. Madeleine, too, claimed that she used arsenic as a cosmetic, though she had told the chemist she needed it for rats, and the defence suggested that her lover might have been an arsenic-eater. Madeleine was luckier than Florence, for in her case the court, swayed by the morality of the day, assumed that if a young girl of good family strayed into an affair she must have been led astray by a vile seducer and was therefore a victim deserving of a certain amount of sympathy.

Without the colouring of 19th-century morals, the case looks rather different. There seems no reason to believe that Emile l'Angelier, a 31-year-old clerk from Jersey, was anything worse than a young man intent on marriage with a young woman from a superior background, while Madeleine was a shallow and selfish girl who fancied herself in love but was happy to send her lover packing when something better offered.

They had met early in 1855 when Madeleine was 19. She was the daughter of one of Glasgow's foremost architects and the family was well above l'Angelier's normal circle. However, Emile saw her several times in the town and was immediately smitten, so he managed to engineer an introduction from an acquaintance of the Smiths. Madeleine must have been taken with his graceful French manners and open admiration for soon they were meeting secretly, at first a few snatched moments in a bookshop near Mr Smith's office, or as she made her way to a music lesson. They began writing to one another and their feelings quickly warmed, but Mr Smith, a strict Victorian patriarch, soon became suspicious and Madeleine wrote: 'I think you will agree with me in what I intend proposing viz: that for the present the correspondence had better stop . . . by continuing to correspond harm may arise.' Her new resolve was shortlived and within a few weeks she was writing: 'I have loved before but never have I loved one better than you – When I set my affections on anyone I am true to them.' In July Emile told Mary Perry, a kindly grey-haired spinster who had befriended him at church and heard all about his secret love, that he and Madeleine were engaged.

Perhaps Mr Smith received more definite proof of his daughter's liaison or perhaps Madeleine plucked up the courage to tell him herself; in any case there was a stern family conclave and Madeleine was forbidden to contact Emile in any way. She gave her word of honour and agreed that she was 'in duty bound' to obey but quite soon she was finding a way round her father's prohibition. Emile's letters arrived addressed to one of the Smith's maids, Christine Haggert, and were removed before the mail was passed on to the family; Madeleine's letters were addressed to Mary Perry. Madeleine's bedroom was on the ground floor, the windows half above ground and half below the pavement, and Emile often visited her at night, when they would hold hands through the pavement railings and whisper sweet nothings. Sometimes they met at Mary Perry's house and at least once Emile was let into the Smith's house when the rest of the family were in bed.

In June 1856, when the Smiths went to their summer house, Madeleine had a room facing directly on to the garden and she could steal out at night to meet Emile. It was then they made love for the first time and Madeleine's joyful letters became sensuous and outspoken – quite shocking by Victorian standards – as she addressed him as 'My own beloved husband' and signed herself 'thy faithful wife' or 'Mimi l'Angelier'. Emile was racked with guilt, blamed himself for what had happened and said that nothing but marriage would efface it from his memory. Madeleine, too, often talked of marriage but knew very well that her parents would never permit it.

Later that year another man entered the picture and everything changed. He was William Minnoch, a well-to-do merchant of 34, slim and elegant, and socially acceptable. He had become friendly with Mr Smith and began to spend a good deal of time with the family, paying special attention to Madeleine. He was often mentioned in letters to Emile, who soon became jealous, but Madeleine reassured him that she had no regard for Minnoch and avoided him as far as possible. It was far from true: at the end of January 1857 she accepted Minnoch's proposal of marriage. She did not share the news with Emile. Instead, she wrote that after many sleepless nights she had decided to tell him that she no longer loved him and that in future they should consider themselves as strangers.

Emile was astonished, angry and wounded and he struck back by threatening to send her letters to her father. Madeleine turned hysterical, begging and pleading with him not to contact her family and bring her to 'open shame'. She protested, 'When I ceased to love you believe me it was not to love another. I am free from all engagements at present. Emile for God's sake do not send my letters to Papa . . . I will leave the house, I will die.' She begged him to come to her. At about the same time she was fixing her wedding day in June and buying arsenic.

One morning in February Emile's landlady, Mrs Jenkins, found him lying in bed looking very ill. He told her that he had been taken ill on the way home with pain and sickness. 'When I was taking off my clothes I lay down upon the carpet,' he said. 'I thought I would have died and no human eye would have seen me.' A few weeks later he was taken ill again and after many hours of vomiting he died on the morning of 23 March. On postmortem, 82 grains of arsenic were found in Emile's stomach, enough to kill 15 people. In his room were found over 200 letters from Madeleine and within a few days she was under arrest.

Her statement, read out in court, stated that she 'never administered, or caused to be administered, to M. l'Angelier arsenic or anything injurious'. She had last seen Emile, she said, about three weeks before his death. She had written to him on 20 March asking him to come and see her the following day, when she planned to tell him about her engagement to Mr Minnoch, but he never arrived.

Madeleine remained cool and composed throughout the trial, apparently confident that she would be acquitted, even when Mary Perry gave evidence that Emile had mentioned being unwell after taking cups of coffee or chocolate on his visits to Madeleine. 'It is a perfect infatuation I have for that girl. If she was to poison me, I would forgive her,' he had said. When Mary asked why he should think Madeleine might want to do him harm, he answered: 'I don't know, perhaps she might not be sorry to get rid of me.'

Madeleine had stated that she used the arsenic she bought on three occasions for cosmetic purposes, mixing it with water and applying it to her face and arms, a habit recommended by a school friend, Miss Guibilei. When Miss Guibilei was produced, she insisted that she had never recommended anything of the sort and had never had any conversation with Madeleine about arsenic.

The defence stressed that, though the letters proved that Madeleine had asked Emile to come to her, there was no knowing what other letters he had received at that time and what plans he might have made. After all, no one had seen him in the vicinity and there was no proof that he had been there. Then there was the question of the prisoner's character: how could a 'gentle loving girl' be suddenly transformed into the perpetrator of such a foul crime? Her outspoken letters had undoubtedly shocked the court but did they think that 'without temptation, without evil teaching, a poor girl falls into such depths of degradation? No – influence from without – most corrupting influence – can alone account for such a fall'. The jury brought in a majority verdict of 'not proven', only possible in a Scottish court, and generally believed to mean that her guilt was likely, but not absolutely certain.

Madeleine seemed unmoved; she only smiled at the announcement while a great cheer rose from the public benches. She certainly did not let the reflection on her good name spoil her life. Though she did not hear from Mr Minnoch again she married a London artist, George Wardle, in 1861.

Jessie Costello

OLD MRS AYERS, a pedlar of sweets who regularly toured the households of Peabody, Massachusetts, had succeeded in selling Mrs Jessie Costello a pound of fudge. Jessie ran upstairs to get some money and Mrs Ayers nearly suffered a heart attack when she heard her screaming at the top of her lungs. Jessie had found her husband Bill lying dead on the bedroom floor, even though he had been fit and well early that morning when he returned from an overnight vigil beside the body of a dead colleague from the Peabody Fire Department.

The autopsy showed that there was nothing surprising about Bill's death: his body contained a quantity of potassium cyanide. When it was found that only the day before Jessie had bought potassium cyanide from the pharmacy, along with oxalic acid, she was arrested. She explained that she bought both substances to make up a mixture that would put a good shine on her boiler and had no idea that potassium cyanide was dangerous. The pharmacist, however, clearly remembered telling her that it was poisonous and Jessie had replied that she knew about it and would take proper care.

Jessie was well-liked in the town; she was a woman with fascinating dark eyes and a ready smile, with an unblemished reputation as a loving wife and mother. On the face of it she was an unlikely murderer when she went on trail in July 1933. When doctors testified that the poison had been taken in capsule form, so that it might have been given under the guise of regular medicine, Jessie protested that she knew nothing about capsules and would have no idea how to fill them. Unfortunately for her, a neighbour remembered seeing Jessie filling medicine capsules when she was nursing a sick friend some time before.

The most damaging witness was patrolman Eddie McMahon of the Peabody police, who revealed to the astonished townsfolk that he had been carrying on an affair with Jessie ever since she had made eyes at him one day when he was directing traffic. After that they met secretly in quiet lay-bys, where they made love in parked cars, or in Jessie's home when her husband was working. When Eddie had appendicitis Jessie had visited him every night and as he recovered from his operation she had even shared his hospital bed with him for a few passionate moments. Jessie refuted his entire story: she scarcely knew the young patrolman and could not imagine why he should tell such lies about her, she said.

The defence tried to suggest, not too convincingly, that Bill had killed himself, even calling as a witness the manager of the local cinema, which shortly before his death had been showing a film called *Payment Deferred*, depicting a death by cyanide. This could, according to counsel, have put the idea into Bill's mind, for Jessie had given evidence that his good spirits were only a front and that he was, in reality, depressed and sickly.

According to the prosecution, Jessie had one eye on her sexy young patrolman and the other on Bill's insurance money; she had the means and the opportunity for murder. For the jury it was not enough. Unable to believe that such an upright citizen – and a handsome figure of a woman, into the bargain – could possibly commit such a crime, they found Jessie not guilty and she walked free from the courtroom. Eddie McMahon, the patrolman who had the bad taste to kiss and tell, lost his job with the police department and Jessie shed no tears for him.

Constance Kent

ON THE morning of 30 June 1860 three-year-old Francis Saville Kent was missing from his cot in the nursery of his house in Wiltshire, England. His nursemaid, Elizabeth Gough, had seen the empty cot when she awoke at about 5 am but assumed that the child's mother had taken him into her room, so the alarm was not raised until nearly 7 am. The house and grounds were immediately searched and the boy's body was found in an outside privy, with a deep stab wound in his side and his throat cut so deeply that his head was almost severed from his body. The time of death had been midnight or shortly afterwards. From the beginning it was assumed that the killer was someone in the household, though Mr Kent tried to suggest that it might be an outsider with a personal grudge against him. At the time, the most likely suspect seemed to be 16-year-old Constance Kent.

Constance was one of Samuel Kent's children by his first marriage. Her mother, who gave birth to 10 children in all, was frail and suffering from mental problems by the time Constance was a toddler and a young governess, Mary Pratt, was employed to look after the children. By the time Mrs Kent died, when Constance was eight, Mary Pratt was running the house and sharing Samuel Kent's bed. Soon afterwards she became the second Mrs Kent and by the time of the murder had four children – Francis, five-year-old Amelia, two-year-old Eugenie and baby Samuel – and was expecting a fifth. Mary Kents' children all slept on the second floor of the house with their parents but, though there were several other rooms available on the same floor, Constance and her two older sisters and younger brother shared the third floor with the servants. This was just one of the ways in which the second family was given preference over the first and at the time of the

480

Constance Kent

investigation there were a number of stories about harsh treatment meted out to the older children. The two eldest girls, it was said, were treated as unpaid servants and Constance was severely punished for any misbehaviour, locked up in the cellar or confined to her room on a diet of bread and watered milk.

Jealousy and resentment, then, were Constance's supposed motives. She had made several comments to friends, suggesting that her home life was unhappy, and everyone remembered the time when she had run away from home at the age of 12, dressed as a boy and taking her brother William with her; the children wanted to join their older brother Edward, who was working in the West Indies. Apart from the possible motive, there was the matter of the missing nightdress. The morning after the murder a bloodstained shirt had been found behind the boiler but in the general confusion it disappeared. Later, when it was found that one of Constance's nightdresses had disappeared, connections were made with the bloodstained garment, though reports suggested that it was the type of coarse garment worn by servants. Constance was arrested and spent a week in gaol until a hearing before magistrates decided that there was no case to answer.

Next it was Elizabeth Gough's turn to come under suspicion. After all, the boy slept in her room and it seemed unlikely that anyone else could have taken him without waking her. Mrs Kent had first seemed surprised that the nursemaid should think that Francis would be with her as she had never taken the child from his bed before. Now she changed her mind and admitted that she might have told Elizabeth not to be frightened if she came and took the child. The case against Elizabeth, too, was abandoned for lack of evidence.

At the inquest it had been reported that the boy had died from suffocation, rather than the cut throat, and that this explained the small amount of blood found at the scene. The findings lent weight to another theory which circulated widely in the county and was discussed in the newspapers. This pinpointed Samuel Kent as the murderer with Elizabeth Gough as his accomplice. The suggestion was that history was repeating itself as Kent found his way to the bed of Elizabeth Gough, as he had once carried on an affair with his children's governess. On one of his surreptitious night-time visits Francis could have woken up and called out, causing Kent, in a panic, to seize the nearest blanket to stop the child's cries and then press too hard, suffocating the child by accident. To avert suspicion from himself, he might then have decided to take Francis into the yard and cut his throat to make it look as though the attacker had come from outside. It was, after all, Kent who had insisted that the murderer must be someone who had quarrelled with him in the past.

Eventually the speculation died down, the Kent family moved out of the area and Constance was sent to a convent in France under the name of Emily Kent. Five years later she was at a convent in Brighton and training to become a nurse when she made a statement before a magistrate in which she confessed to the crime. She had done it 'alone and unaided', she said: 'Before the deed was done, no one know of my intention, nor afterwards knew of my guilt. No one assisted me in the crime, nor in the evasion of discovery.'

Her confession and subsequent guilty plea at Devizes Assize court were accepted and she was sentenced to death, later commuted to life imprisonment – but far from clearing up all the questions about the murder, her confession only added to the mystery. Constance's account of the killing hardly fits the facts. She said that a razor which she had taken from her father's room several days earlier was the only murder instrument, though evidence had shown that the wound in the boy's side could not have been caused by a razor. She said that she had made the second wound because she 'thought the blood would never come', though it seems impossible that a deeply slashed throat would fail to bleed if the child had been alive at the time. Though the doctor who had originally given evidence that Francis had been killed by suffocation obligingly changed his testimony and said that the razor wound was the cause of death, he could produce no good medical reason for the lack of blood.

Constance's only possible motive was in revenge for ill-treatment or neglect by her father and stepmother but she took care to deny this as 'entirely false', saying that she had experienced only the greatest kindness from both of them: 'I have never had any ill-will towards either of them.' Without motive nor convincing explanation of the method, Constance's guilt must be in doubt – but what would prompt an innocent girl to confess, so long after the event? There have been suggestions that in her secluded convent life she came under the influence of religious fanatics intent on saving souls who, knowing her background, managed to convince her that she had, in fact, committed the crime. It is just one more puzzle to add to all the other puzzles in the Kent case.

Adelaide Bartlett

IF ADELAIDE BARTLETT poisoned her husband she was certainly far more inventive than most poisoners, for Edwin Bartlett died from the effects of liquid chloroform. Liquid chloroform had never before been used in a murder and if anyone had been able to produce a credible theory as to how Adelaide managed to administer it to her husband, she would probably have been found guilty. As it was, Queen Victoria's surgeon, Sir James Paget, said afterwards that now that Mrs Bartlett had been acquitted, she should 'tell us in the interests of science how she did it'.

The public had been fascinated throughout the trial as the details of the Bartletts' marriage were revealed. Adelaide, the illegitimate daughter of an English aristocrat and his French mistress, was 19 when her family arranged a marriage with a 30-year-old grocer. Edwin was ambitious, good-natured and an active Methodist and though Adelaide said, 'My consent was not asked and I saw him only once before my wedding day', he seems to have had all the makings of a good husband. Keen that his young wife should continue her education, he sent her first to a finishing school and then to a convent.

When she returned to London the couple seemed to live together quite happily, though Edwin had very strange ideas about sex and marriage. He preferred his relationship with Adelaide to be platonic, so that he could put her on a pedestal and admire her. In fact he went further, believing that every man should have two wives: one to serve as a decorative companion, the other to look after his household and bedroom needs. Adelaide maintained that they only had sex on a single occasion, when she decided she wanted a baby. Though she duly became pregnant, the child was stillborn and the delivery was so long and painful that she decided not to try again.

In their 11 years together the Bartletts moved house several times and in 1883 they arrived in Wimbledon, where they became friendly with the minister of the local Wesleyan church, the Revd. George Dyson. From that moment, Edwin seems to have done everything possible to throw Adelaide and George together. He decided that the minister could teach her more history, geography and Latin and this meant that the two spent many hours closeted together. Sometimes George would spend all day with Adelaide, waiting for Edwin's return in the evening, and he dined with the couple at least three times a week. Edwin was quite happy to see his wife walking hand-in-hand with his friend and even encouraged them to kiss in his presence. He made George executor to his will and it was understood that if anything happened to him, the two of them would 'come together'. Of course, it is quite possible that they had already 'come together', but both always denied adultery, so perhaps their relationship went no further than sexual dalliance.

In 1885 the Bartletts moved back into town and Edwin fell ill. The doctor who was called found that Edwin displayed all the symptoms of mercury poisoning, though he denied ever taking mercury, a medicine used for syphilis. In addition, several of his teeth were in such an advanced state of decay that they needed to be extracted as soon as possible. The symptoms subsided, the teeth came out, but still Edwin remained depressed and lethargic, refusing to get out of bed and insisting that Adelaide should sit up with him at night, holding his foot for comfort. It was Adelaide who insisted on a second opinion because, she said, 'Edwin's relatives would soon accuse me of poisoning him.' The second doctor found little wrong with Edwin and encouraged him to go out more.

George Dyson visited the sickroom often and on 27 December Adelaide asked him to get her a bottle of chloroform, saying that it was the only thing that would ease Edwin's pains and help him to sleep.

Adelaide Bartlett

Dyson told local chemists that he needed the chloroform to remove grease spots and because he was a trusted minister they dispensed a far larger quantity than was normally allowed without prescription. Meanwhile, Edwin was feeling better and by New Year's Eve he was able to do justice to dinner of jugged hare and a supper of oysters and bread and butter, and to order a large haddock for breakfast. Then, in the early hours of the morning, he died. Adelaide told the doctor that she had fallen asleep in a chair by Edwin's bedside, holding his foot as usual, and awakened to find the foot stone cold. She had tried pouring brandy down Edwin's throat to revive him, but in vain.

George Dyson hastened round, not to console Adelaide but to find out what had happened to the chloroform. Heated words were exchanged and Adelaide was overheard shouting angrily 'Oh, damn the chloroform', while George accused her of telling him that Edwin was a sick man, likely to die before long. When the postmortem revealed a large quantity of liquid chloroform in Edwin's stomach George flew into a panic, while Adelaide confided in the doctor, telling him the whole story of the strange threesome. After insisting on a platonic relationship for many years, she said, and after 'giving' her to George Dyson, Edwin had recently decided to assert his marital rights in a most unwelcome manner. Adelaide had decided that she could discourage him by sprinkling chloroform on her handkerchief and waving it in front of his nose to make him drowsy. In the event she had not used it but had admitted her plan to Edwin and given him the bottle, which he put on the mantelpiece near his bed. This 'marvellous' story as *The Times* called it, added more spice to conjecture about the bedroom secrets of the Bartletts.

Adelaide was charged with murder, George was charged as an accessory and on 13 April 1886 they stood side-by-side in the dock at the Old Bailey. At the outset the Crown withdrew the case against George Dyson, who had earlier put all the blame on Adelaide, claiming that he had been 'duped by a wicked woman'. His acquittal was very unpopular with the public but Adelaide's counsel managed to turn it to her advantage by working hard to show how closely their actions were linked, so that the jury would be reluctant 'to send her to the hangman's cord, while he passed unrebuked to freedom'.

It was beyond dispute that Adelaide had had chloroform in her possession, that her husband had been killed by chloroform and that the bottle of chloroform had disappeared after his death, but the central question was asked over and over again: *how did the chloroform get into Edwin Bartlett's stomach?* There were suggestions that Edwin had taken it himself, perhaps intending to take his own life – though a man intending suicide does not usually order haddock for breakfast – or simply trying to put himself to sleep when all else failed. Alternatively, Adelaide might have added the chloroform to a glass of brandy, telling Edwin she was disguising an unpleasant-tasting medicine and encouraging him to bolt it down. This would explain the lack of burns in the mouth which liquid chloroform would normally cause but would almost certainly have made the patient vomit, which did not happen. The prosecution theory that Adelaide had first rendered her husband unconscious with chloroform then poured the rest down his throat seemed unlikely, for medical experts testified that pouring the liquid down the throat of an unconscious person would be an extremely delicate operation. Even when carried out by a doctor, the procedure would probably result in some of the liquid getting into the windpipe and there was no trace of chloroform in Edwin's windpipe.

The jury deliberated for over two hours and when they returned to the courtroom they announced that 'although we think that grave suspicion attaches to the prisoner, we do not think that there is sufficient evidence to show how or by whom the chloroform was administered'. They found Adelaide not guilty to cheers and applause from the public gallery.

Florence Bravo

THE MURDER of Charles Bravo is a mystery that has fascinated students of crime for more than a century. The only certainty is that he was poisoned but which of the women in his household administered the lethal dose will never be known. Charles was a good-looking young English barrister, thoroughly spoiled and accustomed to getting his own way, who married a beguiling young widow, Florence Ricardo, in 1875.

For those strait-laced times, Florence had a colourful past. When she was 19 she married the dashing Captain Alexander Ricardo of the Grenadier Guards, only to find that he was a drunkard who kept a succession of mistresses and was not about to change his dissolute way of life for the sake of his young wife. Florence, neglected and desperately unhappy, began to drink heavily. By 1870 the Captain had retired from the army and could devote himself full-time to women and the bottle, and Florence was at the end of her tether. Her parents suggested that the couple should go to Malvern to take the water cure which had become so fashionable. For the Captain it was a waste of time, but the trip was to change Florence's life. In Malvern she met Dr James Manby Gully, promoter of the famous water cure and medical advisor to such renowned figures as Dickens, Carlyle and Tennyson. Dr Gully was 62, strong, reliable and charismatic, and Florence fell head over heels in love with him. Shortly afterwards she separated from her husband, who obligingly drank himself to death the following year in Germany, leaving his widow a comfortable fortune.

Her liaison with Dr Gully, who bought a house close to hers in London, meant that she was no longer received in polite society and her family had cut her off, so Florence engaged a companion-

Florence Bravo

housekeeper, Mrs Jane Cox. Mrs Cox was the widow of a Jamaican engineer with little money and three sons to support, an unattractive, bespectacled woman whose efficiency meant that everything in Florence's household ran smoothly. The two women became close friends and confidantes and it was through Mrs Cox, who knew the Bravo family, that Florence met Charles. It may be that Florence was yearning for her lost respectability and Charles was certainly yearning for her substantial fortune. In any event, they decided to marry and settle in Florence's imposing London mansion. Florence put an end to her affair with Dr Gully and told Charles all about it. He, in turn, terminated his relationship with a young woman in Maidenhead.

So far as outsiders were concerned the marriage seemed to go well but both Florence and Mrs Cox were later to maintain that Charles was unreasonably jealous of his wife's past relationship with Dr Gully, throwing it in her face at every opportunity, causing bitter rows and occasionally even hitting her. Though Florence had brought most of the money to the marriage, all her property now belonged to her husband and he was mean with it. He persuaded her to give up her horses and her personal maid and his next planned economy was Mrs Cox.

On the evening of 18 April 1876 dinner in the Bravo household consisted of whiting, roast lamb, an egg dish and anchovies on toast. Charles drank several glasses of burgundy while Florence and Mrs Cox demolished two bottles of sherry between them. Florence, who had recently had a miscarriage, went to bed early and Mrs Cox sat with her. Charles was occupying the spare bedroom at the time and shortly after he retired a maid heard him calling desperately for water – though Mrs Cox, in the next room, claimed to have heard nothing. When the maid and Mrs Cox went into his room they found him vomiting out of the window and groaning with pain. Doctors who were summoned questioned the hapless Charles closely about what he had taken, but he insisted that his only medication had been laudanum rubbed on his gums to soothe his toothache. Though Mrs Cox told one of the doctors that Charles had admitted to her that he had taken poison and had asked her not to tell Florence, Charles denied it to the end. As the sickness and pain continued over the next three days, one of the doctors even told him that if he were not honest with them someone might be accused of poisoning him, but Charles still insisted that he had taken nothing but laudanum. He died in the early hours of the morning of 21 April and an autopsy showed that the cause of death was a large dose of antimony administered in the form of tartar emetic, which was easily dissolved in water and tasteless. The inquest, a sketchy affair, decided that the deceased had died from the effects of poison but there was no way of establishing how it had come to be in his body.

Many of Charles's friends were dissatisfied with the verdict and the newspapers began to run stories about the mysterious death of a young barrister. Florence received accusatory anonymous letters. Eventually a new enquiry was ordered and this time Mrs Cox caused a sensation by saying that Charles had told her 'I have taken poison for Gully – don't tell Florence'. She maintained that she had kept quiet about his actual words at first to protect Mrs Bravo's reputation. When Florence gave evidence, she confirmed that Mrs Cox had told her the reason for Charles's suicide after the first inquest. All the other witnesses told stories that contradicted the suicide theory: the maids had never heard the couple quarrelling and Charles's friends and family had seen no signs of depression or unhappiness.

The evidence of George Griffiths, formerly Mrs Bravo's coachman, caused a furore, for it proved that a large quantity of tartar emetic had been available at her home as recently as January. He had bought it to treat the horses, though only a small amount had been used, and he kept it locked in a cupboard in the stables. Griffiths had been dismissed for carelessness after a minor accident with the coach and said that before he left he poured away the remainder of the tartar emetic, but most of his listeners doubted that a discharged servant would have been that conscientious. At the end of the exhaustive 23-day inquest, the jury's verdict was that Charles Bravo had been murdered by the administration of poison but that there was insufficient evidence to decide on the guilty party.

There were plenty of rumours and questions but no answers. It could have been Florence who, trapped in a second unsatisfactory marriage with a husband who was closing the purse-strings on her money and depriving her of one luxury after another, slipped poison into his dinner-time burgundy or his bedroom water-jug. On the other hand, Florence seems to have lacked the strength of character and determination needed by a murderess. Mrs Cox had both and it could be that, faced with the prospect of losing her comfortable lifestyle and having to return without position or money to Jamaica, she decided to dispose of Charles before he could turn her out. Some investigators have even suggested a conspiracy between the two women, with hints of a lesbian relationship, which would explain why their evidence agreed on so many points that were disputed by the other witnesses. If this was the case then guilt must have driven a wedge between them, for after the verdict they went their separate ways: Florence went on drinking and died in 1878 and Mrs Cox returned to Jamaica after all.

Lizzie Borden

LIZZIE BORDEN was acquitted by the jury in Massachusetts, USA, on the charge of murdering her father and stepmother, though legend still holds her guilty and the popular rhyme states baldly:

> *Lizzie Borden took an axe*
> *And gave her mother forty whacks*
> *When she saw what she had done*
> *She gave her father forty-one.*

No one could argue that the Borden household in the little town of Fall River was happy or harmonious. Lizzie's father, 70-year-old Andrew Borden, had made a fortune, first as an undertaker, patenting a popular line in burial caskets, and later as a property speculator. Nevertheless, his meanness was well-known in the town and the Borden home, on 92 Second Street, was a shabby little whitewood house with fewer comforts than those of many of the local millworkers. His first wife had died two years after Lizzie was born and he had made a second marriage, to a fat, plain woman called Abby. She was deeply resented by Lizzie, who called her 'Mrs Borden', refused to eat at the same table and spoke to her only when it was unavoidable. Her anger reached boiling point when Mr Borden bought the house in which Abby's sister lived to save her from eviction and gave the deeds to his wife. Lizzie saw it as proof that Abby was after her father's money. Soon afterwards Abby's bedroom was ransacked and her watch and jewellery were taken. Mr Borden called the police but sent them away again when it became obvious that Lizzie was responsible. It was accepted by the family that she had committed the act during one of her 'funny turns', when she often acted out of character.

In the sizzling hot summer of 1892 strange things were happening in the household, even before the axe murders. Lizzie kept pigeons in the outhouses at the bottom of the garden and intruders twice broke in there. Mr Borden, thinking that they had designs on the pigeons, took the extraordinary course of killing all the birds. Then Lizzie went round the local pharmacists trying to buy prussic acid, only to find that no one would sell her the poisonous substance without a prescription.

The fourth of August was the hottest day of the year. Lizzie's older sister Emma had tried to escape the heat by going to stay with friends in the country. John Morse, brother of the first Mrs Borden, was staying for a few days but was out visiting other relatives. Once Mr Borden had left the house his wife busied herself with housework upstairs and the maid Bridget Sullivan set about washing the windows. Lizzie, who had breakfasted later than the others, was planning to do some ironing.

Shortly before 11 am, Mr Borden returned from town. Lizzie came downstairs to meet him and when he enquired where his wife was, Lizzie told him that during the morning she had received a note from a sick friend and had gone to visit. Mr Borden sat down on the horsehair sofa in the living room and picked up a copy of the *Providence Journal*, but he was exhausted by the heat and soon began to doze. Bridget was feeling ill – the after-effects of some mutton that had upset everyone in the house but Lizzie – so she went up to her attic bedroom for a rest, hearing the clock strike 11 as she mounted the stairs.

Only 10 or 15 minutes later she heard Lizzie calling frantically and hurried downstairs. 'Father's dead. Someone came in and killed him,' Lizzie told her. She would not let Bridget go into the sitting room but sent her for Dr Bowen, the family physician. The doctor was still out on his rounds so she left an urgent message and returned to the house, only to be sent out again to fetch Alice Russell, one of Lizzie's closest friends. Mrs Adelaide Churchill, the next-door neighbour, noticed the comings and goings and saw Lizzie standing by the screen door. She asked her what was wrong and was told: 'Someone has killed father.'

When Dr Bowen arrived he found Mr Borden's body lying on the sofa, his blood covering the floor and walls. The old man's head had been shattered by 10 hatchet blows, so that his face had been destroyed and one eyeball was hanging from its socket. The doctor reckoned that he had been struck while sleeping and that the first blow had killed him.

Mrs Churchill and Mrs Russell were comforting Lizzie in the kitchen, rubbing her hands and dabbing her forehead with a damp cloth, though she seemed remarkably calm and collected. When Mrs Churchill asked her where she was when her father was killed, she said, 'I went out to the barn to get a piece of iron.' Mrs Churchill then asked where her mother was and Lizzie gave the extraordinary reply: 'I'm sure I don't know, for she had a note from someone to go and see somebody who is sick. But I don't know that perhaps she isn't killed also, for I thought I heard her coming in.'

Mrs Churchill went upstairs with Bridget to look for Mrs Borden and as they climbed she glanced through the open door of the spare bedroom and saw the woman's ample body on the floor. She had been attacked from behind with a hatchet as she entered the bedroom and though the first blow must have killed her 18 more blows had been inflicted, leaving the room awash with blood. It seemed strange that Lizzie, when coming downstairs to greet her father, would have noticed nothing.

When John Morse returned to the house, after the police had arrived, he drew suspicion upon himself by his strange behaviour. A crowd of sightseers had already gathered around the house but, instead of hurrying inside to see what was wrong, he wandered slowly round to the back garden, picked some fruit from a tree and munched it thoughtfully before going inside. Then he produced an alibi so glib and exact that it seemed too perfect to be true. When it was checked, however, it was found to be correct in every detail.

The police realized that the murderer was either an intruder who had hidden in the house for some 90 minutes between the two killings without Lizzie or Bridget being aware of him, which seemed unlikely, or someone in the household. Bridget was soon discounted as a suspect, as there were several witnesses to her movements that morning; neighbours had seen her cleaning the windows, both outside and in, and she had even been seen vomiting from the effects of food poisoning. When Lizzie was questioned about her movements she told the police that she had spent 20 minutes in the loft of the outbuilding and had eaten three pears while looking for some weights for her fishing line, but the dust on the floor of the loft bore no footprints.

Enquiries were made about the note Lizzie said her stepmother had received but no note was found, no one admitted sending it and no one had seen it but Lizzie. An axe head, broken from its handle and with its blade smeared with ash from the stove, was found in the basement but there was no proof that it was the murder weapon. A reward was posted for information leading to the arrest of a bloodstained outsider who might have left the Borden household that morning. Interest quickened when a Dr Handy claimed to have seen a 'wild man' in Second Street at around the time of the killings, but faded again when he was identified as 'Mike the Soldier', a well-known local drunk.

At the inquest, Lizzie changed her story and contradicted herself several times. She now said that she was not upstairs when her father arrived home but in the kitchen. 'I thought I was on the stairs but now I know I was in the kitchen,' she said unconvincingly. She now denied that she had ever said she heard her stepmother returning to the house. The authorities were in two minds about charging Lizzie with murder. Though she seemed the only possible killer and the public prosecutor was convinced of her guilt, he was not convinced that there was enough evidence to obtain a conviction. All the same, Lizzie was arrested and stood trial in June the following year.

By then the press vilification of Lizzie, which had at first set people all over America howling for her execution, had caused a backlash in

her favour. Now she appeared as a quiet and God-fearing woman –
secretary of the local Christian Endeavour Society, member of the
Women's Christian Temperance Union, Sunday school teacher –
incapable of such bestial deeds. Flowers and good-luck messages
poured in from all over the country and suddenly she became the
hounded and persecuted victim of the unfeeling state.

Lizzie, now a rich woman, had hired George Robinson, the best
lawyer in Massachusetts and a former governor of the state. One of the
three trial judges had been elevated to the bench during his governor-
ship and therefore owed him a favour. Certainly things went Lizzie's
way when the judges refused to admit the transcripts of her muddled
answers at the inquest, or accounts of her attempts to buy prussic
acid, into evidence. Though blood from the two killings had covered
the rooms where they took place, no one had noticed any blood on
Lizzie at any time and it seemed impossible that she could have
changed and washed without Bridget noticing what was going on, yet
Bridget said that she had seen and heard nothing. Though Alice
Russell had seen Lizzie burning a dress in the stove shortly before the
police were due to search the house – because, she said, it was faded
and had splashes of paint – she was sure there was no blood on the
dress. On the other hand, she had see no paint on it either!

George Robinson appealed to the emotions of the jury by pointing
to the respectable, lady-like woman in the dock and saying, 'To find
her guilty, you must believe she is a fiend. Gentlemen, does she look
it?' The jury could not believe it and at the end of the 10-day trial they
found her not guilty. Her supporters threw a celebration party where
Lizzie was able to chuckle over the newspaper clippings they had
saved for her. Her new popularity did not last long. She bought a
larger house on the more genteel side of Fall River and lived there as
a recluse, giving up all her good works. For a few years Emma shared
the house with her but eventually they quarrelled and Emma left.
Lizzie stayed on, alone but for the servants, until she died in 1927,

Lizzie Borden with her counsel in court

aged 67. Bridget, whom some still suspected of covering up for Lizzie's crimes, returned to Ireland, allegedly with a slice of the Borden legacy.

No one else was ever arrested or even seriously suspected in the Borden case. Five plays and many books have been written about it, giving various explanations of how Lizzie could have carried out the crime. In her book *A Private Disgrace*, American writer Victoria Lincoln puts forward the theory that Lizzie murdered during an attack of temporal epilepsy – the cause of the 'funny turns' well-known to her family – which could result in loss of memory afterwards and explain Lizzie's contradictory statements and coolness when she was accused of murder.

Alma Rattenbury

'I KNOW who did it . . . I did it with a mallet. Ratz had lived too long,' Alma Rattenbury babbled to the police who came to the Villa Madeira in Bournemouth, England, to investigate the brutal attack on 67-year-old Francis Rattenbury, known as Ratz. It was 2 am and Alma was in a state of almost manic excitement, capering about, trying to kiss the police constable, putting one record after another on the gramophone and turning the volume up to full blast. She went on muttering, half incoherently: 'I would like to give you £10 . . . no, I won't bribe you.' At about 3 am, when she was told that her husband's condition was critical, she said: 'I did it . . . he lived too long . . . I'll tell you where the mallet is in the morning. I shall make a better job of it next time . . . I made a proper muddle of it. I thought I was strong enough.' Soon after that her doctor arrived and gave her a shot of morphia so that she could get some sleep.

In the morning the police interviewed the Rattenbury's chauffeur, 18-year-old George Stoner, who said that he had been in his room at about 10.30 pm when he heard Alma calling to him. In the drawing room he found Francis Rattenbury in the armchair, with blood running from his head. Alma had been crying: 'Help me to get Ratz to bed, he has been shot.' He had asked Alma how it happened and she said she didn't know. At 8.15 am, once Alma was up and dressed, Detective Inspector Carter charged her with the attempted murder of her husband and she made and signed a statement as follows:

'About 9 pm on Sunday, 24 March 1935, I was playing cards with my husband when he dared me to kill him as he wanted to die. I picked up the mallet. He then said, "You have not got guts enough to

Alma and Francis Rattenbury with their son on the sands at Bournemouth

do it." I then hit him with the mallet. I hid the mallet outside the house. I would have shot him if I had a gun.'

Alma was then arrested and taken to the police station. As she left the house her companion Irene Riggs, her young son John and George Stoner were all standing in the hall. 'Don't make fools of yourselves,' she told them, and George was heard to say, 'You've got yourself into this mess by talking too much.'

Over the next few days, the strange story of the Rattenburys and their chauffeur was revealed. Alma and Francis had married in 1925; he was a distinguished architect some 30 years her senior. Though the marriage was happy enough at first, they grew apart with the years. Alma was impulsive and romantic, and had achieved some success in writing popular sentimental songs. Ratz was a solitary and rather morose man, prone to fits of melancholy, often talking morbidly about suicide when he had drunk too much whisky in the evenings. He was becoming increasingly deaf and Alma decided that it would be advisable to hire a young man who could act as chauffeur and handyman.

In September 1934 George Stoner, the good-natured and somewhat backward son of a local bricklayer, joined the household. He gave his age as 22, though in reality he was not quite 18. He drove Alma to the London shops, cinemas and theatres and soon he was sharing her bed. It was the shy young man's first experience of sex and he fell deeply in love. When Alma discovered his real age and attempted to end the affair they quarrelled violently and he vowed that he could not live without her. He was often jealous but Alma reassured him that it was six years since she had had sex with her husband and that Ratz had told her that she should lead her own life.

In the spring of 1935 Alma told her husband that she had to go to London for a minor operation and would need £250 to cover expenses. Ratz glumly produced the money, which Alma spent on a five-day spree with Stoner in London, in the course of which she bought him silk pyjamas and shirts, two suits, a coat, underwear and handkerchieves.

She even gave him the money to buy a diamond ring which he could present to her as a token of his love.

The two lovers returned from their trip on Saturday 23 March and the next day Ratz sank into one of his black moods. At teatime he read aloud passages from a book in which the hero considers suicide and Alma tried to cheer him by suggesting that they should take a trip to Bridport next day to visit a business associate. Later that Sunday night someone battered Francis Rattenbury so viciously that he died four days later without ever regaining consciousness.

By this time the police had learned about the strange triangle at the Villa Madeira and George was arrested. He asked detectives, 'You know Mrs Rattenbury had nothing to do with this affair?' He confessed that he had watched through the french windows and saw Alma kiss her husband goodnight, then he had waited, crept in when Mr Rattenbury was asleep and hit him. He then went upstairs and told Alma, who rushed down. 'You know, there should be a doctor with her when they tell her I am arrested, because she will go out of her mind,' he added.

Now both suspects had confessed, both claiming complete responsibility. Yet, when they appeared at the Old Bailey, charged with murder, they both pleaded not guilty. Alma had now changed her story. She said that George had been angry and jealous about the Bridport trip and had cornered her in the dining room, threatening to kill her if she went. She had calmed him down but when he joined her in the bedroom later he was 'looking a bit odd'. He told her that she was not going to Bridport the next day because he had hurt Ratz; he had hit him over the head with a mallet. It had previously been shown in court that George had borrowed a mallet from his grandfather on the Sunday morning, because he needed to drive in some tent pegs.

Alma described how she had tried to rub her husband's cold hands: 'I tried to speak to him and then I saw his blood, and I went round the table and trod on his false teeth and that made me hysterical.' Then she began drinking whisky and after that everything was a blank. She had conveniently forgotten her interviews with the police and her confessions of guilt; her statement was 'absolute double-Dutch' to her, she said.

Alma was represented at the trial by the best lawyers money could buy, while George had to rely on the inexperienced counsel provided by legal aid. He was adamant that nothing must be done to suggest that Alma was in any way involved with the crime. He did not go into the witness box – perhaps because his counsel thought that his evidence would only damage his case, or perhaps because George felt that he might incriminate the woman he loved. His counsel was reduced to suggesting that an addiction to cocaine meant that he was not responsible for his actions. Unfortunately, the prosecution was able to demonstrate that George did not even know what cocaine looked like.

George was found guilty and sentenced to hang. Alma was found not guilty but as she left the court the waiting crowd booed her. Three days after her acquittal, Alma took a train to Christchurch and sat for a while by the river. She wrote a note on the back of an envelope: 'One must be bold to do a thing like this. It is beautiful here, and I am alone. Thank God for peace at last . . .' A farmworker saw her walk towards the river, crouch down, then topple in. She had plunged a knife six times into her chest and three of the wounds had pierced her heart.

George Stoner, in the death cell at Pentonville, sobbed when he heard of her death. A week later he wrote to his lawyer saying that he was innocent of the crime but would never have told the full story if Alma had lived. He said that he had fetched the mallet for perfectly normal reasons and had put it in the coalshed. That night he had found Alma in bed in a terrified state. There was a loud groan from downstairs and Alma went rushing down. He followed and found Mr Rattenbury with terrible head injuries. The mallet lay on the floor and he had kicked it under the sofa. Later, after Alma was arrested and he learned about the statements she had made, he had done everything possible to incriminate himself.

George's appeal was turned down but the Home Secretary recommended a reprieve and he served only seven years in prison before being paroled. He served in the armed forces in the Second World War and took part in the D-Day landings, then, after the war, settled down to respectable married life.

It is hard to judge, in the confusion of contradictory statements, whether the verdict was right or wrong. In his summing up, the trial judge said that it would be unfair to form any conclusion on the basis of a statement made while Alma was under the influence of morphia; however, she made several confessions admitting responsibility, with no suggestion that anyone else was involved. Until shortly before the trial, she was still refusing to blame George. A number of people who had known Alma in the past, when she lived in Canada, believed that she took drugs and her behaviour after the attack seems more in keeping with the influence of drugs than with alcohol. Moreover, she was known to be subject to attacks of excitability 'as though she had taken something'. If she was high on drugs on the night of the murder her husband's constant complaining might have sent her into a fury, and while not fully in control of her actions, she might have seized the mallet and set about him.

Alma's suicide was widely seen as an act of despair by a woman who could not bear to go on living while her lover was sentenced to hang. However, if she were so deeply in love she would have seen that George had the money to furnish the best defence rather than leaving him to the mercies of legal aid. It could be that, having been persuaded to change her story on the grounds that she was a mother whose children would be orphaned if she was executed, she was now unable to face the idea of living with her guilt.

Alice Crimmins

ACCORDING to Alice Crimmins, she opened the door of her children's bedroom in her ground-floor apartment in Queens, New York, on 14 July 1965 to find that although their beds had been slept in, five-year-old Eddie and four-year-old Alice were missing. She immediately phoned her estranged husband Eddie, who was fighting her for custody of the children, to ask if he had taken them. It was Eddie who rang the police to report the children's disappearance. Detective Gerard Piering, who arrived to investigate, took an instant dislike to 26-year-old Alice. With her figure-hugging toreador pants and strawberry blonde hair, her rubbish-bin full of empty liquor bottles and her address book full of phone numbers of past and present boyfriends, she was not his idea of a caring mother and she seemed surprisingly calm about the missing children.

Alice told him that she had given the children a meal at about 7.30 pm, and had put them to bed at 9 pm. She remembered shutting the window because there was a hole in the fly-screen, yet in the morning she had found the window wide open. At midnight she had taken little Eddie to the bathroom but young Alice, known as Missy, had not woken. After she had put Eddie back to bed she had fastened the hook and eye latch which was fitted on the outside of the door to stop Eddie getting up and raiding the refrigerator in the night. She had heard no sound from the bedroom after that, though she did not go to bed herself until between 3.30 and 4 am, so the children must have been taken after that time.

Later in the day, a young boy discovered Missy's body on a vacant lot about seven blocks away. She had been strangled with her pyjama top, which was still knotted around her neck. Little Eddie's body was found a week later in the undergrowth on the embankment of an expressway, some 2 km (1¼ miles) from his home. The body was badly decomposed and it was impossible to tell the cause of death. For months detectives followed up leads that ended nowhere and at the end they were left with Alice as the murder suspect. At first Eddie was also under suspicion but when he produced an alibi and passed a lie-detector test with flying colours, he was more or less ruled out of enquiries. Alice, who had refused to take the test, became the favoured suspect. She was known to lead a promiscuous lifestyle, with various different men sharing her bed in the Queens apartment, and the children's needs often seemed to come second to her own. The latch on the outside of the children's door was probably fitted to prevent them from interrupting Alice's sexual antics rather than to protect the contents of the refrigerator. There had been one occasion when she had left them alone over the weekend while she went to the Bahamas on a boyfriend's boat, though she maintained that this was unintentional: she had been asked to a party on board and had found herself way out in the ocean before she realized what was happening. Her current lover, Joe Rorech, at first admitted that she had talked to him about the custody hearing, saying that she would rather see the children dead than let Eddie have them. Later he said that, when they spent the night together in a motel, she had admitted to killing her little daughter and begged him to forgive her.

A breakthrough in the case came when detectives traced a neighbour with an incriminating tale to tell. Sophie Earomirski first told her story in an anonymous letter but was eventually located and persuaded to testify. At 2 am on 14 July 1965 she had seen a man and woman walking along the road near Alice's apartment. The woman was carrying a bundle wrapped in blankets and leading a little boy by the hand. When the man told her to hurry, she said that she had to wait for the dog because it was pregnant. When the man threw the bundle into the back of a car, the woman – identified by Mrs Earomirski as Alice Crimmins – said, 'My God, don't throw her like that.'

Alice was indicted and charged with Missy's murder. At her trial, pathologist Dr Melton Helpern said that the food in Missy's stomach was at an early stage of digestion, indicating that she had died within two hours of her last meal. As Alice had fed the children at 7.30 pm, it was 'patently absurd to think that death might have occurred in the pre-dawn hours'. Damaging evidence was given by Joe Rorech and by the 'woman at the window', Mrs Earomirski. Her evidence led to discussion about the pregnant dog: Alice's dog Brandy was indeed pregnant at the time but the defence contended that no one had known that on the night of the murder. Alice herself was questioned at length about her many lovers, both before and after her children's death. Though the judge cautioned the jury that they were not trying Mrs Crimmins's morals, her strenuous love-life counted heavily against her.

Alice was found guilty of first-degree manslaughter and sentenced to between 5 and 20 years' imprisonment, but the sentence was later quashed and a new trial was ordered. At the second trial two new witnesses appeared. One was a woman who lived in the same district as Alice and had been travelling in a car driven by her husband on the early morning of 14 July when she saw a man and woman, accompanied by a dog and a small boy. The man had been carrying a large bundle. The other, for the defence, was a young man who remembered walking along the road at the time in question with his family: his wife and young son, his daughter who was carried under his arm like a sack and their plump dog, who might well have appeared pregnant to a casual observer. This time Alice was found guilty of the murder of her son and the manslaughter of her daughter. The appeals continued and eventually the murder conviction was dismissed but the manslaughter conviction was upheld.

Alice was paroled in 1977 but criminologists still debate the case, for the evidence against Alice was never strong. No convincing motive was ever put forward for the killings. If, as was suggested, the children got in the way of her love life, she could have gained her freedom by handing them over to Eddie. The comment that she would rather see them dead than in his custody seems more like the throw-away comment of an angry mother engaged in a dispute with an ex-husband than a threat to murder. Joe Rorech, who said that she had confessed to him, was a man with a lively imagination who later came up with a story about a high-powered political intrigue involving Alice and leading to the abduction and killing of the children by mobsters. As for the 'woman in the window', she may well have seen a salesman's family passing by and embroidered the scene in her imagination after hearing about the crime. If the woman carrying a bundle was Alice, with Missy's body under her arm, then the man accompanying her must have been her accomplice, but no accomplice was ever produced. It may be that, in common with a number of other women tried for murder, her loose morals were her downfall.

Edith Thompson

EDITH THOMPSON was hanged at Holloway Prison, London, on 9 January 1923, at the same time that her lover Frederick Bywaters went to his death at Pentonville. Frederick, who had killed Percy Thompson in the street three months earlier, faced his end bravely but Edith, who had always protested that she had had nothing to do with her husband's death, collapsed and had to be carried to the scaffold. It was Edith's letters to her lover – passionate, fantastic, foolish letters – that had convicted her, making it seem that the crime had been planned in advance, a sinister conspiracy to dispose of an inconvenient husband. Yet the circumstances of the crime suggest an impulse killing, with no careful thought or planning.

Percy and Edith Thompson had married in 1915 and their life together was routine and uneventful; Percy worked as a shipping clerk and Edith was manageress at a firm of wholesale milliners. Temperamentally they were unsuited, for Edith was a thorough-going romantic, given to self-dramatization, while Percy was down-to-earth and unimaginative. However, their life together jogged along uneventfully until the summer of 1921 when handsome, virile Frederick Bywaters, a ship's clerk on the SS *Morea*, was one of a party of young people who joined them for a holiday on the Isle of Wight, invited by Edith's younger brothers.

Freddy was only 19 at the time, eight years younger than Edith, but there was an immediate attraction between them and before the end of the holiday they were exchanging secret kisses. Percy, too, liked the young man and invited him to lodge with them at their home in Ilford until his ship sailed again. The romantic attachment between Freddy and Edith developed, with Percy apparently unaware of what was

Frederick Bywaters and Edith Thompson with her husband Percy (right)

happening. It was a three-cornered argument on 1 August that brought things into the open. A minor disagreement between husband and wife had developed into a full-blown row, during which Percy hit Edith and threw her across the room so that she knocked over a chair and hurt her arm. Freddy came running in from the garden to protect Edith and angry words were exchanged, with Freddy telling Percy that he was making Edith's life hell and should give her a divorce. Percy retorted that she was his wife and that he intended to keep her.

After that, Freddy left the house and went to stay with his mother but he continued to see Edith, usually for brief meetings in teashops, though shortly before his ship sailed in September they managed to share a bed for the first time. It was during the periods of separation that Edith wrote the fateful letters, several dozen of which were produced at the trial. She wrote to him as 'darlint', a diminution of 'darlingest' and her letters were long and effusive, full of gossip and chatter and outpourings of love. She deliberately stirred up Freddy's feelings of jealousy and the tone became more sinister as the months passed: 'Yes, darlint, you are jealous of him – but I want you to be – he has the right by law to all that you have the right to by nature and love and yes, darlint, be jealous, so much so that you will do something desperate.'

She talked openly of trying to dispose of her husband by putting poison or ground glass in his food. She lamented that Percy had become suspicious when his tea tasted bitter 'as if something had been put in it' and that ground glass did not have the desired effect: 'I used the light bulb three times, but the third time he found a piece, so I've given up until you come home . . . I used a lot – big pieces too – not powdered, and it has no effect.' In another letter she wrote, 'he says . . . when he was young he nearly suffocated by gas fumes. I wish we had not got electric light, it would be easy. I am going to try glass again occasionally – when it is safe'. She sent Freddy all sorts of newspaper cuttings about cases concerning death by poisoning and hoped that the proposed crime would not affect his feelings for her:

'This thing that I am going to do for both of us – will it ever – at all, make any difference between us, darlint? Do you understand what I mean? Will you ever think any the less of me?'

In the autumn of 1922 Freddy was back in England and the illicit meetings resumed. The couple met in a London teashop on the afternoon of 3 October and that same evening Edith and Percy went to a West End theatre with some friends. They arrived back in Ilford near midnight and were walking home from the station, talking about a dance they might attend in two weeks' time, when Freddy jumped out of the shadows and grabbed Percy by the arm.

There was a brief altercation, then Freddy pulled out a knife and stabbed Percy several times. A witness heard Edith screaming: 'Oh, don't! Oh don't!' and as Percy slumped bleeding to the ground, Freddy fled into the shadows. Edith, seeing that there was nothing she could do for her husband, ran for help, meeting a young couple with the frantic request, 'Oh, my God, will you help me, my husband is bleeding.' A doctor was summoned but by the time he arrived Percy was dead and Edith demanded, 'Why did you not come sooner and save him?'

The search for the assailant soon led to Frederick Bywaters and the incriminating pile of letters was found in his possession. When she learned of his arrest, Edith sobbed, 'Oh God, why did he do it? I didn't want him to do it.' From the beginning both Freddy and Edith insisted that she knew nothing of his movements that night, and that there was no murder plot between them. According to Freddy, he had never meant to kill Percy. He had jumped out at him in a fury, accusing him of being a cad and demanding that he should divorce Edith: 'I loved her and I could not go on seeing her leading that life. I did not intend to kill him. I only meant to injure him. I gave him an opportunity of standing up to me as a man but he wouldn't.' He said that Percy threatened to shoot him and, thinking that he had a gun, Freddy pulled out his knife – a knife that he always kept in his pocket, like many sailors – and, in fear of his life, stabbed Percy.

Edith's counsel tried to keep the damaging letters out of court as inadmissible evidence but the attempt failed. The prosecution selected all the passages that related to possible murder attempts, though among the thousands upon thousands of words written by Edith she had imagined many different ways out of the love tangle, including divorce, elopement and a suicide pact. Murder was just one of the fanciful ideas she toyed with. Freddy, when questioned about the letters, said that he had never considered that she was serious about poisoning her husband: 'She had been reading books and she had a vivid way of declaring herself,' he explained. 'She would read a book and imagine herself a character in the book.' Edith said that she had only been trying to excite her lover's interest and make him think that she was willing to do anything for him, to keep his love. The evidence of the pathologist seemed to support her story, for no trace of glass or any toxic substance was found in Percy Thompson's body. Later, Edith's counsel was to say that if she had not insisted on going into the witness box against his advice, she would have been acquitted. It was her vanity and her obvious sexuality that put the noose around her neck.

The judge, Mr Justice Shearman, was strongly biased against the defendants and particularly against Edith, an adulterous married woman who had indulged in a 'sordid intrigue'. He reminded the jury that this was 'a vulgar, common crime' and left them in no doubt that the two defendants had plotted the murder together. When the guilty verdict was announced, Freddy exclaimed: 'I say the verdict of the jury is wrong. Edith Thompson is not guilty. I am no murderer. I am no assassin.' Edith, hearing them both sentenced to death, cried: 'I am not guilty. Oh God, I am not guilty.'

An appeal, on the grounds that the judge's summing up had been biased and that the verdict went against the weight of the evidence, was rejected and though several thousand people signed a petition supporting a reprieve for Edith, no appeal was granted. Bywaters protested Edith's innocence to the end. Though he accepted that he must pay the price for his crime, he wrote of Edith: 'For her to be hanged as a criminal is too awful. She didn't commit the murder. I did. She never planned it. She never knew about it. She is innocent, absolutely innocent. I can't believe they will hang her.' But they did.

Marguerite Fahmy

THERE WAS never any doubt that Marguerite Fahmy shot her Egyptian playboy husband Prince Ali Kemal Fahmy Bey in their luxury suite at the Savoy Hotel, London, but the defence centred on the motives and intentions behind the shooting. Marguerite was represented by one of England's most famous legal brains, Sir Edward Marshall Hall, who won the sympathy of the jury by painting a picture of his client as an unfortunate Western woman who had made the mistake of marrying an Oriental whose veneer of civilization was thin and who had abused and degraded her.

The beautiful Marguerite and the exotic Ali made splendid head-lines and the trial, exposing high-society scandal and the bedroom secrets of the wealthy, was one of the most celebrated of the 1920s. The shooting happened at 2.30 am on 10 July 1923, in the middle of a dramatic storm, with thunder crashing and lightning zigzagging the sky. Night porter John Beattie was taking luggage to a room on the fourth floor when he heard the unmistakable sound of three gun-shots. Beattie ran back down the corridor and as he rounded the corner he saw Marguerite throw down a pistol. Ali was lying in the corridor outside his suite, bleeding profusely from a head wound. Marguerite's white evening dress was spattered with his blood. 'What have I done? I've shot him,' the hysterical Marguerite exclaimed over and over again and when the duty manager arrived she clung to him, crying, 'I have been married six months and I have suffered terribly.'

Ali had been captivated by the sophisticated French divorcée 10 years his senior when he first saw her in Cairo, and he had offered to put on a 'fête' on his yacht in her honour. Marguerite was travelling with another man at the time and had turned him down. This only

Marguerite Fahmy

sharpened the interest of the handsome young millionaire who was accustomed to getting anything he wanted and when they met again in Paris the following year he set out to woo her with diamonds, emeralds and expensive cars. When he had to return to Egypt he showered her with effusive letters, calling her 'torch of my life' and referring to her 'bewitching charm' and 'exquisite beauty'. Eventually Marguerite could resist no longer; she joined him in Egypt, first as his mistress but soon accepting his proposal of marriage. As a condition of the marriage settlement Marguerite agreed to convert to the Islamic faith – Ali would lose his inheritance from his mother if he married outside the faith – but she would not be obliged to wear Muslim dress and she would keep the right to divorce her husband. It was a precursor of things to come that, once the ceremony was under way, Marguerite found that Ali had had the divorce condition left out of the agreement.

The couple set off on what should have been an idyllic honeymoon, sailing up the Nile to Luxor on board Ali's luxurious yacht, with its crew of 25. However, the problems began almost immediately. According to Marguerite, her husband was not interested in normal sex and was always pressuring her into acts of sodomy. They quarrelled constantly and often came to blows. Ali wrote gleefully to her sister saying that he was 'engaged in training her' and that with women 'one must act with energy and be severe'. After one argument, when Ali demanded the return of jewellery he had given her and swore on the Koran that he would kill her, she sent a letter to her Paris lawyer, to be opened in the event of her death, stating that she formally accused 'in the case of my death by violence Ali Fahmy Bey of having contributed to my disappearance'. When they arrived in Luxor, Ali locked her in her cabin and instructed the servants to make sure that she did not leave the yacht.

When Ali took a post at the Egyptian embassy in Paris his wife had a little more freedom but the marital rows were now so frequent that hotel guests and theatre patrons were treated to the sight of the ostentatiously wealthy couple screaming insults at one another, with

THE WORLD'S MOST INFAMOUS KILLERS

complete disregard for everyone around them. Once when Marguerite had spent an afternoon at the cinema with a friend and arrived home after Ali, he punched her hard enough to dislocate her jaw. He accused her of seeing other men, she accused him of homosexual liaisons.

In July 1923 the couple went to London for a holiday, booking into a spacious and splendid suite at the Savoy Hotel. One of the first things that Marguerite did was consult the hotel doctor, for she had developed painful haemorrhoids as a result, she claimed, of Ali's unnatural lovemaking. After a week of treatment brought her no relief, the doctor suggested an operation. This caused another rift between the warring couple: Marguerite wanted to return to Paris for the operation, while Ali wanted her to have it in London.

That night they went to the theatre, to a successful production of *The Merry Widow*. The light-hearted operetta did little to improve the atmosphere between them and afterwards the argument raged on over supper in the Savoy Grill. Twice Marguerite refused to dance with her husband, though she did dance with his secretary, and once she shouted that she was going to smash a bottle over his head. When the band leader asked if there was a particular piece of music she would like to hear, she told him she was not in the mood because 'my husband has threatened to kill me tonight'. The band leader, his respectful manner unruffled, said that he hoped to see her again tomorrow.

It was after they had retired for the night that John Beattie was wheeling his trolley past the suite. Suddenly the door burst open and Ali ran out in his night clothes, closely followed by Marguerite. 'Look at my face. Look what she has done,' he told Beattie, who could see a red mark on his cheek. Marguerite had said something in rapid French, pointing to her face, but he could see no marks. Beattie asked them to go back inside and close the door and as he walked away he heard Ali whistling to Marguerite's little dog, which had followed them into the corridor. Seconds later, he heard the shots.

In the witness box at the Old Bailey, Marguerite described the misery of her marriage and her fear of her husband. She explained that Ali had given her the pistol and she had never fired it before the day of her husband's death. In the afternoon, when Ali had become particularly violent and threatened to kill her, she had fired it out of the window to scare him off. Knowing nothing about firearms, she had assumed that, once fired, the gun was no longer dangerous.

On the fatal night, Ali had told her that he would only provide her travel expenses to France if she earned the money. He then began to rip off her clothes. The fight had erupted into the corridor but when Ali had hustled her back into the suite he had advanced on her, saying, 'I will revenge myself.' She had picked up the gun, which was lying where she had left it earlier, but her only thought was to get away from her husband. She had managed to escape into the corridor but he pursued her and seized her by the neck, trying to choke her. She pushed him away but he crouched menacingly in front of her, saying, 'I will kill you.' Hardly knowing what she was doing she pointed the gun, trying to frighten him. She was not even aware that she had pressed the trigger until she heard the gun go off and then she had no idea how many times it fired. Then, when she saw him lying on the ground, she knelt beside him, saying, 'My dear, it is nothing, speak to me.'

The prosecutor, Percival Clarke, asked why she did not leave her objectionable husband once they arrived in Paris where, after all, she had her own flat and influential friends. He would have sent someone to fetch her back from her flat immediately, she explained, and as for her friends 'I did not want my friends to know all about my sorrow'. When he suggested that she must have hated her husband bitterly, she replied: 'I did not hate him, I only hated what he wanted me to do.'

Marshall Hall, in his summing up, relied heavily on raising the jury's repugnance towards the 'treacherous Egyptian beast'. 'Madame Fahmy', he said, 'made one great mistake – possibly the greatest mistake any woman of the West can make. She married an

Oriental . . . The curse of this case . . . is the Eastern feeling of possession of the woman, the Turk in his harem, this man who was
entitled to have four wives if he liked for chattels, which to we Western people, with our ideas of women, is almost unintelligible, something we cannot deal with.' He finished his address with an
impassioned plea: 'Members of the jury, I want you to open the gates
where this Western woman can go out, not into the dark night of the
desert but . . . back into the light of God's great Western sun.'

In the end it was Ali and his 'Oriental ways' that were tried and
found guilty, while Marguerite was declared not guilty of murder
and not guilty of manslaughter. It may be that if evidence about
Marguerite's past character had been introduced in court, instead of
being ruled inadmissible by the judge, the trial might have ended
differently. As the prosecutor had suggested, she was a 'woman of the
world'. Though she had been born to a poor working-class family, had
an illegitimate child at the age of 15 and proceeded to earn her living
from prostitution, she later underwent a metamorphosis at the hands
of a high-class brothel-keeper. Now well-groomed, well-spoken and
fashionably dressed, she was able to attract wealthy admirers. She
married a younger man, mainly to legitimize her daughter, but was
soon divorced and became the mistress of one rich man only to move
on to an even richer one. If these facts had been revealed to the jury,
they might have been less ready to believe in the 'poor, quaking
creature' of Marshall Hall's description and might have formed the
view that she had married Ali for his money and then, not finding
marriage to her liking, had calculated that she would do far better
financially as a widow than as a wife who had left her husband.

Hannah Kinney

HANNAH KINNEY, who was acquitted on the charge of poisoning her husband in December 1840, may have been not guilty of murder – or she may have escaped execution because she was good at putting up a convincing front, so that a number of witnesses were willing to testify that the marriage was happy and Hannah was never seen to scowl.

When Hannah married George in 1836 in Boston, Massachusetts, she already had an interesting past. She was married for the first time at 17 but her husband walked out on her after his business failed, claiming that she had taken lovers. While she was waiting for her divorce to come through she lived in the same Boston boarding house as George Kinney and the two became good friends. At the same time she met up with her cousin, Enoch Freeman, a Baptist minister in Lowell, Massachusetts and married him in 1835. A year later he died, suddenly and unexpectedly. There were unkind rumours in the parish at the time, especially as Hannah had never been liked; she did not, according to many members of the congregation, conduct herself in a manner suitable for a minister's wife. Hannah hastily moved back to Boston and married George Kinney.

She seemed to be dogged by misfortunes, for George's hosiery business collapsed soon after their marriage and she was forced to support the family by running a millinery shop and taking lodgers. George turned moody and began drinking too much. When this led to an argument he would leave home for several days at a time. He finally admitted that he had run up huge debts through gambling and was suffering from a venereal disease.

In August 1840 George took to his bed. Several different doctors were called in, prescribing a range of medicines containing morphine, laudanum and opium. He was also taking a quack remedy for syphilis, some home-made pills of unknown content. On 9 August, shortly after drinking a cup of herb tea, George died. Later a friend who had tasted the tea to check that it was not too hot testified that he was sick afterwards.

Arsenic was found in the body and Hannah was put on trial for murder, though no evidence was brought to show that she had ever bought arsenic. According to the defence, she had nothing to do with administering the poison. Instead, George could have taken the arsenic himself, either intending suicide as a way of escaping from his heavy debts and unfortunate lifestyle, or as a medicine. Men of the time frequently took arsenic as a cure for syphilis and he might have overdosed himself, or died from the effect of arsenic taken as medication and combined with the barrage of doctor-prescribed medicines.

A number of friends and neighbours gave evidence that George Kinney never voiced any criticism of his wife and as he lay dying he said what a good woman she had been, putting up with his difficult ways and supporting the family. To some of them, Hannah had confided that George had died in just the same way as her second husband Enoch and the prosecution saw this as incriminating, but Hannah's lawyers pointed out that it was unlikely that a murderess would make a comparison of her two victims so publicly.

The defence, claiming a 'complete absence of motive', pointed out that 'if this woman is a murderer she is a moral monster, such as the world never saw'. The jury took less than five minutes to decide that she was no such thing.

Elizabeth Fenning

IN 1815, a 21-year-old servant, Elizabeth Fenning, was tried and convicted of 'administering arsenic to Orlebar Turner, Robert Gregson Turner and Charlotte Turner, with intent the said persons to kill and murder'. On 15 July she was hanged at Tyburn in London, still protesting her innocence.

Elizabeth worked as a cook in the Turner household, which consisted of Orlebar Turner, who ran a stationery business, his son and daughter-in-law, two apprentices and two servants. Everyone seems to have found Elizabeth pleasant and hard-working, though she had been in trouble when her mistress saw her going into the bedroom of one of the apprentices late at night. It was Elizabeth, not the young man, who was threatened with dismissal and at her trial it was suggested that her resentment turned to hatred of the family.

The murder method was said to be a dish of dumplings made by Elizabeth on 21 March. They had looked rather unappetising, heavy and dark instead of white and fluffy, but the family tucked into them just the same, along with beef and potatoes. After only a few minutes, all three of them were taken ill with intense stomach pains and vomiting.

The doctor, John Marshall, was called in and found the three members of the family, as well as Elizabeth Fenning herself, all suffering from a serious gastric upset. When he looked round the kitchen, he was shown the pan in which the dumplings had been cooked and found traces of a white powder that later proved to be arsenic. Orlebar Turner remembered that there had been a clearly-labelled packet of arsenic in his desk drawer in early March – he usually kept a small supply to deal with vermin – but it had gone missing since then.

Elizabeth Fenning in Newgate Prison, awaiting execution

When Elizabeth was questioned she said that she knew nothing about the packet of arsenic and that she had made the dumplings the way she always did. If anything was wrong with the food it must be that the milk she had used to make the sauce was tainted. However, testimony from Robert Turner showed that he had eaten only the dumplings, without any sauce, and he had been just as ill as the others.

One of the apprentices, Robert Gadsdon, gave evidence that was damning to Elizabeth. He said that he had seen the prepared dumplings in the kitchen before dinner but Elizabeth had told him not to eat any, as they would do him no good. He had eaten a portion just the same and had been very sick. He added that the defendant usually made excellent dumplings; the previous batch, eaten by Elizabeth, the maid and himself had been quite different in taste and texture.

After the cook's conviction Orlebar Turner, who was not convinced of her guilt, considered petitioning for her reprieve but was warned by the judge that Robert Turner might then fall under suspicion. Two reliable witnesses had made statements saying that Robert had, for some time, been showing signs of mental disturbance and that shortly before the dumpling incident he had asked them to lock him away. 'If I am at liberty, I shall do some mischief; I shall destroy myself and my wife,' he told them. Perhaps, after all, that is exactly what he tried to do.

Jessie M'Lachlan

AT WEEKENDS, when accountant John Fleming left Glasgow, Scotland, for the country, his father James – a bad-tempered and hard-drinking old man – stayed behind. His only company at these times was his bottle and the 25-year-old maid, Jessie M 'Pherson, but this suited the old man well enough as he chose to spend most of his time in the servants' quarters and had an eye for a pretty maid.

When John Fleming arrived home on Monday 7 July 1862, his father told him that he had not seen Jess since Friday and that the door to her room was locked. When it was eventually opened, Jess's partly clothed body was found lying on the blood-soaked bed. She had been hacked to death with a cleaver. Though there were no signs of a break-in, the maid's best clothes and some of the family silver were missing. There were bloodstains on the kitchen floor, though efforts had been made to wash them away, showing that the body had been dragged from there into the bedroom.

James Fleming said that he had heard nothing untoward throughout the weekend. He had not reported the girl's disappearance because he assumed she had gone off with her boyfriend, though it was shown that the boyfriend had called twice during the weekend, expecting to find her at home. When spots of blood were found on two of his shirts, he was arrested.

Then a second suspect appeared, in the shape of 28-year-old Jessie M'Lachlan, a close friend of the dead girl. She was identified as having pawned some of the missing silver, and though she claimed that this was at James Fleming's request, he denied it. When it was found that bloody footprints in the bedroom matched hers, she was arrested. James Fleming was released, in spite of the many inconsistencies in his story. In the days when class distinctions were still treated with reverence, a working-class maid was a much more acceptable defendant on a murder charge than a member of a respected professional family.

From the beginning it was obvious that Jessie was not telling the whole truth and the circumstantial evidence weighed heavily against her, though not nearly as heavily as the judge's summing up, which was strongly biased against her and unwilling to concede a point in her favour. It was only after the guilty verdict had been announced that Jessie made a statement which, she said, was a true account of the crime.

She stated that she had arrived to visit her friend on Friday evening only to find her bleeding from a serious wound across her forehead. Jess told her that the old man had been trying to force his attentions on her for some time and that, during the evening, they had had a row and he had attacked her. The girl's condition had deteriorated overnight and, realizing she was dying, Jessie had been preparing to go for the doctor when James Fleming, alone with her friend in the kitchen, had set about her with the meat cleaver. He said that he had done it because, if a doctor had been called, he would have been blamed for her death. He would make it look like a burglary so that no one would suspect the truth, but if Jessie told anyone what she knew, he would accuse her of committing the crime.

The judge dismissed it as 'a tissue of wicked falsehoods' and sentenced her to death, but afterwards there was such an outcry that this was commuted to life imprisonment. There was still a strong feeling that she had not been given a fair trial but, all the same, Jessie spent 15 years in gaol – a harsh sentence if all she had done was attempt to conceal a murder committed by another.

Candace Mossler

IN THE early hours of the morning on 30 June 1964, several tenants in a block of luxury apartments at Key Biscayne, Florida, were disturbed by a dog barking. It was Rocky, the boxer belonging to multi-millionaire Jacques Mossler, whose barking had caused complaints before. From inside the Mossler apartment they heard a scuffle and thuds, then they heard a man's footsteps running down the corridor. One tenant, just returning home, saw a tall man with long dark hair hurrying from the building.

The evidence of the tenants was to pinpoint the time of Jacques Mossler's murder. He was found in the living room with 33 stab wounds in the upper part of his body. He had also suffered several blows to the head from a blunt instrument, possibly a heavy glass swan that was found lying nearby.

Jacques had been living in Florida for about nine months, while his wife and family remained in their 28-roomed mansion in Houston, Texas. Sixteen years earlier he had married a glamorous divorcée 24 years his junior. Candace had two children, Jacques had four and they adopted four more. Candace was later to claim that Jacques went in for a wide range of sexual perversions but the marriage only seemed to run into trouble when her nephew, Melvyn Powers, came to stay in 1961. After 18 months he was still there and when Candace was unwilling to fix a date for his departure, Jacques had him thrown out.

When Candace and her nephew were tried for her husband's murder, the prosecution alleged that Candace had started a passionate affair with her nephew while under her husband's roof and continued it after he left. While Jacques was away in Europe in the autumn of 1963, it was said, the two were constantly seen together, with Melvyn introducing Candace as his fiancée and telling friends that she was about to get a divorce.

A few weeks before Jacques' death, Candace had taken four of the children to stay with him in Florida. At the end of June she was suffering from migraines and several times she drove to Miami to obtain medication from the emergency department of Jackson Memorial Hospital. It was here that she went in the early morning of 30 June, strangely enough taking the children with her and spending time in a hotel lounge before she went to the hospital. According to the prosecution, all this was in order to give herself an alibi while her lover went to the apartment and killed Jacques.

Detectives noticed that Candace showed no distress over the horrific death of her husband. Though there was no sign that the contents of the apartment had been disturbed she told the police that some of her jewellery had been stolen, along with money from her husband's wallet. When asked who might have killed her husband, she said that he had made a number of enemies in his business dealings and even named some of them. In addition, she mentioned that she suspected Jacques of having homosexual lovers.

At the trial, there was a good deal of talk about the relationship between Candace and her nephew and several men testified that either Candace or Melvyn had offered them money to murder Jacques Mossler. There was evidence that Melvyn had arrived in Miami on the afternoon of 29 June; a friend testified that he had left Houston wearing dark clothes and when he returned the next day he had been wearing light clothes, with trousers that seemed to be made for a much shorter man. A car borrowed by Candace from one of her husband's companies, and which fitted the description of the car driven away from the apartment block by a dark young man on the morning of the murder, was found at Miami's airport, covered with Melvyn's fingerprints, with a car-park entrance ticket stamped at 5.19 on the morning of 30 June. In addition, Melvyn's palm print was found on the kitchen counter, which had been thoroughly cleaned by a servant on the afternoon before the murder.

The lawyers made a meal of the proceedings, dragging them on for 14 weeks and using every trick in the book to win a point. The defence lawyers produced witnesses to discredit prosecution witnesses, did their best to produce confusion over every piece of evidence and exploited the idea of Jacques Mossler's homosexuality (for which there was never any proof), suggesting that he might have been killed in a homosexual quarrel, or murdered by the jealous lover of one of his boyfriends.

It took the all-male jury two and a half days to debate the evidence before bringing in a verdict of not guilty. Candace kissed them all in turn and drove away with Melvyn in an open car, waving like royalty. The two remained together for a time, though in 1971 Candace married a Texan, only to divorce three years later. She died in a Miami hotel room in 1975 and when the contents of her house in Houston were auctioned, hundreds of people came to purchase a souvenir of the woman at the centre of what was known – in spite of the acquittal – as the 'Candy Murder Case'.

Pauline Parker and Juliet Hulme

THE NEW ZEALAND teenagers Pauline Parker and Juliet Hulme lived in a world of their own. They were completely wrapped up in one another, spending long hours writing highly-coloured 'novels' and making plans for their joint future, and they could not bear to be separated. Eventually their parents began to realize that their friendship was so passionate as to be unhealthy.

Pauline was the daughter of Honora Mary Parker and Herbert Rieper, a wholesale fish merchant. The couple had never married but had lived together for 23 years and had three living children, 18-year-old Wendy, 16-year-old Pauline and a Down's syndrome child who lived in an institution. Juliet was a highly intelligent 15-year-old, the daughter of an English research scientist who had brought his family to New Zealand in 1948 because Juliet suffered from tuberculosis and the climate would be beneficial for her.

Now Mrs Hulme was having an extra-marital affair and Mr Hulme was planning to return to England to take up a well-paid job in atomic research. He intended to take his 10-year-old son Jonathan with him, leaving Juliet with her mother, but both parents were so worried about the over-close friendship between the two girls that they decided this would be a good opportunity to separate them for a while. Mr Hulme would take Juliet and Jonathan for a holiday in South Africa, where he was planning to spend some time, then, when he travelled to England with Jonathan, Juliet would return to her mother. The girls were horrified. No one was going to split them up, it was unthinkable. If Juliet was going to South Africa, then Pauline must go too. Both sets of parents were adamant that this was out of the question.

On the afternoon of 22 June 1954, the two distraught teenagers ran

Juliet Hulme (left) and Pauline Parker, after being remanded in Christchurch, New Zealand

up to a refreshment kiosk in a park on the outskirts of Christchurch. They were spattered with blood and sobbing about an accident. One of them said that her mother had tripped on a board and banged her head as she fell and rolled over. 'I'll never forget her head banging,' exclaimed the other girl. Mr Kenneth Ritchie went off along the path, in the direction the girls had indicated, where he found the badly battered body of Mrs Parker. Even at a glance, it was obvious that this was no accident; later, 45 separate head injuries were identified. Mrs Ritchie, left to mind the kiosk, had shown the girls where they could wash and heard them laughing as the water flowed.

The girls were taken into custody immediately and they soon admitted to the killing. They had planned ahead, taking along a brick in a stocking as a weapon. As they walked through the park, Pauline pointed out a pretty stone to her mother and then, as Mrs Parker bent to look, she wielded the brick inside its stocking, knocking her mother to the ground, then hitting her again, passing the improvised weapon to Juliet so that she could take a turn. Juliet maintained that at first she had thought they might use the brick to frighten Mrs Parker into allowing Pauline to accompany her to South Africa, but that after the first blow, she said, 'I knew it would be necessary to kill her. I was terrified, hysterical.' Pauline admitted that she had planned the murder days ahead. She could not say how many times she had hit her: 'A great many, I imagine,' she said coolly.

At the trial, Pauline's diary was the main exhibit for the prosecution. The entries were explicit and chilling. 'Anger against Mother is boiling inside me as she is the main obstacle in my path,' she had written, and 'Why could not Mother die? Dozens, thousands of people are dying every day. Why not Mother, and Father too?' On 21 June she wrote: 'We decided to use a brick in a stocking rather than a sandbag . . . Feel quite keyed up.' On 22 June the entry read: 'The Day of the Happy Event.'

The defence tried to show that the girls were insane and called two doctors, one of them the Parker family physician, who believed that they were both paranoid and suffered from delusions; by their lights they believed that what they had done was right. Two experts on mental illness, however, both gave the opinion they were both completely sane and of above-average intelligence. They had known exactly what they were doing, they had known that it was wrong and what the possible consequences might be. One of the prosecution doctors was convinced that they had a lesbian relationship.

All through the trial the girls were calm; they smiled often and sometimes exchanged a few words. Only once did either of them show emotion: when the revelations from Pauline's diary seemed to indicate that she had had sex with a boyfriend, Juliet's face twisted in fury. When they were found guilty and sentenced to be detained during Her Majesty's pleasure they seemed unconcerned. Pauline was sent to a prison near Wellington and Juliet to Auckland, so the two friends were, at last, separated after all.

Ruth Snyder and Judd Gray

ONE SUNDAY morning in March 1927, seven-year-old Lorraine Snyder awoke in her home on Long Island, USA, to hear a strange tapping in the corridor outside her bedroom – the only sound in an otherwise silent house. She found her mother lying bound and gagged, able only to tap on the floor with the heel of her shoe. As Lorraine removed the cheesecloth gag from her mother's mouth, Ruth Snyder told her to get help from their neighbour, Louis Mulhauser. When he arrived and freed her from her bonds, she babbled out a story about being attacked by an intruder and asked anxiously what had happened to her husband. Mr Mulhauser found Albert's dead body lying across the bed; he had two large wounds in his head and there were also strands of picture wire round his neck.

When the police arrived, Ruth told in more detail her story of being attacked by a big, dark-skinned man with a thick moustache, who had dragged her from her room and trussed her up. After that she must have fainted, for she knew no more until shortly before Lorraine found her. The furnishings in the downstairs rooms were in disarray, with chairs overturned, cushions scattered and curtains torn down. To the practised eye, it looked like an amateur's attempt at re-creating the scene of a burglary, rather than a burglary itself. Ruth at first claimed that her jewellery was missing but, when it was found stuffed under her mattress, she suddenly remembered that she had put it there for safe keeping.

From the beginning, the police disbelieved the burglary story. At the postmortem it was shown that though Alfred had been beaten over the head with a blunt instrument, the blows were not forceful enough to kill him and he had been chloroformed and then strangled.

It seemed hardly likely that a murderous robber would have spent so much time on one of his victims, while leaving Ruth alive to identify him. Then there was the matter of Albert Snyder's insurance policies: quite recently Ruth had raised her husband's insurance from a modest amount to $45,000 and a double indemnity clause meant that if he died by violence the payout would double. When enquiries revealed a close relationship between Ruth and a corset salesman, Judd Gray, they were both taken in for questioning about Albert's murder and the true story was eventually revealed.

Ruth was bored and unhappy in her marriage to a quiet, reliable man 13 years her senior when she met 32-year-old Judd in June 1925. After their first meeting he took her back to his office and they made love, beginning an affair that would lead to murder and execution. Judd called Ruth 'Momsie', she called him 'Lover Boy' and they met frequently, renting hotel bedrooms for a few hours and becoming more and more infatuated with one another. At the same time, Albert seemed to become very 'accident-prone'. He narrowly escaped death when repairing his car with the engine running; after Ruth had given him a glass of whisky he fell asleep and only woke in time to realize that the garage doors were shut and he was inhaling poisonous fumes. Another time he was almost gassed as he was taking an afternoon nap, as Ruth had turned on a gas tap 'by mistake'.

There was no mistake and no last-minute reprieve for Albert Snyder in the early-morning hours of 20 March. When the Snyders returned late from a bridge party, Judd was already hiding in the house. Ruth had seen to it that Albert drank more than usual and once he was fast asleep she tiptoed out of the bedroom and joined her lover. Earlier she had brought a sash weight, the chosen murder weapon, up from the basement and equipped herself with picture wire, chloroform and cotton wool, just in case. Judd crept into the bedroom and brought the weight down on Albert's head but his victim awoke and began to struggle, so that the weight fell to the floor. Albert cried out to his wife to help him but her only answer was to pick up the sash weight and

Ruth Snyder listens to evidence in court

bring it down on his head with all her strength. Still Albert did not die, so she stuffed chloroform-soaked cotton into his mouth and one of them – later each was to blame the other – finished him off with the piano wire. Afterwards the two murderers burned Ruth's nightdress and Judd's shirt – Ruth fetched him a fresh one from her husband's supply, walking past the body to do so – and then they ransacked the rooms to make it look like a burglary.

When arrested, Ruth protested that, though she and Judd had planned the murder together, she had taken no part in the actual killing and in fact had tried to stop him at the last moment. Judd admitted his part in the murder but said that it was all Ruth's fault: 'She had this power over me. She told me what to do and I did it.'

Many men must have indulged fantasies about this masterful woman, for while in the death cell Ruth received over 160 proposals of marriage. 'Momsie' and 'Lover Boy' both went to the electric chair in Sing Sing, dying within a few minutes of one another. A newspaper reporter secreted a camera in his clothes and photographed Ruth's death for posterity.

Bonnie Parker and
Clyde Barrow

HOLLYWOOD has immortalized the legend of Bonnie and Clyde, making them into attractive youngsters, rather naive and confused, trying to escape from the hopelessness of the Depression years. In fact they were tough, vicious killers. They robbed and shot their way across five states of the USA, firing on anyone who got in their way. Genuine gangsters viewed them as 'kill-crazy punks' who gave gangsterism a bad name.

Clyde Barrow, one of eight children, was born on a Texas farm in 1909. He was frequently in trouble as a child and was only nine when he was sent to an approved school as an incorrigible thief and truant. He had a sadistic streak too and neighbours remembered that he took a delight in torturing farm animals. He was 21 when he met 19-year-old Bonnie, a small, fair-haired girl from a devout Baptist family, at the house of a friend. Bonnie took him home to meet her mother who was delighted to see her taking an interest in a young man. Though Bonnie had married at 16, her husband had soon deserted her and had since been gaoled for robbery.

Clyde spent the night on the couch of the Parker house and in the morning he was arrested for five car thefts and two burglaries. Bonnie screamed and cried, beat the wall with her hands and begged the police not to take him. When he was given a two-year gaol sentence, Bonnie smuggled in a gun so that he could make his escape. It was all in vain, for he was recaptured a few days later after an attempted burglary and sentenced to 14 years' imprisonment. This time, the only way he could get out early was by persuading another prisoner to cut off two of his toes with an axe. He was given parole and arrived back at Bonnie's house on crutches.

Once Clyde was able to walk properly he made a brief attempt at honest work, but he was unable to settle down and quite soon he and Bonnie took off together to pursue their criminal career. By this time Bonnie was completely under Clyde's influence, so she was willing to follow wherever he went. In no time she found herself in gaol after an unsuccessful robbery, so she was not present at the first murder committed by Clyde and his associates in April 1932, when they shot a Texas jeweller and made off with $40. After three months she was released without charge and became a useful member of the gang, which was soon getting plenty of publicity. The newspapers called Clyde the 'Texas rattlesnake' and Bonnie was described as his 'quick-shooting woman accomplice'. A raid on a filling station at Grand Prairie, Texas, gave them their biggest haul of $3000 and, with their pockets full of money, they went on a motoring jaunt around Missouri, Kansas and Michigan, staying at luxury hotels and eating in classy restaurants.

Once the cash was exhausted they went back to holding up stores and banks, always in a haphazard, spur-of-the-moment fashion, shooting at the slightest excuse, even when their haul was only likely to be a few dollars. In Sherman, Texas, Bonnie Parker offered the store-keeper a $5 bill for a loaf of bread and a tin of salmon, then produced a revolver and told him to put up his hands. When the store-keeper grabbed a meat cleaver and told her to get out she shot him three times in the stomach.

Bonnie was the getaway driver after the next murder: Clyde and a new member of the gang, 17-year-old W.D. Jones, were trying to steal a brand-new car when the owner rushed out of his house to try to stop them. Clyde shot him in the neck and the three robbers made their escape in the stolen black coupé they were using at the time. It was Christmas Day, 1932.

In March of the following year Bonnie and Clyde were hiding out in

Bonnie Parker playfully 'gets the drop' on Clyde Barrow in a snapshot taken by Clyde's brother Buck somewhere in rural Texas

a Missouri apartment, where they were joined by Clyde's brother Buck and sister-in-law Blanche. Neighbours who had seen guns taken into the house alerted the police and they decided on a raid. Clyde was standing by the garage when he saw one of the policemen jump from the car and he did not wait to ask questions; he blasted the officer with a shotgun. Bonnie, still in her nightdress, began firing a rifle from an upstairs window. In the chaos that followed Blanche ran screaming down the road, her pet dog in her arms. The robbers dived into their car and made off at top speed, amid a volley of police gunfire, rescuing Blanche two blocks away. Both Clyde and W.D. were slightly injured but the policemen fared worse: two were dead and another seriously wounded.

In the apartment the police found a stack of rifles and machine guns as well as rolls of film which, when developed, showed the outlaws in various jokey poses. One showed Bonnie threatening Clyde with a shotgun and in another Bonnie was standing with one foot on the car bumper, holding a revolver and smoking a large cigar. The photographs were published in newspapers up and down the country and Clyde became so angry when reports kept referring to her as his 'cigar-smoking moll' – for he insisted that she had only borrowed the cigar from Buck for the photo – that he threatened the editor of one newspaper with reprisals if this was mentioned again.

Now nowhere was safe for the fugitives and disaster overtook them when their car plunged into a gorge near Wellington, Texas, and caught fire. Clyde and W.D. were thrown clear but Bonnie was badly burned. For a time they hid out in a tourist camp in Arkansas while Bonnie received medical treatment, paid for by several robberies of grocery stores. In July they were at another tourist camp, in Missouri, when they were again surrounded by police and had to shoot their way out. Buck was shot in the head and Blanche was blinded by flying glass so the gang were forced to go to ground in a wood, where the police soon caught up with them. In the gun battle that followed Buck was shot in the hip, shoulder and back and the police found Blanche crouching over him sobbing, 'Don't die, Daddy, don't die.'

Buck died six days later and Blanche received a 10-year gaol sentence. Bonnie and Clyde had escaped once more but their time was running out. They spent the next three months desperately dodging the law but on 23 May 1934 their Ford V–8 sedan was ambushed by six officers. Over 160 shots were fired and the bodies of Bonnie and Clyde were so riddled with bullets that they danced like marionettes.

Even before the bodies could be removed crowds gathered, snipping scraps of bloodstained clothing or locks of hair as souvenirs. Eventually the outlaws' car was towed to the nearest town with the remains of Bonnie and Clyde still in it, and a procession of sightseers' cars following behind. Already their legend was well-established.

Bonnie had predicted their end in her poem 'The Story of Bonnie and Clyde', which she had sent to the *Dallas Evening Journal*. The last verse ran:

> *Some day they will go down together,*
> *And they will bury them side by side.*
> *To a few it means grief,*
> *To the law it's relief,*
> *But it's death to Bonnie and Clyde.*

Elizabeth Duncan, Gus Baldonado and Luis Moya

ELIZABETH DUNCAN looked much like any other American matron nearing 60 – bespectacled, hair carefully permed, conservatively dressed and totally harmless. The reality was quite different, for Elizabeth Duncan was a very dangerous woman, without conscience and with an all-consuming hatred of her new daughter-in-law. Elizabeth was much married, so much so that she lost count of the number of husbands – they were anywhere between 15 and 20, it appears, many of the 'marriages' bigamous. However, the abiding love of her life was her son Frank. She was a devoted, possessive, jealous mother; even when Frank established himself as a successful lawyer she followed him round like a clinging wife. She was in court for every case, standing up and applauding when the case went Frank's way.

Marriage did not feature in Elizabeth's plans for her beloved son but, ironically, it was her actions that brought him and his future wife together. When, at the age of 29, Frank finally decided that it was time to have his own apartment and live his own life there was a furious row and Elizabeth promptly responded with an act of emotional blackmail: she took a handful of sleeping pills. When Frank, suitably contrite, came to visit her in hospital, he met a pretty young nurse, Olga Kupczyk, and the scene was set for a tragic drama. Frank and Olga began dating secretly and in due course Olga became pregnant. When Frank broached the subject of marriage with his mother she flew into such a rage, issuing all sorts of wild threats, that Frank thought it prudent to pretend that he had dropped the idea. Thinking that the main danger was another suicide attempt, he married Olga secretly but continued to return each night to the apartment he shared with his mother.

Elizabeth Duncan was quick to discover Frank's secret and she immediately started hatching schemes to dispose of her unwanted daughter-in-law. She talked them over with her elderly friend Emma Short who might, she thought, take a major role in her plan. Emma could invite Olga to tea to discuss her problems with her mother-in-law, then Elizabeth could leap out of hiding and strangle the unsuspecting Olga. Then she would wait until late at night, drag the body out to her car and throw it into the sea. Amazingly, Emma Short's only objection to the plan was that she disliked the idea of sharing her apartment with a dead body for such a long time. Later she was to say that she did not 'approve' of Elizabeth's murder plans, yet when her friend set off to town with the intention of hiring a hit man to do the job for her, Emma went along for moral support.

Elizabeth took her custom to a run-down café owned by a Mexican family in the least salubrious area of Santa Barbara, California. She knew that several members of the family were on the wrong side of the law: she had seen them in court as Frank defended them. On her second visit she met two young men, Gus Baldonado and Luis Moya, who were willing to take on the job for $6000. Elizabeth, not in the least discouraged by the fact that she did not have anything approaching $6000, talked them into taking a small cash advance and promised the rest when they had fulfilled the contract.

One dark November night in 1958 Olga, who was preparing for bed, responded to a knock on the door. There stood Moya, who told her that her husband was outside in the car, the worse for drink. Trustingly, Olga went with him but as she leaned towards the recumbent form in the back of the car, Moya beat her over the head with his gun and Baldonado pulled her inside. The murder was botched from the start for Olga soon came round and, as a healthy young nurse, she was able to fight hard. By the time she finally sank into insensibility, both young men were covered in blood. They began to panic and, anxious to get rid of the body, they stopped at the first likely spot, a deep dip at the side of the road. Olga was still alive and they tried to finish her off with a bullet, but once again their plan went wrong and the gun failed to fire, so instead they battered her to death with a rock.

At first the police were baffled by Olga's sudden disappearance but when they heard about Elizabeth Duncan's resentment of her daughter-in-law – she had been heard shrieking threats at the young woman – they began asking questions. The answers they received came from Emma Short, who had been present in the café when the murder contract was arranged. Elizabeth was questioned and quickly lied herself into the courtroom. She was found guilty, along with her two hit men, but the executions did not take place until 1962. Frank Duncan, the emotional ties to his mother still strong, fought tirelessly for a reprieve until the very moment she stepped into the gas chamber.

Elizabeth Duncan on the witness stand

Gabrielle Bompard and Michael Eyraud

GABRIELLE BOMPARD and Michael Eyraud were a greedy and unpleasant couple who decided that murder would be more lucrative than their usual petty thefts. Gabrielle was a 22-year-old prostitute who picked up men in high-class bars and hotel lobbies in Paris. Michael was a married man more than twice her age, who had never made a success of any honest job he attempted. When the two became lovers in 1889, they supplemented Gabrielle's income by robbing her clients, who would find it embarrassing to report the circumstances of their loss to the police.

As the summer drew on, Gabrielle spotted a better prospect in Monsieur Gouffe, a 50-year-old bailiff who was a little too fond of alcohol and was always bragging about the amount of money he was taking back to store in his office safe. Gabrielle made a great fuss of him, going out to dinner on his arm, telling him that she was unhappy with Michael and would welcome the attentions of a new lover. Once she had gained his confidence she invited him back to the one-room apartment she had rented for the purpose in a fashionable street.

Gabrielle and Michael had laid their plans carefully. They had chosen the room because there was an alcove behind the bed, masked by a curtain. Inside the alcove Michael had rigged up a system of pulleys and ropes fastened to the ceiling, the idea being that he could hide behind the curtain and pull on one end of the rope. The other end, attached to a hook, was left hanging down at the side of the curtain, where it would not be seen.

Gabrielle welcomed Gouffe with champagne and led him to the

bed. As she kissed him and stroked his hair she undid the belt of her robe and pushed it open, revealing her naked body. While Gouffe had eyes for nothing else, she took the belt from her robe and, in apparently coquettish mood, looped it round his neck, knotting it carefully. As Gouffe lunged for her, Michael reached from behind the curtain and attached the hook to the knotted belt. He then hauled on his end of the rope and Gouffe was jerked into the air, eyes popping and feet kicking.

When they were sure that he was dead, they went through his pockets to find his office keys. They then tied the body in a sack and stowed it in a trunk and, excited by their success, made love. Michael then took the keys and let himself into Gouffe's office but failed to open the safe and fled empty-handed when he was almost caught by the patrolling night watchman. The lovers were still faced with the problem of disposing of a body and the following day they took it on a train bound for Lyons and dropped it off in the river. They then set off for Marseilles and eventually, when they had borrowed enough money for the trip, they travelled to America.

It was several months before the trunk was found and by then the decomposing body was unrecognizable. Scientists were able to establish, from measuring the bones, that the dead man had walked with a limp and suffered from water on the knee, and they could establish his age from his teeth. The information they gained matched the details of the missing Gouffe and identification was completed by comparing the hair of the corpse with that taken from Gouffe's hairbrush. Details of the find were circulated throughout Europe and an assistant in a London store recognized the trunk, which Gabrielle and her lover had bought when travelling in England. He was able to give a good description of his French customers and this was soon matched with the description of the pretty young woman with a voluptuous figure who had been seen several times with Monsieur Gouffe.

Meanwhile the two murderers had reached San Francisco, where Gabrielle left Michael in favour of a young American, telling him that Michael was threatening her life and she needed his protection. However, she found it impossible to settle in America and begged her new lover to take her back to France. Once there, she learned that the police were searching for her and that it was only a matter of time before she was arrested, so she decided to give herself up, claiming that the murder had been planned and executed entirely by Michael Eyraud, who had forced her to take part in his scheme. The hunt for Michael was intensified and he was arrested in Cuba, protesting that Gabrielle's account of the murder was all lies. The crime had been entirely her idea, he said, and she was trying to frame him to conceal her guilt.

The jury found them both guilty but while Michael was to die on the guillotine, Gabrielle was sentenced to 20 years' imprisonment. 'Why not the woman too!' Michael cried when he heard the sentence. Gabrielle escaped death because French society of the time was reluctant to execute a woman and after serving 10 years she was released to sink into obscurity.

Augusta Fulham and
Henry Clark

AUGUSTA FULHAM and Lieutenant Henry Lovell William Clark met at a regimental dance in 1910 and the attraction between them was immediate. Henry, or 'Harry', was a 42-year-old physican in the Indian Subordinate Medical Service with a reputation for drinking too much and carrying on affairs with women among the British expatriate community in Meerut. He had little time to spare for his wife, a nurse several years older than himself, or his four children. Augusta was the good-looking 36-year-old wife of a civil servant and was equally bored with her quiet, retiring husband.

Their affair, with its secret assignations and passionate love letters, provided just the excitement that Augusta craved, though it was a blow when Harry was posted to the hospital in Agra and could only manage an occasional visit to Meerut. It was not enough for Augusta and she coolly decided that the only way to improve the situation was to poison her husband. She persuaded Harry to supply her with suitable poison and he sent a supply of 'tonic powders' containing arsenic. Over the next few weeks Augusta added them to Edward Fulham's food.

When Edward became ill and failed to respond to treatment, his doctor suggested sending him to hospital. His condition improved dramatically but as soon as he returned home, he suffered a relapse. This time, when the doctor insisted on another spell in hospital, Augusta arranged for him to go to Agra, where he would be at Harry's mercy. The day after he arrived Edward told his daughter that he had a feeling that he was going to die. She then watched Harry Clark give him an injection and soon afterwards her father was dead. It was Harry who signed the death certificate, giving the cause of death as heatstroke.

Once Edward was dead only Harry's wife stood in the way of Augusta's plans for a blissful future and she began to press Harry, who was drinking more heavily than ever, to arrange to dispose of the problem. Soon Mary Clark was suffering from gastric upsets. None of the food she was served seemed to agree with her, so she decided to prepare her meals herself in future and her health improved rapidly.

On the night of 17 November 1912, Mary Clark was battered to death in the bedroom of her bungalow in Agra by intruders. Her husband raised the alarm when he returned from an evening out – where he had managed to establish a cast-iron alibi – and discovered the body. Inspector Cecil Smith, head of the local police, was immediately suspicious: nothing had been stolen and without robbery as a motive, it seemed more likely that Mrs Clark had died at the hands of hired killers. When questioned, the Clark's cook became panicky and contradicted himself over and over again, finally confessing that Harry had planned the murder, hiring four young Indians, who had been admitted to the bungalow by the cook, once Mrs Clark had retired for the night.

Inspector Smith soon uncovered the gossip about Harry's affair, so Augusta was questioned and her house searched. Under her bed was a locked tin box which, she said, Harry had given her for safe keeping. Inside were several hundred of the letters she had written to Harry over the past few months. They were full of passionate protestations of love, as well as many references to the plan to murder her husband and the need to get rid of Mary Clark. Augusta was dumbfounded by the discovery of the letters: when Harry had entrusted the box to her, a few days before his wife's murder, he had simply told her that he wanted to keep his private papers out of the house during the investigation. She had thought that her incriminating letters had been destroyed long ago, but Harry could not bear to part with them.

Under questioning Augusta collapsed and told the Inspector what he needed to know and both she and Harry were arrested. Harry remained loyal and wanted to marry Augusta, who was expecting his child, before the trial but she rejected him bitterly, saying that but for him she would still be free and happy. 'He is the cause of all my trouble,' she said. 'He has poisoned and wrecked my life.'

At the trial Augusta gave evidence against her lover while he made a full confession, trying to spare her as much blame as possible and maintaining that they had never intended to kill Edward Fulham, only to make him ill so that he would return to England to recuperate. However, once he had realized that Edward was dying and was beyond help, he had given him a last injection 'out of pity, just to put an end to his misery'.

Both prisoners were convicted and Harry was hanged on 26 March 1913. Augusta was reprieved because of her pregnancy but, though her child was delivered safely, she died in May of the following year.

Myra Hindley and Ian Brady

THE NAME of Myra Hindley still raises an outcry of horror and anger every time it appears in the headlines, as the question of her release from prison is raised yet again. Capital punishment had been abolished in Britain a few months before the 'Moors Murderers' were convicted of their monstrous crimes against children for their own twisted sexual pleasure, so Myra Hindley and Ian Brady escaped the gallows – but some criminologists believe that if the sadistic murders had been discovered earlier, the campaign to preserve the death penalty might have been irresistible.

Before she became infatuated with Ian Brady Myra was a religious girl, a convert to Roman Catholicism, fond of children. As a teenager she was keen on dancing and swimming and was generally well-liked. She had a strong personality and was often the dominant partner in a relationship but there was no warning of the perversions to come. Ian Brady, on the other hand, seems to have been twisted from childhood, when he enjoyed torturing cats and killing birds. By the time he was 20 he had quite a history of petty crime and a spell in Borstal behind him but he had settled into a job as a clerk in Gorton, Manchester. In 1961 Myra joined the firm as a typist and was immediately attracted to the tall, reserved young man with the deep-set, brooding eyes. She did her best to attract his attention but it was a year before he started asking her out.

As soon as she became involved with Ian her family noticed changes in her. She was no longer interested in religion, she became secretive and began locking her things away, and she no longer enjoyed mixing with people. It was hardly surprising: Ian was 'educating' her, introducing her to the books on torture and killing that he enjoyed. He was a great admirer of Hitler and together they listened to Nazi marching songs on the gramophone.

No one knows when he first broached the idea that Myra should entice a child into her car, a child who would later be killed. When first 12-year-old John Kilbride then 10-year-old Lesley Ann Downey went missing, no one connected their disappearance with the couple who kept themselves to themselves. Everything changed when the two murderers, perhaps needing an extra boost to the excitement of killing, tried to involve David Smith, Myra's brother-in-law. For some time Ian had been introducing Smith to his ideas: they had practised shooting revolvers out on the moors, read pornographic books together and planned an armed robbery on a bank. The robbery was never carried out and it seems likely that Ian was only testing out his friend to see how far he was prepared to go. He boasted to Smith that he had committed three or four murders and fancied that he had a receptive audience and that Smith would be a willing convert.

One night in October 1965 Myra arrived at Smith's door, asking him to see her home because the street lights were out and she was nervous to walk alone. When they reached her council house, Myra asked him in to collect some miniature bottles of liqueur Ian had for him. While he was waiting for them, he heard Myra calling 'Dave, help him!' Thinking Ian was being attacked, he ran into the living room to find Ian standing over a prone young man, bringing an axe down on his head and shoulders over and over again. When at last his victim was dead, Brady said cheerfully: 'That was the messiest yet. It normally only takes one blow.'

Myra brought plastic sheeting and blankets and they set about wrapping up the corpse and cleaning up the blood. Then Smith helped Ian to carry the body upstairs to the spare bedroom, where it would remain until they could borrow a pram to get it to the car. Afterwards Myra made tea and reminisced, laughing merrily, about the time she had been sitting in the car on Saddleworth Moor with a body in the boot. She had been waiting for Ian to finish digging a grave, but a policeman had stopped to ask if she was in difficulties.

Smith left in the early hours of the morning, dazed and shocked, and a few hours later he went to the police, carrying a breadknife and a large screwdriver for protection, in case Brady saw him and decided to attack. When they heard the story the police went to Myra's house and though Myra tried to stall them, claiming that the key to the locked back bedroom was at her office, Ian eventually admitted, 'There was a row last night' and gave them the key. In the bedroom, just as Smith had described, was the body of Edward Evans, a 17-year-old engineering apprentice. In Myra's car they found a detailed plan for disposing of Evans's body and the selected spot for burial.

In a thorough search of the house, police found left-luggage tickets for Manchester Central Station hidden in the spine of Myra's prayer book. The contents of the two suitcases retrieved from the station included photographs of a naked child, a gag in her mouth, her eyes full of terror and bewilderment. She was identified as Lesley Ann Downey, who had disappeared on Boxing Day 1964 after visiting a fairground. Tape recordings found with the photographs were to reveal new horrors: the murderers had recorded the cries and pleading of the little girl as she was violated and killed. There were photographs of Myra in several identifiable spots on Saddleworth Moor and an exercise book containing a number of names, including that of John Kilbride. Questioned about whether this was the child who had disappeared on 23 November 1963, Ian answered that it was another boy, someone he had known in Hull.

The police began the grim job of digging on the moor and on 16 October 1965 they discovered the naked body of a child in a shallow grave, along with clothes and a plastic necklace identified by Mrs Ann Downey as belonging to her daughter. John Kilbride's grave was located from one of the photographs Ian took of Myra standing proudly at the spot. His clothes and spectacles had been buried with him.

Throughout the trial Ian tried to shield Myra and she protested her

The search for the Moors Murder victims with – inset – three missing children: (top left) John Kilbride, *(top right)* Keith Bennett, *(bottom left)* Pauline Reade

innocence, but no one believed her. Some listeners thought that she had been completely under Ian's spell, others thought that she was the dominant partner; either way, they believed her guilty. The tapes recording Lesley Ann Downey's ordeal were played in court, while some of the jurors wept openly. At first the child was heard pleading 'Don't undress me, will you', and 'I want to see my mummy . . . Honest to God I have to go because I am going out with my mamma. Please, please help me, will you.' Later she was crying and screaming in pain: 'Please take your hands off me a minute please . . . I can't breathe . . . Please God. Why? What are you going to do with me?' Myra was heard telling her to stop crying and keep quiet: 'Shut up or I will forget myself and hit you one.'

Ian Brady was found guilty of three murders, Myra Hindley of two; in the case of John Kilbride she was found guilty of harbouring and assisting Ian Brady, knowing that he had killed the boy. Ian was sent to Durham gaol, Myra to Holloway and at last the two soulmates were separated. Though at first they maintained a frequent and warm correspondence and begged to be allowed to see one another, in time the bond was loosened and broken.

Though Ian became resigned to living the rest of his life in prison, Myra has constantly sought freedom. In 1973 she involved a prison officer, Patricia Cairns, with whom she had a lesbian relationship, in an escape attempt, resulting in a six-year prison sentence for Cairns. Since then she has worked hard to convince everyone that she is a reformed character, turning back to Catholicism and earning a BA Honours degree from the Open University. In 1987, perhaps hoping to gain sympathy for her cause, she responded to a letter from the mother of another missing child by admitting knowledge of the killing of 12-year-old Keith Bennett, who disappeared in 1964, and 16-year-old Pauline Reade, missing since 1963. Myra was able to take the police to Pauline Reade's grave on the desolate moor but Keith Bennett's body was never found.

It remains to be seen if she will ever succeed in gaining her parole, as feelings on both side run high. Lord Longford and other reformers have worked hard on her behalf, but each time the subject of her release comes up Lesley Ann Downey's mother spearheads the campaign to make sure that Myra Hindley remains in prison. As she says, she herself has a sentence that will be with her for the rest of her life.

Betty Jones and Karl Hulton

BETTY JONES, who had left the quiet Welsh village where she grew up at the earliest opportunity, was working in London as a stripper under the name of Georgina Grayson in 1944. When she met Karl Hulton, who called himself Ricky Allen and told her he was a Chicago gangster, she thought that this was her chance to see some real excitement at last. She liked the idea of being a 'gangster's moll' and told him she wanted to do something dangerous. When Ricky showed her his gun she was both scared and fascinated.

Using a stolen army truck as a vehicle, the two embarked on a series of robberies. The first victim was a woman driver who was forced out of her car by Betty. Ricky then hit her over the head and knocked her to the ground, kneeling on her while Betty went through her pockets. They left the girl lying bleeding by the road. Another girl, who accepted a lift from the couple, was hit over the head with an iron pipe, half strangled and thrown unconscious into the river.

On the night of 6 October, Betty flagged down a private hire car driven by 34-year-old George Heath. According to the statement she gave to the police later, Ricky had waited until they were on a quiet road, then told the driver to stop so that they could get out. As the driver leaned over to open the door, she 'saw a flash and heard a bang'. Then Ricky had taken over the driving and, once George Heath had stopped breathing, Betty searched his clothes for money and valuables, taking his watch, cigarette case and matching lighter as well as money and petrol coupons. After that, Ricky had dumped the body in a ditch, where it was found next morning. They then went for a meal.

The killers might never have been traced if they had disposed of the car immediately but Ricky was found driving it the following day.

He gave Betty as his alibi for the previous evening and she was asked for a statement. Later that day she told a friend, a reserve policeman, about the investigation and added: 'If you'd seen someone do what I've seen done, you wouldn't be able to sleep at night.' When the conversation was reported, Betty was taken in for questioning. Soon, both Betty and Ricky were giving their versions of the murder. Ricky maintained that robbing the cab driver had been Betty's idea; when he protested that he did not want to go ahead, she told him to give her the gun so that she could do it herself. When the police took him to the spot where the body had been found, he said, 'I wouldn't have been here but for that girl.' He claimed that he had never meant to shoot Heath and that the gun had gone off accidentally while he was distracted by his girlfriend's chatter. According to Ricky Betty had helped him to carry the body over to the ditch, but although police evidence confirmed that the body had not been dragged across the grass Betty always denied helping him.

In court, 18-year-old Betty said that she had only gone along with Ricky because he had often threatened her and she was frightened of him. However, other witnesses said that they had seemed perfectly at ease with one another and Betty had not shown any sign of fear. The jury found both defendants guilty, though in Betty's case they added a recommendation for mercy. Both were sentenced to death by hanging but two days before the execution date Betty's sentence was commuted to life imprisonment. She remained in prison for nine years.

Martha Beck and
Raymond Fernandez

DELPHINE DOWNING, a widow with a three-year-old daughter, contacted a lonely hearts club in the hope of finding a congenial man for friendship with a view to marriage. She felt that she had found him through her correspondence with Charles Martin; he sounded like a kind, caring man who would make a good father. When he came to visit her at her home in Michigan, USA, he brought with him his sister, the rotund and smiling Martha. Delphine was surprised but pleased, thinking that he was concerned for her reputation. A man whose intentions were not respectable would hardly bring his sister along.

In the weeks that followed Delphine allowed herself to be charmed by Charles, who thoughtfully took over management of her financial affairs. She may well have been taken aback by Martha's obvious jealousy once she realized that her brother was sleeping with Delphine, but she assumed that Martha would get used to the idea in time.

Neighbours used to seeing Delphine every day were surprised when she suddenly disappeared without a word. Charles told them that she had gone away for a while, leaving him and Martha to look after her house. One of the neighbours, not as impressed by the odd couple as Delphine had been, notified the police. They arrived as Charles and Martha were returning from an evening at the cinema and asked to look round the house. In the cellar they found a patch of recently laid cement and when they dug down the bodies of Delphine and her daughter Rainelle were uncovered.

When the couple were questioned they were revealed as Raymond Fernandez, who had long made his living from swindling women who answered 'lonely hearts' advertisements, and his mistress Martha Beck. Raymond, born in Hawaii of Spanish parents, moved to Spain in the 1930s, gained a reputation as a war hero during the Civil War and married a Spanish woman. In 1945 he worked his passage to the USA on an oil tanker. His defence lawyers were later to maintain that an accident on this voyage, when a hatch cover fell on his head, had changed his personality for the worse. Arriving in America, he soon found his niche as a confidence trickster. By 1947, with something like 100 victims already behind him, he went on holiday to Spain with Mrs Jane Thompson, travelling as a married couple. After a quarrel, Mrs Thompson was found dead in her hotel room. Spanish police were anxious to question Raymond about her death but he had already left for America, where he produced a fake will and took possession of Mrs Thompson's apartment.

It was in this apartment that he first met 26-year-old Martha Beck. Her name had come from a lonely hearts club but, as a divorcée with two children to support and very little money, she was no use as a potential victim. The vastly overweight Martha had little in the way of physical attraction to offer either, but she and Raymond soon recognized one another as soulmates. Martha's appetite for perverted sex was as insatiable as his and she threw herself wholeheartedly into his business as a swindler, convincing him that, working as brother and sister, they could find even more gullible women to deceive.

From the beginning, Martha's jealousy got in the way. Raymond's success in conning money out of his women friends meant that he had to win their love, but Martha could not bear the thought of him making love to another woman. In August 1948, he made a bigamous marriage in Illinois with Myrtle Young, but the bride found herself sharing a bed with Martha rather than with her new husband. When Myrtle refused to stand for this any longer Martha gave her a large dose of

Raymond Fernandez (third from left) *and Martha Beck* (right) *are examined in the Municiple Court, Michigan*

barbiturates and, while she was still in a befuddled state, put her on a bus to Arkansas where she collapsed and died.

In December the couple were in Albany, New York, where Raymond persuaded 66-year-old widow Janet Fay into signing over all her assets and a substantial insurance policy to him. Martha admitted to hitting Mrs Fay over the head with a hammer in a fit of jealousy, then Raymond finished the job by strangling her with a scarf. They put the body in a trunk which they stored in Raymond's sister's cellar while they arranged to rent a home in Queens, New York. They moved in, complete with trunk, and buried the body in the basement, covering it with cement. A few days later they left the house.

As far as Delphine Downing was concerned, it was never known for certain which of the two actually committed the murder. Delphine had been given barbiturates and then shot. It may have been Martha who fired the shot, in another of her jealous rages. On the other hand, Raymond at one point in the investigation claimed that he had shot her to hasten her death, as she was already dying from the drug overdose. Little Rainelle had cried so inconsolably after her mother's death that Martha drowned her in the bath.

The couple were charged with the three murders – Janet Fay and Delphine and Rainelle Downing – though they were suspected of 17 more. A long battle ensued over where the couple were to be tried as, though they had been arrested in Michigan, the first murder had been committed in New York. The choice was a significant one, for in Michigan the most the killers could expect was a life sentence, while New York still had the death penalty. New York won.

Their trial began on 9 June 1949 and when Martha was brought into the court she broke away from her guards, ran to Raymond and kissed him, exclaiming, 'I love you and I always will.' Their only hope was to convince the jury that they were not responsible for their actions – Raymond because of his head injury, Martha because of a disastrous childhood, when she was reputedly raped by her brother. Every detail of their sordid sex life was revealed in evidence and the courtroom was crowded with spectators who wanted to catch a glimpse of the 'monster' and his 'fat ogress'.

The trial lasted 44 days and at the end of it Raymond Fernandez and Martha Beck were both found guilty of murder in the first degree. On 8 March 1951 they both went to the electric chair at Sing Sing. Shortly before the execution Raymond sent Martha a loving message and she said: 'Now that I know Raymond loves me, I can go to my death bursting with joy.'

Delfina and
Maria de Jesus Gonzales

IN THE early 1960s the white slave traffic was booming on Mexico's west coast. Teenage girls looking for work answered advertisements for employment as maids and were abducted, never to be seen again. Enquiries kept leading back to a smoothly dressed woman with a mole on her cheek who had been seen several times in the company of girls who subsequently disappeared.

Faced with yet another missing teenager in January 1963, the police department in Guadelajara decided to devote extra resources to stopping this trade in human flesh once and for all. A watch on local brothels was mounted and the woman with the mole, Josefina Gutierrez, was arrested. Realizing that the game was up and determined not to shoulder the blame alone, she told them that she collected victims for two sisters, Delfina and Maria de Jesus Gonzales, who owned a ranch in a remote spot near the town of San Francisco del Rincorn. They entertained customers there and also provided girls for the brothels of the area.

The Ranch El Angel was difficult to find and by the time the police arrived the sisters had heard they were planning a raid and had gone into hiding, leaving the ranch in the charge of a group of armed 'minders'. Inside the police found 13 young girls, all weak from ill-treatment and drugs. They had a terrible tale to tell. When a girl was first 'recruited' she was beaten and gang-raped, then turned over to a succession of customers. She was regularly fed drugs to make her more amenable and flogged unmercifully if she did not obey every command. If she became pregnant, the foetus was forcibly aborted by the simple expedient of a vigorous beating administered to the stomach.

Some of the girls had become mentally unbalanced from their suffering, others were riddled with venereal disease, but at least they were alive. They told the investigators that once a girl lost her looks, fell ill or became so hopelessly addicted to drugs that she was no longer useful, she was killed and quickly buried behind the ranch. A team of diggers was brought in to turn over the ground near the ranch and they uncovered the remains of more than 80 girls, together with many aborted foetuses. There were also 11 male bodies which belonged to migratory Mexican workers who were returning home from seasonal work in the US, their pockets full of money. They were easy prey when they stopped in at the ranch to hire a girl for the night; their drinks were drugged, their money was taken and by morning there was a fresh grave outside.

The evil sisters had been plying their trade for 10 years, paying protection money to various influential citizens so that they were always tipped off when a raid on one of the brothels was about to take place and could thus remove the young prisoners in advance. This time there was no protection: their hiding place was soon discovered and the Gonzales sisters were brought to trial. They tried to evade responsibility, telling the court that all the bodies belonged to girls who had died from natural causes while in their care – they were poor, undernourished girls who were already suffering from disease when they arrived – but the testimony of their pathetic victims made nonsense of their story. They were convicted and sentenced to 40 years' imprisonment. The investigation did not end with their trial and a number of local worthies were ultimately to pay the price for their co-operation.

Carol Bundy and Douglas Clark

THE KILLINGS that became known as the 'Sunset Strip Slayings' first hit the headlines on 12 June 1980, when the bodies of stepsisters 15-year-old Gina Narana and 16-year-old Cynthia Chandler were found alongside a Los Angeles freeway. Both had been shot in the side of the head. Twelve days later two more bodies were discovered in different places. Both 24-year-old Karen Jones and 20-year-old Exxie Wilson were prostitutes who worked Sunset Strip in Hollywood: Exxie Wilson's head had been cut off and removed. The body of 17-year-old Marnette Comer was half-mummified by the time it was found in late June and an unidentified corpse was discovered a month later on Sunset Boulevard.

All were the victims of 32-year-old Douglas Clark and his girl-friend Carol Bundy, a 37-year-old nurse and mother of two. They had met at a country and western bar and he had moved in with her immediately, teaching her all sorts of new ways to enjoy sex. He brought girls back to her apartment – one of them only 11 years old – and had sex with them in front of Carol, who recorded the event with pictures.

Douglas had always entertained fantasies about murdering women during the sex act and once he decided to turn his fantasies into reality it was often Carol who enticed girls into the car where he would force them to have oral sex, then shoot them in the head at the moment of climax. He took Exxie Wilson's head home and stored it in the deep freeze until he was ready to take it out and use it for sex acts. Carol stood the head on the kitchen counter and gave it a full make-up. 'We had a lot of fun with her,' she said later. 'I was making her up like a

Barbie.' Afterwards they scrubbed the face clean and packed it in a box, then dumped it in an alleyway.

It was Carol who gave the game away. At the country and western club she met up with an ex-lover, John Murray, and as the evening wore on and she got slightly drunk she started hinting at the things she had witnessed. Murray put two and two together and guessed that her new boyfriend was the 'Sunset Strip' killer. Afraid that he might go to the police, Carol decided that he, too, must be killed. His body was found a few days later, with nine stab wounds and without a head. The head was never recovered; Carol said she had thrown it into a ravine to delay identification.

Two days after Murray's body was discovered Carol broke down in front of a friend and confessed what she had done, crying that she had been trained to save lives, not to kill. The friend, horrified, went to the police and the lovers were both arrested. The gun that had killed five of the six victims was found, along with undergarments collected from the girls as souvenirs.

Douglas Clark was charged with six counts of first-degree murder and Carol Bundy with two murders, that of John Murray and the unidentified girl found on Sunset Strip. Douglas tried to convince the jury that the murders had been carried out by John Murray and Carol, and that she had killed her partner in crime so that he could not testify against her. No one believed him and he was sentenced to die in the gas chamber.

At first Carol pleaded insanity but changed her plea to guilty early in the trial. She was sentenced to 27 years to life on the first count of murder and 25 years to life on the second, the terms to run consecutively.

Fred and Rosemary West:
The 'House of Horror Murderers'

Although the mass murderer Harold 'Doctor Death' Shipman was the most prolific serial killer in British criminal history, certainly the most horrific mass murders of recent years were those that took place in the "house of horror" in the peaceful town of Gloucester, at the hands of husband and wife killers Fred and Rose West.

What made the West murders even more repulsive – if there could be anything more repulsive than the abduction, torture and dismemberment of innocent girls and young women – was that one of the victims was their own daughter. If only for this reason, it was a case that made an impression on the public consciousness as powerful as that of the notorious Moors Murderers thirty years earlier.

In fact the West's daughter Heather was the final victim in a total of twelve murders which were centred on the house at 25 Cromwell Street, stretching back twenty years from her death in 1987 to Fred West's killing of his first wife Rene in 1967. And it was Heather's disappearance that first alerted the police, and led to them digging up the back garden of the house in February 1994, an event which in turn captured the attention of the local press.

Journalists from the paper, the Gloucester Citizen, began to look through their records for any mention of the occupants of the house, Frederick and Rosemary West, and found a report from the previous summer of a court case involving the couple in the sexual assault of a young girl. The Wests were cleared after the key witness declined to give evidence, but the discovery of the clipping in the Citizen archive was enough to get the newshounds on the trail.

What the newspaper folk didn't know at this stage was that after the allegations were made against the Wests, their six youngest children were taken into the care of the local Council social services, while an older girl – Heather – had disappeared in May 1987, aged 16, but had not been reported missing. Her parents told people that she had left home and was working in a holiday camp in Devon, but the other children would jokingly refer to her being 'buried under the patio.'

It was these murmurings that came to the ears of the police after the children were put into care, and when Detective Constable Hazel Savage, who had previous dealings with Fred West, looked a little further into Heather West's records she found there were none. Via her national insurance number, there was no trace of her either working or claiming unemployment benefit, in fact there was effectively no trace of her at all.

So it was, in response to Detective Savage's suspicions and the 'patio' rumours, that the police began to dig up the West's back garden, and made their first gruesome discovery; the first of Heather's remains. The next day Fred West was taken into Gloucester police station for questioning, where he admitted almost immediately to killing Heather, but went on to insist that his wife Rose had nothing to do with it, and indeed knew nothing about it. This, it transpired, was far from the truth, the result of a hurried pact he had made with his wife the night before – that he would take all the blame – when they knew the police were on the case. Rose West was, in reality, very much involved with the crimes about to be (literally) unearthed at 25 Cromwell Street.

But what the police pathologists discovered triggered far more concern than they had anticipated – with the remains they presumed to be those of Heather West was a third leg bone, elevating the inquiry from one concerning a single family homicide to one of multiple murder.

From here on in, Fred West gradually revealed the full horror of the crimes perpetrated in Cromwell Street. First of all he admitted to the killing of two other girls, both of whom had disappeared in the late 70s, Shirley Robinson and Alison Chamber, showing police where he had buried their remains in the garden.

Then, in response to the authorities bringing in a 'counsellor' normally used to dealing with juvenile cases, he went on to admit to another six killings, buried under the cellar and bathroom of the house. Subsequent confessions by West revealed he had also buried a victim at another address in Gloucester, the eight year old daughter (of whom West was not the father) of his first wife. He also admitted to killing former girlfriend

Ann McFall and his first wife Rena, both of whom he had buried in the Gloucestershire countryside.

It was only these last two who were definitely killed and disposed of without Rose West's involvement, at a time before she got involved in Fred's life, 1967 and 1970 respectively. But it transpired, despite her pleas to the contrary and Fred's claims of her non-involvement, that Rosemary West was thoroughly involved in the abduction, torture, sexual abuse and death of the ten females of whose murder she was charged and convicted at Winchester Crown Court in October 1995.

Initially Rose had been put into a police safe house in nearby Cheltenham, but was still under suspicion, and eventually charged with sex offences and taken into custody. She was subsequently charged with murder, after Fred had reneged on his original pact of silence before hanging himself in his prison cell on New Year's Day 1995.

Rose West's trial revealed the true horror of how the pair abducted vulnerable females, mainly teenagers, submitted them to rape, further sexual abuse and torture, before killing them and burying their dismembered bodies. Two graphic accounts illustrating the couple's perverse evil highlighted the evidence against West: the testimony of Fred West's eldest daughter Anne-Marie (Rose's stepdaughter), telling how her parents had continually sexually abused her since she was eight years old, and that of Caroline Raine, an early victim who the two abducted and abused but then set free – a mercy they did not extend to later unfortunates.

Rosemary West was found guilty on all ten counts of murder by a unanimous decision of the jury, and committed to life imprisonment. In this case, the life sentence was deemed by decree of the Home Secretary to literally mean life – Rose West would never be released.

The 'House of Horrors', scene of world media attention since the first bodies were uncovered, was demolished by the local Gloucester Council in October 1996. Meanwhile, the counsellor who interviewed Fred West said that he claimed there were 20 other bodies to be taken into account, but as time goes on there is less and less chance of police ever finding them – Rose West has shown no signs of any further revelations as she languishes in Durham Prison.